The March to the Marne

The French Army
1871–1914

The March to the Marne

The French Army
1871–1914

DOUGLAS PORCH
Lecturer in History
University College of Wales, Aberystwyth

CAMBRIDGE UNIVERSITY PRESS

Cambridge
London   New York   New Rochelle
Melbourne   Sydney

PUBLISHED BY THE PRESS SYNDICATE OF THE UNIVERSITY OF CAMBRIDGE
The Pitt Building, Trumpington Street, Cambridge, United Kingdom

CAMBRIDGE UNIVERSITY PRESS
The Edinburgh Building, Cambridge CB2 2RU, UK
40 West 20th Street, New York NY 10011–4211, USA
477 Williamstown Road, Port Melbourne, VIC 3207, Australia
Ruiz de Alarcón 13, 28014 Madrid, Spain
Dock House, The Waterfront, Cape Town 8001, South Africa

http://www.cambridge.org

© Cambridge University Press 1981

This book is in copyright. Subject to statutory exception
and to the provisions of relevant collective licensing agreements,
no reproduction of any part may take place without
the written permission of Cambridge University Press.

First published 1981
First paperback edition 2003

A catalogue record for this book is available from the British Library

Library of Congress catalogue card number 81–10139

ISBN 0 521 23883 8 hardback
ISBN 0 521 54592 7 paperback

Contents

Preface		*page* vii
1	The army and the republic	1
2	The army and the nation	23
3	The high command	45
4	The Dreyfus affair	54
5	The Radical solution	73
6	The *affaire des fiches*	92
7	Anti-militarism and indiscipline	105
8	The colonial army	134
9	The army and the Nationalist Revival	169
10	The three-year law	191
11	The spirit of the offensive	213
12	The heavy artillery	232
13	Conclusion	246
Appendix 1	War Ministers 1871–1914	255
2	Army corps areas	256
Notes		257
Select bibliography		281
Index		291

For Françoise

Preface

'It is desolating to realize that upon these frivolous old gentlemen, with their false mystery and their half developed "science" of war, rested the continued existence of European democracy', wrote British historian Philip Guedalla of the French high command in 1914. Such opinions were not untypical in the aftermath of the Great War. The deficiencies of the French army in the opening months of that conflict were only too apparent. Indeed, France had an army which appeared unable to decide in which historical epoch it lived – its firepower was that of the 20th century, but its uniforms were virtually unchanged since the Second Empire, while its tactics were essentially those of the French Revolution.

The French army's shortcomings were especially apparent in three areas: the high command contained a disturbing and almost fatally large number of incompetent generals whom Joffre was forced to sack in the heat of battle and exile to Limoges. In the process, the French language acquired a new word – *Limoger*. Secondly, the army remained committed to the doctrine of the offensive. Largely ineffective frontal attacks cost the French almost 2,500,000 casualties in the first 15 months of the war. Lastly, these tactical mistakes were compounded by an almost total absence of heavy artillery. French attacks were broken up by German artillery firing from distances beyond the reach of the light French 75s.

How does one explain the poor, not to say disastrous, performance of the French army in 1914? Historians, led by those of the 'nation-in-arms' school, see these mistakes as the inevitable result of France's reliance on her professional soldiers: 'The professional army implies the premature offensive of 1914, and this springs fatally from its very nature', wrote Monteilhet, whose pioneering work on French military institutions has set the tone for subsequent studies. The 1914 offensive, his theory goes, was the result of a struggle over military organization between conservatives and republicans which dated from the French Revolution. The history of the French army since 1871 is seen as a battle between the professional army and the 'nation-in-arms'. The French army, officered by men whose aristocratic origins and political views made them unsympathetic to the republic, fought to maintain an elite, professional army, highly trained and skilled in manoeuvre, capable of applying offensive doctrines of warfare. Republicans struggled to introduce a militia, or at least an army made up primarily of reservists, less adept at manoeuvre and able to fight only from behind breastworks and fortifications. After 1899, the Left made a concerted effort to 'republicanize' the forces. This failed. With the Nationalist Revival of 1911–1914, the professional army was victorious. The unrepublican, and disastrous, doctrine of the offensive, based on a totally unrealistic appraisal of French military capabilities, triumphed with the three-year service law of 1913. Joffre, Foch and others ignored that the French were outnumbered and outgunned, disdained the use of reserves and took the offensive against a superior enemy.

This, then, is our received view of the French army in 1914. Like many models it appears logical on the surface. But the more I study the French army in this period, the less the facts appear to fit the theory. Was the officer corps dominated by aristocrats? Is it fair to say that officers were anti-republican after 1871? Of what did the Radicals' attempts to 'republicanize' the army after 1899 consist? Did the Nationalist Revival restore the 'professional' army after 1911? Was the Dreyfus affair simply a hiccup in civil-military relations from which the army quickly recovered? In an army as confused and disrupted as was the French army in 1914, can the tactical offensive and the lack of armaments really be said to be the product of a coherent policy? And many more. These may seem small points, perhaps, but when the nails begin to fall out, the entire edifice is in danger of collapse. In short, I believe that there is need for a book which attempts to explain the army's shortcomings in 1914 and to give a more balanced appreciation of the place of the army in the society and politics of post-1871 France.

I should like to thank the many people who have given me help and encouragement over the last few years: L. H. Gann, Patrick Bury and Christopher Andrew to whom I owe a great debt for their encouragement and helpful advice. Monsieur Jacques Millerand for permission to see his father's papers which, when I saw them, were not yet classified. I should also like to thank the University College of Wales, the Sir Earnest Cassell Trust, the Social Science Research Council, the *Centre national de la recherche scientifique* and the Hoover Institution for grants which enabled me to complete my research. Lastly, I should like to thank my wife, to whom this book is dedicated, for her patience and understanding through the bouts of bad temper and ruined holidays.

I

The army and the republic

'At this moment', Leon Gambetta wrote to his father on 19 February 1871, 'I have only one preoccupation: after our fruitless efforts to drive out the foreigner, to try to save at least our republican institutions.'[1] Few rated his chances of success. Only days earlier the French electorate, asked to choose between peace or war, handed a crushing mandate to the 'Prussians of the interior', monarchists determined to smother the Third Republic in its cradle. Over the next eight years a combination of Gambetta's political sagacity, and extraordinary ineptitude on the part of his opponents, transformed the Third Republic from a provisional political experiment into France's longest lasting regime in modern times. However, one question mark dangled over their otherwise total victory, one vital institution remained possibly steeled against political progress: the army.

The relationship between the French army and the regime provides one of the central themes in the history of the Third Republic. Historians have argued that the republic and its army were uneasy bedfellows from the beginning. A high command inherited from Louis-Napoleon combined with an influx of aristocratic and increasingly Jesuit-educated officers with thinly disguised royalist opinions to create an officer corps with a distinctly anti-republican disposition. To this political and social antipathy was added an organization which was warmed-up Second Empire, and which favoured the dominance of a professional military caste over the more democratic organization of the 'nation-in-arms', blocking the penetration of republican ideas. Even Gambetta and his supporters, visibly shaken by the Commune, bartered a few of their political principles for security from social upheaval. The army remained, like Banquo's ghost, an unwelcomed guest at a republican feast. 'The basic trouble with the new army was that it was not a "new" army, but an old one', wrote American historian Edward L. Katzenbach.

There were the same old generals, with many of the same old ideas, leading the same old units. The new legislation on effectives, organization and cadres passed in the 1870s may have paid lip-service to certain republican ideas or even introduced ideas favoured by the republicans . . . but, on the whole, the spirit behind the reforms was that of the old professional army. Republican elements and ideas were treated with suspicion. Thus, what happened in the years between 1871 and 1876, when France was a republic without republicans, was that an anti-republican officer corps managed to get so thoroughly entrenched that in France from this time on the army was never to be, in a strict sense, a political reflexion of the state . . . The situation which made for a Boulanger affair and a Dreyfus case and which eventually sent four thousand odd officers over to Vichy was that the army of the republic was to remain an army which was by no means solidly republican.[2]

The striking resemblance between the old army and the new had been spotted early on. The new era of national dedication and reconciliation behind the army announced by Marshal MacMahon's June 1871 Longchamps review, when 120,000 troops filed past in an atmosphere shimmering with patriotic emotion, caused the more cynical spectators like the novelist 'Gyp' to conclude that 'it was still the magnificent army of the empire'.[3] The high command formed the army's most obvious link with the past. Gambetta lamented that the top army posts remained in the hands of 'the vanquished and incompetent men of the last war', and reckoned that of 18 metropolitan army corps commanders, only one, General Clinchant, was a republican.[4] Although France had a republic, the National Assembly, dominated by monarchists, was prepared to express its gratitude to the old army for suppressing the Commune by putting it back on the payroll. The postwar Rank Revision Committee reduced in rank 14 generals named by Gambetta and placed four on the retired list, creating a discontented group of 'Gambettist generals' who saw their demotion as punishment for serving the republic, while at the same time returning the forces to the safe hands of the conservative old guard, the best insurance against radical change and 'republicanization'.

However, the political motivation of the Rank Revision Committee has almost certainly been exaggerated. In the first place, serving in the republican phase of the war constituted no disgrace, and a number of generals who had done so immediately moved into high positions in the new army: Borel was named chief of the general staff and served as war minister between 1877 and 1879, while Clinchant, Ducrot, Bourbaki and Chanzy occupied corps commands. Trochu, who had commanded Paris during the Prussian siege, took an influential place on committees named to study army reform. Others, like Farre, Billot and Saussier, all sympathetic to the republic, were given posts of responsibility which became those of high command after 1879. If many old generals returned from captivity to important commands, it was largely because the new regime needed experienced military technicians to reconstruct a badly disabled defence machine and the republican phase of the war had thrown up few obvious candidates. But those who had been impressive – Clinchant, Billot, Chanzy and Saussier – were assigned important positions in the forces, regardless of political sympathies. While Freycinet thought General Bourbaki belonged to nature's second XV, his brillant pre-war record and exalted reputation among his colleagues insured for him a high post. Competence, then, weighed more heavily than politics in the naming of generals to top commands.

While republicans read sinister intentions into the rank reshuffling in 1871, such readjustments are the rule rather than the exception following a prolonged conflict. The creation of new armies required more officers to staff them and the subsequent rank inflation had to be pricked at the war's end. The British army in 1946 saw brigadiers reduced to majors, while similiar readjustments occurred in the American army. In this context, the demotions ordered by the Rank Revision Committee seem measured. In 1871, the task was complicated by the two phases of the war, imperial and republican. Desperate for officers to lead the new formations, republicans often catapulted professional soldiers who had managed to escape capture to high rank; sergeants became captains as did many men, not a few foreigners among them, with spurious military antecedents or on the basis of tenuous personal recommendations. Some infantry lieutenants complained that they had returned from captivity to find their old sergeants promoted to captain.[5] Emile Mayer, an artillery officer and veteran of 1870 who eventually quit the army, complained that these hastily promoted NCOs usually proved 'mediocre' officers.[6] 'There were some extraordinary, scandalous and intolerable results', wrote General du Barail, war minister in 1874, of this wartime 'orgy of promotions'. '[But] as no officer thought that he had been unjustly promoted, [the Committee] was assailed by a wave of anger and a deluge of recriminations'.[7] This was not an easy problem to sort out, and after rewarding depressingly few cases of outstanding service, the Committee usually fell back on seniority as their major guideline, demonstrating a not uncommon professional reaction against queue jumpers out to violate the army's most sacred promotion rule. With Marshal MacMahon temporarily settled into the presidency, the cronyism of the old army on more than one occasion reasserted itself in the selection of men for high posts. But the personal relationships of the old army, the traditional deference paid to seniority and the sheer absence of obvious replacements for the old guard played a far more important role than politics in the Committee's decisions. A few ambitious officers attempted to make political capital out of what was basically a professional rearrangement, representing themselves as abused because they had fought for the republic. 'Following the rapid and even scandalous promotion of some, career ambitions were stimulated', wrote Emile Mayer. 'The decisions of the Rank Revision Committee stirred up the military world.'[8] Colonel Carrey de Bellemare, who escaped from the besieged Metz to serve the republic as a major general, went a long way towards creating the 'Gambettist generals' when he unsuccessfully appealed his reduction to brigadier to Gambetta. Du Barail reckoned that Bellemare's motives were more personal than political.[9] But the fact remains that many of the 'Gambettist generals' were generals none the less – something most of them had not been in January 1870.

Whatever the intentions of the Rank Revision Committee, historians have argued that the result of its decisions was to entrench at the top of the military hierarchy an anti-republican elite which communicated its conservative prejudices to successive generations of officers. 'The men in command of the French army over the next two or three decades would all have begun their careers under Napoleon III or before', wrote Ralston.[10] Raoul Girardet makes the same point: 'One must remember that the upper ranks, colonels and generals, had all been educated under the empire and they could not fail to retain most of the reflexes, tastes and prejudices of their first military education, inevitably bound up for many of them with a certain nostalgia for a regime which raised the glory and the prestige of the uniform to such heights.'[11]

But we cannot rely on such statements to explain the political attitudes of French officers after 1870. Governmental instability meant that *all* French regimes since 1789 had inherited an army 'educated' under previous governments. Nor was the Third Republic the first government to be made nervous by the prospect of political disloyalty in the barracks. Relations between the *ancien régime* and the army had never been particularly close, which explains in part why so many officers were quick to desert the Bourbons for the prospect of a command in the revolutionary armies after 1789.[12] Robespierre's distrust of his generals was such that more than one chose desertion as a preferable alternative to the scaffold while even Bonaparte found his marshals unwilling to support him in 1814. The spectre of the army's desertion of Louis XVIII during the Hundred Days of Napoleon's return from Elba haunted civil-military relations throughout the Restoration. The executions of Marshal Ney, 'Bravest of the Brave', Colonel La Bedoyère, the first officer to rally to Napoleon in 1814, Generals Mouton-Duvernet and Chartran in the aftermath of Waterloo, and the gaoling and exile of several others, were measures hardly calculated to establish an atmosphere of trust and confidence between soldiers and the government. 15,000 Napoleonic officers were sent home on half pay in 1815, their places often taken by aristocrats chosen for their loyalty rather than their military qualities. Despite efforts by ex-Napoleonic Marshal Gouvion-Saint-Cyr, war minister in the moderate Richelieu government of 1817, to guarantee the rights of old soldiers, Napoleonic veterans were tolerated rather than encouraged: promotion and postings went to émigrés and loyalists, while messes were often dangerously divided between royalist 'gentilshommes' and Napoleonic 'vilains'.

After a series of plots led by regular soldiers or ex-Napoleonic 'demi-soldes' failed to topple the Restoration, the government and the army settled back into an uneasy truce which was shattered by the July Ordinances of 1830. After only half-heartedly opposing the insurgents on the 28th, the Bourbon army simply melted away. Most officers must have reasoned with Major Barrès, a Napoleonic veteran who once already in 1820 had narrowly escaped dismissal for refusing to toast the king with sufficient vigour:

To accept battle would have been to doom to certain death the fifteen officers and two hundred men whom I had with me and to doom to destruction the barracks, the valuable stores and the neighbouring houses. Torrents of blood would flow and my memory would be held responsible for all these calamities; and for whom? For a perjured king, for an inept government imposed on France by foreign bayonets. Until then I had served faithfully and conscientiously. I had nothing with which to reproach myself as regard to the Bourbons, but this wretched, ill-advised sovereign had broken his oath, had he not freed me from mine?[13]

The first attempts by the young July Monarchy to curry favour with the army by reinstating many of the 'demi-soldes' sacked in 1815 badly misfired. Regular officers were less than content to see the Napoleonic veterans slip into jobs which they had hoped to occupy themselves. The government quickly realized that the loyalty of the army would be won by guaranteeing its future, not by pandering to the political traditions of the past. An 1832 law regularized the promotion procedure, thereby removing complaints of political favouritism so often levelled at the Restoration. An 1834 law further stabilized an officer's position by declaring that his rank was his property and could be taken from him only in exceptional circumstances. This removed the threat of arbitrary or politically motivated dismissals, not uncommon in the past, and gave an officer the status and security of tenure of a civil servant.

Loyalty to the state had replaced the Bourbon's notion of loyalty to the sovereign. The divisive years of the Restoration had undermined comradeship and professional standards and placed an officer's job in jeopardy. Soldiers now declared themselves to be political non-combatants, men who served France, not a particular regime. Even Louis-Philippe's son, the Duc d'Aumale, respected this social contract in 1848 when as Governor General of Algeria he gracefully retired rather than precipitate a civil war.

Republicans after 1870 not infrequently cited the army's participation in Louis-Napoleon Bonaparte's *coup d'état* of 2 December 1851 as proof of its essentially Bonapartist inclinations. By appealing to the conservative instincts and ambitions of a few Algerian generals led by Saint-Arnaud, the Second Empire rode to power on the point of a bayonet. Any hesitation on the part of the soldiers in case this enterprise was in any way illegal was smoothed by Louis-Napoleon's constitutional position as commander-in-chief. 'Solicited by both parties, the army, in the very name of the obedience owed the constitutional authorities, could not refuse to take sides', wrote Girardet.[14]

Yet rather than a break with the political neutrality of the past, a blot on an otherwise clean copybook, the *coup d'état* of 1851 was perfectly consistent with the army's attitude toward politics. The army did not care who sat in the Tuileries or the Elysée, so long as the government was strong and showed a demonstrable affection for the forces. Saint-Arnaud's objection to the Second Republic was not that it was a republic, but that it was a weak republic. Weak regimes opened the future to question, tempting officers to warm themselves by the fires of the nation's political passions. His 2 December 1851 coup, which installed Louis-Napoleon as emperor, did not herald the entrance of the army into politics. Rather, it signalled the end of a political debate in the barracks which had undermined discipline and even witnessed NCOs running for parliament. One of Louis-Napoleon's first acts was to bar officers from sitting in the Corps Législatif, something which had been done neither by the Bourbon Restoration nor the July Monarchy.

The army was wedded to order, not to a particular regime, and the officer corps would have disintegrated under any attempt to impose a political view. A long history of changing regimes had left a residue of political traditions and tastes among a socially diverse soldiery. After the Bourbon Restoration had attempted unsuccessfully to direct the opinions of the officer corps down the narrow channels of political loyalty, subsequent regimes were content with political neutrality. Divergent political views had long been tolerated in the army – both monarchs and marshals had conceded an officer's right to keep his own discreet counsel. Artillerymen and sappers were distinguished throughout the nineteenth century by their republican sentiments, prominent in political demonstrations under the July Monarchy and voting 'no' in Louis-Napoleon's 1852 referendum called to endorse the empire, and yet they enjoyed the special favour of the Emperor. The medical corps, army administration and supply corps were also reckoned to contain many officers sympathetic to the Left.[15] Cavaignac, le Flô, and Lamoricière, all keen republicans, enjoyed rapid promotion under Louis-Philippe, while Trochu, an Orleanist, found this no impediment to his career under Napoleon III, until he published *L'Armée française en 1867*, critical of army organization rather than of the regime's politics. Even officer purges following each change of regime were only partly political: in 1815, the Bourbons had to scale down the vast army bequeathed to them by Napoleon, while, in 1830, pressure for promotion meant that some officers had to make way for ambitious youngsters whose careers had stagnated during 15 years of peace. In 1848, only 84 officers lost their jobs, and in 1851, Louis-Napoleon sacked a few outspoken republican officers. Nor were many officers sorry to see the back of Louis-Napoleon in 1870, for far from absorbing the 'reflexes, tastes and prejudices of their first military education', they felt that Louis-Napoleon had thrown open promotion to favouritism and neglected vital military reforms, leading France down the road to defeat and social revolution.

The army's tradition of political neutrality was sorely tested in the decade following the Franco-Prussian War. The republic had risen from the cinders of the empire on 4 September 1870, as news of the surrender of Sedan reached Paris. But five months of defeat and frustration which culminated in the crushing monarchist victory in the February 1871 elections for the National Assembly threw the future of the regime into doubt. The monarchist triumph proved ephemeral, however. The by-elections of July 1871 returned 99 republican deputies and only 15 monarchists, initiating the swing which eventually was to win the republic for the republicans. Four days after the vote, the monarchists received a disastrous setback when the Comte de Chambord, the Bourbon pretender, announced that he would only rule beneath the white banner of the *ancien régime*. This declaration, which was clearly unacceptable to the Orleanists and Bonapartists, not to mention the republicans, was tantamount to an abdication. The Right realized that time was not on their side. Fearing that new elections would return a 'red' assembly, they resisted demands from the Left that, having ratified the peace treaty, it should step aside and make way for a newly elected body. In such a finely balanced contest, a war of nerves between Left and Right, both sides quickly realized that the attitude of the army might prove crucial. 'It is upon it, upon its bad disposition carefully maintained and stimulated towards the republicans, that the reactionaries of all kinds are speculating', Gambetta wrote in December 1876.[16]

The traditional respect of the man on horseback for order, the unsavoury reputation as dangerous radicals which clung to republicans like Gambetta, and the traditional links between the power elite and high command seemed to throw the advantage in this tug-of-war for the army's loyalties to the monarchists. Certainly in the imperious General Ducrot, hero of Sedan and the siege of Paris and commander of the 8th army corps at Bourges, they found a keen supporter. Montaudon, Lebrun, Douai, Picard, Bourbaki and Espivent were among the most important of a number of other generals counted in the anti-republican camp. Gambetta did not fear a *pronunciamento* from a gaggle of army chiefs – such an initiative was unlikely and certainly out of character. However, he did fear that if the quarrel between monarchists and republicans ever reached a show-down, the attitude of the generals could prove decisive.[17] 'We are not on the verge of a coup d'état and we are working to make it impossible', Gambetta declared. Republicans sought to guarantee the political neutrality of the army. To do this, they must win a number of senior officers to their camp and to assure the mass of the forces that there was no incompatibility between a republican regime and the professional interests of the army.

Many generals had serious reservations about the new regime, but Gambetta could count a few recruits among senior officers. Clinchant, commander of the first army corps at Lille, was the only republican corps commander, but, lower down, de Galliffet, de Bellemare, Saussier, Pajol, de Wimpffen, Billot, Boulanger and Thibaudin formed a phalanx of brigadiers and colonels destined for high command in a republic controlled by republicans. While the high command was certainly not republican, neither was it wholly reactionary, and its divisions denied the Right its support. Already in July 1872, British military attaché Colonel Connolly noted that the high command was slipping towards political neutrality: 'In short, those who are ready to sacrifice their personal feelings to the cause of order and stability are in the great majority.'[18] Right-wing generals spoke only for themselves, not for the army. 'Everyone listened to General Changarnier speaking for the army', wrote War Minister General du Barail, 'without dreaming that if he left a great name and a great reputation in the army, he had been absent for almost a quarter-century and had no solid, firm support as he claimed. As for myself, the indispensable agent [for a coup], no-one asked my opinion.'[19] 'My old friend Changarnier was no more than a pretentious and destitute old man', wrote Charles de Rémusat.[20]

In the over-heated political atmosphere of the republic's first decade, the surprising thing is not that a few officers took an active interest in political affairs, but that the vast majority of officers, generals included, respected the army's apolitical traditions. And even of those who jumped into the political lists, the Right by no means held the monopoly. Of 16 army officers who sat in the National Assembly in 1873, nine sat with the Right and seven with the republicans, and this became eight to seven with the November 1873 resignation of General Ducrot.[21]

In 1876 and 1878, Gambetta's two secret studies of the political opinions of the officer corps revealed the army's political divisions while pointing up that republicans were winning converts. Beneath a grumbling crust of colonels and generals lay a mass of officers sympathetic to the republic. 'Some of the major generals are legitimists, some are Orleanists, most are Bonapartists', wrote one of Gambetta's military informers in November 1877.

If republicanism is beginning to make converts among the brigadiers it still has some way to go: they share the same opinions as the major generals. Among the colonels, lieutenant colonels and majors, there are still several legitimists, Orleanists and Bonapartists. The rest are republicans. Among captains, lieutenants and sub-lieutenants the only Bonapartists are Corsicans and the only legitimists are graduates of the rue des Postes [a Jesuit preparatory school for Saint-Cyr] and not even all of them. Ninety-nine per cent of the rest are republicans.

The *Times* special correspondent wrote on 5 November 1877:

Wherever I have been, I have constantly heard this: 'We are in daily communication with the officers of the garrison, and we are perfectly certain that the mass of them will be no party to a crime against the nation. A very large proportion of the younger officers are known to be republicans, and in every command there are colonels and general officers who are known to be with us.'

Other civilians were struck by 'the republican sentiments' of army officers, especially artillerymen and sappers.[22]

The reason for the budding affection between the republic and its army was a simple one: soldiers were increasingly convinced that republicans sought to resurrect French military power. Already from his captivity, Galliffet had admired the heroic defence directed by the men of Tours. He expressed his 'shame at the capitulation of Sedan and Metz' and of the generals 'who abandoned without orders the field of battle at Sedan . . . Gambetta and Trochu have all my respect; their energy doubles my shame.'[23]

With the bulk of the professional army locked up with its emperor at Sedan and Metz, the republic was declared on 4 September 1870. Gambetta, who once had called for the regular army to be scrapped and French defence entrusted to a *levée en masse* on the outbreak of war, at last had an opportunity to put his ideas into practice. The experience convinced him that something might be said for military preparation after all. Together with Freycinet, defence delegate in the new Government of National Defence, Gambetta attempted to piece together a force from the remnants of the professional army, *gardes mobiles* and assorted adventurers including Garibaldi and the rump of his Red Shirts. Perhaps the guillotine was the missing ingredient, but the miracles of 1792–93 were not repeated. Augustin Cochin described the Government of National Defence as 'Waterloo combined with 1848 . . . not the Great Republic but a watered-down parody of it.'[24] Ignorant of the art of war and the demands of army organization, the two amateurs blundered from defeat to defeat, organizing operations without consulting their generals and hamstrung by the shortage and diversity of their armaments. Without experienced officers and NCOs, enthusiastic recruits faltered under fire. Von Moltke was not the Duke of Brunswick. The Prussian juggernaut rolled on and French soldiers ran away in increasingly larger batches. Following the battle of Le Mans in January 1871, General Chanzy estimated that fully 70,000 French soldiers had deserted,[25] virtually the equivalent of the entire German force confronting him.

The reorganization of the army was the first priority of the new republic. Defeat had been a hard school for the Gambettists but it had given them an experience and maturity in military questions which would often not be matched by their opponents. 'Let it be understood', Gambetta said in his first post-war speech at Bordeaux in June 1871, 'that every boy born in France is born a soldier as well as a citizen.' Seven years later at Romans, his attitudes remained unchanged: 'This army must be the first concern of the republican party . . . the armed representation of the elite of the French nation.'[26] Contacts between officers and republican politicians were extended. Gambetta's newspaper, *La République française*, devoted column after column to military reform while soldiers were invited to write in their grievances, republicans realizing unlike most conservatives that the army's major concerns were professional and not political. This was good politics as well as being in the national interest. Officers would queue up behind the party which opted to keep the army strong and bolster the prestige of its leaders. 'The day that the republic will give [lieutenants a pay rise]', he wrote, 'it will have all their sympathy and their support.'[27] The more intelligent officers realized early on that Gambetta was a man eager for reform.[28] A new spirit was abroad in the army, more studious, more professional than before 1870. And while it is true that there was nothing specifically 'republican' about the new reforms, it is nonetheless certain that the impetus for innovation came in great part from a group of dynamic younger officers sympathetic to the new regime, led by Lewal, Berge and de Galliffet. While it would be an exaggeration to claim that the middle and lower echelons of the officer corps were republicanized, the enthusiasm for reform demonstrated by the Left did much to reconcile the army to the republic and to reinforce the army's tradition of neutrality in affairs of state. The future General Weygand confirmed that in the days before the Dreyfus affair, officers were confident of the republic's sympathies: 'Whatever the political rivalries were at the time, we heard nothing in our provincial garrisons, where we lived in the belief that questions touching the army unified everyone and that the Third Republic, triumphant from the defeat, placed in the first rank of its concern that of national defence.'[29]

The slide of the army towards political neutrality was also aided by several political factors. The war and the Commune forced officers to take decisions with political implications. But if, as Patrick Bury suggests, the defeat of the republicans of the Commune by republican troops strengthened rather than weakened the cause of the republic in the country at large,[30] it must have done much to calm fears in the army that the Third Republic would call up the disorder and divisions of its predecessors. Following the suppression of the Commune, the issue which remained to be settled, as Thiers took great pains to point out in his last speech as provisional president in 1873, was no longer that of conservatism or radicalism, but of monarchy or republic.[31]

From the summer of 1871, the conservatives rather than the republicans began to take on the image of the factious party, the men who placed their beliefs and ideas before the national interest. Their clamour to restore the papal domains seized by Italy in 1870 drew the attention of many to the fact that the party of peace was quite prepared to fight for the Pope but not against the Prussians. Their calls for a restoration made them appear the revolutionaries, not the republicans. 'The republic exists', Thiers declared on 13 November 1872. 'It is the legal government of the country; to want something else would constitute a new revolution of the kind most of all to be feared. Do not let us waste our time proclaiming the republic, but let us employ our time in giving it the characteristics which are necessary and desirable.' Monarchies invite popular revolutions, Thiers was fond of repeating. The republic guaranteed stability and so was the best insurance against disorder.[32] From the moment of his first speech at Bordeaux in June 1871, Gambetta was also busy shedding his reputation as a dangerous radical and stressing the commitment of his party to order and stability. The 'commercial traveller of the republic' stumped the country repeating the message that his was 'not a party of revolution, but of conservatism', the guarantor of order, 'not the order of silence and fear ... but order based on legality, on legitimacy established by the general will'.[33] It was to be a republic of toleration tailor-made for men who desired political stability and economic prosperity. In a country whose powers of recovery from the rigours of war, occupation and a crippling indemnity imposed by the enemy appeared hardly short of remarkable, the message struck home.

The monarchists also forfeited much sympathy in the army: even Marshal MacMahon, sympathetic to the Right, made it plain that his troops would only serve under a tricoloured flag.[34] The death of Napoleon III in 1873 was reckoned to remove the last traces of temptation from officers nostalgic for the empire: 'It is true that the Emperor was very kind to me,' said Galliffet, 'but he is dead now and I owe nothing to his son. I would only act on his behalf in so far as my chiefs gave me the order, for discipline alone is my watchword.'[35] Zulu assegais ended the life of the Prince Imperial, Louis-Napoleon's only son and heir, a few years later, removing the Bonapartist threat once and for all.

The neutrality of the army was to prove vital to the Left in their struggle to preserve the republic. The monarchist dominated National Assembly, chafing under the leadership of Thiers, ousted him as a provisional president in May 1873. In his inaugural letter, the new president, Marshal MacMahon, promised to restore the 'moral order' of the country threatened by 'a faction which menaces the repose of all peoples and seeks your dissolution only because it sees in you the principal obstacle to its plans'. The Duc de Broglie was named to head a 'gouvernement de combat' pledged to 'struggle against those passions inimical to all social order and incompatible with any government'.[36] Prefects and sub-prefects were replaced by men loyal to the 'moral order', while conservatives tightened their grip on other branches of the administration. Military governors of the 43 departments still under martial law were ordered to keep a close eye on the press – in Paris, Gambetta's friend, radical journalist Arthur Ranc, fled to Brussels rather than face the death sentence imposed upon him by General Ladmirault. Festivities were banned on 14 July, 22 September and 4 September. The Right appeared to be preparing the ground for a restoration.

However, the foundations of the 'moral order' were less than firm. In the first place, de Broglie lacked the political expertise to command a cabinet whose loyalties were seriously divided between Henri V, the Duc d'Orléans and the young Prince Imperial. Gambetta was far from depressed: 'After all,' he told Freycinet, 'we now have a more clear-cut situation . . . The people can see who are their friends. There are now only two parties: those who want to destroy the republic, and those who wish to preserve it.' 'The new regime might pose as the restorer of moral order and seek to silence its adversaries', writes Bury. 'But it could not dispel an economic recession nor could it claim to be the saviour of a society in the throes of revolutionary violence.'[37]

Secondly, in MacMahon they had perhaps found a man sympathetic to the Right – 'Nous sommes ici pour tenir la place' his wife was reported to have said – but one who was equally determined not to overstep the bounds of legality: on assuming office, he is alleged to have asked to see a copy of the regulations. When the Comte de Chambord came unannounced to Versailles hoping by his sudden appearance to win over the Marshal and take the Assembly by storm, MacMahon refused to receive him, leaving the pretender to remark that he had come to see the Constable of France and found instead a police inspector. If the National Assembly elected to restore the monarch 'even by a single vote', the Marshal would step aside and would ensure the support of the army. But he was adamant that the army would remain strictly neutral, above the political debates which agitated the country, and would be no party to a *coup d'état*. If the 'moral order' meant a return to conservative principles for the country, in the army it translated into a strict adherence to its apolitical traditions – both Carrey de Bellemare and Ducrot were rebuked by the war minister for their political utterances.

The attitude of the new president was crucial and should have served as a warning to Chambord that without a dramatic change in France's internal situation or a renunciation of his rights, there would be no coronation in his lifetime.[38] But hopes for a restoration soared in the summer of 1873 as rumours of a 'fusion' hammered out in Vienna between Chambord and the Duc d'Orléans spread. The coronation carriages were ordered and shopkeepers' storerooms filled with restoration china and white flags to go on sale the day Henri V entered Paris. On 19 October 1873, the royalist Council of Nine announced that all obstacles to the restoration had been removed. Gambetta and Thiers were certainly in touch with a few generals, although the extent of their plans to resist a restoration with the aid of sympathizers within the forces is not known. 'There was no reason to fear sedition', wrote MacMahon's biographer. 'The Marshal knew that by remaining within the limits of the law he would command the army's absolute obedience. He was legally the mandatory of the Assembly and he himself saw many of the corps commanders [and] reminded them that they must accept the decisions of the majority of the Assembly even though it was a majority of only one.'[39] Gambetta and Thiers need not have worried: in the stubborn Chambord the republic found an incongruous but consistent ally. On 27 October he wrote to the Catholic deputy Chesnelong that a Bourbon could not abandon 'the standard of Arques and Ivry'. On 30 October the letter appeared in the legitimist *Union* and the monarchist campaign collapsed in a heap.

Republicans set about strengthening their grip on the reprieved regime. The de Broglie government fell in May of the following year, while by-elections continued to register republican gains. A series of laws voted in 1875 re-established the Senate and ended the republic's provisional status. Increasingly unsettled by a leftward shift in the political balance of power, MacMahon dismissed the Simon government on 16 May 1877: 'I am a man of the Right,' he told Simon, 'we can no longer work together. I prefer to be overthrown than to remain at the orders of M. Gambetta.' Unable to patch together a conservative ministry, the president prevailed upon the Senate to dissolve the Chamber of Deputies and call new elections which he hoped would return a majority more favourable to the Right.

The 'Seize mai' crisis was to prove the longest and most crucial test which the young republic had yet faced. At issue was the constitutional power of the president to dismiss a government irrespective of its parliamentary majority. The crisis contained the threat of civil war which became more apparent in October when, despite the enormous pressure exercised by prefects and ministry officials, the country returned a Chamber dominated by republicans. Fears grew on the Left that the old Marshal, exasperated at the election results, might call in the army to break the deadlock. The threat was a plausible one: many of the Marshal's cronies, including the incorrigible conspirator Ducrot and General Rochebouët (a Bonapartist turned legitimist who once already in 1851 had manoeuvred with Louis-Napoleon on the fringes of legality), occupied vital military commands.

Although republicans drew up contingency plans to organize resistance around Lille and Dijon under the protective wings of Generals Clinchant and Galliffet, Gambetta did not fear a *coup d'état*. The high command was badly divided by politics. Active legitimists and Bonapartists might support a military solution to France's constitutional crisis, but their divisions were fundamental. Orleanists opposed any action which would probably only benefit the Bonapartists, and the Duc d'Aumale, commander of the 7th army corps at Besançon, paid a secret visit to Gambetta on 18 May to tell him so. The French army also counted enough republican generals to make the success of any coup problematic. But more important than the diverse political views represented in the high command which acted as a brake on conspiracy was the army's long tradition of non-interference in affairs of state, a tradition of which the Marshal himself claimed to be the prime custodian and ultimate guarantor. 'Legality' was the Marshal's watchword and the cornerstone of French civil-military relations at least since 1815. It would have been exceedingly difficult for Ducrot or anyone to rally the forces for an adventure so alien to the army's traditions and one in which legality seemed on the side of the Left: 'We are in occupation of the heights of the law from which we can fire at our ease upon the miserable troops of reaction who are floundering in the plain', Gambetta wrote to his mistress Léonie Léon.[40] Nor did conspirators have any solid guarantees that their orders would be obeyed by the mass of officers and NCOs among whom Gambetta enjoyed no little prestige. 'I do not believe [in a coup]', Gambetta wrote to Ranc in August 1877. 'The army is solid and the generals are very divided. It is impossible to risk such an adventure without the assurance of being followed by everyone. Thus, the rumours will continue, but even the most timid will not be taken in. Believe me that in 1873 our precautions are seriously taken to wreck any such attempt, if it is made.'[41] The situation, the *Times* was quick to point out on 3 November, did not remotely resemble that of December 1851. Even had MacMahon wanted to imitate Louis-Napoleon, he did not 'command the requisite weapons': War Minister Berthaut was no Saint-Arnaud; Voisin, the Prefect of Police, no Maupas; nor Ladmirault, the military governor of Paris, a Magnan. 'But of course he is too honourable to use them even if they lay ready to his hands', it concluded.[42] After several unsuccessful attempts to patch together a viable government, MacMahon finally gave in and named Dufare to form a ministry.

The new prime minister wasted little time in purging the administration and the prefectorial corps of men favourable to the *ordre moral*. Nor did the high command escape a minor house-cleaning. Ducrot's active intervention on behalf of the Comte de Chambord since 1871, while not strictly illegal, was more than enough reason to send him into an early retirement. Following the republican victory in the Senate elections 1879, War Minister General Gresley demanded that right-wing generals Bourbaki, du Barail, Bataille, Lartigue and Montadon be relieved of their duties, on the convenient pretext that they had commanded army corps for more than the three years allowed in law. MacMahon protested that this constituted undue interference in military affairs and resigned, probably with relief, on 30 January.

Republicans had at last captured the republic, but had they captured the army? While not politicized in an active sense, the army was more than reconciled to the regime, it was even sympathetic to it. The fundamental moderation displayed by the Left did much to conciliate the soldiers. A few officers might hold royalist or Bonapartist sympathies out of personal conviction or family loyalty, but for most the army was a hermitage, a cloister of peace in a world agitated by politics. This attitude was well illustrated by General Chanzy who, upset with the religious policies of Gambetta's *Grand Ministère* of 1881, exchanged his post as ambassador to Russia for the quiet of the 6th corps command. The *entente* between the republicans and its pretorians rested upon this understanding: the republic looked after the professional interests of its soldiers and allowed them a large degree of institutional autonomy in return for their discreet loyalty. Some did grumble when the government placed Algeria under a civil administration ending almost 50 years of military rule. However, the 'Africains' had always been a minority in the forces and after 1870 not a particularly popular one. In Algeria, the political role of the army opened it to charges of maladministration and corruption which were too often justified. It had also stimulated a taste for politics in a few generals like Cavaignac and Saint-Arnaud which they had on occasion imported into France. Lastly, the 'Africains' were thought to have acquired far too much influence in the old army and were heaped with blame for the disastrous handling of the French forces in 1870. Algeria may have preoccupied the July Monarchy and Second Empire, but now it was a mere sideshow. 'European' warfare, not bush skirmishes with the Arabs, was the army's prime mission, and the energies of officers were directed towards preparing the *revanche*. The Third Republic's decision to hand over Algeria to a civil governor was perfectly consistent with its policy of shoring up the army's apolitical traditions and strengthening its continental posture, and was greeted with complete indifference by the majority of soldiers. General Saussier, Governor General in 1879 when the transfer took place, quieted the rest.

The Boulanger crisis proved that the republic's foresight had paid off. 'General Revanche' had earned much respect as war minister in 1886 through his efforts to strengthen patriotism in the army. However, his subsequent attempts to use his military position as a springboard to political prominence elicited only profound distaste in the army. Generals were permitted to cultivate political contacts, but not to appeal to the mob. Boulanger was a vulgar careerist with a talent for self-advertisement, as many of his more prescient colleagues had long suspected. Neither Boulanger nor his supporters made any serious attempt to canvass support in the army, for they knew that it would have been a waste of time. In November 1888 a few officers were transferred from Paris suspected of harbouring pro-Boulangist sympathies, but, as Ralston points out, the evidence against them was based on the flimsiest of rumours.[43]

But if the army and the republic were friends at first, the influx of aristocrats into the officer corps induced a gradual change of atmosphere. Old prejudices and antiquated attitudes imported into the army from outside soon altered the confidence which reigned in military matters, introducing discord between the army and its new masters. 'It is certain that with the departure and the replacement of the leaders of the old army whose social origins were more diverse, the links between the higher echelons of the army and the leading conservative milieux were constantly strengthened and multiplied', wrote Raoul Girardet.[44] 'The army, because of its social prestige, attracted the aristocratic classes as it always had before the French Revolution and after it', wrote Edward Katzenbach. 'And because the monetary recompense was small, the bourgeoisie was, for the most part, content that the army should remain the domain of the elite. It was entered in the upper ranks through Saint-Cyr, and Saint-Cyr remained an exclusive school.'[45] Bédarida concludes that this aristocratic invasion altered the officer corps from a middle-class institution to one 'half-aristocratic, half-bourgeois' with developed clerical prejudices.[46]

The old army had never been an aristocratic closed shop. Even during the *ancien régime*, nobles never succeeded in excluding their social inferiors: 30 years after a 1715 ordinance restricting the officer corps to the nobility, 4,000 bourgeois were still counted in its ranks.[47] The Ségur ordinances of 1781 were no more successful and vanished with the enormous expansion of the army after 1789. The flood of aristocratic cadets into Saint-Cyr in the early years of the Bourbon Restoration soon fell back into a stream which fluctuated between 20 and 35 per cent of each year's intake, but usually fell short of 30 per cent.[48] The army continued to recruit fully two-thirds of its officers from among NCOs, for the most part men of modest origin for whom a captaincy crowned a successful career. Poor pay and slow promotion made the army an unattractive career for ambitious and well-connected sons of the middle classes, who left the epaulette largely to those who had little career choice. Saint-Cyr was not a socially exclusive school, but filled largely by sons of officers, gendarmes and minor civil servants, 54 per cent of whom in 1869 were too poor to pay for their own studies.[49] In 1870, the complaint most often heard was not that French officers were distinguished, but that when compared to their Prussian counterparts they were positively common. If one assumes that roughly one-third of Saint-Cyr graduates before 1870 were aristocrats, and that the academy furnished one-third of the officers for the infantry and cavalry, then roughly 11 per cent of infantry and cavalry officers in the Second Empire were aristocrats. These figures are, of course, approximate but underline the fact that aristocrats in no way dominated the French army, as they did in Prussia.

Historians have argued that this situation changed after 1870 with the influx of aristocratic and increasingly religious-educated officers. However, the claim that the army was transformed into the aristocracy's last refuge, a mud redoubt in a republican Sahara, is not supported by the figures. French historian Raoul Girardet, who accepts the established premise, notes that between 1868 and 1883, 30 per cent of Saint-Cyr cadets bore aristocratic *noms à particule* – roughly the same number as for the Second Empire – and that their numbers decreased thereafter.[50] In 1899, at the height of the Dreyfus affair when an aristocratic army was supposedly poised to topple the republic, *Le Temps* claimed that 11 per cent of lieutenants were aristocrats.[51] While the percentage of aristocrats among major generals, the French army's top rank, rose to 29, this hardly justified de la Gorce's accusation that 'the army . . . had become at the end of a quarter century of evolution, the most [socially] closed body in the nation'.[52] Aristocratic presence in the army of the republic was not significantly higher than it had been before 1870.

Nor did aristocrats impose their particular tone on the officer corps. Even in the cavalry where many of them were concentrated, the social origins of officers remained diverse.[53] The atmosphere of the army remained very middle-class and its increasing proportion of married officers were concerned principally with mundane professional and parental duties and with making ends meet until the end of the month.

Two things must be noted about the *nom à particule*: firstly, it was not a legal sign of nobility, but had been adopted by many socially conscious bourgeois in the 19th century to give the impression of aristocratic descent. Despite their high-sounding names, Marshals Franchet d'Esperey and de Lattre de Tassigny had not one drop of noble blood, but were descendants of the bourgeois Desperey and Delattre families which had changed their names during the Restoration.[54] Nor was a *nom à particule* a guaranteed stamp of opposition to the republic. The new regime counted among its partisans a number of backwoods aristocrats including Clemenceau and Freycinet. The same was true for the army where intellectual fashion, a developed sense of duty and patriotism, and sheer opportunism had long joined family tradition in determining aristocratic attitudes to France's frequent changes of regime. Saint-Aulaire, a Jesuit-educated aristocrat whose family espoused decidely royalist views, argued that in questions of career, pragmatism was more important than politics: 'Our political opinions are less frequently determined by constitutional theory than by more or less conscious considerations of our personal interests.'[55] Robespierre and the Terror were propped up by a posse of aristocratic generals quick to abandon the *ancien régime* – de Saix, Kléber and

Bonaparte to name a few. The alacrity with which aristocratic army officers rushed to occupy seats in France's various legislative bodies after 1789 offers poor proof of the anti-parliamentary attitudes attributed to them. Professional concerns traditionally had been more important than politics in determining French officer attitudes to a regime, and the Franco-Prussian War did nothing to alter this. The international situation had changed beyond recognition, and French defence had to be altered to match the new Prussian challenge. Any anti-republican prejudice which lingered in the officer corps soon evaporated in the winds of military reform. Most officers, aristocrats included, realized that in a moderate republic lay the best hope of a militarily strong France. The aristocratic de Freycinet, architect of national defence in 1870–1 and several times war minister before 1900, had no trouble in convincing aristocratic generals like de Gallifet, de Wimffren, Carrey de Bellemare, de Miribel and others to cross the chasm which supposedly divided republicans and aristocrats in the name of national defence.

The increasing number of Saint-Cyr cadets educated in religious schools is cited as yet another indicator for opposition to the republic in officer ranks. The staunchly republican General Iung, one of Boulanger's staff officers, complained in 1892 that, since the passage of the Falloux Law of 1850 permitting the unchecked expansion of parochial schools, the number of cadets from religious schools had skyrocketed – from 25 to 35 per cent between 1865 and 1886.[56] After 1872, Jesuit colleges like Paris' Ecole Sainte-Geneviève on the rue des Postes, the Collège Saint-Joseph at Rheims and Toulouse's Ecole de l'Immaculée Conception, le Crousou, specialized in preparation for Saint-Cyr with no mean success. By 1954, the famous rue des Postes counted 457 generals and 72 admirals on its class lists, including Lyautey, Franchet d'Espérey, Fayolle, de Lattre de Tassigny and Leclerc de Hautecloque.[57] The Left complained that religious education had transformed the French high command into a 'Jésuitière' where opposition to the republic was not only encouraged but *de rigueur*.

However, the political connotations of a Catholic education cannot be taken for granted. A large number of military and naval cadets and their families chose parochial schools because of their success record in entrance examinations to the military schools. In 1903, even Radical Navy Minister de Lanessan recognized that if a substantial number of his naval cadets came from religious schools, it was largely because only two state lycées in the entire country, at Rochefort and Brest, prepared young men for entrance. Likewise, parents eager to push sons into Saint-Cyr could make no better choice than Sainte-Geneviève.[58] School fees also weighed heavily. Parochial schools were usually prepared to tailor school fees to fit modest incomes, while hard-up students in a state lycée had to secure a competitive scholarship. For poorly paid officers, school costs were a decisive factor in their choice. But while quality of preparation, cost and location of schools usually played an important, if not crucial, role in the selection of school, the Left argued that religious education reflected the anti-republican bias of the families of many officers. The 1904 *affaire des fiche* demonstrated that republican suspicions focused on officers who educated their children 'chez les pères'.

Admissions to Grandes Ecoles, 1892–1901[59]

Type of secondary school	Ecole polytechnique %	Saint-Cyr %	Ecole navale %
State	85.04	75.41	66.98
Jesuit	13.11	17.86	21.91
Other (usually parochial)	1.85	6.73	11.11

In the keen competition between Jesuit colleges and state lycées like Paris' Louis le Grand to fill the benches at Saint-Cyr, the state schools were clearly winning, and by several lengths. When placed beside those of General Iung, Bush's figures show that by the 1890s the number of places allocated to graduates of religious schools at Saint-Cyr was on the decline. This was due to a number of factors: more effective preparation offered by lycées, especially after 1905 when the entrance examination at Saint-Cyr and the *Ecole navale* were brought into line with the 'Math A' curriculum taught in state lycées, as opposed to the more arts-orientated parochial schools;[60] increasing government pressure placed on officers and civil servants to send their sons to state schools, made obvious with the *affaire des fiches*; and poor army career prospects which meant that by the end of the century many religious colleges were discouraging their best graduates from entering Saint-Cyr.[61] But the fact remains that in 1899, at the height of the Radical campaign against clerical influence in the army, fully 43 per cent of male secondary school students were taught in religious institutions,[62] while the number of their graduates at Saint-Cyr hovered just below 25 per cent. The belief that Jesuit schools were sending a steady stream of anti-republican cadets into Saint-Cyr and that officers with a religious education were *a priori* lost to the republic appears exaggerated. Gambetta's informant in 1878 noted that by no means all 'Postards' were anti-republican, while it can hardly be argued that a seminary education improved the disposition of Emile Combes and Joseph Stalin towards the Church.

As further evidence of clerical bias in the army, historians have pointed to the *ordre moral*'s re-introduction of military chaplains in 1874 and the religious ties of the general staff, criticized by left-wing Radicals in 1899 as a 'Jésuitière'. But this overlooks the fact that officers regarded the re-introduction of military chaplains as a nuisance. Chaplains had been unpopular in the army since the Bourbon Restoration used them as spies and they were swept away with few regrets in 1830. 'The 1874 law was proposed as a clerical measure by a reactionary Chamber', Choisel told the parliamentary army committee on 13 March 1877. 'It was not supported by the army.' War Minister General du Barail, regarded as pro-clerical by the Left, labelled the law 'useless' since every garrison town had plenty of priests to minister to the faithful in uniform. He also thought it 'impolitic' for threatening to add substance to the Left's claim that the army was priest-ridden.[63] The young conscript Vallery-Radot noted in 1874 that while soldiers were given every opportunity to attend mass, 'the army remains largely indifferent to religious practice'.[64] Du Barail, in fact, enforced a strict neutrality in religious matters, refusing to allow official army representation at secular funerals, too often transformed into political jamborees in which the Left was eager to associate the army, while sending a stiff rebuke to General Ducrot, who went on a pilgrimage to Lourdes with a religious medal pinned to his uniform, for wearing 'unauthorized decorations'. The real objection to chaplains, however, was professional: officers disliked the presence of men whose first loyalty was to the spiritual rather than the military hierarchy. From 1874, military newspapers began to carry reports of disputes between commanders and chaplains, usually touched off by clerical opposition to duels or by a chaplain's refusal, often supported by his bishop, to bury a dead duellist. Although petty, these incidents were nonetheless important indicators of the basic belief of most officers that while religion reinforced discipline, chaplains undermined it. In 1877, War Minister General Berthaut directed that 'in the interest of religion, the priest must not become involved in the daily life of the barracks'.[65] Officers greeted the 1880 repeal of the chaplain law with relief.

Most officers shared their countrymen's basic good sense in the application of religious principles to daily life, refusing to mix professional concerns with priests. Although officers involved in the Dreyfus cover-up were believed to be Jesuit-inspired and trained and although Radicals accused Jesuit Father Stanislas du Lac, former rector of Sainte-Geneviève and personal confessor to army chief Boisdeffre, of masterminding the plot against Dreyfus, examination of the background of officers involved in the affair shows that few had a religious education. Boisdeffre had spent two years at the Jesuit college of Vaugirard, but had left for the lycée at Alençon. None of his immediate staff was Jesuit-educated and only nine or ten of 180 officers at GHQ were former Jesuit students. Thus, the general staff was far from being the 'Jésuitière' its critics claimed. Only one Jesuit pupil sat with the *conseil supérieur de guerre* and none on the Rennes court martial which re-condemned Dreyfus in 1899.[66] The influence of the Church on the high command, then, appears to be much weaker than supposed and historians, as often with the Third Republic, have confused the opinion of those who claimed to be speaking for the army, as the Assumptionists, with the opinion of the majority of officers.

Thus, it would be inaccurate to interpret the friction which opposed the republic and its soldiers at the time of the Dreyfus affair as originating in the reactionary beliefs of the high command or in the social origins and religious sentiments of the officer corps. Despite the apparently provisional nature of the new regime in 1871, the army's tradition of complete neutrality in affairs of state held firm. The major complaint of left-wing politicians at the turn of the century was not that the army was politicized, but that it was not politicized enough. This, they argued, was the fault of the moderate republicans who through their organization of the forces had insulated it against the penetration of republican ideas and the sanitizing influence of parliamentary politics.

2

The army and the nation

The reorganization of the army was the first priority of the National Assembly. Military organization had always been a controversial topic in a nation troubled by revolution, but defeat and the Commune gave the debates a special urgency and forced deputies to reconcile their political prejudices with the demands of national defence. The result, according to the Left, was an unsatisfactory compromise which, while it paid lip service to republican principles, allowed a conservative officer corps to retain its stranglehold on the army and pervert the spirit, if not the letter, of the reforms. 'The National Assembly had proclaimed national service and had preserved the old organization of the professional army, thus earning a victory for democracy in the field of ideas, but a practical defeat', wrote Monteilhet. 'The nation was militarized by obligatory service but remained enclosed in the too narrow professional cadres of Louis-Philippe and Napoleon III.'[1]

Since the Gouvion-Saint-Cyr law of 1818, completed by the 1832 Soult law, the army had recruited largely by selective conscription. Each year a limited number of conscripts who drew a 'bad number' in the annual draft lottery were inducted for a period of service which varied with the arm but was seldom less than four years and often seven. Frequent garrison changes which separated the conscript from his home and family and poor employment prospects outside combined to insure that many soldiers re-enlisted when their first service term expired. Long service, voluntary enlistment and replacement, a system whereby conscripts could purchase a substitute, combined to produce a small professional army expert at fighting limited wars and in quelling civil insurrection, but ineffective against a large conscript force – a shortcoming which reformers set out to remedy in 1871. An 1872 law declared all young men eligible for military service and set conscription at five years, after which young soldiers were poured into reserve. An 1873 law divided France and Algeria into 19 army corps each with a commander named for a maximum of three years while an 1875 law set limits on the numbers of professionals and conscripts called to the colours in peacetime. Historians have claimed that together these laws reflected the conservative preference for a large professional cadre backed by long serving conscripts. Monteilhet argued that the 1872 law was simply its 1832 predecessor with a few phrases changed, a new skin pulled tightly over the dry bones of the old army: 'The archaic edifice of the professional army under illusory cover of the nation in arms'.[2] He complained that the resurrection of the old army had both political and military consequences: it created an opposition knot of armed hostility to the republic which threatened the regime's stability and crippled its institutional development. Secondly, it threw up the harmful and unrepublican doctrine of the offensive which was to cost so many French lives in 1914. 'The philosophy of the offensive was born in 1873 from the desire to retain the professional army, using the reserves only as a last resort', he wrote. The history of the French army between 1871 and 1914 was a battle between the professional army and the 'nation in arms'. 'The professional army was in the end victorious.'[3]

However, one must be careful not to draw too precise a correlation between politics and military organization. In the first place, many conservatives called for universal military service and a root and branch army reform. Trochu, an Orleanist, provided republicans with many of their ideas on military reorganization, while early meetings of the *conseil supérieur de guerre*, created in 1872 to oversee army reform, saw politically conservative soldiers, like MacMahon, at loggerheads with Thiers over reform.[4] Republicans pushed reform, but by no means all reformers were warm republicans. The boundary over army reform was not drawn at the political frontier between the republic and the *ancien régime*, but zigzagged to take in men who, despite their political preferences, believed a strong national army vital for French security and prestige. Secondly, the idea of a 'republican' military organization is a misleading one. Post-1870 reformers were faced with the task of creating a defence machine capable of meeting the Prussians on equal terms. By their very success, the enemy had largely dictated the military model. The republicans basically sought to apply, with minor modifications, a system developed and perfected by an autocratic monarchy. 'I am of the old school,' Thiers told Freycinet in 1872, 'and I see that according to your book (*La Guerre en province*), you are for the Prussian system.'[5] Monteilhet agreed that 'from 1871 to 1914, in its institutions, its doctrine and its regulations, the French army lived, thought, acted in the furrow of the Prussian army'.[6] When one examines the general lines of post-1870 reform, it is difficult to conclude anything other than that the reformers won the day.

While historians have drawn attention to the similarities between the old and the new army, the changes brought about by the new legislation were nonetheless fundamental. The major defects of the pre-1870 recruitment laws had been replacement and the lack of an adequate reserve. Replacement had provided an escape hatch for the wealthy, diluting the idea of national service and limiting conscription to the poor, while the lack of a trained reserve left the army unprepared for total war and in 1870 crushed by the sheer weight of Prussian numbers. Replacement was abolished in 1872, but critics complained that it was resurrected in the form of the 'one-year volunteers', young men destined for the liberal professions who served only one year on the payment of 1,500 francs towards their training costs and who subsequently joined the reserves as second lieutenants. While this system did not guarantee equality, there was a crucial difference between replacement and the one-year volunteers: before 1870 young men paid to avoid military service while after 1870 they paid to be trained. And while it is certain that the one-year volunteers provided a concession to wealth, intelligence and education quickly became even more important criteria. Republicans increasingly stiffened the requirements for one-year volunteers, whose numbers fell from 10,000 in 1874 to 4,700 in 1881.[7] From 1880, the examination was made more difficult with 1,680 points rather than 1,300 required of successful candidates. Those who passed the test fell from 6,302 in 1877 to a mere 975 in 1886 which, together with those accepted on the basis of their diplomas, meant that only 3,392 were admitted in 1886,[8] less than three per cent of the contingent. This hardly constituted an abuse substantial enough to undermine the principle of national service. The one-year volunteers were swept away with the three-year service law of 1889.

The second defect which the new legislation set out to correct was the old army's lack of a trained reserve. Historians of the 'nation-in-arms' school have claimed that the creation of a viable reserve had foundered traditionally on the military prejudice against the citizen soldier. While the belief that they hold a monopoly on professional competence is perhaps almost universal among regular soldiers, professional prejudice only partly explains why France did not have a trained reserve in 1870 and why attempts to integrate the reserves fully into defence plans after that date encountered serious difficulties. Louis-Napoleon managed to quell military opposition to the 1868 Niel law which aimed to create a trained reserve, but he failed to quiet opposition in the country which on both Left and Right revolted at the idea of being forced to submit to regular army discipline. Consequently, in 1870, with the bulk of the army locked away in Metz and Sedan, the republic's remaining military force resided in the untrained *garde mobile*. Those counting the cost of rearmament after 1871 realized that the reserves were the cheapest way of maintaining army strength. But unless properly trained and led, they were about as useful on the outbreak of war as a brace of blunderbusses. The 1872 law required conscripts released from service to return for two training periods of 23 days each, the first in the unit which they would join on mobilization and the second in a training camp. Men over 30 were assigned to the territorial army and owed two training periods of 13 days each. Reserve officers and NCOs were named among old national guards, ex-one-year volunteers and retired officers and NCOs.

War Minister Freycinet placed the final touches on reserve organization. The three-year service law of 1889 raised the total manpower available to the army by one-third and resulted in the creation of the 'mixed' regiments, composed both of one reserve and two territorial battalions. These mixed regiments proved difficult to train and administer, as training requirements and status of officers differed for each group, complicating their assignment to the separate reserve and territorial battalions within the regiment. A 19 July 1892 law abolished the 'mixed' regiments by transferring the three youngest classes in the territorial army into the reserve, creating the reserve regiment.[9] These reorganized reserve and territorial regiments were tested by Freycinet in the 1892 manoeuvres: 'We were all struck by the martial aspect of the men, by the endurance they showed and the spirit with which the reserves and the territorials executed the various movements', Freycinet wrote, perhaps over-optimistically.[10] Others reckoned that the reserves needed a stronger regular cadre, and a 25 July 1893 law named 10 generals and 20 brigadiers to reserve commands, while allocating two senior officers and captains in each regular regiment to stiffen reserve units. Supporters of this law claimed that this lent more experienced officers to the reserves, helping them over the rough spots of inexperience and integrating the reserves more closely into the defence structure. Critics countered that this reform created a class of idlers within the regiments, swelling the number of regular cadres. At the same time, steps were taken to integrate reserve and territorial officers into the defence network: in August 1878, they were given their ranks as their personal property, a measure applied to regular officers since 1834 to prevent arbitrary or politically motivated dismissals. Prefects were encouraged to invite them, in uniform, to official functions, reserve officers could advance to the rank of major[11] and Boulanger set aside a small number of *légions d'honneur* for them.

In its general lines, the reserve organization was an incontestable success. Despite a shaky start, reservists and territorials effectively joined the regular army in 1914. But the war also revealed defects in reserve training and leadership, due partly to Radical reforms after

1900, but also to a shortage of reserve cadres. Critics had noted a discouragement among reserve officers for some time, and generally blamed it on professional disdain for their part-time colleagues.[12] 'Because, by force of tradition, one wanted to conserve the national guard under the name of the territorial army, one has not only created distinctions prejudicial to the solidity of the forces, to their training and good wartime administration, but also one has dug a sort of moral trench (between regular and territorial officers)', wrote the *Progrès militaire* on 20 January 1886. Only in the artillery, where reserve and regular officers were often graduates of the *Ecole Polytechnique*, was this friction thought absent.[13] The boredom and sterility of training periods were also blamed for the lack of enthusiasm of young men for reserve command. But while reserve officers perhaps did not find all of the encouragement they might expect from their professional colleagues, the fact remains that the inadequate incentives the government offered reserve officers were a more important factor in the shortfall of reserve cadres – after deducting the trifling prestige, officers found that training periods and uniforms put them considerably out of pocket. The recruitment of reserve cadres depended less on the attitude of professionals toward them than on the concessions offered them by the government and the prestige the army enjoyed in the nation. In Germany, high army prestige ensured the recruitment of quality reserve cadres: 'The doctorate is the calling card, but the reserve commission is the open door', it was often said across the Vosges before 1914. In France, however, the recruitment of reserve cadres was hampered by a general lack of incentives, both financial and patriotic, which became more pronounced following the Dreyfus affair when reserve officer vacancies grew alarmingly.

Long service was a third concession generally reckoned to have been made to the old army. Five years' service was adopted largely through pressure by Adolphe Thiers, once Louis-Philippe's chief minister and first provisional president of the Third Republic, who believed firmly in the value of a long-service professional force as a bulwark against revolution. Having done little more than delay the adoption of other reforms, he stuck on this issue. Trochu's call for three years' service was rejected by 455 votes to 227, and a popular compromise offered by General Charenton suggesting a system in which conscripts would serve not less than one year and not more than four was narrowly headed off by Thiers, who threatened to resign if anything less than five years was adopted. This proved successful blackmail against republicans who saw in Thiers the only man with the prestige and experience to limit the German peace demands as well as the best guarantee against a monarchist restoration.[14]

But if five years' service was a victory for the conservative notions of a long-service professional army, it was a hollow one, for no French conscript ever served five years; all served considerably less. While ostensibly placating Thiers, the National Assembly took steps to insure that short service would be the rule by allowing the war minister to release conscripts before their legal service had expired and refusing to vote the funds necessary to keep conscripts for long periods. The longest serving conscripts in the class of 1873, for instance, served only three years and eight months.[15] Regimental commanders sent many conscripts home in the winter months because they could not afford to feed them. In January 1879, 20,794 men were given a four-month winter leave and the following year the figure rose to 34,337.[16] On 20 October 1880, the war minister decreed that soldiers would serve only 40 months with four months' winter leave in their last year. This was soon reduced to 36 months – three years' service.

The financial limitations imposed forced the army to fall back on its pre-1870 practice of dividing the contingent into two portions by the drawing of lots, one group to serve six months before joining the reserves while the second group remained in barracks until released by the war minister. Monteilhet concluded that this system was another conservative concession to the old army while it demonstrated further the ability of Assembly reactionaries to dilute the principle of national service.[17] But rather than being imposed by conservatives, this system was the logical outcome of the reformist desire to frustrate five years' service through financial starvation. Far from reminding officers of the comfortable old days, this system was generally unpopular in the forces, especially in the infantry which incorporated the six-month soldiers while the bulk of the contingents' second portion went to the cavalry, artillery and engineers. Infantry officers complained that the arrangement meant numbers well below establishment, a constant turnover of recruits and the virtual impossibility of forming conscript NCOs, vital for the reserves.[18] By 1880, officers were demanding a regular and evenly applied three-year service as preferable to the system of winter leave which 'disrupted the rhythm of regimental life, left companies short-staffed and lowered the efficiency of corporals and NCOs sent on leave'.[19] The fact that these demands were not met earlier had less to do with conservative pressure than with Gambetta's fears that an official declaration of three years' service might provoke Bismarck. In any case, many officers were disappointed when Laisant's 1876 three-year service measure was defeated largely due to Gambetta's refusal to support it.[20]

The five years' service measure was a product of conservative pressure but survived in its legal form because of short-term republican political concerns. The 1872 law did not create the army of longserving regulars favoured by the Right, but progressively introduced the three-year service army called for by reformers. War ministers steadily reduced service time and cut the number of men placed in the second portion of the contingent in half, from 40 to 20 per cent, until General Ferron abolished the second portion altogether in 1887.[21]

Conscript Class – Infantry Contingent:[22]

	1st portion	2nd portion	total
1872	84,147	53,203	137,350
1873	85,375	56,910	142,285
1874	85,600	46,400	132,000
1875	85,700	41,663	127,363
1876	76,749	56,152	132,901
1877	82,130	41,813	123,943
1878	104,096	31,504	135,600
1879	105,000	43,535	148,535
1880	120,800	30,200	151,000
1881	112,400	28,100	140,500
1882	116,000	29,000	145,000

The application of universal service combined with the gradual replacement of officers of the old army brought about a definite change of atmosphere in the forces. Boulanger's painting of sentry boxes blue, white and red symbolized the republic's conquest of the army and the arrival of a new generation of officers who rejected the blind discipline of the pre-1870 force. 'The period which corresponded to Boulangism modified the conception of discipline evolved after the 1870 war', wrote Emile Mayer. 'The influence of peace had relaxed the rigours of discipline. Universal service imposed on all French youth, the incorporation of the elite on equal footing with the rest of the nation, had brought about some progress in the current educational processes and above all had modified the general outlook of the army.'[23]

Permanent garrisons and regional recruitment, republicans argued, would forge links between the army and the nation. The recruitment debate had raged since the French Revolution when the provincial legions of the *ancien régime* had gradually been absorbed into the nationally recruited and numbered Napoleonic regiments. Restoration attempts to found departmental legions broke up on the rocks of desertion and indiscipline, and the experiment was quickly abandoned. Government officials feared that locally recruited regiments might falter in a civil crisis. Regional recruitment was largely maintained, but its effects were mitigated by frequent changes of garrison. Soldiers argued that this system eliminated local influence in the regiment, minimized regional differences in size, education and military aptitude of recruits and eased the problems of replacement in wartime, while constant movement encouraged regiments to discard excess baggage and to remain battle-ready.

Republicans argued that this system created a pretorian force whose attitudes and recruitment had separated army and nation. The army of the empire had been little more than a mercenary band. How could decent folk look with pride to an alcoholic and syphilis-ridden soldiery closest to barmen, police constables and country girls short of cash? Reformers argued that regional recruitment would strengthen the links between the population and the forces while achieving the goal of 'making for the entire country a military school, which, rather than remaining a school of debasement, will become a true school of public morality'.[24] Lewal agreed: 'It is the military family living side by side with the civilian family; it is more than the juxtaposition, it is the blending, in their normal existence of two parts of the same family', he wrote.

Cohesion and solidarity will be strengthened, *esprit de corps* more developed with the additional element of local pride, the officer's position more solidly based, the constant relations with civil society will raise their prestige, and their material position will be better. Soldiers, in constant contact with their families and friends, will behave better. Morality and the worth of the army will be better off.[25]

Regional recruitment encouraged NCOs to re-enlist, vital for a short service army, allowed officers to keep an eye on soldiers while on leave, encouraged regimental pride, would solidify links with reservists and territorials, facilitate mobilization and discourage desertion.[26]

The 24 July 1873 law decreed that regiments were to be recruited nationally, but the provision was increasingly ignored.[27] By 1877, all but infantrymen were serving within their military regions. Gambetta reckoned that regional recruitment and permanent garrisons had cemented links between the army and the nation, adjourning any sedition: 'Monsieur Gambetta considers that the recently adopted system of army organization in geographical divisions has kept the soldiers, now mostly young men, in communication with the sympathy of the people', wrote the American ambassador to Paris on 8 June 1877.

Many of the higher officers are republicans and others would not favor a movement which could be of profit only to Bonapartists. These facts are known to those about the Marshal, and will probably prevent any attempt at a coup. But if attempted, it will fail ignominiously. Every city will arise in indignation, and proclaim the downfall of the government... M. Gambetta then went on to explain that... since the war the army had been renewed from beginning to end; that it was no longer composed of old soldiers having no home and no opinion, but of young men... who had all sorts of moral and material connections with the country and who could not be used as mercenaries to overthrow its institutions. Among superior officers, there are many republicans who would resist any usurpation.[28]

Disparities in population and the need to concentrate large numbers of troops in the north-east meant that comprehensive regional recruitment was never possible. But regional recruitment was quietly encouraged both for reasons of politics and practicality. An attempt by General Berthaut to change the law officially was rebuffed in 1877, but the war minister submitted proposals again in 1881.[29] In April 1886, Boulanger ordered recruitment by regions whenever possible and by 1889 fully three-fifths of French soldiers served close to home,[30] although none were allowed to serve in their actual home subdivision.

The combination of regional recruitment and permanent garrisons transformed civil-military relations at the local level. The increase in the number of regiments meant that towns which had never before seen soldiers now hosted garrisons. This not only placed many backwaters in touch with outsiders for the first time, but brought trade, prosperity and the breath of France into formerly closed communities.

Competition for barracks was keen among provincial towns, and municipal councils vied with their neighbours in offering land and local funds to supplement barracks construction. Du Barail managed to squeeze extra cash out of the Saumur town council by pointing out that Angoulême was prepared to lay out substantial sums to have the cavalry school transferred there.[31] 'Once upon a time, the presence of the army in a town, except in a few patriotic departments, was an unwelcome blessing', the *Avenir militaire* wrote on 16 May 1876. 'The army formed a separate caste; soldiers living apart from the population were looked upon askance. Today things have changed. Obligatory service, although attenuated, has meant service for many young men who generally return home the better for it.'

Once regarded as undisciplined rogues, soldiers now became an accepted and acceptable feature of provincial life. The army was integrated into local events, mounting a decorative guard on official buildings and participating in local fêtes. Officers organized local sporting societies while retired officers and NCOs provided physical instruction in many state schools: 'In this way, [students] will be given the first ideas of discipline without which neither armies nor nations can survive', wrote the *Avenir militaire* on 21 July 1876. Councils proudly named streets after the local regiment and parents eyed officers as good matches for their daughters. Indeed, many observers pointed to a marked increase in shotgun marriages as proof that regional recruitment and permanent garrisons had perhaps brought soldiers and locals into too close contact.[32]

Far from entrenching the old army, national service, regional recruitment and military reform, combined with successful republican attempts to stimulate patriotic sentiments in the country, drew a once outcast army into the pale of French society. With universal service, as with schools, roads and railways, republicans looked to pour the foundations of a strong nation. Three years with the regiment forged a greater sense of national unity, melting rich and poor, Bretons and Basques, Provençals and Parisians into one community. The laws reaped the benefit of what American historian Eugene Weber calls 'that great explosion of change after 1880' which eroded barriers of remoteness centuries thick. By 1889, conscription, once detested as a 'blood tax' levied by an alien and distant government, was a duty accepted almost everywhere in France. In the Pyrenees, Auvergne and Savoy where, before, young men fled rather than go to fight, conscripts now reported docilely for induction. The army was no longer the occupying force imposed by Parisians and prefects, but a joint stock company in which all Frenchmen held shares. Rather than create a gulf between the nation and the army, the Third Republic's conscription laws joined the two in a bond broken only by the Dreyfus affair. 'By the 1890s, there is persuasive evidence that the army was no longer "theirs" but "ours"', wrote Eugene Weber.[33] Gambetta, Freycinet, Trochu and other reformers who preached that successful military reform was not simply a question of substituting a few generals but of reconstructing the army on a solid national foundation, had largely achieved their aim.

The trauma of the Franco-Prussian War convinced most Frenchmen that a thorough reform of the army was vital. Defeat came as a severe blow to a nation which believed itself the cultural and military master of Europe. Happy and secure memories of the volunteers of the Year II, Napoleon's near invincible grognards and the almost unbroken string of victories over Arabs, Russians, Mexicans and Austrians turned to dust in the humiliation of the cruel amputation of two provinces and the huge indemnity imposed by Bismarck on the bayonets of an occupying army. Frenchmen of all persuasions lost little time in searching for the causes of their defeat. While all recognized that the war had been disastrously handled by empire and republic alike, they unanimously agreed that the basic causes of the defeat went deeper than bad organization and bad leadership. Freycinet wrote in his *La Guerre en province* in 1871 that France had been inferior to Prussia 'in number, in armament, in organization'. Numerical inferiority had been exacerbated by lack of training, while an almost total absence of arms standardization meant chaos on the battlefield. 'Far and away the greatest difficulties sprang from lack of organization', Freycinet wrote. 'In the last analysis, it was that which defeated us.' Poor discipline and staff work and support services in disarray were especially to blame. 'The French soldier is much easier to direct when fortune is kind than when she frowns', he continued. 'Victory sustains the soldier's morale; defeat disheartens him, discourages him and makes his job odious to him.'[34]

Lack of discipline and sound military organization were simply the fruits of imperial corruption. Freycinet continued:

Is it possible for an entire nation to give itself over for 20 years to the pursuit of riches, to sink itself in frivolity, to lose the habit of austerity and virtue, and for the army, which after all is born of the people and represents them, to do likewise without losing some of its traditional good qualities? ... This national enervation is the primary cause of our military weakness; it is that which explains the gradual abandonment of science and hard work within the ranks, the slow disappearance of the spirit of discipline, ... and finally the deplorable management which resulted in France's finding herself at the crucial moment equipped with incomplete cadres, empty arsenals, and antiquated methods.[35]

For once Left and Right united to heap blame on the empire for lulling into a twilight of decadence characterized, according to Jules Simon, by 'a combination of ridiculous luxury, shameless speculation, and dubious customs'. Colonel Fleury, the Emperor's aide-de-camp, confessed that the late government 'wasn't a proper empire, but we had a damn good time'. The first principle of Clausewitzian philosophy held that the army always mirrored the state of society. The year 1871 found most of French society, in a moment of rare lucidity, staring into the mirror to discover that it was middle-aged and unhealthy, easy pickings for a young and confident Germany.

Having diagnosed the disease, the physicians were unable to agree on a cure, although everyone peddled his own brand of patent medicine. In attempting to categorize this supermarket of military theories, one can say that they fell broadly, very broadly, into three political categories – conservative, moderate republican and radical. Conservatives formed a ragbag of Legitimists, Orleanists, Bonapartists and simple reactionaries like Thiers who supported the republic for want of a better alternative. Bundled together by their fear of social upheaval, they looked to re-create the old army whose success record at putting down Paris' periodic revolts was above average – or at least better than their performance against the Prussians. While conceding that some tinkering might need to be done with military organization, the army should be kept as exclusively professional as possible. Long service would guarantee that conscripts not only received military training, but also a military 'education' – in short, blind obedience. It weaned soldiers away from their civilian trades, substituted a military vocation and encouraged them to re-enlist, assuring the army a strong corps of long-serving NCOs. Thiers told the parliamentary army committee that a few disciplined troops were much more valuable than 'a mass of reservists who aren't worth a damn'.[36] However, as noted before, the influence of this group was limited almost exclusively to Thiers' delaying tactics.

While by no means all partisans of national service and military reform were republicans, this group rallied support for the reform and modernization of the forces. Moderate republicans and thinking soldiers could not fail to point out that a small professional army, while perhaps impressive on parade, was virtually useless in national defence. It was 1870 that confirmed the modern trend towards mass armies, to which France must conform or else measure her weight in the European balance of power in grams rather than kilos. However, 1870 also demonstrated that the question of mass armies went beyond the simple acquisition of more bodies for the forces. While the republican phase of the war had been carried forward on a gratifying wave of patriotism and little else, the arrival of the Prussians revealed that in some areas of France patriotic spirit was in short supply. Far from greeting the invaders in sullen silence, some inhabitants, even in the traditionally patriotic east, offered aid and comfort. Many countryfolk were simply indifferent to the fate of France, or worse, preferred the Germans to marauding French or *francs-tireurs*, too much like the *armées révolutionaires* of the Year II. Behind the battle lines, patriots were often turned to the enemy by peasants fearing reprisals, while away from the front life was hardly affected by the nation's agonies.[37]

Moderate republicans like Gambetta realized that the 1870 defeat stemmed to a disquieting degree from a failure of patriotism. Despite the cataclysmic events of the Revolution and disruptions of the empire, the notion of the fatherland had yet to percolate through to large sections of the rural masses. The tentacles of state centralism did not reach into Auvergnat hamlets, Pyrenean valleys or the flat pinelands of the Landes. Language and sheer distance stood between the peasant and any sense of national community, locking him into a remoteness which equated outsiders with bandits and taxmen. After 1870, soldiers noted with bitterness the 'aggressive and cowardly' hostility and the 'little developed ... military spirit and patriotism' in several parts of the country.[38] Republicans must reach into rural heartland with roads and schools, to forge one nation from this Babel of patois and provincialism. The army was a key piece in the jigsaw of a modern, civilized and republican France: 'The gymnast and the soldier must everywhere stand side by side with the teacher,' Gambetta told a Bordeaux audience in June 1871, 'so that our children, our soldiers and our fellow citizens are all able to hold a sword, fire a rifle, make long marches, spend nights out of doors, to support bravely all hardships for the fatherland.'[39]

For all who had fought with the republic, the great lesson of the war was the need for discipline. In the small army of the Second Empire, discipline was acquired by each soldier as part of his profession, like marksmanship, and Algerian generals led the army in devising special methods to instil it in recalcitrants. However, for a variety of ideological and electoral reasons, republicans insisted that soldiers be treated as citizens, with rights and duties. Social discipline must become the basis of military discipline. While Thiers argued that social upheaval was inevitable and sought to create an elite force to quash it whenever it raised its head, republicans believed that the army could be used to heal the wounds of several generations of revolution and help France towards a new national consensus. Reformers offered an answer to conservative charges that France's political, religious and regional divisions precluded any consensus strong enough to persuade Frenchmen to bury their quarrels in the interest of national defence and internal stability. Thiers had argued that short service suited countries united behind definite national goals, but France had only a *frondeur* passion for equality: 'Military education is even more necessary when there is no dominant national passion', read an 1879 report which repeated Thiers' arguments verbatim. 'Italy has a passion for unity, Germany for conquest, Russia for race. France has the passion of the republic. This passion is self-sufficient and can no longer give any resilience.'[40] The war minister, General Gresley, had crossed out this argument and scribbled in the margin: 'And Alsace-Lorraine!' Clearly, many believed that there was no conflict of interest between short service and discipline because France had what Thiers might have called, had he been more honest, a 'passion for revenge'. Reformers believed that military spirit and patriotism were not antithetical, but should fuse to form a new national consensus behind a strong army.

La République française, mouthpiece of the Gambettists, led a chorus of politicians and soldiers who called for the transformation of the army into a school of civic instruction. Military service must be sufficiently long to allow conscripts to develop a strong national feeling. 'Military training is not everything', Freycinet wrote in January 1872. 'There is another kind of instruction still more important – civic instruction. In one year, social classes cannot arrive at any real understanding of each other. The time is too short for them to forget mutual rivalries in a common love of country.'[41] General Trochu, whose attempts to organize the defence of Paris with a pick-up force of professional soldiers, volunteers and national guards had confirmed his pre-war views on French military decadence, supported Freycinet. 'Character debasement, laziness, public corruption and social indiscipline contributed more to our defeat than the bad organization of our arsenals, the weakness or incompetence of our leaders, the small number of soldiers and our losses', he maintained.[42] 'If we consider the present state of the nation, the divisions, the failures, the passions apparent everywhere which do not seem to diminish, one can say that indiscipline is the principal obstacle to all efforts of governments, legislators, reformers to re-establish order and harmony, to return the country to stability and peace', he continued. His solution was 'social regeneration through the army'.[43]

While superficial conservatives attributed von Moltke's successes to the aristocratic caste mentality of the Prussian officer corps and the rigidly hierarchical nature of the Prussian state, Trochu reckoned that Prussia had succeeded in inculcating its population with a true 'military spirit', creating a disciplined society where respect for the army was high and where military service was the necessary adjunct of citizenship. He complained that France had a 'warrior spirit . . . an effervescent force', in contrast to the Prussian 'military spirit . . . a tranquil force, effective, disciplined, solid and lasting, [which] alone . . . can sustain a nation in great adversity, armies in perilous retreat after lost battles, and give to both the moral resilience and aptitude to prepare for revenge'. Trochu shared with Gambetta and Freycinet the belief that the 'professional education' of the old army should now be accompanied by a 'civic education . . . which associates within the new army rich and poor, literate and illiterate with the defence of the country'. The French army should become 'the school of national discipline and . . . the school to regenerate the public spirit destroyed by our revolutions'. 'In France,' Trochu claimed, 'military spirit, as far as it goes, is found only in the regiment. In Prussia . . . it is everywhere. The reason for this temperamental difference is very obvious. In France, it is the nation which, eventually, formed the army. In Prussia, it is the army which, rapidly, formed the nation.'[44] The *Avenir militaire* also called for the army to be tranformed into 'a vast school . . . Universal service is a solution to the social question.'[45]

The idea of the 'army school' inspired by defeat was adopted by republicans and a new elite of young reforming officers, like Colonel Lewal, first commandant of the new war college and future war minister, and Lieutenant colonel Berge, who rose to corps commander subsequently artillery chief. 'The army must become a beneficial corporation,' Lewal wrote in 1873, 'a school of morals which returns to the country better, more law-abiding men more respectful towards authority, friends of order and honest men.' The barracks must become a schoolroom where soldiers learn to read and write and officers lecture men on their 'military and civic duties. They will look to stimulate honesty and patriotism.'[46] Berge deplored the separation of the army and the nation which had increased since 1815 and which he said could be bridged only by 'radical reform' in the army,[47] including universal military service. While some conservatives warmed to calls to discipline and hierarchy, the views of Trochu, Lewal, Berge and many other military reformers went beyond a narrow expression of class egoism[48] or a soldier's obsession with order for order's sake. Military efficiency and ultimate victory depended upon France's social regeneration. 'We must develop education . . . and above all military civic education . . . before reducing service to three years', War Minister General Farre told parliament on 15 June 1881.[49]

Boulanger was perhaps the best known of a series of war ministers – Farre, Berthaut, Campenon, Thibaudin, Lewal and Freycinet – who worked to associate the army with the patriotic aspirations of the new republic. The army became the symbol of a France united behind the spirit of regeneration: Alsace, Lorraine and national self-respect would be reconquered on the points of bayonets. The army's new role as vanguard of patriotism constituted a decisive break with its recent past. This is not to say that officers before 1870 had not been patriotic. But theirs was an elitist, inverted patriotism which associated French glories with the traditions of the regiment and the great deeds of professional soldiers; it was patriotism by proxy – soldiers formed a class apart and the two communities united, like ratepayers and dustmen, by toleration rather than esteem. Republicans sought to transform barracks into seminaries of French patriotism and its officers into missionaries of national unity. In this they were remarkably successful. But the process was to prove a slow one because it required a thorough reform of the outlook and attitudes which characterized the old army.

An obvious stumbling block to republican plans to transform the army into the forge of national unity was the embarrassingly low intellectual level of the officer corps. This stemmed in great part from the low prestige attached to service in the old army and a career structure which discouraged study: the talents of intelligent, efficient officers in the post-Napoleonic French army were seldom harnessed to improve military quality and they formed an eccentric and generally discouraged minority. Colonel Lewal complained that the prestige of the officer corps had bottomed out in France because of 'the spectacle of its idleness and poverty of its knowledge'. In North Africa especially, courage and cunning were thought more than acceptable substitutes for intelligence. The French army had never cavilled overmuch about officer education. Half of Napoleon's generals, according to Jomini, could not even write their own names, and they had conquered Europe. The inability to write persisted well into the 19th century, especially among officers promoted through the ranks. Sergeants promoted second lieutenants were expected to know how to read, write and keep simple accounts and have a very basic knowledge of history and geography. Probably half of French officers had only this basic education, but even these minimum standards were sometimes winked at. British officers had generally avoided their socially inferior French counterparts in the Crimea while observers had been struck in 1870 by the superior bearing and education of Prussian officers: the Prussian Crown Prince was appalled when faced with a captured zouave captain unable to write.

The problem, however, was not simply one of low social recruitment. The officer career structure actively discouraged study. Lewal complained that regimental libraries were intentionally kept small for easy transport while the promotion system favoured age rather than application – inspecting generals were not interested in 'general education or knowledge indispensable to an officer'.[50] Under the Second Empire, military decadence reached its peak. Saint-Cyr was more interested in turning out 'men of the world' proficient in dancing than 'serious officers', while in the regiment officers worried more about home comforts than military efficiency. Lewal claimed that 40,000 francs was spent annually to subsidize the theatre at the Châlons training camp, while only 100,000 francs went towards training the entire army.[51] 'To convince officers to educate themselves for their own good and for the good of the army, to satisfy their conscience or their ego, was like preaching in the desert', Lewal wrote. Trochu, Lewal, Berge and others argued that the army lived by its legends, occasionally bolstered by a shamelessly exaggerated bush victory over poorly armed, disorganized natives. No-one questioned the courage of French officers; Crimea and Italy had proved that. But 1870 revealed that bravery was no substitute for efficiency. Lewal wrote:

The coup de force, brillant action, audacity alone won praise and made reputations, distorted further by distance... During the great war in Europe, people were surprised at the shortcomings of those whom public opinion had thought so competent and esteemed so highly ... One thought that energy, courage, training, audacity would overcome all obstacles and that the *furia francese* would supplement, as before, foresight, ability, science. The last war demonstrates rather cruelly how wrong we were.[52]

The political implications of the poor quality of military leadership for reformers were obvious. Many doubted whether, given the intellectual doldrums of the French officer corps, the army was capable of becoming the school for patriotism and military regeneration – the first requirement for the school of the nation was competent teachers worthy of respect and emulation. 'As things now stand', General Billot wrote on 2 July 1874, 'the intellectual level of the army is absolutely inferior to the intellectual worth of the enlightened section of the nation.'[53] 'Military command must be exercised by the nation's elite', the *Avenir militaire* pleaded on 21 March 1884. 'The officer corps must form an aristocracy not of birth, but of intellect and morals. Officers are the teachers of youth . . . The Prussian army . . . owes its success, apart from secondary factors, to the exceptional worth of its officer corps.' On 11 May 1884, the newspaper complained that officers were not intelligent enough to deal with conscripted university students who held them up to ridicule.

Reformers looked to raise the intellectual standards of the officer corps and establish a career structure which rewarded intelligence and industry. Military schools were the first to feel the winds of reform. General Trochu complained that the scarcity of military schools and the low quality of the education which they offered had contributed generously to the defeat. In 1870, Prussia counted 23 military schools; France had only six. 'Among all these reforms, perhaps the most important . . . is the establishment of military education', Trochu wrote.[54] In Prussia, seven military schools sent a steady stream of well-educated men into the officer corps; France depended largely on Saint-Cyr. German second lieutenants destined for the artillery, engineers and cavalry received additional training in one of the special schools which prepared men for these arms. The German scholastic edifice was capped by the Berlin *Kriegsakademie* which recruited the best officers for staff training. The educational standards imposed on all Prussian officers guaranteed an elite and intellectually homogeneous corps. All NCOs were trained in six special schools which assured high standards in the lower ranks. Military traditions were further encouraged in a number of army-run schools for sons of NCOs destined for the forces.[55]

In contrast, French military schools reflected the army's intellectual decadence and sharp inter-arm rivalry. History, geography, maths, physics, chemistry and German were included in the entrance examination for Saint-Cyr, but standards were kept low enough to give every applicant a fighting chance. Nor was the school curriculum particularly stimulating. 'Saint-Cyr hardly prepares [an officer] for intellectual development', General Billot complained in 1874.[56] Trochu lamented that the academy was ruled, not by a military spirit, but 'a schoolboy spirit ... the continuation of school', instancing the rough jokes and even riots as proof that life at the school was often like a scene from *Zéro de conduite*. 'In the past, the schoolboy spirit, which forms the basis of the secular traditions of our school at Saint-Cyr, was apparent not only in the odious coarse jokes of which I have spoken, but in the periodic revolts which gave the war department a rough passage', he wrote in 1879.[57] In 1840, 40 of 130 students were sent to the regiments as privates after a riot at the school; eight years later, another 70 students were sent down to the ranks. Soon after General Louis Hanrion arrived to take command in 1872, he was presented with a substantial bill for damage caused by cadets on the Paris train, mostly by sabre thrusts applied to upholstered parts of the carriages.

The smack of firm command brought order and a more professional atmosphere to the academy: Hanrion placed NCOs on the Paris trains to keep order and in the barracks to prevent harassment of first-year cadets. Civilian teachers unable to keep order in the classroom were replaced by officer instructors. Cadets were allowed to move freely between classes, punishment records henceforth followed students to their regiments – a measure which Hanrion reckoned curbed tempestuous spirits. Cadets were billeted according to height, so mixing social classes and students from Jesuit and state schools. War Minister du Barail abolished the separate infantry and cavalry sections at Saint-Cyr in 1873, encouraging future cavalrymen to work hard for a place in a cavalry regiment and eliminating rivalries between the two sections.[58] Brigade manoeuvres were instituted and from 1876, cadets were dispatched to autumn manoeuvres. Academic standards were improved so that places at the *Ecole de guerre* would not be monopolized by the well-educated ex-Polytechnicians.[59] At the *Ecole polytechnique*, the 'côte jésuite', a speech traditionally delivered by the bottom-placed polytechnician from a state lycée to the highest-ranked ex-Postard in his class calling upon him to set aside his clerical prejudices, was abolished in 1879, regarded as degrading and damaging to student solidarity.[60] These reforms cut down friction between cadets, encouraging a spirit of fraternity among future officers and an atmosphere of serious preparation at the academy. The number of students at Saint-Cyr and the *Ecole polytechnique* doubled and applications to Saint-Cyr tripled. Rising entrance standards reflected reforms, and preparatory colleges began to point to Saint-Cyr entrants as indicators of academic achievement.

'NCO schools' were also established for each arm and for the administration to filter officers promoted through the ranks, so bridging the enormous educational crevasse which in the old army had separated academy-trained officers from ex-sergeants. The army's educational pyramid was capped by the 1876 creation of the *Ecole de guerre*, modelled on Berlin's *Kriegsakademie*. Entry into the general staff was reserved for graduates of the *Ecole de guerre*, channelling the educated and hardworking toward the top of the military hierarchy. Regimental libraries and military publications expanded substantially. Officers who once frittered away time in bars and brothels were now expected to acquire a knowledge of their profession. Map exercises and Kriegsspiel, which had confused Louis-Napoleon's generals in 1868, became a regular feature of officer training, and war ministers like General Lewal encouraged officers once under threat of no promotion by MacMahon to write on military subjects.[61] While one must not exaggerate the results of this revival of professional interest, the general quality of the officer corps improved substantially.

Historians who argue that the army of the republic was simply the old army of the empire superimposed onto the edifice of the 'nation in arms', a *crème chantilly* which embellished but added little substance to national defence, little appreciate the enormous changes wrought by reformers on the ways and habits of the old army – changes which forced officers to come to terms with the new world, even if reluctantly.

The army which the republic inherited in 1871 was a patchwork of arms and services, balkanized by inter-arm prejudice and rivalry and under a war ministry which coordinated rather than commanded. Lacking an efficient peacetime command structure, the imperial army had been little more than a loose association of arms and regiments periodically brought together to fight a war. Frequent changes of garrison kept regiments slowly drifting across France like Bedouin tribes, confining officers to the cheap hotels and cafés of dreary garrison towns, immersed in the minutiae and parochial concerns of the regiment. Reformers set out to transform the army into an effective organization, narrowing the divisions of arm and education, and to settle it down, allowing regiments to put down roots among local populations. The task was not simply one of administrative rearrangement; the army had to be firmly integrated into the social and institutional structure of the nation.

Improved standards of officer education, a heightened sense of professionalism and a tighter command structure poured cold water on the embers of inter-arm rivalry. Tribalism in the old army had reflected differences in the professional status and to a certain degree the social origins of the officer corps: studious staff officers, well-bred cavalrymen, educated and middle-class artillerymen and sappers, rough infantrymen and even rougher colonial officers, administrative and supply officers hardly regarded as soldiers at all, and, at the bottom of the military pecking order, transportation officers, all ex-NCOs with meagre career prospects. These divisions went beyond the exchange of good-natured jibes, splintering the old army into rival factions, each protecting its patch. Before the war, these rivalries had hamstrung efficiency and reform; on the battlefield, they boiled into bitter recrimination. Combat officers seethed against the incompetence and negligence of administrative officers, when most of the blame lay with a faulty military organization. The staff corps was accused of being more in touch with the theories than the realities of war. Artillery officers were more concerned with protecting their guns than the infantry while the cavalry excited both annoyance and admiration by its incompetent reconnaissance and wasteful, if courageous, attacks. Left alone, the infantry fell in heaps.

The republic looked to homogenize the officer corps, levelling standards, integrating officers into a smooth-running machine where division of labour was a function of cooperation rather than discord. The staff corps was reformed and thrown open to honest competition. Once independent administrative and supply officers were incorporated into the chain of command, their depots decentralized and service improved. In 1889, Freycinet raised infantry pay and abolished salary differentials among the arms, throwing out favours to the 'armes savantes' which were especially resented by infantrymen who felt their light pay packet a mark of second-class status. This capped a series of reforms which had struck at the exclusivity of the artillery and engineers since du Barail had named General Séré de Rivière, 'open-minded and free of the prejudices of the past', to head the engineers in 1874.[62] Lewal ended the separate promotion classifications for artillery and engineering officers in 1885, integrating them into a promotion structure based on corps committees. All combat arms were now represented on the technical committees which laid down policy in each arm to coordinate planning and inter-arm cooperation. 'He [Lewal] continues an enemy of arm exclusivity, pursuing his ideas and never missing an occasion to apply them', the *Avenir militaire* wrote of these reforms on 1 April 1885. 'No more [inter-arm] rivalry in the army, unity of command . . . unity of origin, pay and aptitude . . . We hope this logic builds a real army.'[63] The following year, Boulanger, answering critics who complained that the 'army should have a uniform, not a series of costumes', put artillery and engineering officers in red trousers like everyone else.[64] He also ordered garrison manoeuvres for all arms: 'If the general staffs carry out the minister's orders,' the *Progrès militaire* wrote on 19 June 1886, 'the arm rivalry of troops stationed in the same garrison will nearly disappear.' Military circles and messes which aimed to establish 'comradeship and solidarity . . . between all members of the great military family' had been growing since 1871. Under Boulanger, they became permanent features of every garrison – with a strict prohibition on German beer![65] The pay, uniforms and promotion opportunities for doctors, pharmacists, veterinarians, telegraphists and eventually administration officers were gradually brought into line with those of combat officers.

These reforms were not simply cosmetic; they successfully transformed the character of the officer corps, strengthening the links of professional solidarity. A new type of French officer emerged in the 1880s – better educated, more professional and more distinguished than his pre-1870 counterpart; an officer not so much of a new *class*, as historians have suggested, but of a new *sort*. The officer was no longer a nomad, shunned by the respectable, but a salaried civil servant, a stable representative of the national government like the postmaster, the chief of police or any one of the army of minor officials who invaded the provinces. Despite his low pay, the officer was now socially acceptable, a worthy match for the daughter of a respectable bourgeois. 'It was not so long ago that many officers, the last holdouts of the old school . . . found the idea of presenting themselves into a family perfectly noxious', the *Avenir militaire* declared on 16 May 1875. 'Consorting with women of doubtful morals, spending all day in the café, gambling, conversation peppered with oaths and vulgarities – all this a soldier considered infinitely preferable to the company of good society, especially civilians . . . These opinions, thank God, have had their day.'

These reforms combined with judicious appointments to the high command brought the French military revival to a peak. The 1891 manoeuvres in which 100,000 French soldiers participated were taken as proof that the French army not only matched but might also have outstripped its Teutonic rival. The German military attaché in Paris told von Hohenlohe-Schillingsfürst that 'the French army was superior to ours for the moment, that the armament and the powder were very good, and that the infantry was well up in its work';[66] while the English observer, Sir Charles Dilke, complimented the high degree of tactical cooperation among the arms, the endurance of the troops, including the reserves, and the expert handling of the artillery.[67] The future Marshal Foch, who organized the final parade, considered the 1891 manoeuvres as the first work of France's military renaissance. 'For the first time since 1870,' he said, 'the French army had demonstrated the results of 20 years of labour, showing itself educated, well-trained, equipped with excellent armaments, led by excellent cadres, in excellent spirits – in a word, a redoutable instrument of war.'[68] Others thought these claims inflated: British General Rawlinson, on a continental military tour in 1893, noted that: 'The Germans are miles ahead of the French in organization, equipment and training, and both are miles ahead of us.'[69]

In retrospect, the decade preceding the Dreyfus affair appeared to be the army's golden age. The republic had arranged a truce with its soldiers based on a realization that national sovereignty could be guaranteed only by continued cooperation. While the army was not republican in the sense that it was actively politicized, it realized that its interests and those of the regime were one – the regime created the political climate in which the soldiers could best carry out their professional duties. 'In the course of my inspections, I found everywhere much dedication, much confidence and unlimited patriotism', wrote General Billot in 1889 in a report obviously destined for his political chiefs. 'The corps commanders have begun to prepare the mobilization plans with great competence and vigorous initiative. The general staffs ... have worked with unflagging ardour and enthusiasm. In the regiments, the new units have been methodically and intelligently organised. Every possible preparation has been undertaken.'[70] But this truce between the army and the republic was a delicate one, for the potential for a misunderstanding was great. And nowhere was it greater than in the high command.

3

The high command

The Prussian victory of 1870 had been the victory of the big battalions. But more, it had been the victory of the German General Staff and its architect von Moltke. The French army laws of 1872, 1873 and 1875 had given France soldiers, but they did not give her an organization capable of preparing them for war and directing them in battle – a high command. The reason for this was political: the deputies who had called up new regiments, divisions and army corps at a stroke were reluctant to hand them over to men whose willingness to submit to the will of parliament might someday come into question. The history of civil–military relations in France between 1871 and 1914 is largely a story of the efforts of soldiers and deputies to reconcile the requirements of military efficiency with the demands of parliamentary control.

In retrospect, the surprising thing was not that the French army was defeated in 1870, but that it managed to perform as well as it did, for the organs of coordination and control were rudimentary in the extreme. The war minister was chief of the army, but his ministry, run on principles which had changed little since Louvois' time, was geared to the comfortable routine of peacetime administration. Ten 'directions' staffed by civilians who were often insensitive to army needs reserved to themselves most of the major and many of the minor decisions affecting the forces. Consultative committees made up of soldiers existed for the infantry, cavalry, artillery, engineers and staff corps, but the power of committee chairmen or even of the war minister to push entrenched directors toward reform was limited. Each director, each committee worked in isolation and no body existed to coordinate policy or to draw up an overall plan of army needs. 'The ministry reigns, the bureaux govern', the *Avenir militaire* complained on 26 August 1876.

Within this ministry, war planning was a haphazard affair. Critics complained in 1870 that the army had no plan of campaign. Rather, it had several. The Depot de la guerre amassed topographical and statistical information and prepared a smorgasbord of war plans which were available to any general who cared to consult them. Few did. Other 'directions' held plans prepared by keen officers and presented to inspecting generals or to the Emperor himself which were promptly filed away and forgotten. Prussia's defeat of Austria in 1866 demonstrated that a strategy based on a small professional army and a strong network of frontier fortresses was no longer adequate, but political pressure, financial stringency and military conservatism all combined to obstruct reform. In the absence of any rational attempt to devise a strategy in keeping with French military realities, officers called for an offensive against Prussia which the army was organizationally incapable of carrying out.[1]

The French army in 1870 had generals, but it lacked a high command. A December 1859 law had divided France into six army corps, but these in no way resembled wartime commands. Corps commanders could not inspect their corps in peacetime, nor would they lead them on mobilization. The omnipotence of the ministry directors deprived the corps commanders of much of their authority: 'The initiative of the marshals and generals placed at the head of the six great regional commands was nil', wrote Marshal Bazaine. 'They had to be prompted by the minister of war.'[2] On the outbreak of war, divisions and corps had to be cobbled together from scratch and generals hastily named to lead them. Regional commanders had no control over the supply and administrative services upon which mobilization depended, while regimental movement meant that the 'depots' which transfused men and *matériel* into each unit were often located at the other end of the country. 'The operations began', recalled Trochu. 'The first battles, so decisive for the morale of the army and the nation, were fought and no one knew the exact location of the depots and concentration points. Men and *matériel* arriving simultaneously from every direction jammed the railways, searching for and not finding the corps, the divisions the brigades to which they belonged. The confusion was indescribable.'[3] Bad organization had not been so costly during the relatively leisurely preparation for Crimea and Italy: French commanders could always count on the inefficiency of the enemy or the stoicism and bravery of their own troops to counter shortages of bullets or to rescue a misdirected manoeuvre. However, in 1870 the French faced an enemy whose high command had left nothing to chance.

The young Third Republic, like its predecessors, believed the war minister to be the army's natural chief. This command concept also guaranteed that the forces took orders directly from the government. However, in practice this notion of the war minister as the army's first soldier contained many drawbacks. In the first place, the war minister seldom remained in office long enough to establish his authority or to realize a coherent programme of reforms. Political life in the Third

Republic was characterized by frequent changes of cabinet. But this image of governmental instability was deceptive. One-third of the deposed ministers usually surfaced in the new cabinet. 'Governmental instability, ministerial stability, these are the two inseparable characteristics of French political life', the historian Auguste Soulier wrote.[4] Many ministers were virtually permanent occupants of their ministries. Finance ministers averaged five and a half years in office and foreign ministers seven and a half, lending much needed continuity to those offices. No such stability was to be found at the war department, where

Ministerial careers, February 1879–June 1940

Terms of office	1	2	3	4	5	6	7	8	9	10	Total
Ministers	217	103	71	48	28	17	13	17	14	33	561

the war portfolio changed hands more than any other in the Third Republic. Between 1871 and the outbreak of war, war ministers

War Ministers, June 1871–September 1914

Terms of Office	1	2	3	4	5	6	7	Total
Ministers	12	13	3	–	–	1	2	30

averaged barely one year in office. Eight years – 1877, 1879, 1883, 1885, 1887, 1893, 1895, 1899 – witnessed as many as three war ministers. In 1898, five different men occupied the rue Saint-Dominique, while 1911 and 1913, crucial years of military preparation, saw four war ministers each.[5] Only three ministers served in more than three cabinets between 1871 and 1914. 'Three-quarters of them did not have the time to apply the reforms which they had prepared, nor dispose of the funds which they had requested', wrote General du Barail, speaking from bitter experience.[6]

Secondly, the war ministry was seldom in the best hands. Senior generals were reluctant to risk brilliant military careers in parliamentary cloakrooms. Few were comfortable in the intrigue and invective of the political milieu, nor did they measure up to the exacting oratorical standards expected of deputies. A successful military career was capped by one of the more prestigious corps commands or a seat on the *conseil supérieur de la guerre*, not by a tenuous few months on the rue Saint-Dominique where a soldier would almost certainly be forced to take decisions which would make him unpopular in the army. Consequently, the war ministry went by default to rather junior divisional commanders – Borel, Gresley, Farre, Campenon, Thibaudin, Boulanger, Lewal, Loizillon – who had neither the authority nor the longevity to impose their will on service directors or senior generals, as du Barail discovered in 1873: 'Hardly 53 years old! That is almost a babe in arms for a minister in a gerontocratic institution where seniority is the only means of promotion which avoids criticism and rivalry.'[7]

For soldiers accustomed to traditional commands, a few months in the war ministry could be an exhausting experience. General du Barail, a cavalryman, found little good will among the civilian directors in the ministry who did little to disguise their contempt for soldiers. Only graduates of the *Ecole polytechnique* earned their grudging respect. 'The Chamber is sovereign by right . . . the bureaucracy is sovereign in fact', he wrote. His task was complicated by the fact that he was forced to reside with the government in Versailles leaving the rue Saint-Dominique to his administrators: 'The ministry in Paris therefore escaped from my direct control', he wrote. 'It took a great amount of time to obtain the slightest information. Also, all questions had to be asked in writing so that the replies were brief and unsatisfactory.' The directors were generally hostile to reform, especially the 14 July 1873 law which substituted 19 army corps on a war footing for the six administrative corps of the empire, for they stood to lose many of their powers to the corps commanders. 'The legislative power laid down the basis for this reform. It remained with the executive power to apply it, but the ministry bureaux could not be brought to draw up the decrees. The service chiefs, when pressed, simply replied that it was "an enormous task and could not be done too quickly".' The war minister was forced to draw up the decrees himself.[8] In this atmosphere, it is hardly surprising that many reforms foundered on the rocks of an administrative *non possumus* or slipped away with the deposed minister to his new provincial command.

Reformers determined to strengthen the control of the war minister over his directors and to transfer many of the decisions from the ministry to corps commanders, who would now have control over their own transport, supply and medical services. 'It is administrative centralization which I condemn and whose abolition I want', demanded Trochu.[9] Du Barail began by replacing his civilian directors with soldiers who, it was hoped, would pay their military superiors more respect. General Séré la Rivière was named to head the engineers whose refusal to cooperate with other arms was notorious. War Minister Lewal named officers from different arms to sit on the various arm committees in an attempt to increase inter-arm cooperation. Boulanger obliged officers serving on arm committees to alternate between ministry service and troop command to give them more practical experience. He also set out to streamline the ministry by creating seven technical sections to replace the 70 committees set up to study individual problems. These technical sections would form the link between the directions and the arms committees and so end the state of war which too often existed between the 'directions' and the arms committees.[10] Corps commanders were given far more authority to make decisions – in 1882, the once independent supply and medical services were brought under the command umbrella.

This programme of ministerial reform and decentralization was only a partial success. War ministers remained birds of passage too often ignored by entrenched officials, and new men imported into the ministry to shake out old habits soon fell into the comfortable administrative routine. The French army still possessed nothing comparable to the great German General Staff to centralize strategic planning and to prepare the army for war.

The changing role of the war minister more than anything else pushed parliament towards the creation of a permanent and powerful general staff. The war ministers of the republic's first decade had been considered as technicians. MacMahon insisted on naming the ministers of war and the navy himself irrespective of the political leanings of the cabinet. Du Barail noted that his cabinet colleagues considered him to be 'a negligible quantity because I was not a deputy' and so he dealt with his morning mail while they discussed politics.[11] The job of the war minister was to administer the army and remain above politics. However, with MacMahon's resignation in 1879, republicans insisted on appointing men known for their republican sympathies who would guarantee the army's loyalty. General Farre, war minister in Freycinet's 1879 ministry, was the army's first 'republican' minister of war. Throughout the 1880s and 1890s, generals named to the rue Saint-Dominique were selected from among those known for their republican sentiments: Campenon, Logerot, Lozillon, Mercier and Billot had all distinguished themselves as loyal supporters of the regime. However, on at least two occasions, war ministers selected on the basis of their political convictions attempted to use their office to carve out political reputations.

A political manifesto issued by the Prince Napoleon in January 1883 led to a demand from the Left for the exile of all members of former ruling houses. As a compromise, Prime Minister Jules Ferry ordered the retirement of three Orleanist princes serving in the army. War Minister General Billot resigned rather than carry out this order against three men whose conduct had been above reproach. After Generals Campenon and Thoumas declined an invitation to take over the war ministry, Ferry was obliged to name General Thibaudin to carry out the execution. Thibaudin was desperately unpopular in the army even before taking office. Alleged to have fled captivity in 1870 after pledging his word of honour not to escape, he had enlisted with the Government of National Defence under a false name and risen to command the 14th corps before the Rank Revision Committee had reduced him to colonel. He had since distinguished himself by his left-wing views and so won a following among Radical politicians. Once in government, his imperious conduct raised the hackles of senior generals, including Galliffet, while Ferry worried that his blatantly political speeches overstepped the bounds of restraint normally expected of a war minister. The prime minister sacked him after Thibaudin refused to attend a ceremony to honour Alfonso XII, the King of Spain, an honorary colonel of Uhlans and denounced by French patriots as a friend of Germany. Thibaudin was fêted by the Left for his patriotic act but never again held an important military command in the two years before his retirement.[12]

But it was General Boulanger, war minister in the 1886 Freycinet government, which made the republic rethink its appointments policy. Like Thibaudin, Boulanger had attracted the attention of the Radical Left. His noisy patriotism and vigorous programme of military reform had won him respect in the army as well as in the country at large. But like Thibaudin, he forfeited much good will when he manoeuvred to sack General Saussier, the military governor of Paris, a long-time republican and one of the most respected generals in the army, and by gratuitously stripping the retired Orleans princes of their military ranks in direct contravention of the 1834 law. Moderate republicans began to have second thoughts about 'General Revanche', but his following among the Radicals obliged them to include him in the new Gobet ministry which replaced Freycinet in December 1886. Gobet fell in May of the following year, and the new prime minister, Rouvier, sought a majority to the Right rather than pay the price of Radical support in the form of Boulanger. The ex-war minister was given command of the 13th corps at Clermont-Ferrand, but his departure from the Gare de Lyon occasioned a rowdy demonstration of support. Boulanger had become a symbol of a groundswell of disenchantment with the regime, of a longing for a leader more dynamic than the succession of agile but uninspiring provincial lawyers who headed France's all too transient governments, a champion patriot who would restore the nation's sadly depleted stock of self-respect. But when his name appeared on the ballot in five departments in the by-elections held eight months later, he was struck from the army rolls and chased into exile by government threats of prosecution. A Boulangist movement flickered briefly but attracted no soldier except the retired General

Thibaudin who stood unsuccessfully as Boulangist candidate for the Seine in 1889.

The Thibaudin and Boulanger episodes brought home forcefully the danger of naming politicized and *arriviste* generals to the rue Saint-Dominique. It also pointed up the shortcomings of the official notion that the war minister was a mere technician whose tasks were limited to those of administering the army.[13] In the republic of the republicans after 1879, the question of the army's loyalty was a seldom spoken but nonetheless lingering one in the minds of many deputies. The war minister must be a republican, a full member of the cabinet responsible to parliament and prepared to apply its political decisions in the forces. If soldiers were unsuited to this task, then it must fall to a civilian.

A civilian minister of war had long been on the list of reforms demanded by republicans. However, the ever cautious Gambetta passed over Freycinet in 1881 for General Campenon, fearing that a civilian war minister might suggest to nervous soldiers the ugly spectre of politics in the barracks. Also, as the army's hierarchical chief, it was inconceivable to many that the war minister could be anything but a general. But eight years and nine turnovers in the army's top job led to a reassessment. A soldier in the ministry of war was certainly no guarantee against the intrusion of politics into the army – the increasingly political tasks required of the war minister had done much to alter the notion that the war minister was a technician above party squabbles. Politics and soldiers were best kept separate. Nor did the succession of junior generals strengthen the prestige and authority of the war minister as army chief.

The appointment of Freycinet as war minister in 1888 forced the government to come to terms with the problem of the high command. Ministerial instability, generals with little authority over ministry officials or their more senior colleagues and the increasing awareness that the war minister's job was more political than technical had led to a growing demand for the creation of a general staff on the German model. The war minister was the army's political chief, but Charles de Freycinet was obviously not the man to lead the army in the field. The forces needed a permanent commander-in-chief and a great general staff.

Freycinet was the Third Republic's most successful war minister. As Gambetta's right arm in the Government of National Defence, he had acquired a first-hand knowledge of the problems of directing a military machine in wartime. His prestige was high both in parliament and in the forces, so that he was perhaps the only man able to create a strong high command while soothing republican fears of a concentration of power in the hands of a few generals. In 1874, General du Barail with the support of MacMahon founded the general staff of the war ministry, but this in no way resembled von Moltke's creation. Fearing that a strong chief of the general staff would challenge the authority of the war minister, du Barail passed over General Ducrot in favour of a brigadier. The chief of the general staff, then, was to strengthen the position of the war minister, not weaken it. While the chiefs of the general staff were responsible for drawing up war plans, increasingly they came to be regarded as the minister's private secretary whose major task was to insure the smooth functioning of his ministry. For the next 15 years, chiefs of the general staff were little more than senior clerks who changed with each ministry. They were able neither to coordinate the various 'directions' of the rue Saint-Dominique nor to impose a unified strategic plan or system of tactics in the army.

On 6 May 1890, Freycinet created the post of chief of the army general staff. Both the change of title and the nomination of one of the army's senior generals to the new post indicated a strengthened role for the chief of the general staff. General Miribel, considered the army's best strategist, was responsible to the war minister, but he had the stability and authority to draw up a war plan, to impose a tactical system and an armaments policy in the army. On the outbreak of war, the chief of staff would be placed under the commanding general of the eastern armies.

Freycinet also turned his attentions to the *conseil supérieur de la guerre* where he found his commander-in-chief and army commanders. The *csg* had been created in 1872 to provide a cast of senior generals to be consulted on important defence questions, to lay down policy to be followed by the ministry, to provide an element of continuity to counterbalance ministerial instability and, as inspecting generals, to assure the uniform application of doctrine in the forces.[14] Its beginnings were not auspicious: 'Our meetings were irregular', du Barail remembered.

> The debates were confused and never methodically directed. If they sometimes touched on questions of vital interest, they also wasted time on minor questions which could better have been left to the bureaux, or on discussions which had nothing to do with the army. Monsieur Thiers invariably chaired these *csg* meetings and, when he was in good spirits, they were transformed into an interminable meeting where one discussed everything but the army ... and rarely, I must confess, did we arrive at a practical solution.[15]

In 1888, Freycinet revived the *csg* which had been virtually moribund since 1874. Henceforth, he declared, the *csg*'s 12 senior generals would be consulted on all questions of organization and training, mobilization, defence and armaments, as well as 'all measures which could affect the organisation of the army and its mission'. However, the *csg* was to be more than a mere consultative committee, it was to become a de facto high command. The war minister was the *csg*'s president, but the vice-president was the designated commander of the principal north-east army group. The remaining generals would take charge of the field armies in wartime and, in peacetime, inspect the corps which would make up their commands.

'The 6 May decree concludes the evolution of our military institutions', the *Progrès militaire* declared on 7 May 1890, while the *Avenir militaire* opined two days later that 'one could not do better in a republic'. But while the high command was definitely strengthened, the Freycinet reforms left many questions unresolved. This situation bore testimony to the fact that the changes in the high command were the products of both a political compromise and of a philosophy of command in a state of transition. Rather than create a high command, Freycinet had created several high commands the bounds of whose authority remained nebulous. Consequently, the power of the *csg* to initiate and veto reforms, the relationship between the designated generalissimo and the chief of the general staff who prepared the plans of war which he was to execute, and the authority of the chief of the general staff over the ministry directors were questions which were decided by personalities rather than by regulations. Some war ministers like General Zurlinden stood in awe of their military superiors on the *csg*, while others like Cavaignac, son of the republican general of 1848, intentionally snubbed them. The strong-willed Miribel refused to defer to Saussier, the designated commander-in-chief between 1888 and 1898, while Boisdeffre, who succeeded Miribel in 1893, was more prepared to treat Saussier as his superior. Miribel was also the only chief of staff who succeeded in asserting his authority over the directors in the ministry.[16] But the reforms were unambiguous on one point – the authority of the war minister had been weakened. The Dreyfus affair offered the republic an occasion to regain much of the ground lost to the soldiers, to re-establish the authority of the war minister, and through him parliament, over the high command. The Dreyfus affair demonstrated that, even after 25 years, the question of who ruled the army remained to be settled.

4

The Dreyfus affair

In the two decades following the Franco-Prussian War, France had undergone a military renaissance, made possible by the republic. Moderate republicans led by Gambetta had created the political climate without which the enormous expansion and reorganization of the forces would have been impossible. By 1890, it appeared that the army had been successfully integrated into French society and the high command into the institutional structure of the French state. However, the *entente* between France and her army rested on fragile foundations. The Dreyfus affair demonstrated that the potential for misunderstanding between soldiers and politicians was still great.

After 1870, patriotism and the spirit of *la revanche* had combined to raise the prestige of the army within the nation. However, the slow but steady growth of anti-militarism in the century's last decade announced a change of public mood in France. The first indication that the spirit of national sacrifice bred by the *année terrible* was fading came with the 1887 publication of Abel Hermant's novel *Le Cavalier Miserey*, the first of a string of anti-militarist novels which resurrected the old middle-class complaints of the corruption and degradation of barracks life. Henri Fevre's *Au Port d'armes*, Lucien Descaves' *Sous-offs* and Georges Darrien's *Biribi* gave the French public a series of simple conscript heroes fed into a machine which still bore the stamp of the *ancien régime* – aloof and indifferent officers who allowed ignorant NCOs to enforce a brutal and capricious discipline against a sordid background of filthy barracks, greasy soup and a debauched and depraved soldiery. In the century's last decade, anti-militarism varnished only French society's upper strata. When Miserey asks himself: 'Isn't there something more to life than rising at reveille, going to class and looking after your horse, to eating soup and going to bed?' he was expressing an opinion held almost exclusively by middle-class young men disturbed at the prospect of serving three years as privates next to uneducated peasants, beyond the reach of parental protection and influence. By the 1880s, rural conscripts regarded a few years in the regiment, if not with pleasure, at least as a not unwelcome break from the back-breaking tedium of farm labour. While army standards of cuisine and hygiene might be sniffed at in the comfortable suburbs of Alençon or in the Faubourg Saint-Honoré, they were certainly superior to those of much of France. In the 1860s, a soldier's daily ration amounted to 1.4 kilograms of food, above the national average of 1.2 which included the gargantuan feasts of the bourgeoisie. In the first decade of the Third Republic, the army diet was stretched to include more than half a pound of meat a day, half a pound of white bread, still a luxury in most districts, two pounds of vegetables including potatoes, coffee, wine and sugar. Compared with farm labour, the army's work routine was almost leisurely: soldiers rose at 6 am and worked until 9 am, when they ate. After a mid-morning break, they spent the remainder of the day in classes, training or duties until 4.30 pm, when they again sat down to soup. 'Every day, meat and soup, without working in the army', ran a Flemish conscript song. Army sickness and mortality rates, while higher than in the German army, were below the national average.[1] Small wonder that many conscripts, after completing their term of service, were reluctant to return to the farm and instead fell into posts as minor officials or domestic servants swelling the rural exodus.[2]

Middle-class anti-militarism grew in the 1890s as Alsace-Lorraine became a ghostly memory and the spirit of *revanche* was re-programmed toward colonial expansion and subsequently anglophobia. France was slipping toward a *fin-de-siècle* decadence in which café intellectuals were already expressing a fashionable lack of concern for things martial. 'Personally, I would not give the little finger of my left hand in exchange for these forgotten lands [Alsace-Lorraine]', wrote Rémy de Gourmont in the 1891 edition of the *Mercure de France*. 'I need it to shake the ash off my cigarette.'[3] After a decade of hibernation, pacifism was enjoying a new vogue in university circles. The philosopher Frédéric Rauh led an intellectual chorus which cried that patriotic duty must be examined under the microscope of individual conscience. Historians argue that these changes in the intellectual climate were given a special urgency with the passage of the three-year service law of 1889 which abolished the one-year volunteers. Girardet writes that the effect of the 1889 law on the development of anti-militarism has been exaggerated, as *Le Cavalier Miserey*, the first expression of middle-class anti-militarism, appeared in 1887.[4] But this view overlooks the fact that from 1881 officials began to close the loopholes which allowed the rich to sidestep military service, slashing the number of student deferments and reducing the one-year volunteers to a mere handful. Faced with the reality of the *conseil de révision* and the stark prospect of from ten months to three years in a barracks peopled and ruled by the lower social orders, bourgeois youth snapped up anti-militarist doctrines which rationalized their natural reluctance to leave home. The Dreyfus affair brought bourgeois anti-militarism to the boil. The endless parliamentary wrangling, the press diatribes, Zola's trial and Henry's suicide were avidly followed and passionately debated by middle-class France. Charges of treason levelled at top officers confirmed many in the view that the army was corrupt, badly led and rotten through.

Politicians on the Left were ready to turn this increasing disenchantment with the army to their advantage. Anti-militarism, they argued, was the fault of the army and would vanish only with reforms which whipped the ideals and methods of the forces into line with those of the republic. 'Anti-militarist and anti-patriotic propaganda is a fact whose importance no one can deny, but whose gravity must not be exaggerated', wrote Adolphe Messimy, a Dreyfusard captain who left the army in 1899 to launch a parliamentary career which eventually took him to the war ministry.

Have our officers over the last 25 years always understood how difficult and delicate, in a country totally free politically, is the task of exercising for 3 or 4 years absolute authority over all French youth? Have they done everything in their power to make themselves understood and loved by the young men placed in their charge? Have they not had in the past a very substantial part of the responsibility in the passing disaffection from which the entire army has suffered? . . . The day – and it is fast approaching – when the republic will have officers completely faithful to the regime, grasping the aspirations and the sentiments of the men they command, aware of the delicacy and gravity of the difficult role they must fulfil, anti-militarism will have had its day. We firmly believe that this day is imminent.[5]

'What is the anti-militarist thesis?' asked War Minister General André. 'The barracks is a school of laziness, of debauchery and of crime where poor soldiers, submitted to the arbitrary authority of arrogant and disdainful superiors, lose all self-respect and individual worth.' He vowed 'to improve the soldier's material conditions, make the regulations more humane, ease the relationship with his superiors, make him see the need for and the utility of discipline, to inculcate and develop in him the idea of devotion to his comrades and to the community'.[6]

The growth of anti-militarism which revived suspicion and distrust of the army in some restricted but influential circles and the exploitation of this new mood by politicians of the Left during the Dreyfus affair has served to obscure the cause of the misunderstanding which arose between the republic and the army. The affair did not originate in the social and religious attitudes of the officer corps, the resistance of old France to the modernization and 'republicanization' of the army. On the

The Dreyfus affair

contrary, many of the officers involved in the Dreyfus cover-up were known for their republican sympathies. The Dreyfus affair was rather sparked by an institution founded and nurtured by republican reformers and regarded as distinctly middle class in its composition and outlook – the general staff.

Following the dismal performance of the staff corps in the Franco-Prussian War, reformers regarded the creation of a general staff on the Prussian model as a top priority: 'Our armies were beaten less by the genius of Moltke than by an institution: the great general staff', wrote Lieutenant colonel Bonnal, a staff college professor.[7] In the old army, the staff corps had been creamed from the top of each Saint-Cyr class, but the talent and abilities of these men had been poorly utilized. After a two year course at the staff school on the rue de Grenelle which was considered excessively theoretical, the students joined the staff corps at the age of 21 or 22. The rest of their careers were spent in routine clerical work, so that they were deprived of the regimental experience which was vital if the orders and plans which they drafted were to reflect military realities. In 1870, the shortcomings of the staff corps were only too obvious.

After the war, the staff corps was disbanded and replaced by a staff service: the *Ecole de guerre* founded in 1876 recruited lieutenants and captains by competitive examination, which meant that the staff college took in the best of the young officers from the combat arms who had already acquired several years' experience in regimental service. After two years' instruction in military history, tactics and other appropriate subjects, they were classed as brevet staff officers and spent the remainder of their careers alternating between staff service and troop command. This system aimed to centralize tactical thought and to give the army a doctrine and a central nervous system, with each military muscle responding to the messages of the high command. It offered its officers the right combination of practical experience and theory, unobtainable in the old staff corps, and it was meritocratic. By recruiting officers from all arms, it sought to break down the prejudices which divided the army.

Girardet, however, was probably right in reckoning that one of the paradoxical effects of republican reforms was to increase the distance between officers and men, between professionals and conscripts.[8] Rather than break down old prejudices and misunderstandings which had separated staff and line officers into rival camps, staff officers in their turn became the army's new elite, proud of their status and singular *esprit de corps*. Jean de Pierrefeu, a reserve lieutenant assigned to general headquarters in 1915, discovered that general staff officers considered themselves an elite whose major concern was to 'flee the stiff and mechanical habits of the line'. Among this priestly caste, saluting and standing to attention were considered vulgar barrack manners, reserved *'pour le peuple'*. 'No matter how low your rank, from the moment you are a general staff officer, you are of the same world as your most eminent leaders. By admitting you, they confer a certain social equality.'[9] The Dreyfus affair revealed the extent of the growing distrust of line officers for the professional snobbery of staff men: 'At first we wanted to believe, and we all believed, in a conspiracy against the army, against the last bastion of order', Lyautey wrote in October 1898 of the burgeoning scandal over Dreyfus' conviction.

Today we must acknowledge the evidence: dragged along little by little by the deplorable habits engendered by the milieu, by a false conception of the military ethos, our great general staff became entangled in a web of lies, of compromises, of unspeakable blunders. From now on, it is a ruined citadel incapable of resisting the skilful attacks of anti-social forces.[10]

The refusal to review Dreyfus' conviction and the false evidence manufactured to throw sand in the eyes of justice did not reflect an officer corps seeking any excuse to defy the republic, but rather an incestuous and exclusive general staff. Lyautey wrote in 1899:

Even before I left France, . . . I had good reason for retaining only moderate confidence in certain methods of the personnel of the rue Saint-Dominique and the general staff, mutual admiration coteries, lovers of clichés and formulas removed from the currents of popular opinion assured by troop command, good at book learning, carrying to the ministry and to the high command petty schoolboy jealousies, flattering the prefects, eager to please, shrinking personality and freedom of spirit. This is why, as I set foot on the boat [for the colonies] four years ago, I felt as if I were escaping from jail.[11]

Lieutenant colonel Emile Mayer, too, felt that staff officers, because they spent little time in troop commands, had not shared the change in attitudes toward discipline and authority which universal service had introduced into the army in the 1880s.[12] Galliffet also laid the blame for the Dreyfus affair at the feet of the general staff. 'The General has followed the affair', wrote Abel Combarieu, President Loubet's secretary, in 1899. 'From the first day, he blamed the "practices of the general staff".'[13] The general staff was united neither by social background, nor by secondary education, nor by political or religious conviction. Created by republicans and reformers to open the army to fresh ideas and place its leadership in the hands of a class of dynamic technocrats, general staff officers soon became inward-looking bureaucrats sunk in routine, in their personal careers and in defending their privileges against poachers. These were the raw ingredients of the Dreyfus affair. In 1890, Freycinet had attempted to give the army a stable high command by creating the general staff of the army to coordinate and centralize the task of war planning. However, parliamentary instability, the weakness of the war minister and the absence of any clear lines of authority to the generalissimo or the war minister increased the pretentions to autonomy of the general staff. The question of who rules the army was still an open one and one which became increasingly relevant as the Dreyfus affair gathered steam.

The events of the Dreyfus affair are by now well known. On 15 October 1894, Captain Alfred Dreyfus, an artillery officer attached to the general staff of the army, was accused of selling military secrets to Germany. In February 1895, after an humiliating ceremony in the courtyard of the *Ecole militaire* during which his stripes of rank were torn from his uniform and his sword broken, he was shipped to Devil's Island to begin a life sentence for treason. Dreyfus was momentarily forgotten by all except his brother Matthew who for the next two years led a solitary campaign for his brother's rehabilitation. By 1897, Matthew Dreyfus had succeeded in convincing at least two important people of his brother's innocence: Auguste Scheurer-Kestner, vice-president of the Senate, and Georges Clemenceau, who had lost his seat in 1893 as a result of his involvement in the Panama scandal and who had turned to journalism for his living. Quiet efforts by Scheurer-Kestner to convince influential politicians to re-open the Dreyfus case, seconded by a press campaign led by Clemenceau in his newspaper *Aurore* and by the prestigious *Figaro*, failed to produce a groundswell of popular support for a re-trial. However, it did result in the trial of Major Esterhazy, a fellow staff officer, in January 1898 for Dreyfus' crime.

Esterhazy's acquittal and the persistent refusal of War Minister General Billot and Prime Minister Jules Méline to acknowledge any irregularities in Dreyfus' conviction pushed the 'Dreyfusards' to step up their campaign. On 13 January 1898, Emile Zola threw down the gauntlet with 'J'Accuse', a scathing attack on General Mercier, war minister at the time of Dreyfus' arrest, and the high command whom he accused of conniving at the conviction of an innocent man. Moral indignation on the Left now boiled over into a political crusade. Zola's trial served to rally French intellectuals to the Dreyfusard cause while the attacks on the army by anti-militarists like Urbain Gohier increased in violence. The fact that Dreyfus was a Jew led to accusations that he had been the victim of anti-semitism which was alleged by Dreyfus' champions to be rampant in the army. Attacked *en bloc*, the great majority of officers rallied round their chiefs. They were joined by a coalition of right-wing Catholics, anti-semites led by the unsavoury Edouard Drumont, and the apolitical who always preferred to believe the government rather than the opposition. The issue, they claimed, transcended that of the innocence or guilt of one man. The 'honour of the army' was under attack from irresponsible radicals who would like to bring the institutional structure of the republic tumbling down. The battle lines were clearly drawn between the reactionary France of cutlass and cleric fighting to retain their privileges and the progressive forces of *literati* and representatives of the industrial proletariat, between, in the words of Philip Guedalla, 'those sections of society who could read and write and those who found it preferable to watch and pray'.[14]

Under the Dreyfusard onslaught which persisted through the spring and summer of 1898, the siege mentality of the general staff deepened into paranoia. The reason for this was simple: the case against Dreyfus was built on forged evidence. The *bordereau* found in the dustbin of the German embassy in 1894 led to a demand by General Mercier to find the traitor. The fact that the information leaked to the Germans concerned the artillery and that the handwriting on the *bordereau* resembled that of Dreyfus led to a snap arrest. Mercier was convinced that he had found his man and, to shore up his sagging position in the ministry, he staked his reputation on it. Major du Paty de Clam was told to build the prosecution case, but as Dreyfus awkwardly refused to confess and as no other evidence of treasonable activity could be uncovered, the officers of the general staff, certain of Dreyfus' guilt despite the inconvenient lack of evidence, decided to manufacture some. Du Paty and Colonel Sandherr, head of the statistical section of the general staff, built a dossier against Dreyfus with documents which were either ambiguous or forged. For reasons of state security, it was claimed, this dossier could not be shown to the defence counsel, so that Dreyfus was condemned on the basis of evidence which he was not permitted to refute.

Dreyfus' conviction was not the result of a conspiracy against the republic or of an anti-semitic plot. It was a blunder produced by a blinkered bureaucracy in which notions of justice and common decency had been sacrificed to a misconceived sense of loyalty, careerism and political ambition. But once Dreyfus had been convicted by such irregular methods, it became quite impossible for the men involved in his conviction to admit that there might have been a mistake. When Lieutenant colonel Picquart took over the statistical section from Sandherr in July 1895 and with it the Dreyfus dossier, he quickly concluded that Esterhazy, not Dreyfus, was the real traitor. But when he communicated his suspicions to Boisdeffre, chief of the general staff, and Gonse, his assistant, he was transferred to the southern Sahara. Major Henry of the statistical section set about producing more forgeries, the most spectacular of which was a letter from the Italian military attaché in Paris to his German colleague in which Dreyfus was named as their contact in the rue Saint-Dominique. The *faux Henry*, as the note came to be called, did much to convince War Minister Billot that Dreyfus had been fairly convicted and that Picquart needed a change of air. The general staff, in an attempt to justify Dreyfus' conviction, had become entangled in a web of criminal conspiracy. The exposure of the *faux Henry* and the subsequent suicide of its author in 1898 not only brought the high command into disrepute but also paved the way for the transfer of the political balance of power to the Left.

That the Dreyfus affair which began as a moral crusade to establish the innocence of one man came to have such sweeping political consequences was the direct result of the political alignment of the 1890s. Throughout the preceding decade, the republic had been ruled by an uneasy coalition of moderate and Radical republicans against their enemies on the Right. However, Radical involvement in the Boulanger episode and in the Panama scandal served to discredit this group, which lost heavily in the 1893 elections. At the same time, Pope Leo XIII's call for Catholics to rally to the republic made possible the formation of conservative cabinets made up of moderate republicans and Catholic 'ralliés'. Anti-clericalism, which had formed one of the main links between Gambettists and Radicals in the 1880s, dropped from fashion in the 1890s as prime ministers like Casimir-Périer, Dupuy and Méline sought to avoid questions of principle in the interest of parliamentary stability. The reopening of the Dreyfus case, even after the discovery of the *faux Henry*, threatened the stability of this moderate–conservative alliance, so that Prime Minister Méline insisted doggedly that the Dreyfus affair did not exist.

If the government majority had an interest in preserving the *status quo*, the Left equally had an interest in upsetting it. It was no accident that the campaign for revision was stimulated by Georges Clemenceau who saw it as a means by which the Radicals would pry their way back to power while he might regain his lost parliamentary seat. Jean Jaurès likewise sought to use the affair to unify the socialists and to convince their more extreme elements to drop their pretentions to revolution and rally to the republic. The attack on President Loubet by a young royalist aristocrat at Auteuil on 4 June 1899 allowed the radicals and socialists to unite beneath the banner of 'the republic in danger'. The Left was given a new lease of life and Waldeck-Rousseau formed a government in that month which included Radicals and even a socialist.

The moderates might have been able to retain power had they possessed a war minister capable of putting his house in order. But here the weakness of the war minister and the generally poor quality of the men who held the job proved fatal. General Billot, war minister for two years in the Méline government, should have settled the case in 1896. But to do so would have meant the sacrifice of his old comrades Mercier, Boisdeffre and Gonse, so he grasped at the straw of the *faux Henry*. His successor, Godefroy Cavaignac, also allowed himself to be taken in by the *faux Henry*, so that when it was revealed in August 1898 to be a forgery, he was forced to resign along with Boisdeffre. Prime Minister Brisson turned to General Saussier as the only soldier with the prestige required to settle the question of Dreyfus' guilt. But the old general refused to step into a hornets' nest. Consequently, Brisson fell back on the usual expedient of inviting rather junior generals to take over the rue Saint-Dominique, with predictable results. Generals Zurlinden and Chanoine lacked the prestige and courage to mount an assault upon a shaken but still well-entrenched bureaucracy. In 1898, Prime Minister Dupuy turned to the man whose creation of the general staff had contributed to the confusion of the Dreyfus affair and whom he believed commanded the prestige both among soldiers and politicians to settle the issue once and for all. But while few equalled Freycinet's skill at political manoeuvre, the time for negotiation was long past. Freycinet abandoned the field to the minister of commerce Camille Krantz, a second-rate politician whose inability to deal with a problem of such dimensions quickly became apparent.

The growing political violence which culminated in the attack on President Loubet in June 1899, the volley of charge and countercharge rebounding between partisans and enemies of Captain Dreyfus soon loosened the bolts which held the union of centre parties fast. An old Gambettist moderate, Waldeck-Rousseau, formed a government of republican defence in June 1899. Left alone, he might have remained content with forcing a few generals to respect the army's traditional apolitical role.[15] However, his basic moderation was challenged by the covey of Radicals nesting in his cabinet and by those in Parliament whose support he needed for a working majority. A prisoner of the Radicals, he slid slowly leftward towards eventual resignation in 1902.

Waldeck-Rousseau's first choice of war minister was a judicious one which reflected his preference for a strong but temperate hand in the rue Saint-Dominique. The nomination of 70-year-old General Galliffet, called out of retirement to the army's top post, was not, however, immediately popular: as inspector general of cavalry he had for years pushed reforms through over the protests of his colleagues and, with strong personality and biting wit, had won few friends in the army. His political background baffled politicians. An aristocrat who had been close to the Imperial family, Galliffet had distinguished himself by his bravery in 1870 and by the zeal with which he attacked Communard barricades, winning the hatred of the Left and the title 'Butcher of the

Commune'. However, Gambetta's patriotism and devotion to rebuilding French defence won Galliffet for the republic. It also made him a sworn enemy of anyone who sought to cut the regime's life short: 'I cannot countenance his arrival in power', Galliffet said of Boulanger. 'In the first place he is an infantry general. Secondly, he sits badly on a horse, Lastly, he pretends to play a role for which I was created.'[16] Waldeck-Rousseau had wanted to place General Brugère, chief of the general staff known for his republican sympathies, in the war ministry, but because he was away from Paris and the ministry needed to be formed quickly, the new prime minister settled on Galliffet.[17] The old general shared Waldeck-Rousseau's moderate views, pointing out that he supported neither the Dreyfusards nor their enemies but was determined to place the general staff house in order and judiciously reshuffle a few top men. 'We are going to navigate on an ocean of sabres', he told President Loubet. 'As I understand nothing of politics, I agree with you that my presence in the preparatory [cabinet] meetings is unnecessary', he wrote to Waldeck-Rousseau. 'It remains understood, of course, that we shall protect and defend the army while keeping it strictly within its duties . . . The military profession does not combine well with a political sauce.'[18] On 22 June 1899, Galliffet wrote to the Princess Radziwill in Berlin: 'The government will give me *carte blanche* and not interfere in anything to do with the rue Saint-Dominique.'[19] 'I am resolved, when I speak to the Chamber, even if I am alone, to fight for my theory of non-reprisals for several reasons, the principal one being that they are demanded by the worst enemies of the social order, religion and the army', he repeated on 22 September.[20] Others thought Galliffet's motives less pure: 'While he often claimed to have accepted the portfolio from the hands of Waldeck-Rousseau only to save his comrades from peril and restore the army's lost prestige, given over to its worst enemies, his senile zeal for power is explained by slightly less elevated motives', wrote Ernest Judet in Galliffet's 1909 obituary. 'In fact, he was furious at the law which threw him into retirement at 65, vigorous and bubbling over with ideas . . . When he eventually understood that his notoriety and prestige were being exploited to prepare the infamies which André later zealously executed, he stole away with pride mixed with disgust.'[21]

For the new prime minister, the nomination of Galliffet, a good republican and a man of order with an impeccable military record, would assure moderate opinion and soldiers that the army was insulated against precipitous change. 'Make them understand that Galliffet will not only cover me with the army, but will cover the entire cabinet and the republic, and all before Europe', he wrote to Joseph Reinach, a Dreyfusard deputy and Galliffet's one-time aide-de-camp.[22] But the presence of the old general in a left-leaning cabinet which contained Alexandre Millerand, the first European socialist to sit in a bourgeois government, moved the Left to fury. 'Cancerous militarism in its most violent and cynical form, the militarism of the *coup d'état* and civil war, seemed until now to have had in this country one incarnation: Monsieur le Marquis de Galliffet, Father Superior of Martiques', foamed the Radical-Socialist journalist and deputy, Camille Pelletan. 'No matter what is convenient at the moment, the public conscience, which accepts subtle compromises only with difficulty, will not tolerate the representatives of democracy rallying around the pitiless general of 1871.'[23] When Galliffet made his first appearance in the Chamber, he met with an avalanche of shouts accusing him of being an 'assassin'. 'Obviously there are a few I forgot to assassinate', he replied with characteristic aplomb. His coolness under a barrage of parliamentary heckling and his firm hand in the war ministry soon squeezed a grudging admiration from deputies who resented non-specialists poaching in their preserve, so that Galliffet, initially regarded as the cabinet's biggest millstone, became one of its major strengths.[24]

The government's early statements indicated that it was content to restore the army to its traditional apolitical role, ending the effervescence in the ranks which on occasion had bubbled up into statements of political ill-humour. 'Among our primary interests closest to national conservation and dignity, we place the army, which the Third Republic has rebuilt upon foundations so strong and broad that it is the very expression of the security and pride of France', read the government's 26 June 1899 declaration to the Chamber. 'We, together with its most illustrious chiefs and its surest leaders, believe that an unshakeable attachment to discipline is the first and essential guarantee of its own grandeur. We shall defend it with the same energy against attacks on it and the solicitations which are the least merited of insults.'[25] Some of the generals whom the affair had made objects of controversy – Pellieux, Zurlinden and Roget – were shifted from Paris to less sensitive provincial commands. A decision on the future of General Mercier had to be postponed, for it hinged upon the verdict of Dreyfus' second court martial scheduled for August 1899.

The accusations, denials, forgeries and patent falsehoods which had so far tattooed the affair had served only to raise the political temperature in France without enlightening public opinion. Paul Déroulède's 23 February 1899 attempt to prod General Roget's troops to switch the regime following the funeral of President Félix Faure characterized the atmosphere of fantasy breathed by many on the political fringe. The Rennes re-trial was intended to settle the issue once and for all. However, differences between the Prime Minister and the General over the purpose of the trial soon surfaced: while Waldeck-Rousseau was prepared to push for an acquittal, Galliffet simply wanted a review which, regardless of its outcome, satisfied opinion. He also betrayed a slightly naive belief in the impartiality of military justice. 'We are not and we never were the ministry of obligatory acquittal', Galliffet wrote to Princess Radziwill on 7 September 1899. 'We have nothing to do with that. I respected and made others respect the independence of military justice.'[26] To do so, however, he had to resist strong pressure from Waldeck-Rousseau to order a verdict *à la carte*, a practice quite common in civil courts.[27]

The Rennes verdict which, by a 5-2 vote, found Dreyfus guilty with extenuating circumstances did not sweep the affair under the carpet. On the contrary, it dropped like a thunderbolt on public opinion: 'The first reaction is one of stupefaction', wrote Abel Combarieu.[28] Many saw the trial as proof that soldiers were incapable of judging an old comrade fairly. The court martial had been subject to tensions which civil judges might have overcome more easily: the Rennes court, for example, met not just to judge Dreyfus but also to judge the propriety of General Mercier's involvement in the affair. The decision of the United Appeal Courts to repeal Dreyfus' 1894 conviction and to convene a second court martial was based in part on the secret and illegal communication to the judges of the 'Ce canaille de D . . .' letter by the General when he was war minister in 1894. On 5 June 1899, the justice minister recommended that Mercier be prosecuted. The court of middle-ranking officers was well aware that an acquittal of Dreyfus would mean the arrest of the popular general and was no doubt slightly intimidated by his active role beside the prosecution throughout the trial. The Rennes verdict was an indictment of the French judicial system which allowed witnesses to make long speeches, piling up evidence based on rumour and speculation without proper scrutiny either by the judges or by the defence. Demange, Dreyfus' defence attorney, could only argue that no hard evidence had been offered against his client. But faced with a barrage of accusation and the knowledge that Dreyfus' innocence was Mercier's guilt, the court found against the prisoner.[29]

The court martial over, Dreyfusards clamoured for an appeal. Galliffet disagreed: 'One feels that the moment has arrived to calm tempers, to put an end to our quarrels to allow us to consider the country's needs', he wrote to Waldeck-Rousseau.[30] Clemenceau, Jaurès and others wanted a clear statement of innocence from a new trial. They also wanted to draw out the affair, prolonging the political debate and shifting the parliamentary balance of power further left. However, concern with the bad publicity which the Dreyfus scandal provided abroad and for the state of Dreyfus' health were joined to Galliffet's contention that a new trial would not necessarily produce a different outcome. When on 19 September a reluctant President Loubet pardoned Dreyfus, few were satisfied. 'Dreyfus' partisans declared that they intended to push for rehabilitation not implied in the pardon', wrote Combarieu. 'While the adversaries, what a noise they will make.'[31]

Attempts by Galliffet to order the affair out of existence in the forces were no more successful than Waldeck-Rousseau's administrative burial. On 21 September, Galliffet issued his famous order to the army: 'The incident is closed!' But his confidence in the salutary effect of his order was misplaced. Pelletan waxed sarcastic: 'Attention! On my command, by the left flank, Forget! That is what was missing from the military regulations.'[32] The Left, enraged by Dreyfus' new condemnation, renewed its demands for a sweep of soldiers accused of perjury and treason. Galliffet's order was received no better in the army. Dreyfus' re-conviction was hailed by officers who saw the Rennes verdict as a slap in the face for the army's detractors. 'The perversion of the ideal of France is the immediate goal,' wrote Major de Civrieux, 'the Dreyfus affair is the means.' News of the Rennes verdict exploded in his Algerian mess: 'A great shout went up immediately', he wrote. 'The young officers jumped onto the tables singing the Marseillaise. Everyone shouted for bottles of champagne. News of the taking of Metz would not have unleashed greater enthusiasm in this remote garrison.' With perhaps more foresight than Galliffet, however, de Civrieux speculated that the 'incomprehensible verdict', far from putting an end to the affair, had in fact prolonged it.[33] Galliffet's faith in the impartiality and independence of military justice blinded him to the fact that, as long as the conviction of Dreyfus stood, the army would remain at the centre of a heated political battle which could only sap morale and efficiency. Bound by the narrow rule which excluded politics from the barracks, he refused to allow the government to intervene to liquidate the affair, ironically opening the army to the very political reprisals from which he claimed to be defending it – the likes of which had not been seen since the opening months of the Bourbon Restoration.

By the end of the year, Galliffet's stock with the army and the parliamentary Left was running low. Suspicious of his conservative past, the Left called his reforms purely cosmetic and blasted his refusal to make a clean sweep of officers involved in the Dreyfus cover-up. Millerand was already pressuring Waldeck-Rousseau to name a war minister inclined to more Jacobin methods in dealing with the soldiers. Officers, meanwhile, in their ignorance of the probable alternatives, thought that common sense had deserted their old comrade-in-arms. Galliffet had from the outset felt the pressure of his ambiguous position:

'The newspapers, such as the *Gaulois*, call on me to play Boulanger, while those on the Left invite me to decapitate every general who displeases them', he wrote to Princess Radziwill on 14 July 1899. 'I do not want to come down on one side or on the other, but only to do my duty which will often be difficult. Everyone is mad . . . the public is idiotic. If I lay hands on a guilty general, I am accused of massacring the army. If I do nothing, I am accused of treason. What a dilemma!'[34]

The immediate object of the debate was Galliffet's treatment of the high command. On 24 June 1899, only two days after Galliffet's entry into the ministry, General de Négrier, designated successor to Saussier as vice-president of the *conseil supérieur de guerre*, France's top military post, told senior officers while inspecting the 15th infantry division that the patience of the high command over the government's refusal to take firm action against the army's detractors was fast reaching the breaking point. The colonel of the 10th infantry regiment at Auxonne allegedly told his soldiers after Négrier's inspection:

I am charged to tell you that because of the attacks of which the army has for some time been victim and which the government believes its duty to tolerate, the members of the *conseil supérieur de guerre* have decided, immediately after the Rennes court martial has pronounced on the Dreyfus affair, to ask the government what measures it plans to stop the attacks on the army and in case no notice is taken of their request are disposed to take action.

Galliffet immediately recalled Négrier and a presidential decree placed him in retirement. 'Négrier is playing at Boulanger', Galliffet told Waldeck-Rousseau. 'He is preparing himself and the troops under his inspection for the role he wishes to play. Rather than appease the army, he pushed it toward indiscipline. He brands the government in the eyes of the army, etc.'[35]

The Négrier affair served as the excuse for a reorganization of the *conseil supérieur de guerre*. Among its 12 members were the designated army commanders, and although neither the armies nor the army staffs existed in peacetime, Freycinet had named them the permanent inspectors of the troops who would make up their wartime commands. Traditional opponents of strong military leadership on the Left claimed that inspecting generals had thus carved out *de facto* territorial commands against the will of parliament: 'They have become in *fact*, if *not in right*, the true authorities between the minister and the commanders of the army corps', read an official report.[36]

General Galliffet . . . pointed out that the moral authority and the legitimate and necessary influence of the [war] minister had diminished fatally with the increased power of the army inspectors. He believes that future army commanders, to prepare themselves for their wartime role, need only know the situation of their three or four corps from the point of view of provisions, mobilization, matériel, transport etc. and the disposition of the general plan of mobilization and assembly. He believes they do not need to occupy themselves, however superficially, with the direct command of the soldiers. He believes it *urgent* to return the army inspectors to a more basic understanding of their true mission.

Galliffet's 24 October decree ended the csg's permanent residence in Paris and banished its members to the provinces as corps commanders. In future, csg meetings would be called only by the war minister. In this way, although council members still made inspection tours, the fact of belonging to the council was not to be considered a superior rank in an army which admitted no rank above that of major general. 'If the army inspectors continued to sit permanently in Paris, the influence of the csg would soon be dominant. You could envisage conflicts.'[37] On 27 February 1901, André abolished their right to inspect the corps which would make up wartime commands, so eliminating an important element of central control and standardization, in the conviction that local commanders could best judge their own troops.[38] Many officers felt that military efficiency had been sacrificed on the altar of Radical paranoia. 'The [army] commanders must know their mission beforehand', General Zurlinden wrote in 1903.

They must be given the time and the means to prepare for it. But in order to insure the interests of France, threatened by these designations, to pander to republican sensibilities and to give the government a free choice, they are named only provisionally in peacetime so that the government can re-examine its choice at the beginning of each year.[39]

In the same 24 October decree, Galliffet added Giovanninelli, Hervé and Langlois to the lengthening list of generals he had already retired, and one which included Zurlinden, Négrier and Pellieux, the Paris commander. But many in the army and on the Right were angered by these dismissals which, they claimed, transgressed the officers' sacred right to job security. The Left, however, countered that, with the possible exception of Zurlinden, Galliffet had refused to touch the officers most inculpated in the affair. On the contrary, on 20 December 1899, Waldeck-Rousseau pushed a bill through parliament which amnestied those involved in the Dreyfus cover-up. While Galliffet was determined to re-establish discipline in the forces, he never believed that generals were planning or even capable of a *coup d'état*. He was, however, convinced that, since his retirement in 1895, the army had accumulated a crop of mediocre leaders.

Each day the masons enrol more soldiers, sometimes those one thinks the least likely candidates. The upper ranks of the army are shaken and worn out.

They eat too much, run after little girls and try to increase their emoluments and that is all. The colonels (some of them), the majors and captains are much better, but by the time they arrive the army will have been completely nationalized. The affair will have contributed greatly by the mistakes of many. I say this without passion, without anger and without awarding responsibility more or less deserved.[40]

With Galliffet's every word, a reputation died: Zurlinden was 'an imbecile', Brugère 'neither an enigma nor a character ... a soldier who staked out his career at the Elysée', and Jamont 'a first-rate coward'.[41]

His poor opinion of the top leadership helped to fashion his last great reform and the one which ultimately did the army greatest damage. Promotion had long been a sensitive issue in an army led by ambitious men. An 1832 law had laid down the basic ground rules in an attempt to reduce the political favouritism rampant in the Restoration army. Freycinet further regularized promotion procedures in 1889 by establishing a series of hierarchical committees to assess officers' ability. Officers were therefore judged by their immediate superiors and political and personal favouritism took a back seat to professional competence. The war minister seldom exercised his right to add to the promotion lists.[42]

But Radical republicans claimed that this system perpetuated the 'reactionary cliques' which ruled the rue Saint-Dominique and worked to open promotion to outside influence. In Galliffet, they found an ally: 'In the promotion committees and above all in the inspection committees, favouritism was scandalous', he wrote. 'Generals like Brugère, Négrier, Hervé, just to name a few, worked to create a clientele without taking note of professional considerations.'[43] 'These promotion lists ... in practice imposed on the government of the republic the nominations for which it has the responsibility without having the choice', read Galliffet's 29 September 1899 decree which gave the war minister the exclusive right to name colonels and generals. He then seized control of the promotion of junior and middle-ranking officers, and on 9 January 1900 he declared the promotion committees merely consultative, arguing that they favoured officers in the chain of command against talented men in ministries, embassies or on other special assignments.[44]

While the Left condemned the pernicious effects of the promotion committees in the hands of reactionary generals, Langlois leapt to their defence: 'A legend which holds that promotion committees obeyed clerical influence must be destroyed', he wrote. 'Nothing is further from the truth.' André was but one of a long list of 'republican' generals which included Billot, Saussier, Dessirier, Brugère and Peigné who had shinned to the top of the military pole. 'The members [of the promotion committees] honestly worked for equity.'[45] The charges levelled against the clerical or political bias of the promotion committees were exaggerated by the Left. The French army was not split along political lines, and professional considerations weighed far more heavily than those of politics or religion in questions of promotion. In the French army, as in most French institutions, senior officers built up a clientele of younger favourites whose promotion they actively sponsored. But officer favouritism usually operated independently of political opinions, and fell upon promising younger protégés. For instance, Galliéni, a good republican of modest origin, pushed the aristocratic Lyautey who made little attempt to disguise his distaste for the regime. The entourage of General Castelnau, the *capucin botté* who travelled everywhere with his personal Jesuit chaplain, included a Protestant and an avowed atheist.[46] The immediate staffs of Boisdeffre, Joffre and other generals were a mixed bag socially and politically. Competence rather than conviction formed the principal criterion for promotion. And of necessity, for in pushing 'his' officers, an inspecting general was not simply creating a clientele for its own sake, but was out to prove that his inspection system was superior and the officers under his command better trained.[47]

This system, however, had two defects: first, it favoured officers in staff jobs who were called to the attention of influential inspecting generals by their senior officers. For instance, of captains who received discretional promotions to major in 1893, 42 per cent in the infantry, 28 per cent in the cavalry, 62 per cent in the artillery and fully 94 per cent in the engineers occupied staff, administrative or teaching posts.[48] For this reason, although Galliffet's reforms were denounced by General Grandin as 'the crowning of the most abominable acts yet made against the dignity and political neutrality of the army', they received a cautious welcome in some garrisons.[49] While one could argue that staff men were placed in their jobs because they had proved themselves, many line officers felt that troop command did not receive its just reward. The second defect of the French promotion system was that it was weighted against imaginative, outspoken candidates in favour of good but more pedestrian men.[50] Difficult personalities like Lyautey might have trouble finding a patron and eventually perhaps be forced to resign or go to the colonies, which practically became a catchbag for maladjusted officers. The result was an officer corps of guaranteed solidity but which, with few exceptions, lacked genius in its upper ranks. 'I am convinced that our promotion system is detestable', wrote Emile Mayer in 1898.

It is by pure chance, and to a certain extent by fraud, against all the rules, that men of real worth slip into high commands ... The summits of the

The Dreyfus affair

military hierarchy are almost always occupied by generals against whom no-one has any complaints, and who are more or less neutral, unobtrusive. Any officer really worth something may not stand out from the mass because he is not blessed with the attractive qualities which are appreciated in ordinary life ... What is more; these true warriors are often badly brought up.[51]

Galliffet certainly intended his reform to be moderate and progressive. As no war minister could possibly know even a fraction of the 25,000 army officers, he was obliged in the vast number of cases to follow the advice of the promotion committees.[52] However, by leaving the final decisions to the war minister, he was well aware that he had unlocked the door to political abuses which were bound to follow in the overheated political atmosphere of the Dreyfus affair. 'It is probable that André will abuse the right which he is demanding [total abolition of the promotion committees],' Galliffet wrote to the Marquis de Laguiche on 12 October 1900, 'but the laws and the regulations must be framed as if the minister were good.'[53] Galliffet was right on both counts.

By the spring of 1900, Galliffet increasingly felt the strain of shielding the army from a government and a parliament clamouring for more drastic reforms. 'I am a liberal, at least I think I am, but I am also a soldier', he wrote to Princess Radziwill on 1 May 1900.

I want the army to remain outside politics, but also to bar politics from the army – and I cannot at any price associate myself with a measure which would lift one stone from the 'block' which the army must be and remain. But I am not sure whether the republican party shares my view on this subject. Not too long ago, they were asking only silence from officers on political matters. Today, they seem disposed to reward officers who will post their republicanism. This would be absurd and dangerous.[54]

The increasing leftward slide of Waldeck-Rousseau's government had been made inevitable by the prime minister's need for Radical support. However, it was no doubt hastened by right-wing demonstrations at Reuilly and Auteuil on 9 August 1899, and by a report by the Paris Prefect of Police, Lépine, that Rightists and army elements were brewing a *coup d'état*.[55] 'The Rennes verdict, whatever it is, will be full of complications', read an unsigned note dated 13 August, probably from a police informer. 'The army does not like Galliffet who, out of friendship for Waldeck, is ruining a brilliant military past. The ministry will be overthrown in three months or they will carry out a *coup d'état*.'[56] On 24 September, the high court declared charges that a military coup was being prepared unfounded. However, Waldeck-Rousseau remained convinced of a military conspiracy. General André recorded the following conversation with the prime minister on the eve of his appointment as war minister:

Our adversaries, he claimed, had prepared a coup for the day of the Rennes judgement. A little later, the trial in the high court proved that the conspiracy was everywhere. And not everything was exposed in this trial! ... I can tell you that there was open talk among the conspirators that everything was ready for a national insurrection and that they planned to join the action of the army to that of a riot. We headed off all of this in time, but the spirit of rebellion persists and is looking for any moment to act.[57]

Increasingly ill-at-ease in the government and worried by the continued attacks on the army, Galliffet was probably looking for an excuse to walk to the wings. On 16 May 1900, he told Princess Radziwill that Waldeck-Rousseau must soon choose between him or Millerand.[58] When on 28 May Galliffet refused to press charges against Captain Fritsch of the army's statistical section for giving confidential letters on the government's investigations into the Dreyfus affair to the editor of *Eclair*, he was not supported by the prime minister who in the Chamber of Deputies denounced Fritsch as a 'felon'. 'I can no longer digest the enormous snakes and toads which you make me swallow', he wrote in a huff. 'I resign.'

With Galliffet's resignation, the Dreyfus affair might be said to have been brought, at last, to a close. Dreyfus was not to be cleared of charges of treason until 1906 and repercussions from the affair, especially in the army, were to continue for some years. But if, as most were willing to concede, the essential issue in the affair had long ceased to be the innocence or guilt of Dreyfus and had become a raw struggle for power between Left and Right, the Dreyfusards had clearly won – the Radicals now had a stranglehold on the government and the war ministry. Galliffet had hoped 'to liquidate the affair and to protect the best interests of the army'.[59] He had done neither. His basic belief in Dreyfus' guilt, his blind faith in the impartiality of military justice, his refusal to punish those responsible for the conspiracy against Dreyfus had simply prolonged the affair to the disadvantage of the moderates and ultimately of the army. His restructuring of the high command returned the army to the confusion and lack of direction which had characterized it before the Freycinet reforms, except that now the high command was not only disorganized, it was discredited, in Lyautey's view 'a ruined citadel incapable of resisting the skilful attacks of antisocial forces' or of providing the army with effective leadership.

5

The Radical solution

The Radicals whom the Dreyfus affair catapulted into power were not a political party bound by a programme – indeed, they did not formally organize until 1901. They formed a confederacy of latter-day *sans culottes* keen to root out reaction. The *ancien régime* no longer existed, so they had to invent it: the Church and the army provided fodder for their political guillotine. Paris settled back into another Year II which, if less violent than its predecessor, was to last substantially longer than twelve months.

The view that the Radical victory allowed France to shake off the dead hand of reaction, consolidate the republic against the intrigues of right-wing conspirators and inaugurate a new era of democratic progress has long been held as an article of faith on the Left. However, rather than look forward into the 20th century, the 'Dreyfus revolution' stared fixedly into the past, allowing Radical revolutionaries to beat the dead horses of clerical reaction and military conspiracy, reopening old wounds and rubbing them liberally with salt. Priest-baiting was substituted for old-age pensions, idolatry for income tax. Jean Jaurès and the Socialists who had joined the 'Dreyfus revolution' when the cry 'the republic in danger' went up, began to realize around 1906 that their Radical allies had become obstacles to social reform.

By hitching the Socialist Party wagon to the Radical republic, Jaurès hoped to defuse the revolutionary pretensions of many of his fiery associates, linking socialism with the political questions of the day, giving it a stake in power and gently weaning it away from revolutionary bluff. But Jaurès failed to appreciate the nature of his temporary ally's political support: the Radical party did not simply represent petit bourgeois democracy, the last evolutionary step before the peaceful conquest of power by the workers; it was rather a 'state of mind', strong among a class of small farmers and shopkeepers wedded to private property and deeply suspicious of the capital. 'The Socialist leaders have always followed a dream – absorb Radicalism', wrote Radical politician Joseph Caillaux.

They believe that they can absorb the majority of Radicals the day that they can convince them that promised Radical reforms have been achieved ... I have noted on dozens of occasions that Radicalism is not a party, but a state of mind: that of the petite bourgeoisie and the majority of peasants. It is possible that in the future this state of mind will change names – in the past it was called liberalism, opportunism, etc. But it is impossible that Socialism will capture it, except on one condition: that Socialism changes cloaks, that it renounces collectivism and Marxism ... Only then will Radicalism be absorbed by Socialism.[1]

These attitudes explain both the violence of Radical invective against the army and their inability to achieve any significant military reforms. For them, the compromises of Gambetta and Freycinet with the professional army were not a step toward political maturity and a solid national defence, but a pact signed with men whom tradition and temperament would always banish to the other side of the barricades. Ancestral memories of the June Days of 1848, Saint-Arnaud's 1851 sweep of the Legislative Assembly which announced seemingly endless military parades and foreign wars, and the brutal repression of the Commune headed a lengthening list of complaints against the men on horseback, to which real or imagined conspiracies against Marianne – 16 May 1877, Boulanger and Dreyfus – came to reinforce prejudices and deepen the desire for revenge. The liberal political traditions of the special arms, the revolutionary battle honours which decorated many regimental standards, the gratitude of a post-1870 generation of officers for the republican-led military revival were nuances lost on a Radical leadership for whom suspicion of soldiers and priests was an inherited characteristic. The 'military spirit' which cemented a solid hierarchy of drill and discipline was decried as a wall raised against politics and democracy, isolating soldiers against change and keeping alive loyalties to an imperial past. The Radical republican believed civic spirit a more acceptable basis for army organization, reviving the patriotic pride which the men of 1792 carried with them into battle, breaking down the barriers of caste and uniform and blending soldier and citizen into a coalition for national defence.

Radical calls for civic spirit to replace, rather than reinforce, the military spirit dear to post-1870 reformers did not announce that the Left had at last hit upon a coherent philosophy of military organization, but rather betrayed a lack of appreciation of the profession of arms of which the Left had long been secretly proud.

The Waldeck-Rousseau ministry appointed to liquidate the affair set out to transform what Radicals still saw as the antiquated and caste-ridden army of the empire into a force worthy of a republic. The job was taken up in succession by Emile Combes and Georges Clemenceau

– men whose dislike of the uniform combined with uncompromising and at times vindictive personalities to reduce regimental messes to jelly. With an evangelical fervour born of a devotion to the republican principles of the Great Revolution and a desire to 'épater la bourgeoisie', both men deployed their forces against the 'enemies of the people', using shock tactics and intransigence to pull down the pillars of the establishment. They sought to conquer power through its destruction, calling, like Marx, for the gradual abolition of the state.

Radicals were neither revolutionaries nor anti-militarists. On the contrary, by attacking bureaucracy and state centralization they claimed to be combatting revolution. 'He who kills bureaucratic routine will kill the spirit of revolution in France', Clemenceau declared. 'Bureaucratic routine is stronger in the army than anywhere else . . . We have changed the barracks stones. The time has come to change the spirit of men as well.'[2] Radical leaders became the champions of the people against the institutions of the state, espousing a belief in individual freedom which rubbed shoulders with chaos. They aimed to rule for their friends against their enemies, and sought out ministries which carried influence and patronage rather than simple power.[3] Their ultimate failure to carry out their avowed political revolution in the forces betrayed their basic priorities; behind a smoke-screen of reformist rhetoric, they worked to hold sway behind barrack walls.

The increasingly leftward slant of Waldeck-Rousseau's ministry left only one obvious candidate to replace Galliffet at the war ministry – General André. André came late into the affections of the Radicals. A graduate of the *Ecole polytechnique*, decorated for bravery for his actions against the Communards, André had acquired a reputation as a competent but undistinguished technician who owed his promotion to his friendship with Sadi Carnot, his classmate at the *Ecole polytechnique* who became president of the republic. In 1897 he was named to command the 4th corps artillery, and for the next two years he was on the best of terms with his superior, General Mercier, whose anti-Dreyfusard opinions he shared. Promoted to major general in 1899, André attracted the attention of the Left with an order forbidding several right-wing publications in the NCO mess: 'We congratulate General André because we are now reduced to congratulating officers who simply do their duty', the *Radical* wrote on 30 December 1899. In February 1900, Galliffet pointed out to Waldeck-Rousseau that André was virtually the only general who would willingly push through two-year service, but he placed the prime minister on his guard: 'Everyone or almost everyone in the Chamber if not favourable is at least not hostile to two years' service', he wrote. 'I cannot accept it *under any circumstances*. You need a *General* favourable to this law. I see only André (guided by you). The man – whom I do not recommend but who "recommends" himself – has nothing to offer, commanding no esteem and determined to succeed by aiding the executioner. God protect you from him.'[4] 'The ministry is now homogeneous, for André, a poor soldier, is a mason, sectarian, a Dreyfusard and a Brissonnist', Galliffet wrote to Princess Radziwill on 1 June. 'He has been and always will be inspired by Monsieur Brisson whose creature he is... Never having gone to war... he knows nothing of men or matters... No longer fearing me, the ministry will slide daily toward the extreme left... [it] detests priests as much as it detests soldiers.'[5] Colonel Legrand-Girard, serving in President Loubet's *maison militaire*, thought André 'the candidate of the masons, sectarian and slightly mad', and found it ironic that Mercier's protégé had become a Radical disciple.[6]

In his first meeting with Waldeck-Rousseau, André made it clear that he shared the Prime Minister's fears about the treasonable potential of the high command. When asked: 'how can one remedy the situation?' André replied:

I see two ways, Monsieur le Président: one revolutionary and rapid, the other calm and slow ... The first would be to handle the army like one handled the judges in 1878: suspend for a limited and brief period the 1834 law on the position of officers and the rights of rank as one did for the inviolability of judges and ... purge. – The second? – Eliminate the same people but without touching the arch-saint. This will require patience, diplomacy, great prudence and above all a long time.

After discussing the prejudices faced by republican officers, allegedly discriminated against in the army-controlled promotion committees, and the army's supposedly strong clerical sentiments, Waldeck-Rousseau told André to adopt 'provisionally the second remedy: the progressive and prudent, although energetic, move toward purge'.[7]

André's goals were essentially two: to strengthen the position of the war minister vis-à-vis the high command and to republicanize the officer corps by bringing its political ideas, life style and social recruitment into line with the new requirements of the Radical republic. Determined to prove that the war minister and not the general staff ruled the army, André lost little time in fulfilling his promise to 'adapt the army to modern ideas, attitudes and institutions'.[8] Blocked by the 1834 law from purging officers considered disloyal, he moved to fill top positions in the ministry, the general staff and the military schools with men whom the republic could trust. These were the positions of influence in the forces, the hilltops from which republicans could keep watch on the reactionary plain below, and consequently the positions most coveted by officers keen to push their careers. André brought with him to the rue Saint-Dominique a hand-picked core of officers dedicated to republicanizing the army, which included Colonels Percin and Sarrail and Captains Targe, Mollin and Humbert, with whom he prepared the decrees, circulars, transfers and ultimately the promotion lists which gradually tilted the balance of forces in the government's favour. A clean sweep of the general staff was his first priority: 'It is the brain of the army', André told the Prime Minister. 'It is what moves and governs the entire body. It is the source of the evil.'[9] Freycinet's regulations which allowed the chief of the general staff to name his own collaborators were thrown out so that André could axe staff colonels Hache, Meunier and Castelnau, basically because they were practising Catholics. Colonel Legrand-Girard complained that André named 'mediocre' replacements whose only title to favour was their friendship with Picquart.[10]

André's action locked him in a test of strength with the chief of the general staff which, ultimately, was to prove fatal to the authority of the high command. General Delanne resigned his post rather than accept subordinates thrust upon him by the war minister. When André refused Delanne's resignation, Delanne countered by refusing to recognize André's nominations and ordered his staff to do likewise. André took his case before parliament arguing that, while the chief of the general staff had the authority to name his own bureau chiefs according to the 3 January 1891 law, this authority was 'under the war minister'. The Chamber of Deputies gave André a vote of confidence while the *Radical* denounced what it called 'a praetorian sedition'. The generalissimo, General Jamont, also resigned, claiming that he could work with no other chief of the general staff than Delanne. André also refused to accept Jamont's resignation until, after much searching, pro-republican Generals Brugère and Pendezec 'who have always observed the most correct attitudes'[11] agreed to replace the two disgraced officers. André named Jamont and Delanne to simple brigade commands.

André's showdown with Jamont and Delanne was to have fatal consequences for the authority of the high command. Brugère and Pendezec were well down the seniority list, an indication that the power and independence of the high command had been down graded.[12] Consequently, that of the ministry directors was increased and the initiative for reform passed from the high command to the rue Saint-Dominique. As if to underline the fact that strong personalities were no longer in fashion in high military circles, men like artillery director General Deloye were also put out to pasture: 'You will have learned from the newspapers that Deloye has at last been jettisoned', Captain Targe wrote to the Dreyfusard activist Louis Havet. 'I trembled until the last moment, for he is from Montélimar which entitles him to all of the republic's favours. One more stage has been completed. It remains to clean out the stables to which we now have the keys.'[13]

The military schools attracted the special attention of reformers. Believing reform of the officer corps had to begin at the bottom, André named a new crop of instructors charged with converting future officers to the republic. 'The least that we can ask today from our officer corps is absolute loyalty to the republican government', the future Radical war minister Berteaux told the Deputies in 1902. 'To arrive at this result it seems to us that we must not neglect the assistance provided by military school teaching. In this teaching, a large place must be consecrated to civic and moral education ... We must develop the ideas of liberty, progress, fraternity and solidarity which inspired their grandfathers, our glorious generals of the First Republic.'[14] Colonel Lavisse, superintendent of the infantry school at Saint-Maixent, and his successor Colonel Sarrail, engaged university professors to lecture future infantry officers on economic and social problems, while Colonel Sauret at the Artillery and Engineering School called his instructors to 'an ideal of democratic progress that will allow them to consider themselves government delegates for the formation of cadres for the republican army'.[15] 'The schools' teaching staff is less concerned with forming officers than with turning out teachers fired with a secular, civic and republican spirit', wrote Captain d'Arbeaux.[16] Even the political views of the civilian examiners were closely scrutinized by the André cabinet. 'Can you inform me of their ideas? ... Do they teach in religious schools?' Targe wrote to Havet. 'I am sorry to trouble you, but the question is of the utmost importance. It would have been useless to name good instructors at Saint-Cyr if candidates are examined by clericals and nationalists.'[17]

Radical republicans regarded Saint-Cyr as a hot-bed of political reaction and disliked the 'undemocratic' promotion of its graduates. Officers promoted through the ranks could seldom hope to reach colonel: 'Great discontentment reigns in the officer corps at this moment among officers promoted from the ranks', the *Avenir militaire* wrote on 24 November 1893. 'The unfavourable application of the present law is beginning to create an unfortunate division in the officer corps whose unity – the principal force of armies – is undeniable.' Radicals claimed that this resulted from the expansion of Saint-Cyr, which now furnished 60 per cent of second lieutenants. Their solution was to slash places there by 50 per cent between 1900 and 1910, reversing the percentages and so giving ex-NCOs a better chance at discretional promotion.[18] Between 1899 and 1903, 56 per cent or 2,732 of the second lieutenants commissioned in the four combat arms were graduates of either Saint-Cyr or the *Ecole polytechnique*; the remainder,

2,117, were former NCOs. After 1904, when André's reforms had begun to bear fruit, the percentages were tipped in favour of NCOs. Between 1904 and 1909, 59 per cent or 2,459 of second lieutenants commissioned were ex-NCOs.[19] Many of these were not graduates of NCO schools. After 1904, one-tenth of second lieutenancies went to adjutants promoted directly from the ranks. In 1910, the figure grew to one-fifth.[20] André's decision to promote adjutants directly to second lieutenant is cited as another example of the reformers' desire to democratize the officer corps. However, the truth is that André was forced to do it to make up for the shortfall of applicants to Saint-Cyr and to fill the vacancies left by the increasing number of officer resignations.

Radicals argued that the forces formed a caste apart, separated by class, by belief and by life style from republican France. Officers should renounce privileges, rites and traditions inherited from a monarchist past. Rather than await a military fourth of August, however, reformers struck at practices designed to reinforce the social standing of the epaulette and the solidarity of the officer corps. A 1 October 1900 decree abolished the 1,200 franc dowry required of officers' brides, claiming that it transgressed every citizen's right to marry freely. On 21 September 1907, the *France militaire* reported that officer marriages had increased by one-third since the abolition of the dowry. However, Legrand-Girard saw the measure as a transparent attempt to lower the social standing of the officer corps: 'As for the marriages contracted by the officers, they are not good', he wrote in 1908.

For the last five years, as colonel and general, I have seen the requests for permission to marry appear on my desk. I am the son of a petit bourgeois without fortune, but not even three of these marriages would have suited me, without feeling that I had done myself a disservice in associating my officer's existence with those whom I see joining us. They are probably decent people, but without education and seldom able to raise the moral and intellectual level of their husband. We are going downhill, that is beyond question.[21]

André's second blow at officer corps solidarity swept away the obligation imposed upon unmarried officers to share a common mess, with the argument that officers should abandon their self-contained world to seek contact with fresh civilian currents of opinion. A third measure permitted officers to wear mufti off duty. When President Loubet questioned the advisability of this measure, coming on the heels of Galliffet's orders to the contrary, André threatened to resign if it were not signed into law, reinforcing the opinion of Loubet and his military adviser that the war minister was 'an absolute madman'.[22]

Fast on the heels of the abolition of the dowry and the breaking-up of the bachelor officers' mess came a spate of decrees which stripped officer existence of all trappings of elegance. Tennis courts, skating rinks, hunting wagons and other carriages for officers, in short, many things which allowed officers 'to appear', were axed as a 'useless' drain on the budget. D'Arbeaux complained that officers now hitched rides on ambulances and meat wagons.[23] Reformers also attacked the use of soldiers as batmen – an estimated 40,000 according to Messimy. In 1900, André abolished the reduced railway fare for batmen attached to officers on mission, and in 1906, War Minister Picquart outlawed batmen altogether for non-mounted officers: 'This had an enormous effect in the army, where small military households, especially poor officers, were hard-hit', wrote d'Arbeaux, who also claimed that the measure was not aimed at rescuing men for combat, for batmen reported for training, but rather at lowering officer prestige. 'All this tends to reduce our situation by withdrawing the few material advantages which allow us to hold our own', echoed Legrand-Girard.[24]

Together, André's reforms aimed to alter the customs, traditions and personnel of the French army. However, they failed to produce the fundamental changes looked for by Radicals. Brugère and Pendezec got on with the war minister little better than their 'reactionary' predecessors. Brugère soon quarrelled with André who refused his resignation but forcibly kept him on without allowing him access to many papers vital to mobilization. His successor, General Hagron, resigned in 1907 to publicize Radical refusal to keep the army battle ready. Colonel Castelnau's transfer certainly did not put paid to his career, while André reinstated both Négrier and Langlois, retired by Galliffet.

André's failure to live up to his revoltionary promise can be attributed both to Waldeck-Rousseau's delaying tactics and to the war minister's own political ambition. 'The brutality of my acts will set everyone against me, and I shall fall under a deluge of abuse', André told Emile Mayer upon taking office. However, the prime minister blunted the edge of his fanaticism, passing things through the parliamentary army committee in André's absence and obliging the war minister to acquiesce or resign. '[André] soon acquired the habits and perhaps the taste for power. His revolutionary ardour of the early days seemed to calm down.'[25] Combes, too, noted that André's Senate ambitions had improved his disposition toward officers and the opposition.[26]

However, Radical plans to recast the army did not break up exclusively upon the rocks of Waldeck-Rousseau's delaying tactics or of André's political ambition. In 1902, Emile Combes succeeded the old Gambettist in the chair, bringing with him a reformist zeal and an even more left-leaning coalition removing all cabinet barriers to a thorough shake-up of the forces. The failure of the Radicals to push through many of their military reforms was more a reflection of their unrealistic aims than of moderate sabotage. Their military school measures provide a case in point. Attempts to disband Saint-Cyr hit a brick wall of opposition both on the Right and from socialists like Jaurès. Radicals hoped to throw the balance of recruitment to the NCO academies, both to break the vice grip of the allegedly upper-class Saint-Cyr clique on the senior ranks and to bring more 'democratic' elements into the officer corps. The promotion of ex-NCOs was hampered not simply by their inferior education and training but also by their age. While Saint-Cyr graduates were commissioned at 20 or 21, ex-NCOs became second-lieutenants between the ages of 26 and 28,[27] meaning that they were overhauled by retirement in middle ranks. In 1904, Radicals proposed that future Saint-Cyr cadets be required to spend a year in the regiment as privates and a year after graduation as sergeants, ostensibly to bring them into contact with the soldiers they would one day command. However, the primary aim of the reform was to delay their commissioning, so cutting the age gap between the two officer groups. 'In these conditions, every intelligent young man will not hesitate to enlist at 18 years of age and will not waste his time in school preparing for Saint-Cyr, lest he fail his entrance exam for the school and considerably compromise his future', the *France militaire*, a newspaper generally favourable to Radical reforms, wrote on 8 January 1904.

Conclusion: [the proposed reform] would be the veiled abolition, purely and simply, of our two *grandes écoles*, in a short time by a devious route ... One hardly sees any advantages in this new organisation, neither for the youth of the cadres nor the education of the officers ... still less for the worth of our national army and our knowledgeable officer corps in comparison with that of foreign military powers.

The two-year service law of 1905 did oblige Saint-Cyr cadets to spend one year in the ranks as privates, but it did nothing to facilitate the access of ex-NCOs to top ranks.

Nor did the increased numbers of ex-NCOs in the officer corps substantially alter its social colour. Sarrail complained that colonels filtered Saint-Maixent applicants to assure that only those with wealth or an aristocratic *particule* were successful.[28] While this charge was exaggerated, NCOs with secondary education inevitably enjoyed a better success rate in the entrance examinations. The result was that Saint-Maixent and Saumur became a repository for men who had failed to enter Saint-Cyr, the *Ecole polytechnique* or the *Ecole navale*, and who signed on to be promoted through the ranks. 'Whatever one may say, whatever one may do, with the present recruitment conditions for student officers, Saint-Maixent is an anti-democratic school', Sarrail wrote in 1904. 'From a social point of view, Saint-Maixent must not be the port for all who dreamed of *Navale*, Saint-Cyr, *Polytechnique* and, for whatever reason, . . . could not achieve their desire.'[29] Messimy recognized that attempts to promote NCOs in the cavalry had transformed Saumur into a school much more socially exclusive than the meritocratic Saint-Cyr: 'It is through the ranks that the "children of the valiant" prefer to enter the army', he noted in his 1907 budget report.[30] General Langlois, too, observed that Radical attempts to open the officer corps to democratic elements promoted through the ranks had had 'diametrically opposite results'.[31]

Raoul Girardet maintained that these reforms led to 'a new and very rapid fall in the military society's centre of gravity toward the milieu of the middle, even the lower, bourgeoisie'.[32] This conclusion, however, must be treated with caution. As noted before, the recruitment, and certainly the atmosphere, of the French officer corps before 1900 was very middle-class. Rather than democratize the officer schools and subsequently the officer corps, Radical reforms simply lowered the quality of officer recruitment. The lower classes were not suddenly sucked into the officer corps in any significant numbers. Rather, the NCO academies became a god-sent dumping ground for middle-class boys whose lack of intelligence barred them from more ambitious careers. The quality of military school entrants had been slipping for some time, but Radical reforms combined with the general abuse heaped upon the army to bring standards crashing down. Where 1,920 candidates applied for admission to Saint-Cyr in 1897, only 982 did so a decade later. Saint-Cyr admitted one in five candidates in 1890 and one in two in 1913. Saint-Maixent turned almost no one away.[33] The average Saint-Cyr admission score of 11.2 out of 20 in 1902 dropped to 8 by 1912.[34] Few good applicants appeared at Saint-Cyr and the education there was considered mediocre, especially after 1905 reforms re-orientated the curriculum toward the new 'social role' expected of officers.[35] Saint-Maixent weighted entrance examinations strongly in favour of practical experience and boosted scores for seniority, campaigns, wounds or special functions, but still entrance standards fell.

Saint-Maixent: average entrance examination scores[36]

		1882	1886	1890	1898	1902
Written	Literature	16	20	14	15	11
	Maths	20	16	6	6	4
Oral	Literature	10	10	8	8	7
	Maths	24	24	12	13	8
Total (out of 100)		70	70	40	42	30

NCOs were prepared in their regiments by lieutenants who often had no specialized knowledge of their subjects. The result, according to Senator Charles Humbert, an ex-officer, was 'a deplorable mediocrity'. Four out of 20 was considered a pass mark.[37]

Saint-Maixent: comparative value of each part of entrance examination (in %)[38]

	1882	1886	1890	1897	1902
Military Instruction	6	22	34	41	68
General Instruction	72	57	46	56	23
Colonel's Appreciation	28	21	20	3	9

The decline of educational standards at Saint-Cyr was not simply an unfortunate and unforeseen consequence of the Dreyfus affair. Rather it was the consequence of a deliberate attempt by Radical reformers to lower the social and intellectual level of the officer corps. Messimy, the Radical spokesman for military affairs, told Parliament in 1907 that an officer needed no more than a good primary education,[39] while the parliamentary committee charged to look into officer education declared in 1906 that officers needed only 'une certaine intellectualité'. The avowed intention of debasing officers' educational standards was to be able to amalgamate Saint-Cyr and Saint-Maixent, thus ending the divisions in the officer corps between 'democratic' ex-NCOs and elitist Saint-Cyrians who monopolized promotion to senior ranks.[40] Unity of origin had been demanded by the Radical left since the 1880s, but the cry was taken up in earnest after 1900. Multiple entry into the officer corps had been possible since before the French Revolution, and in modern military organization is considered a progressive step, preventing any one group from completely monopolizing commissions and allowing men of differing abilities to seek their natural levels in the hierarchy. Most ex-NCOs had limited career ambitions, and few seriously coveted the stars scattered among their colleagues from Saint-Cyr or the *Ecole polytechnique*. However, with a genius for exploiting non-issues Radicals exaggerated the tensions which, many claimed, were not between Saint-Cyr and ex-NCOs but between staff officers, whose easy access to high rank was resented, and the rest. But by fanning latent resentment between Saint-Cyrians and ex-NCOs, Radicals clearly hoped to drive yet another nail into the coffin of officer corps solidarity. Jaurès, who proposed a university education for officers, blasted Radical levelling as 'pseudo-democracy'. 'By deflating [Saint-Cyr's] pretensions, the educational standards will suffer. In this way, officers from both schools, by becoming more similar, will soon make up . . . an honourable and democratic average, democracy being reduced in the army to the Orleanist formula of the "juste milieu".[41] He especially attacked the 1906 school committee report which claimed that officers needed only 'une certaine intellectualité'. Radical 'mediocrity' would soon taint the army:

> The men who dare not candidly admit the value of higher education, a good, truly intellectual military preparation, but will not repudiate it altogether, oscillate between arbitrary combinations. They do not abolish the schools which provide it, but they undermine them and seek to substitute fictitious equivalents for a solid background ... Each school must attain the highest standards possible within its given framework. And if to do this the schools must be unequal, the dogma of alleged equality must not take precedence over the higher law of national security.[42]

The only school which evaded the general decline in standards was the administration school at Vincennes. Paradoxically, however, this principally reflected the declining status of a career in the combat arms and to a limited but not unimportant extent contributed to lowering still further the quality of the officer corps. 'Our system comes down to draining off the best line officers for administrative and noncombatant jobs', Patrice Mahon wrote in 1912.[43] Candidates for the administration school at Vincennes averaged 14.5 out of 20 in the 1913 entrance examinations, compared with 7.5 at Saint-Cyr in 1912.[44] Its applicants virtually tripled after 1900, and by 1910 it had ten candidates for each of its 50 places.[45] The *France militaire* noted on 25 March 1904 that Vincennes was the only school which had escaped the general decline in standards. The administration and the intendance, whose officers were once regarded as unfashionable if not slightly ridiculous military appendages, now began to siphon off many of the best officers, boosted by reforms which improved their status and promotion prospects.

Military recruitment from the prestigious *Ecole polytechnique* also trailed off after 1900. The artillery especially began to feel the squeeze with the decline of the prestige and educational levels of the officer corps. At the *Ecole polytechnique*, cadets first in the order of merit picked the plum state jobs, leaving the artillery and engineers the scrapings of each year's class. The *Porte-Voix* estimated on 15 November 1909, that fully one-tenth of each class left the *Ecole polytechnique* before graduation because their class rank was too low to qualify them for anything but an army career. In 1900, 42 per cent of artillery second lieutenants were ex-Polytechnicians. In 1902, this figure had dropped to 40 per cent and in 1903 to 35 per cent. By 1910, only 25 per cent of artillery second lieutenants were ex-Polytechnicians, and by 1913 only 20 per cent.[46] A large number of ex-Polytechnicians also resigned from the officer corps after 1900 – a full 50 per cent in 1911, according to Captain d'Arbeaux.[47]

The decline in officer standards was soon reflected in the *Ecole de guerre*, to which the best officers applied in their fifth year of service, around the age of 25 or 26. Arès estimated in 1912 that fewer than a fifth of the 90 officers at the school could write correctly and lamented the sharp decline in officer quality since 1900.[48] The poor entrance results of 1913 were a matter of public concern and the war minister complained that those of 1914 'once again reveal serious shortcomings in a great many candidates'.[49] This low educational standard soon told even in ministerial reports in which, for instance, General 'Lyauté' frequently would not have recognized his own name.

André's blows at the social exclusivity of the officer corps also appear to have bounced off harmlessly. He exaggerated the importance of the 1,200 franc dowry required in officer marriages which was more a practical than a social measure. Few households could survive on a captain's pay, and interest from an invested dowry formed an essential contribution to an officer's monthly budget. While the dowry was no longer obligatory, commanders retained the right to approve the marriages of their subordinates and usually insured that the bride was able to pay her way.[50] The abolition of the obligatory mess for bachelor officers hardly affected officer solidarity. French army messes were pale copies of those in the British and Prussian armies where they played an important part in the social cohesion of the regiment. Before 1870, officers' messes existed only in the Imperial Guard, and despite their extension in the Third Republic, they were never more than places to eat. Rather than break up officer solidarity and force officers to make civilian friends in garrison towns as reformers had hoped, the effect was often the opposite: messes continued to eat together or re-form elsewhere in a more exclusive form.[51] On 23 January 1912, War Minister Millerand re-established obligatory mess, arguing that it was cheaper, kept officers deficient in either morals or cash from frequenting low taverns and furnished 'a school of comradeship, solidarity, guardian of the *esprit de corps*. . . . Experience has proven that when a common mess is lacking, young officers form groups based upon their [military] school, wealth or social standing.'[52] Although Galliffet charged that André's decree which permitted officers to wear mufti off-duty had been motivated by 'the revolutionaries'' hatred for 'the officer in uniform', and pushed officers to further expense, it simply recognized what had been common practice among officers at least since Lieutenant Canrobert in civilian dress had been pursued through the streets of Perpignan by ageing General Castellane in 1834. Officers also contested the war minister's decree abolishing batmen before the *Conseil d'état* and won.

While the practical application of André's measures was limited, the psychological effect was more profound. The military debate of the turn of the century cannot be understood, as historians have claimed, simply as a struggle between two ideals, one republican and the other imperial. The great declarations of principle, the parliamentary rhetoric which swept across the pages of the *Journal officiel* declaring war on the professional army and announcing the era of the 'nation in arms' have seduced modern historians, as they once locked Dreyfusards into a holy war against reaction. Trenches taken were duly marked on the campaign map of the *Bulletin des lois* and accolades were showered on those who led the charge. And yet, these great debates were almost a side show, a parliamentary Dardanelles with each side engaged in political butchery for some prestige objective. 'Republicanization' and 'the nation in arms' were battle cries calculated to rally support, pyrotechnic displays to convince soldiers in the trenches that the enemy was being softened for the final assault. But the real war of attrition was fought elsewhere, a sapping operation in which the objectives were prestige and *esprit de corps*. Its weapons were not limited to parliamentary speeches, but also employed decrees, circulars and committee reports – leaflets to demoralize a besieged population. The Radicals were expert at this sort of psychological operation and, as with most Radical reforms, André's decrees aimed to produce more publicity than practical results. But that in itself was important, for Radicals pursued a petty vendetta in which the weapons were trivial insults and demeaning decrees. Action taken against an officer who refused to shake the hand of a mason or whose wife snubbed the divorced spouse of a colleague assumed exaggerated importance in a political world which lived on non-issues and among officers whose poor pay packet traditionally had been topped up by ladles of prestige.[53]

Rather than confront army reform head on, Radicals looked to make service to the republic a purgatory, forcing officers to conform or resign. The church inventories became one such test, a calculated humiliation which offered many officers a choice between two kinds of disobedience: to the command or to their conscience. For the Radicals, it proved only a partial success: most officers carried out their orders to disperse the faithful who sought to prevent government agents from carrying out their inventory of church property following the 1905 Separation law – even Sarrail was surprised that the revolt had been so limited; other officers developed 'diplomatic illnesses' and so avoided the issue.[54] A small but not insubstantial number simply declined to break down the church doors, and court martials refused to find them guilty, forcing War Minister Etienne reluctantly to discipline them himself.[55] The inventories infuriated many soldiers, but not, as Radicals planned, because a Catholic officer corps had been ordered to act against the Church. Despite a few 'private disasters' of conscience-stricken officers Lyautey claimed that most officers were 'indifferent' to religion. What they objected to was being forced to chase women and children from Church premises, acting as agents for a policy deliberately designed to divide the nation: 'Like me, you believe that the Combes, Pelletans, Jaurès, who have cast the country into this politic of hate and division, are state criminals', Lyautey wrote bitterly to Etienne.[56]

The completion of the inventories did not end the army's trials. The 1906 arrival of the Clemenceau government placed in the chair the Radical's master of psychological warfare, an avowed enemy of the army whose refinements of humiliation made those of Combes and André appear clumsy by comparison. With great skill, he had rallied French intellectuals to a war of principle while probing for the nerve which would leave his military adversaries shrivelled and defenceless. Lieutenant Colonel Picquart, re-integrated by Etienne in 1906 with the rank of brigadier, was promoted major general and named to head the rue Saint-Dominique. The elevation to the top army post of an old Dreyfusard given extraordinary promotion was considered a slap in the face by officers, as was Clemenceau's conscripting of the high command for the ceremony transferring Zola's ashes to the Pantheon. One journalist claimed that Picquart's nomination 'shows that an officer can rebel against his superiors and ten years later become their supreme commander'.[57] 'How can one explain, except by the desire to flout the command, the choice of General Picquart as the war minister and the imperative invitation to generals on mission to return to Paris for the deification of Monsieur Zola?' Captain d'Arbeaux asked.[58] On 16 June 1907, Clemenceau announced that, as two-year service meant fewer troops, the number of *légions d'honneur* given to officers would be slashed. However, Picquart was successfully prevailed upon to cede one of his remaining decorations so that the foreign minister, who had used up his quota, could decorate Tomps, the *sûreté* agent who had attempted to accuse the high command of buying witnesses at Dreyfus' Rennes retrial. Clemenceau capped his work by reorganizing the order of official precedence which had been the rule since the French Revolution, so that generals were now ranked behind prefects and colonels behind sub-prefects. For officers, this decree illustrated just how far army prestige had plummeted since 1900: 'One considers that the republic is saved when a 50-year-old colonel bows to a sub-prefect who can be half his age and whose appointment is the result of family connections', complained d'Arbeaux.[59]

Other Clemenceau decrees aimed to raise the republic's prestige vis-à-vis its soldiers: generals were forbidden to ride in the presidential carriage but had to ride on horseback at the door 'in the place of the squire'. Corps commanders were no longer allowed to review their troops upon taking command, while an under-secretary in the education ministry was awarded the right to military honours.

This deliberate campaign to strip the military profession of its compensations served to point up the poverty in which most officers lived. While low pay had always been a source of discontent in the army, officers felt somewhat compensated in prestige. Few officers had signed on for the money, but had joined from a mixture of motives which might include family tradition, a developed sense of duty or a taste for adventure. For many promoted through the ranks, the epaulette represented a social promotion, a step up from the farm or the shop. Most governments, including the republic, had allowed the army its little patch of prestige, encouraging the glory of the regiment both from a sense of national self-preservation and as a way to recruit an army on the cheap. After 1900, however, Radicals, set on deflating military glory, relegated officers to the status of minor civil servants. Stripped of their glory, the hard facts of military life took their toll on morale.

The French officer corps had always been one of the worst paid in Europe. Slow promotion increased the pay gap, for French officers were often older than men of equivalent rank in foreign armies. As a one-year volunteer in 1874, Valléry-Radot heard the pecuniary lamentations of an old school friend, then a second lieutenant: 'Do you know how ten out of 15 officers live?' he asked.

> The government pays a second lieutenant 171 francs a month. The *pension* or the mess costs us 80 francs, our room 25, the tailor 20, the shoemaker 10. You can count five francs for the washing, five for the batman and five for gloves. Total: 150 francs. Now, one must pay a host of petty expenses: shirt, képi or sword knot to buy, a dinner of welcome for a second lieutenant who arrives, or of farewell for one who is leaving. This costs 15 francs on average. This leaves one six francs in pocket. A lieutenant is paid eight francs more.[60]

If bachelor officers could just scrape by, married captains with a few children were reckoned to be constantly out of pocket, unless their pay was supplemented by independent means like a generous dowry.[61] Without independent means, married captains could not afford the two-year course at the *Ecole supérieure de guerre*, depriving the general staff of many potentially valuable recruits. 'A bachelor officer can just scrape by,' General Pédoya noted in 1908, 'but if he is married, he can support his family only with difficulty. He lives in perpetual discomfort, sometimes even in misery . . . They make a hole in the dowry, when there is one, or resolve to live a life of privation and sacrifice.' He claimed that many workers would turn up their noses at a lieutenant's pay while 'many foremen or shop assistants would not be content, after 30 years' service, with a captain's emoluments'.⁶²

Officer's annual pay, 1908 (in francs):⁶³

French		German	
Major General	18,900	Corps Commander	32,475
Brigadier	12,600	Division Commander	21,619
Colonel	8,136	Brigadier	15,643
Lt Colonel	6,588	Colonel	12,767
Major	5,508	Lt Colonel	10,098
Captain	3,492–5,004	Major	7,908
Lieutenant	2,520–2,988	Captain	5,533–7,033
Second Lieutenant	2,340	Lieutenant	3,563
		Second Lieutenant	2,813

The social trappings of regimental life made economies difficult to realize: officers were obliged to pay mess dues and contribute toward the cost of receptions, retirement parties and other regimental festivities. Military charities required a contribution while officers, especially in small garrisons, dared not refuse civilian collections: 'If they are in a small-town garrison and they refuse to contribute to their charities, their reputation will suffer', Pédoya noted.⁶⁴ Officers' wives were forbidden to work, even at respectable jobs like school teaching, and therefore could not help to ease the family's financial embarrassment. The derisory indemnities offered to French officers for unavoidable expenses like new uniforms, garrison changes, weekend sporting festivals at which officers were frequently called on to act as judges, or periods in training camps, on manoeuvres or, increasingly, on strike duty, deepened their penury. Garrison changes, especially with a family, could be ruinous: a German captain sent to a new post 300 kilometres distant collected the equivalent of 708 francs in expenses; a French captain was paid only 115 francs.⁶⁵ Pédoya claimed that in his career he had changed garrisons 34 times. Communities which used the army's services to fight forest fires or repair damage done by floods or avalanches were expected to pay expenses, but few did. The *Porte-Voix* complained on 20 May 1913, that indemnities covered perhaps one-quarter of the required expense. 'The uselessly extended stays in the work yards deserted by strikers, the camps and manoeuvres, are the ruin of officers', d'Arbeaux complained.⁶⁶

Without prestige, poor pay seemed yet another Radical torpedo fired against officer status, especially when civil servants were holding their own against rising prices. 'In the colonies, as in France, the officer can no longer hold his social position', said d'Arbeaux. 'Lacking money, he lives increasingly on the fringes of the middle class, which scorns him while envying him.'[67] Pédoya, who left the army to capture a senate seat on the Radical Party ticket, was pessimistic: 'With his present pay, an officer without independent means cannot live honourably in the army.'[68] '[Army] pay . . . does not compare, the statistics prove it, with the gains made by workers or most civil servants over the past ten years', the *France militaire* wrote on 9 January 1912. 'This overriding question constantly dogs the officer and deprives him of the lightness of heart, that *allure*, that freedom he needs to be ready always to defend the fatherland. . . . As a consequence, the military ideal is devalued, submerged by a sort of bourgeois ideal, tied to the hard facts of everyday life.'

Nor could officers look forward to a particularly comfortable retirement. Army pensions compared badly with those paid to civil servants: for instance, a captain retired on 2,300 francs while a lycée professor was paid 4,500.[69] 'It is very sad to see the difficult situation in which many retired officers find themselves', wrote the *Porte-Voix* on 21 January 1912, citing the cases of some officers forced to work as gamekeepers to survive. 'There are many majors and captains who hide their misery in an out of the way place or who, to make ends meet, take on the most humble jobs.'

Pensions (in francs)[70]

	France (30 years)	Germany (30 years)	Britain (30 years)
Major General	7,000	14,964	21,000
Brigadier	6,000	10,834	17,500
Colonel	4,500	8,672	12,500
Lt colonel	3,700	8,672	9,125
Major	3,000	6,604	7,500
Captain	2,300	5,396	5,000
Lieutenant	1,700	2,905	5,000

André's four years in office were unhappy ones for the army, for his measures exacerbated rather than remedied many of its problems. Chopping and changing the high command lowered the prestige and quality of its personnel with no significant reduction in bureaucracy. On the contrary, the drop in the quality of the men at the top of the army did much to increase confusion in war planning, armaments and training. Attempts to change the character and outlook of the officer corps lowered its morale and the quality of its intake, but there is no hard evidence that André's measures appreciably altered its social composition. By treating the army in this petty and vindictive way, the Radicals had contributed to a decline in military efficiency both in the ministry and in the regiments. But none of André's acts was to create as much controversy as his deliberate attempts to subject promotion to political influence.

6

The *affaire des fiches*

Political influence in army promotion formed the Radical's most serious strike at army morale. While other measures might be ignored or dismissed with a grumble, direct intervention in an officer's career was obviously calculated to break the back of officer resistance to the 'republicanization' of the forces. 'To attain my goal,' André wrote, 'my first preoccupation was to seek out among the anonymous and silent mass of officers, those whose republican sentiments could single them out for my attention ... How did one recognize them? I resolved to fix my attention upon those recommended by no one.'[1] Galliffet's modest promotion reforms were transformed into a full-scale revolution. As further evidence that the war minister was the army's commander-in-chief, André took promotion out of the hands of the military hierarchy and brought it into the ministry. In 1901, he abolished both promotion committees and general inspections. With only a seniority list before him, the war minister was free to promote whomever he chose, often without much attention to professional standards. The minister's cabinet made no secret of the fact that they, and not the colonels and generals, were now the army's promotion brokers and that they intended to reward political loyalty. Captains Targe and Humbert were detailed to draw up the promotion lists, 'so as to bring [republican officers] to the top ranks and in this way to block the road to the students of the Jesuites', Targe wrote to Louis Havet. 'Above all, one must think of the future ... We must reserve all our favours for those who will count in the struggle and who can continue the work we have begun.'[2] As commandant of Saint-Maixent and later as infantry director, General Sarrail pushed republican officers to the head of the promotion queue,[3] while General Percin, André's permanent secretary, claimed that at least two-thirds of the officers whom he promoted were competent and that, in any case, he reserved the right to advance his 'political friends'.[4]

If officers had any doubts that promotion was being handled in an arbitrary and political fashion, these were soon dispelled by the *affaire des fiches*. The 4 November 1904 revelation by Guyot de Villeneuve, deputy for Neuilly, that André had turned to the masonic Grand Orient for information on the political opinions and religious beliefs of some officers and their families, and that this information was carefully filed in the ministry and taken note of for promotion, could not have come as too great a shock to officers who since 1900 had flocked in increasing numbers to masonic conclaves. 'How otherwise, given the inertia of the high command, could I have accomplished my task?' André argued in his defence. 'I was forced to use every means at my disposal to gain information... I maintain that I was imperfectly informed through the normal channels... That is why I was obliged to look for information elsewhere. I believe that the sources should be diverse to complement each other.'[5] Despite what Combes termed as André's 'mediocre defence', the Left rallied to support the war minister, especially after the nationalist deputy Syveton topped an already tempestuous session by striking André in the heat of the debate. 'As for material damage [breaking of desks, etc.] they surpassed the maximum achieved up to today', the *France militaire* noted of the 4 November session. Despite a vote of confidence which Combes confessed was 'without political significance' because Syveton's 'inept brutality' had won the war minister a last-minute reprieve, André acknowledged that he no longer had the 'moral authority' to continue, and a month later tendered his resignation.[6]

The 4 November debate rocked the garrisons: 'The debates... have produced in the civilian and military population a certain emotion', read a police report from Poitiers.

The officers above all, among which the reactionary element dominates, seemed preoccupied. They can be seen in the streets discussing events with the undisguised hope that their chief, the war minister, will be defeated. In the artillery barracks in particular, groups of officers seemed joyous and gaily discussed the downfall of the war minister, which they considered certain – their disappointment was great when they read the result of the vote of confidence in the papers. From this moment, there were no more secret meetings, no more happy discussions. They now speak only of work and nothing abnormal has happened.[7]

Officers at Belfort were 'worried' as they scanned the files published by the *Figaro* to find their names. 'It seems that the officers in Belfort would quarantine any comrade guilty [of giving information on the political views of officers], and would make his life so intolerable that he would be obliged to leave the garrison.' Although the Nord had witnessed no serious incidents, police noted 'the situation in the regiments is very strained'.[8]

Elsewhere, however, officer discontent over the *fiches* erupted in agitation, duels and court actions: Major Bader of the 37th infantry at Nancy fought and wounded a local mason who described him in a *fiche* as 'reactionary, a police agent and a nasty character'. Duels between officers and masons, some of them officers accused of spying on the army, were reported in Bastia, Montélimar, Toulouse, Toul, Biarritz and Marseille, while officers accused of reporting on comrades were often forced to change regiments. At Le Mans, three colonels brought court action against a local mason who had passed information on them to the ministry and were each awarded a token 400 francs damages. At Aix-en-Provence and Châlons-sur-Saône, masonic lawyers guilty of passing information were disbarred by their colleagues. At Clermont-Ferrand, students demanded the resignation of a professor alleged to be a masonic spy, as did Lyon lycée students. A police guard was placed on the house of a prominent Angers mason after a poster, one of many which appeared all over France, denounced him as a 'casserole' – a spy. However, army agitation was greatest in Tours, where the 9th corps commander, General Peigné, was accused of sending reports on the political opinions of his command to the Grand Orient and even of transferring officers suspected of 'reactionary' sentiments to eastern garrisons: 'Resign! Resign! The spy is not worthy of commanding the 9th army corps!' read posters in Tours in a successful campaign to have the General transferred.[9] Otherwise, the *affaire des fiches* left in its wake a petty war of insults, demands for disciplinary action and transfers.

The *affaire des fiches* has been interpreted as the most blatant bid by the Radical Left to apply political considerations to officer promotion in its avowed campaign to 'republicanize' the officer corps. By exposing promotion abuses, the argument goes, the Right ended André's long reign over the rue Saint-Dominique, weakened the Combes ministry which toppled a few weeks later and ushered in the more moderate Rouvier and Sarrien governments which limited the more pernicious political influence in promotion. This view needs re-examination. While the existence of the *fiches* was exposed by the Right, the affair, as will be seen, had been provoked by a group of left-wing officers in André's military cabinet who felt that the war minister was dragging his feet in republicanizing the army, and it was the Radicals rather than their opponents who profited.

Idealists, like Captains Targe and Mollin, who set about their tasks with evangelical fervour were soon brought face to face with political realities. As André gradually acquired a taste for power, was integrated into the political system and even set his ambitions on a senate seat, his reformist passion gave way to a desire for political survival. The very republican Captain Mollin, married to the daughter of Anatole France, denounced the number of petty opportunists drawn into the war ministry by the promise of revolutionary spoils. Their influence increased especially after André announced that he was concerned only with major questions, leaving the day-to-day running of the ministry to Percin. Under Percin, junior officers and minor officials in the ministry doled out favours and retribution often on the basis of personal friendship or professional connections, to settle some private dispute rather than according to any concerted plan to republicanize the army. 'Percin has become the real minister, and as he cannot do everything, his cabinet officers become little subministers', wrote Colonel Legrand-Girard. 'I am told that there have been some abuses.'[10] Real power in the André ministry lay with underlings like Mollin, Targe and Humbert who drew up promotion lists with prejudiced or inaccurate information supplied by the Grand Orient, or, according to Mollin, with an uneducated gendarme named Thérèz who amused himself by transferring officers whom he or one of his friends or acquaintances disliked, muttering: 'je me venge'. 'It is undeniable that General Percin lost control and granted him all sorts of favours', Mollin wrote. 'The gendarme only had to insist a little in giving him any order to sign, no matter how arbitrary or abusive, and he signed it.'[11]

Radical politicians complained, and historians have since agreed, that a decade of Radical rule failed to 'republicanize' the officer corps. This was bound to prove an elusive goal. In the first place, the vast majority of army officers were already good republicans. Even the republic's most severe military critics, like Lyautey, rejected the notion that any other form of government would suit modern France. All they demanded was that the regime's elected representatives and officials act with more responsibility and less egotism. Secondly, any attempt to 'republicanize' the officer corps was bound to stumble over the contradictions of the Radical Party. For Radicals, to republicanize the army meant to politicize the army, to end the long-standing convention which made the army immune from the swings and shifts of France's political fortunes. For idealists like Targe and Mollin, the goal set was the capture of all top army jobs and ultimately of the entire officer corps by men of pronounced left-wing views. But for the majority of Radical politicians who understood like Joseph Caillaux that their party represented more an 'attitude' than a coherent political philosophy, and that votes and power followed favours, not lectures on constitutional theory, the aim was to make officers directly dependent on the party in power. In this respect, the army was successfully 'republicanized', for soldiers now began to look to the party, and to their favourites in power, as the arbiter in all questions of career. Even conservative soldiers were prepared to bury their convictions to salvage their careers by a visit to an old Saint-Cyr classmate sitting in the war ministry. The idealists were bound to be disappointed – barely two years into André's four-year ministry, Targe complained that they were stripped of hope: 'For the last three months we have been followed by the police, our mail is opened, our private life exposed. And these people dare to call themselves Dreyfusards!' Targe wrote in August 1902 to Dreyfusard Louis Havet

> People say that we lacked flexibility: it is certain that we opposed the Minister when he wanted to compensate the Ducassés, the Gueslins, the Bourgognes, the Ragets, etc. The Minister has not understood that we do not serve his *person* but an *idea* and that when he departed from that idea, our duty was to separate ourselves from him. But whatever the bankruptcy of the man, and it is greater than we can imagine, the idea remains and we shall continue to serve it.[12]

Combes decried the fact that his Radical colleagues were more interested in extending their political patronage into the forces than in rewarding *bona fide* republican officers, and wrote in an undated memorandum, written probably in 1903, that:

> Three years ago we believed that the hour had arrived to give the republic to the republicans. In the army, the ministerial cabinet was pushed to it by necessity – they tried for about one year. In the last two years, the old parties have regained all of their power and all of this great effort has succeeded only in leaving the army perhaps worse than it was before, because the republican element is now discouraged and given over to the reprisals of the reactionaries.[13]

It was these divisions and disagreements between republicans and opportunists, between idealists and politicians, which gave birth to the *affaire des fiches*. André faced increasing criticism from within his cabinet, especially from Captain Charles Humbert, the future senator, who charged publicly that André was an 'opportunist' and favoured reactionary officers. When Humbert actively intrigued to have André replaced by Percin (many thought to further his career rather than from a devotion to the republican 'cause'), André transferred him to the provinces. Humbert resigned from the army, but continued to press Percin to jettison the war minister. Encouraged by Humbert, Percin visited Galliffet in 1902 to tell him that Captain Mollin was in charge of an information network which passed through Vadécard, General Secretary of the Grand Orient, and asked Galliffet if he should resign in protest. The old general suggested that his resignation might be attributed to other reasons, and counselled him to remain in the ministry. Galliffet told Waldeck-Rousseau, newly resigned, that the *fiches* were 'extraordinary and inadmissible': 'I readily admit that prefects representing the central government are consulted for important promotions', he wrote. 'They offer guarantees and they are responsible, but no-one can imagine that one takes notice of information from anyone who walks through the door. Spying should not be encouraged.' Although Combes later claimed that he knew nothing of the *fiches*, Waldeck-Rousseau wrote on 30 December 1902: 'Saw Combes. My opinion is that the procedure carried out at the war ministry is inadmissible and will unleash legitimate anger when it is discovered. Combes agrees.' The new prime minister promised to look into the matter after the senate elections.[14]

In 1902, several of the *fiches* kept in Percin's office in the war ministry went missing. These re-emerged two years later in the *Figaro* to coincide with Guyot de Villeneuve's revelations based on *fiches* passed to him by Jean Bidegain, an employee at the Grand Orient who collected information on 19,000 French officers. The role of Percin and Humbert in the leaks was never established, but they certainly attempted to profit from André's embarrassment by posing as men outraged by the practice. But a letter of 26 March 1904, published later by the *Humanité*, and the appearance of Mollin's book which pointed out that only Percin had access to the file in which the *fiches* were kept, threw suspicion upon André's chief aide as the man behind the affair.[15]

While these revelations ruined Percin's standing in the army, they did nothing to loosen the grip of politics on promotion. Rather than an attack by the Right on a left-wing minister, the *affaire des fiches* boiled down to an attempt by a left-wing general and an ambitious captain to ditch a minister whom they saw as a road-block to their own ambitions. Rather than end favouritism and political influence in promotion, André's departure simply accelerated it, inflicting a defeat on those who had hoped to reverse the growing influence of politics in the barracks. Before 1899, attempts to gain information on the political views of officers, even through official channels, stood condemned, so that Gambetta had to keep very quiet about his two 1876 and 1878 investigations. In June 1900, when Waldeck-Rousseau reluctantly gave André permission to mobilize police to keep an eye on the army, they were at first reluctant to do so: 'Monsieur Waldeck-Rousseau, to whom I renewed my objections, ordered me, although without enthusiasm, I admit, to honour the request of General André, who, he told me, needed to be informed and that the Minister of the Interior must help him as much as possible', the Director of the Sûreté wrote to the Minister of the Interior on 4 November 1904.[16]

The debates over the *affaire des fiches* brought official surveillance into the open and institutionalized it, restating the view that promotion should be reserved for the republic's faithful. A Senate resolution of 30 March 1905 called on the government 'to be guided, in the promotion of officers, both by their professional qualities and by their devotion to the republic'. Berteaux, André's successor in the war ministry, instituted a regular system of prefects' reports on all officers offered for promotion and for the *légion d'honneur* – a system which, Millerand claimed, was 'very influential'.[17] Berteaux even defended the republican obsession, so evident in the *fiches*, with acquaintance with not only an officer's religious opinions, but also those of his wife and the type of school to which they sent their children. Even impartial observers considered this unfair: a wife's opinions are not necessarily shared by her husband, while selection of a school was often determined by the course of study, the location or the fees, which were often cheaper in parochial schools than in state lycées. Berteaux, however, held firm: 'I believe that the wife, in particular the Frenchwoman, exercises a very great influence on her husband', he told the senate. 'If the wife is reactionary, the husband must be at least three times more republican for me to be perfectly satisfied about his opinions.' Fortunately for them, the Socialists did not apply the same criterion in the selection of their leaders or Jaurès, whose wife was a devout Catholic, would not have advanced beyond a modest local secretariat. As for the selection of schools, Berteaux reminded senators that: 'It is the State's duty – and the minister of education has reminded prefects that it is also their duty – to know the republic's civil servants' attitude to education.'[18] Officers were left in no doubt that their political opinions and religious beliefs were a matter of record at the war ministry and weighed in the promotion scales.

The *affaire des fiches* convinced soldiers that promotion was now a free-for-all, an arbitrary affair in which men with the best connections stood to gain most. As influence replaced ability in the promotion stakes, officers rushed to curry favour with well-connected deputies and journalists and with left-leaning officers who might mention their names in the right places: de Civirieux noted that after the initial shock of the *affaire des fiches* had passed, officers sought to ingratiate themselves with 'the favourite and the delegate of power'.[19] The war ministry was flooded with officer recommendations – between 15,000 and 20,000 annually by 1910.[20] 'When generals were all-powerful in the classification committees, they were surrounded by crowds of courtiers', wrote Captain d'Arbeaux.

When the minister had power of promotion for the entire army, these courtiers sought out journalists and politicians. Favouritism, therefore, has changed shape and become essentially political and open to outside influence. It has become much more common-place. Recognizing the power of political intervention, officers have become clients of influential deputies. Name me an officer who does not know a deputy, a senator or a journalist.[21]

André admitted that his promotion system had been abused: 'Despite my good intentions [in promoting republican officers] things sometimes went too far. Sometimes also, one mistook an upstart for a dedicated republican because of signs of loyalty too ostentatious to be true.'[22]

In 1906, War Minister Etienne tried to staunch the flow of unsolicited officer recommendations and tried to convince officers that their military superiors, not their political friends, would decide their careers. 'People have told you that the decisions of the war minister are purely arbitrary', he stated in a circular.

This is untrue. The war minister makes his own decisions. He takes advice from those whose job it is to examine, to regulate the worth, the titles and the merits of officers. The promotion list is for the minister, I ask you to believe it, a constant concern and particularly worrying. In any case, you understand the promotion procedure. The colonel who, having heard the officers in his regiment, marks them. The brigadier afterwards makes his recommendations. Then it is the turn of the major general and then the corps commander. This work arrives at the ministry and it is on these bases that we make our choice.[23]

The truth was somewhat different. Even the moderate Etienne, chosen to restore badly shaken army morale in the wake of the Tangier crisis and the *affaire des fiches*, allowed extraordinary abuses to continue. The 1906 promotion lists were drawn up by Captain Jouinot-Gambetta, nephew of Léon Gambetta and a member of Etienne's staff in the ministry, his friend the young diplomat Saint-Aulaire and his girlfriend Blanche, over lunch Chez Maxim's:

Over coffee, smoking oriental tobacco ... inspired by patriotism, [we] drew up the lists free, if not of all spirit of friendship, at least of that partisan spirit which, before Etienne's arrival, sacrificed the elite of our officers. I set a bad example of friendship, but an example which did not fly in the face of justice, by recommending my college friends, like myself old students of the Jesuits, treated odiously during the André regime. Jouinot-Gambetta put them down immediately. 'Uncle Leon said: *le cléricalisme, voilà l'ennemi!* I don't give a damn. I don't give two damns. The only enemy for me is the Prussian.'[24]

'What Third Republican politicians really missed was frequenting Chez Maxim's', concluded Saint-Aulaire. One could say the same for French officers. On 1 April 1912, the *Porte-Voix* claimed that four-fifths of officer promotions were the result of political connections.

The *affaire des fiches* had a second unhappy result for military efficiency. To appease officer fears that uncomplimentary and inaccurate information was included in their files, a 13 January 1905 decree obliged all commanders to show every officer his efficiency report. A 22 April 1905 law extended this right to all civil servants. The result was a flood of banal information, usually erring on the side of praise, which offered little appreciation of professional competence. As a result, political and ministry connections became even more important in promotion: 'Now, with few exceptions, all officers have excellent reports and I must admit that this has reached amazing proportions since the ministerial order requiring the communication of dossiers to the officers concerned', Picquart confessed in the *Aurore* on 1 January 1906. In the absence of sound professional judgement, 'the spirit of coterie, personal or political relations plays a decisive role. In any case, the example comes from higher up.' He also confessed that in the promotion melée following the abolition of the classification committees, 'many more officers than one imagines' had been promoted through a mix-up of names. On taking over the war ministry in 1911, struck by the inferiority of the men who had risen to the top of the army, Messimy also found himself utterly disarmed when he attempted to single out competent men for promotion: 'I was struck by your arguments and the difficulties you face in selecting men for the high command', Lyautey wrote to Messimy in August 1911. 'I realize as do you that the banal complimentary reports of the corps commanders, even the verbal appreciations, leave the minister little informed.'[25] 'The experience acquired since 1905 has clearly shown that the obligation to show the [efficiency] reports annually has undermined the commander's freedom of expression to such a point that, in general, these reports have become more or less uniform and no longer furnish the minister the positive information which is indispensable to him', read a 1912 decree by Millerand which made officer files confidential and at the same time abolished prefectorial reports on the political and religious opinions of officers.[26]

Increasingly, under Radical administration, competence took a back seat to connections in army promotion. The result, however, did not always please left-wing idealists: captains charged with drawing up the promotion lists and other ministry officers well-placed to make their preferences known, like Sarrail who was infantry director from 1907 to 1911, were vulnerable to pressure from all directions – politicians, journalists, old comrades and friends. Left-wing deputies may have found access to the war ministry easier,[27] but, as Combes complained, left-wing politicians did not always push left-wing officers. Delighted at the uniformed petitioners who now sat in the anterooms of their political surgeries, they were often more concerned with building up their own clientele than with worrying over much about the intimate political convictions of the supplicants. Officers too quickly learned the rules of the new game, posting a new-found republicanism or slipping into a political neutrality calculated not to embarrass their patrons. Picquart complained that many officers had been 'transformed by the circumstances into loyal republicans',[28] a phenomenon observed by many: Captain d'Arbeaux noted that 'republican officers multiplied to the horizon once rewards were showered on the pioneer workers'.[29] De Civirieux noted sourly how, when André visited his garrison in November 1900, officers who before had denounced him in unprintable language, rushed to shake his hand: 'I then understood the devotion which a regime making such dreams possible can inspire in its favourites pulled from obscurity.'[30]

Langlois argued that promotion reforms had left morale in ruins, rewarding mediocrity rather than merit, encouraging a growing number of resignations and weakening the high command: 'What has been the result?' he asked in 1907.

First, it has weakened the command, which no longer has any influence on an officer's career. They see that success no longer depends on professional competence. Some, systematically shunted aside, slowly lose their enthusiasm, their zeal, become discouraged, work less, become mediocre officers or simply leave the army: the number who have left is frightening and, we must be honest, they are often the best . . . Other officers with fewer scruples become the lapdogs of politicians and debase themselves thus increasingly losing the virtue needed in a leader – character. These men are showered with favours. As a result, for several years now, one finds incapable men who inspire neither affection nor confidence at the head of some of our largest commands. Knowing that they are distrusted, they become hard and unfair. Lastly, so as to avoid stirring up trouble, they are not firm enough and indiscipline increases daily.[31]

While statistics are lacking, contemporary observers frequently bemoaned the number of good officers who left the army in these years.[32] Undoubtedly, many with a civilian alternative resigned; others, like Major de Civrieux, took advantage of the 30 March 1902 finance bill which allowed officers to take three-year furloughs. 287 officers were released on three-year furlough in 1905, and by 1909, 963 officers were either listed as on furlough or as non-active. These prolonged leaves were usually a form of disguised retirement: for instance, of 54 infantry captains on three-year furlough in 1905, only eight had returned to active duty by 1909.[33] While not every officer who left the army in this period did so for exclusively political reasons, the Dreyfus affair and subsequent Radical military reforms cast a long shadow in the regiments, accounting in great measure for the declining quality and quantity of recruitment to Saint-Cyr. The events of these years certainly discouraged the future General Veron, who only rediscovered his military vocation in the trenches of the western front: 'Was I going to enter a career at a time when the best men were abandoning it?' he quoted his mother as asking him. 'Follow a profession which now consists of confronting strikers, of breaking down church doors and chasing nuns? And what freedom can one find in a career where the officers, like all civil servants, were obliged if they wanted promotion to give humiliating proof of their fidelity to the regime – even if it meant joining a masonic lodge?' The *affaire des fiches* was the last straw. 'I was not the only one of my generation whose military vocation was shattered.'[34] By 1907, officers combining intelligence with most of the martial virtues had become France's endangered species.

The promotion squabbles introduced divisions in the officer corps – not, as historians have suggested, between officer cliques split into political camps, but between officers with connections and thus with a future, and those with none. 'There are now two clear factions in the army', declared a 30 December 1904 report. 'That of officers who, whatever their political preferences, do their duty as they see it, and that of the *arrivistes* who try to advance in rank any way they can.'[35] Divisions were no less acute between the lower ranks and senior officers. In keeping with Radical policy which branded the officer corps as reactionary and in an attempt to cover their professional deficiencies, generals were often overly strict with officers. Captain d'Arbeaux blasted the 'egoism of generals' who sought excuses to inflict punishments on subordinate officers.[36] 'General X speaks to soldiers only in the most affectionate terms: "My comrade"', wrote an anonymous officer in 1909. 'But as soon as he turns to the officers, his face and language change: he becomes brusque, haughty, difficult... The way in which those generals carry out their inspections, you would think that the officers are imbeciles or evil-doers.'[37]

The poor quality and political promotion of the high command had repercussions throughout the military hierarchy. 'People known throughout the army for their professional incapacity are named to the highest commands', Langlois lamented.

The results are fatal. The best officers, shoved aside, become discouraged. Some leave the army, most lose little by little their enthusiasm... Other officers, less good, finding no military explanation for the promotion of comrades judged mediocre, attribute it to hidden influences. From this moment they are no longer interested in serving well but look only for patrons outside the army... and too often they succeed. Appetites which destroy comradeship grow: distrust and jealousy increase among officers and the spirit of solidarity without which all is weakness gradually disappears, giving place to a narrow and vile egoism. As the influence of superiors on the officer's career is nil, officers begin to accuse their leaders of lacking energy in defending their interests ... Unjustifiable choices in the eyes of officers have given them as superiors men they judge incompetent.[38]

Promotional favouritism and political spying introduced a new note of caution and hesitation into relationships among officers. Suspicion replaced comradeship in the mess, splintering officers into factions. 'For some time now ... the relationships among officers have taken on another character', noted the *France militaire* on 22 November 1904. 'When they do not know each other, they go cautiously, each looking to discover the thoughts of the other, and only shake hands with half-confidence. Conversations in the mess, once frank and gay, have become prudent and measured.' 'The great majority of officers mistrust their comrades and disdain their leaders', wrote Major de Civrieux in 1908.[39] Captain d'Arbeaux conceded that the Radicals had successfully cracked the cohesion of the officer corps: 'Nothing any longer binds officers together: neither the cohesion which results mechanically from garrison life (except in Algeria and in a few garrisons, notably cavalry ones), nor confidence in their leaders, nor the community of an ideal.'[40]

The *affaire des fiches*, then, had two important consequences for the army: it convinced soldiers that promotion was now reserved for the well-connected. Officers increasingly sought out influential deputies or journalists, which did little to encourage professional standards or high morale. Secondly, the decision to allow officers access to their efficiency reports resulted in superiors making only banal comments, calculated not to offend, which offered little appreciation of an officer's merit. After 1911, generals and ministers sifting efficiency and inspection reports in an attempt to single out officers worthy of promotion found that they offered few worthwhile comments upon which to base a decision. The most useful indication of professional competence, the truthful appreciation of an officer's immediate superiors, was no longer available.

The *affaire des fiches* also served to point up the hollowness of radical claims to 'republicanize' the forces. The question of 'who rules the army' had long ago been settled in favour of the republic. To pretend otherwise was simply to tilt at windmills. But it was resurrected as an excuse to disorganize the high command and break the morale of the officer corps. 'Republicanization', in the final analysis, came down to the simple expedient of handing over promotion to political influence. But the army remained unreformed, and this was a pity, for, as many officers recognized, the army could have benefited from a thorough shake-up. Not because it was unrepublican, but because it had become bureaucratic, self-satisfied, sluggish. But Radicals were not reformers, they were destroyers eager to make political capital by prolonging issues, drawing out crises to convince the electorate that only they could cork a smoking reactionary volcano. As a result, they squandered much potential goodwill among the more open and imaginative officers, like Lyautey from whom they took many of their ideas and complaints. 'The "revolution" has not been carried out', Lyautey wrote to Max Leclerc in May 1904. 'The present minister amuses the gallery by punishing people. It is insufficient and a bad method. They have not carried out a basic reform, and for the first time in my life I want to become war minister to take a hatchet to the institutions.'[41]

The self-esteem, professional interests, notions of hierarchy and discipline – virtually everything which soldiers held dear – had been savaged by the party in power. It was a shortsighted, not to say foolish, way to deal with problems of civil-military relations in France, for it encouraged suspicion and mistrust and automatically rejected men of good faith who might have been encouraged to collaborate in a genuine reform, as Lyautey recognized: 'one must first help [the army], cleanse its wounds, calm its nerves, reassure it, restore its self-confidence and then one could launch out, but again with many precautions, softness, consideration and above all consideration for those of good faith, for their worthy private interests', he wrote to Etienne. 'You understood that within this army there was much goodwill and a profound good faith, that it needed above all to be loved.'[42]

7

Anti-militarism and indiscipline

In the post-Dreyfus years 1906 marked a political turning point. The alliance of republican defence which bound Radicals and socialists with the cry 'no enemies to our left', began to unravel as the representatives of the working class called into question the sincerity of their bourgeois allies. The 1905 formation of the *Section Française de l'Internationale Ouvrière*, France's first unified socialist party, strengthened, at least temporarily, the position of the intransigent Guesdist wing. Jaurès and friends submitted to the directives of the 1904 Amsterdam congress which forbade socialist collaboration with bourgeois governments. The revolutionary Left turned its back upon the reformist Left, the socialists upon their erstwhile Radical allies. This political divorce was celebrated with a festival of labour unrest. The 18 March 1906 Courrières disaster, in which 1,100 miners perished, sparked an era of confrontation between the government and the militant *Confédération générale du travail* which witnessed a rocketing number of strikes. Into this minefield of labour relations stepped Georges Clemenceau, first as interior minister in the March 1906 Sarrier government and finally as prime minister from October of that year. Not a man known for his willingness to compromise, Clemenceau waded into a delicate situation, setting off explosions which increasingly wrenched the unions from France's body politic. As his friends dropped off on the Left, Clemenceau was forced to form his majority to the Right. The old Jacobin was transformed into a man of order, the revolutionary into 'France's first cop', the Dreyfusard into the enemy of the Left.

Clemenceau's wanderings toward the Right did little to improve his standing with the army. The new prime minister posed as the champion of order, not of tradition, and refused to make it up with the enemies of his youth, the sword and the altar. Consequently, the forces continued to suffer the privations of the siege war laid against their prestige. Even as Père-la-Victoire, Clemenceau's appeal resided largely with his ability to impose his authority upon the generals, while more orthodox conservatives like Poincaré believed their duty lay with giving the soldiers a free hand, protecting them from the retributions and malicious attacks of the Left.

Soldiers saw Clemenceau's increasing use of the army to control strike violence as yet another blow struck against their status. Traditionally, the French army had two roles: defending France against foreign enemies and against internal disorder. The first task united soldiers; the second demoralized them. The Left frequently charged that soldiers liked nothing better than to skewer disorder on the ends of their bayonets. During the church inventories especially, they chided that sulking officers marched against strikers 'with joy',[1] paradoxically transforming the Left into the champion of military discipline by insisting that conservative officers should give the example of obedience to soldiers they would later lead against strikers.[2]

The use of the army to police the interior was a traditional job assigned to the forces and had dictated many organizational refinements in the nineteenth century. The Commune was only the last on a long list of military police actions which stretched back to the *ancien régime*. But the army had never relished usurping the gendarme's role. Despite the soldier's instinctive horror of disorder, his antipathy for the revolutionary Parisians and their anarchistic slogans, the psychological balance in a civil disturbance was always precarious. 'The soldier dreads civil war', wrote Marshal Canrobert, recalling his experiences in 1830. 'He does not know if the cause he is defending will be victorious, or if perhaps tomorrow he will be serving the insurgents ... He becomes restless, manifesting a lethargy and mistrust which sometimes lead him to desert, to disobey and to panic.'[3] French soldiers were not Cossacks, blindly faithful to their Paris masters, but sniffed the political winds, cautiously weighing the balance of forces and firepower. In 1830 and 1848, this fence-sitting was enough to send two dynasties scurrying to foreign exile. Even the slaughter of the Commune, announced by Thiers as a holy war against socialism and disorder, was a painful chore. 'The soldiers themselves are silent', wrote Catulle Mendès after the orgy of bloodshed. 'Victorious, they are sad; they do not drink or sing. Paris has the atmosphere of a city taken by dumb men.'[4]

The use of the army to quell domestic disturbances created tensions which the organization sometimes could not absorb. But such tasks also challenged the French army's traditional image as the symbol of national unity. The ugly memory of the Commune behind them, soldiers turned East, confident that all Frenchmen were united behind their army in a patriotic bond. Conscription and the adulation showered upon the army by the government, convinced officers that they were no longer outcasts, but warriors who embodied the aspirations of the

Fatherland and the goodwill of its citizens. The growth of industrial and social unrest and Clemenceau's increasing use of the forces to control it resurrected old tensions and doubts, casting the army in the role of the working man's villain and shattering the image of a body above class and political faction.

The advent of the Radical government coincided with a marked increase in the use of troops on strike duty: the 528,000 francs spent in 1900 to send soldiers to control striking workers virtually tripled in two years to 1,542,635.[5] In 1906 the *Confédération générale du travail* launched a campaign for the 8-hour day and to organize civil servants, which embittered relations between the government and the unions.[6] The number of strikes grew spectacularly. To the government, and especially to Clemenceau, the army's *raison d'être* appeared to lie almost exclusively in its repressive potential. To the complaints of officers and NCOs that strike duty was for them financially ruinous, or that it was a perversion of the army's professional role, was added the admission that the task was quite impossible. 'From every point on the horizon, by the railways, marvellous instruments of despotism and domination, arrive battalions, squadrons, even batteries', wrote Major de Civrieux of the army's intervention in strikes.[7] These military invasions were usually enough to transform a fairly modest dispute into a full-scale walk-out which almost inevitably led to violence, before which officers untrained for such missions and seldom given clear instructions beyond being told to use as little force as possible felt almost entirely disarmed. Local police were noticeably reluctant to be associated with soldiers representing government repression, while those imported from safe rural areas like Brittany seemed intimidated and out of their depth in a situation which contrasted so violently with their quiet country beat.[8] 'Since Monsieur Thiers . . . times have well and truly changed', wrote an officer who signed himself Lieutenant Z.

If one is attacked, which is always possible, what does one do? Either give the assailants free rein, or fire. It is not by ordering 35 men to strike out with rifle butts that one can force back 2,000 . . . A troop commander in a strike is always in a difficult position. Always questioning his conscience . . . and fearing to be blamed if he acts too much or too little, almost sure to be accused if any serious incident occurs . . . The unfortunate man wants only to see the storm pass.[9]

Dismounted troops faced special difficulties, for strikers appeared intimidated only by cavalry: 'Experience has for some time demonstrated the efficiency of cavalry in popular disturbance', wrote the *Avenir militaire* on 26 May 1905 in a statement whose truth was vividly illustrated by Lieutenant Z's description of a charge mounted by dragoons to rescue a platoon of infantrymen about to be beaten to a pulp by strikers.[10] De Civrieux's description of strike duty sounds like 1830 without the gunfire: 'On the public square . . . the company is drawn up', he wrote.

All around, people shout insults, paving stones, bricks, broken bottles fly. And rigid before the execution of his orders, without daring to infringe them, [the officer] sees his subordinates knocked out, covered with blood! Ah! if his conscience is not troubled, he has no heart. For the duties of an officer are two-fold, and those which he owes to his men, whose life depends on him, are as sacred as the obligation to obey unworthy orders, too often followed out of fear for his own interests.[11]

That the army on occasion opened fire on strikers, as at Raon-l'Etape, Narbonne and Villeneuve-Saint-Georges, is not at all surprising. One may well wonder, however, why bloodshed did not follow more often from the clumsy use of soldiers to control strikes.

Army resentment over increasing strike duty concentrated on the government, which it charged with allowing the situation to bubble over and calling in the army to take the scalding. D'Arbeaux remarked bitterly that if provocative politicians, incompetent magistrates and pusillanimous police performed their jobs properly, then officers could get on with theirs – war preparation.[12] 'It is the army which has paid with its blood for all the incoherent policies of public officials and of the government', wrote the *France militaire* on 26 April 1906, following a particularly violent week of strikes in the North in which one officer was killed and several soldiers and police seriously wounded.

Many officers realized that the use of soldiers to control strikes had also linked the army to repression in the minds of an increasingly large section of the working population. De Civrieux, called out in October 1903 to deal with a miners' strike in Flanders, denounced the companies as 'rapacious' and 'morally irresponsible' and found that his sympathies lay with the strongly religious strikers.[13] 'If, in the beginning, the army accepted without repugnance the new role assigned to it, little by little officers have become embittered at being made to appear before the proletariat as adversaries', wrote d'Arbeaux. 'Whatever his opinions, the frequency of these interventions in strikes has encouraged a discontentment not lacking sources. . . . The slightest work stoppage brings the soldiers, while the end of the stoppage does not see them sent home. The idleness favours the birth of uncomfortable reflections in the spirit of men who saw the profession of arms as something different.'[14] He claimed that discontentment over strike duty was a major catalyst in the campaign which began in 1910 to win the vote for officers so they could better defend their own interests. The senator for the Seine,

Montfort, also argued that 'the use of soldiers in the repression of strikes is always perilous, in that the result can be to create a profound division between the army and a part of the nation'.[15]

The seemingly spectacular growth of anti-militarism after 1900 was a product of several factors, including the gradual erosion of *la revanche* and the revival of a pacifist tradition dormant since the Second Empire. But the use of the army to control strikes and the violence which ensued had been crucial in calling the attention of union leaders to the strategic position occupied by the army on the road to working men's rights. The 1 May 1891 massacre of strikers by troops at Fourmies opened the debate on the Left, which denounced the army as a weapon in the hands of industrial capitalism. 'Modern armies are no more than police forces', Paul Lafargue wrote in the *Socialiste* on 1 May 1891. 'The Fourmies massacre will have enormous reverberations in the army. It will awaken in the soul of the soldier, himself working-class, that feeling of his duties toward his class which brutal and ferocious discipline attempts to snuff out.' Fourmies and the bloody confrontations which followed forced socialists to define their attitudes on a whole series of questions, including patriotism.

A history of the socialist Left before 1914 is largely a history of its attitudes toward the army. The motions voted in party congresses, the heated debates on attitudes to war between Hervé, Guesde and Jaurès, and the positions defended by party newspapers, eventually united most left-wing leaders behind Jaurès' deep patriotism and fear of German domination. The vast groundswell of support for the war in 1914 announced to political leaders, nervously clutching the Carnet B (the list of socialist leaders to be arrested on the outbreak of war), that this conclusion had long ago been reached by working men and women. However, the fundamental moderation of socialist leaders like Jaurès often contrasted sharply with the militant language of party meetings and newspaper articles, giving many reason to believe that an insurrection was being prepared – a feeling reinforced by growing army indiscipline and desertion. The fact that hardened anti-militarists were concentrated in the trade unions and *Bourses du travail* wrapped up anti-militarism and the army's strike breaking role in one neat package.

The anti-militarist resurgence was sparked largely by anarchists and the socialist fringe in the *Bourse du travail*, an organization founded in 1886 to agitate for better pay and working conditions while providing meeting halls, libraries and classes for working men. The 1901 death of Ferdinand Pelloutier, the moderate president of the *Fédération des bourses du travail*, and his replacement by the militant Georges Yvetot, announced a distinct change of tone in that organization. A May 1901 declaration called upon unionists to oppose all wars while the following year's conference approved the diffusion of anti-militarist propaganda.[16] The turn of the century also saw the establishment of the *Sou du Soldat*, a fund to aid needy union members in uniform which soon stretched beyond its original purpose to funnel anti-militarist propaganda through militants called to the colours. 'Founded originally to encourage comradeship and solidarity, the "Caisse du Sou du Soldat" rapidly became one of the most redoubtable arms in the hands of the revolutionaries and the anti-patriots', read a January 1912 police report.

In fact, the *Confédération général du travail* does not hide the final result it expects from this institution ... One of its two secretaries, Yvetot, wrote the following in the *Voix du peuple* of 15 July of last year: 'In time of strike, as in wartime, the syndicalists will remain men, brothers of all those who suffer, work and think. And when these speak out, when they rebel, justice demands that our children, our brothers and our friends who are soldiers COME OVER TO OUR SIDE WITH ARMS AND AMMUNITION.'[17]

An anti-militarist group formed in Paris in 1899 and in 1902 took the title of *Ligue antimilitariste*, while the 1904 Amsterdam congress witnessed the founding of the *Association Internationale Antimilitariste* – led in France by Gustave Hervé and Miguel Almereyda, who sought to prepare a 'military strike and insurrection'.[18]

However, government repression and socialist hostility put paid to anti-militarist plans. Twenty-six *AIA* leaders including Hervé were sent to jail on 30 December 1905, after the publication of a tract calling on conscripts to revolt and turn their rifles upon their officers. Although they were amnestied six months later and feebly attempted to publish more propaganda, a pitifully small following, financial difficulties and fear of arrest all but reduced them to silence. Nor did the *Bourses du travail* prove particularly effective catalysts of revolution. The government estimated in October 1907 that only 58 of 139 *Bourses* were anti-militarist. Most workers yawned at the mere mention of anti-militarism and so stayed away from anti-militarist meetings. Syndicalist leaders also feared that the government would cut off the subsidies which made up one-half of the budget of the *Bourses*, including the leaders' salaries: 'The militants of the *Confédération générale du travail* or of the *Bourses*, terrorized by the executions in their ranks, are no longer eager to show off their anti-militarist and anti-patriotic sentiments', read an October 1907 report. 'They fear firstly for their organization which will be deprived of municipal or departmental subsidies. Next, they fear for themselves, for they were paid with these subsidies and fear that they will be replaced if imprisoned.'[19] However, the police found little comfort in their successful repression. On the contrary, they feared that they had simply driven the anti-militarists into the rank-and-file trade union movement where they were virtually impossible to ferret out. 'There was another way to continue their propaganda and inculcate in the workers their anti-militarist and anti-patriotic ideas', the report continued.

This means was not difficult to find, given that the great majority of leaders and workers belonged to the *Parti socialist unifié*, the unions or the *Bourses du travail*. It was sufficient, for the propagandizers, to be named to direct discussions in the union conferences, fairs or meetings. Here, while speaking of political, economic or union questions, they always found a way to speak of anti-militarism. And the workers, above all the youth, drawn by a political or economic subject, were always present in large numbers. That is why one never, or almost never, holds exclusively anti-militarist meetings today. The result is the following: anti-militarism is unknown, therefore unattackable now because it is no longer localized in specifically organized groups. Only occasionally does an imprudent man, or a 'trouble-maker' overstep the bounds and commit an infraction . . . Long tolerance has permitted anti-militarism to conquer a great portion of the working masses, who are in the habit of confusing syndicalism with anti-militarism.

The police assertion gained credence with the upsurge in anti-militarist activity after 1905. The 1906 *CGT* congress at Amiens declared:

That anti-militarist and anti-patriotic propaganda must become increasingly intense and audacious. In each strike the army is for the bosses. In each war between nations or in the colonies, in each European conflict, the working class is a dupe and sacrificed for the profit of the parasitic and bourgeois ruling class. For these reasons, the 15th congress approves and advocates all anti-militarist and anti-patriotic action and propaganda.

The 1908 Marseille congress voted 681 to 421 that 'the workers will reply to a declaration of war with the declaration of a revolutionary general strike'. Urbain Gohier continued his fanatical tirades against the army in *La Guerre sociale*, backed up by Hervé in the *Pioupiou de l'Yonne*, in which seldom an issue went by without a call for soldiers to desert. And he seemed to get results: the number of young men who deserted or failed to report for military service doubled in ten years. The 5,991 men listed as missing in 1902 rocketed to 13,000 in 1912. By 1912, fully 76,723 men had deserted or failed to don a uniform, the equivalent of two army corps.[20]

However, the impression given of a socialist wave rolling inexorably toward the sabotage of the national ideal was a deceptive one. Beneath the noise of press diatribes and party motions, moderate socialists worked successfully if not to silence their fiery colleagues at least to empty their threats. At both the 1906 Limoges congress of the *PSU* and that of 1907 at Nancy, Jaurès carried the debate on the general strike in the event of war with the argument that Hervé's solution would add a 'foreign tyranny' to a capitalist one.[21] The superior quality of the socialist leaders meant that they, rather than the union leaders, gradually established themselves as the true spokesmen for working men. Hervé's influence further declined when Guesde's attempt to have him evicted from the April 1909 Saint-Etienne congress was sabotaged by Jaurès and Vaillant. Whether Hervé now felt himself in the debt of the moderates or, as some suggested, the failure of the October 1910 railway workers walk-out had convinced him that the general strike was little more than a pipe-dream, Hervé changed his tactics. 'If the railway workers strike failed, if other attempts at revolution are doomed to the same fate, it is because the army is with the bourgeoisie. We must bring them over to our side.'[22] Rather than attack the army, socialists must work to win soldiers to the revolution. 'One has never made a revolution against the army', the *Guerre sociale* declared on 11 October 1910. 'The revolution with the aid of the army is made easier when the Revolutionary Party has at least a portion of the officers with it: No revolution against the army! If we want to foment revolution, let's have the army with us – the soldiers at least, for with the leaders . . . it is always possible to work things out.'[23] On 11 January 1911, the *Guerre sociale* condemned desertion as against the interest of the revolution – soldiers must remain to spread propaganda among their comrades and, if possible, win their stripes so as to be in a better position to offer leadership on the fateful day of insurrection. Militants were encouraged to seek positions as reserve officers: 'The social revolution needs artillery officers.'[24] Hervé perversely welcomed the use of the army in strike control to extinguish the remaining sparks of patriotism in the working population. Although Hervé claimed that 'my new militarism is not a rejection of the old (anti-militarism), but on the contrary an accentuation and an extension', his change of heart coincided with a general re-orientation of socialist anti-militarism which, rather than attack the army *en bloc*, sought to point out individual scandals.[25]

The victory of Jaurèsian conservatism did not mean an end to agitation: anti-militarist demonstrations continued, notably in January–February 1912, to protest the conviction of Private Rousset for the murder of another soldier in what many believed was a frame-up almost as serious as the Dreyfus affair, and against the three-year service law of 1913. But claims to be able to prevent mobilization remained pretentious bluster: anti-militarists were too fractured by ideological and personal quarrels to cobble together a common front. 'In the last trial of the anti-militarists, it was easy to see how they, belonging to different groups, share few sympathies and have few contacts', read a January

1908 police report. 'The young people who appeared before the judges are members of the "jeunesses révolutionnaires" of the neighbourhoods and have no more relations with pure socialist groups – who hardly tolerate them – than with the anarchists who do not like them at all.'[26] Even the growing number of desertions could not be attributed directly to their actions. In December 1909, when Private Gosset of Brest's 6th colonial infantry regiment claimed that he had been helped to desert by Delpech, general secretary of the *Fédération des bourses du travail*, Delpech denied it vehemently: 'A convinced anti-militarist . . . I personally am absolutely opposed, on principle, to desertion.' Jouhaux, general secretary of the *CGT*, confirmed that 'those who desert are lost for syndicalism'. A thorough police investigation of several suspected 'desertion agencies' in Paris and the provinces revealed that they did not exist: 'There is no organization charged to push soldiers to desert, and no fund has been created with this in view', read a December 1909 Paris report. The Marseille police chief claimed that his anti-militarists had moved to Toulon, while Toulon police noted that 'nothing proved that it (*Jeunesse Libre*, a local anti-militarist group) has provoked the desertion of soldiers in the garrison'. Police in Brest and Cherbourg also found that while local groups distributed the *Guerre sociale* and paid lip service to desertion, they did nothing to encourage it directly.[27] The growing desertion statistics seemed to have less to do with anti-militarist propaganda than with the two-year law of 1905 which for the first time required Frenchmen living abroad to report for military service. Few, Jaurès claimed, were particularly keen to make the trip home. Other 'deserters' were counted among reservists who had changed address and did not receive their annual training notice.[28] However, many complained that the amnesties voted by Parliament at the beginning of each legislative session – an average of every 27 months – simply encouraged young men to cross the border. Those of 1904 and 1906 stipulated that once a deserter married or turned 30, he was no longer liable for service.[29] 'Almost everything is permitted, and that which is forbidden will be quickly pardoned', said Georges Bonnefous of the principle underlying the amnesties.[30]

Anti-militarism was a force whose importance was grossly exaggerated before 1914. On the outbreak of war, anti-militarists could not move a man to stop mobilization. While officials estimated that 13 per cent of men called up would refuse to report, only 1.5 per cent in fact held back. Frenchmen everywhere rushed to take up arms with an enthusiasm which soothed the worst fears of even the most pessimistic prefect of police.

These years of anti-militarist propaganda and agitation, however, were not without importance. For if anti-militarists made but a weak impression in the working class population they aimed to convert, they did dent army morale. Not that officers were surprised to hear themselves denounced in colourful terms. They might even laugh at the obvious exaggeration: 'Officers are only drawing-room officers, fit only to drink champagne. Corporals are brutes who torture soldiers. The army is created to protect the capitalist bourgeoisie. The barracks is a school of crime, theft and syphilis', ran the script of an anti-militarist play put on for the benefit of Cherbourg conscripts.[31] More sobering was the realization that the government's image of the officer corps and military life was only slightly different. While police kept a close watch on anti-militarists in the trade unions, Radicals stimulated the anti-militarist debate for their own electoral reasons, repeating the old argument that anti-militarism was the fault of the soldiers. Anti-militarism, like anti-clericalism, was kept alive as a political issue. Radicals denounced reactionaries in the officer corps and the evils of military life while making only half-hearted attempts to correct what they saw as its major faults. This deepened the pessimism of professional soldiers who felt unjustly persecuted and inadequately defended.

While the ardent anti-militarist campaign ultimately proved a phantom threat, for many at the time anti-militants seemed to be converting great masses of French soldiers. The indiscipline increasingly encountered in many regiments after 1900 was seen as a direct result of growing anti-militarist influence in the ranks. The revolt of the 17th infantry regiment in 1907 and the 1913 riots which surrounded the three-year law debates were only highpoints, 50 foot waves in a sea whipped by political winds. Other incidents, many insignificant and unrecorded, indications nonetheless of a simmering contempt ready to burst to the surface each time leave was refused or discipline imposed, accumulated the poison in regimental life. The anti-militarist demonstrations which accompanied the annual departure of conscript classes in large cities, the political tracts in the barracks, trivial excuses for a chorus of the *Internationale* in the canteen, the sarcastic comments and refusal to salute, drained the confidence of officers and NCOs forced to cope with unenthusiastic conscripts plunged into sullen revolt. Soldiers suspected that the campaign of disorder was organized and directed by anti-militarists, especially as it first infected reservists recalled for training. From 1903, if not before, many reservists considered a training period incomplete unless marked by some manifestation of discontent over what they considered overwork or by general rowdiness which officers repressed with difficulty.[32] Many attributed the revolt of the 17th infantry in 1907 to the spirit of indiscipline introduced by reservists: 'For two years now, the regiment has not been the same', reported a senior officer of the 17th in 1907. 'Anti-militarism has made great and destructive progress . . . and the poison becomes stronger with each training period for reservists and territorials.' In 1905, officers only with difficulty persuaded reservists to march and even then 100 left manoeuvres early, without permission, and took the train back to Béziers 'to avoid the rain'. In 1906, 478 reservists reported sick on the day of departure. In 1907, 'the departure of the 17th was deplorable. In the town itself, the reservists sat on the pavements, in the doorways and refused to march. Several, taking advantage of the darkness, remained at Béziers.' Ninety-two dropped out with fatigue before the end of the manoeuvres compared with 15 the previous year.[33] The fact that reservists had been released on the day of the mutiny did not go unnoticed: 'The principal cause of the mutiny', reported Sergeant Roger, 'seems to be the training period of the reservists of the 17th, liberated on 20 June, who during their stay at Béziers and Agde pushed their regular colleagues to revolt.'[34]

Reservists were not infrequently in the forefront of disorder, confident that their civilian status would protect them from military reprisals: in 1906, the war minister forbade officers to keep reservists confined to the guardroom beyond their legal training period. 'The means of repression no longer exist', lamented the *France militaire* on 19 September 1906. In 1906, reservists in Brioude and Romans refused to march and sang the *Internationale* while reservists in the 75th infantry revolted and demanded to be sent home early.[35] 'The reserve call-up only served to demonstrate the progress of anti-militarist doctrines among several of them', the *France militaire* declared on 4 September 1906 of that year's reserve call-up. 'In a certain number of garrisons, one was treated to the scandalous spectacle of several men given over to demonstrations which only show that they have been contaminated by the theories dear to Monsieur Hervé and his acolytes.' In 1907, reservists at Saint-Dié sang the *Internationale* after complaining of bad quarters and roughed up a lieutenant sent to silence them.[36] Other incidents involving reservists were reported at Châlons-sur-Marne, Tarbe, Grenoble and Ajaccio.[37] Elsewhere, reservists made anti-militarist speeches, handed out political tracts and insulted or attacked officers.[38]

Nor were soldiers spared anti-militarist contamination: 65 soldiers of the 33rd artillery regiment rioted in January 1903 and smashed barracks windows, in what André soft-peddled as a 'schoolboy stunt'. Soldiers in Tours rioted in February crying 'Down with the army! Long live socialism!', as did soldiers in the 17th chasseurs at Lunéville who protested that they were worked too hard. In April, colonial hero Colonel Marchand complained publicly of the negligent appearance and disorderly behaviour of soldiers on leave in the large cities. Other incidents of indiscipline were reported in such cities as Angoulême, Epernay, Rennes, Rochefort, Clermont-Ferrand, few of which were active centres of anti-militarism. André generally displayed an indulgent attitude and soldiers were let off with only light punishment. However, when students at the *Ecole polytechnique* refused to take a written examination in 1902, he banished several to the regiments as privates, claiming that he intended to be 'as severe for the sons of the bourgeoisie as for the children of the people'.[39] The departure of conscripts, especially in Paris' *Gare de l'Est*, became the scene of demonstrations each October, with conscripts intoning the *Internationale* egged on by an admiring gallery of left-wing militants. While these incidents were much publicized and discussed, one must be careful not to exaggerate the effects on military discipline. The peace of the barracks square was only rarely interrupted by a major incident. But evidence suggests that almost everywhere the atmosphere had changed for the worse. The 17th infantry provides an example: 'The attitude of the soldiers has completely changed in the last two years', complained Madame Racaud, the canteen keeper of the 17th. 'Often in the canteen things became unbearable and we had to put our calm clients in a separate room. They rioted, breaking and shattering everything while singing the *Internationale*. I often had to intervene, but I finally gave up even though I lost a lot of money. Bad manners, disorder and excitement were everyday occurrences. We had to put up with everything.'[40]

By 1906, the general decline in discipline had attracted the notice of War Minister Etienne, who acknowledged that indiscipline had reached worrying levels: 'My attention has been called to a certain relaxation of discipline which seems to have occurred for some time now in several metropolitan and colonial units', read his 14 August circular. 'The statistics ... show a marked increase in the number of serious punishments, removal to discipline battalions and trials by court martial.' He called upon commanders to enforce 'an exact and absolute discipline', while respecting 'humanitarian' principles. 'If Monsieur Etienne deigned to speak of recent acts of indiscipline, the situation must really be serious', the *France militaire* wrote with a touch of sarcasm on 4 September 1906.

The pressure of indiscipline gradually building up in the army passed the danger mark with the Viticole crisis which in 1907 brought the Midi to the boil. The revolt had been brewing at least since 1904 in the four departments – Gard, Aude, Hérault and the Pyrénées-Orientales – which made their living almost exclusively from the cultivation of an inferior red wine. The situation gradually worsened as competition pushed many growers fraudulently to add sugar or water, bringing prices crashing down. Small proprietors with less than eight hectares were just able to break even, but those with larger spreads lost considerable sums. Land values at Narbonne dropped 80 per cent and at Béziers 70 per cent. The protests which began in 1906 with the refusal of some land owners to pay taxes became more serious in May 1907, when meetings organized by the Viticole Committee under a local wine grower, Marcellin Albert, and the socialist mayor of Narbonne, Ferroul, called for an extension of the tax boycott, the resignation of several municipal councils and an end to the fraudulent doctoring of wine. Mass demonstrations in Béziers, Perpignan, Narbonne and Carcassonne climaxed on 9 June with a 600,000-strong protest meeting in Narbonne. Clemenceau brushed aside warnings that serious trouble was brewing, explaining to Caillaux, 'You don't know the Midi. All this will end in a banquet.'[41] He obligingly laid on special trains to bring the demonstrators to the station just behind the barracks of the 100th infantry regiment, whose soldiers were recruited almost exclusively from Narbonne and the surrounding area. A large number of soldiers perched on the barracks wall had watched the arrival of the trains and listened to demonstrators calling on them to revolt for much of the afternoon. When a group of sergeants ordered the men off the wall, no-one budged. Furious, a sergeant Capo dragged a conscript off his perch, and was immediately set upon by several soldiers. The other sergeants retreated under a hail of stones and abuse. Attempts by officers and NCOs to restore order were made more difficult by a crowd of onlookers 400 strong, some of whom urged the soldiers to revolt: 'The authority of the NCOs who intervened to re-establish order was completely ignored', wrote the regimental commander Colonel Rabier.[42] Fearing that an immediate attempt to discipline the soldiers would provoke new trouble, no disciplinary action was taken for three days. When the regiment was ordered to the training camp at Larzac, three men were left behind in the guardroom and six more were confined on arrival at destination. Soldiers later said they were tired of being confined to barracks for days in anticipation of strike duty. On 11 June, soldiers of the 122nd infantry at Montpellier sang the *Internationale* and the *Carmagnole* in the regimental canteen to protest against their confinement to barracks, while on the 15th, similar incidents were reported in the 12th infantry at Perpignan,[43] the 58th infantry and 7th engineers at Avignon, the 11th infantry at Narbonne, the 2nd engineers at Montpellier and the 13th chasseurs at Béziers.[44]

Military misbehaviour burst into open mutiny at Agde. On 18 June, Clemenceau fought and won a parliamentary debate on his handling of the Viticole crisis. Strengthened, he ordered the arrest of the leaders of the Viticole Committee. Riots erupted in Narbonne and were put down, not without bloodshed, by troops ferried in from Aurillac and Rodez. Given the general state of unrest and the 17th infantry's tarnished disciplinary record, officials had for some time planned to transfer it beyond temptation. On 3 June, they had imprudently announced that the regiment should prepare for departure, providing ample time for the spread of rumours that its destination was the Hautes-Alpes or the Vosges. Soldiers allegedly told civilians not to permit the regiment's departure, so that when the 17th was ordered to nearby Agde for firing practice on 18 June, a large crowd surrounded the barracks crying: 'Don't leave! Down with Clemenceau! Down with Picquart!' Only at 2 am was a detachment of more than 100 police and a squadron of cavalry able to open a path to get the regiment out.

Once at Agde, the troops were billeted in an old convent and a disused barracks, the ground floor of which was occupied by the *Bourse du travail*. The poor conditions of the billets did little to bolster sagging morale, as mutinous troops later pointed out. Others suspected that the proximity of the *Bourse du travail* placed soldiers in contact with anti-militarists eager to cause trouble: witnesses later claimed to have heard troops boast that 'tonight we shall revolt; we shall be led by the people from the *Bourse du travail*'.[45] Galliéni, who led the official enquiry, gave them a great deal of credit in sparking the revolt. Certainly, many civilians, whether militant anti-militarists, people agitated by the crisis or simple troublemakers, bought drinks for soldiers inexplicably allowed to roam the streets, urging them to 'protect civilians'. Indiscipline increased on the 20th, fed by rumours that soldiers had fired on a crowd at Béziers, so that reservists, thought the most troublesome, were released and marched back to Béziers. The revolt was touched off as police and soldiers rounding the conscripts up confronted a crowd milling outside the barracks. Some claimed that a bugle was blown as a signal for the revolt to begin. Whatever the truth, soldiers rushed down the stairs into the arms of civilians who 'seemed to be waiting for them'. A group made immediately for the magazine where arms and ammunition were distributed. Officers and NCOs who attempted to stop the revolt were shoved aside by soldiers shouting: 'They are killing our parents.' By midnight, the entire regiment was on the road back to Béziers where they were met by General Lacroisade at the head of the 81st infantry sent to stop them. 'We want to go to Béziers to defend our parents who are being murdered', the soldiers shouted, and rather than risk a confrontation, Lacroisade let them pass. Once in Béziers, however, the soldiers were met by their relatives and local political leaders who urged them to return to duty. After several hours of negotiations, the soldiers gave in. Lacroisade allowed them to go home for the day and on the 22nd led them back to Agde. The regiment was later transferred to Gap and between four and five hundred soldiers were shipped to Tunisia.

The revolts of the 100th and 17th regiments confirmed for many Frenchmen that army morale had sunk dangerously low. In Parliament, they served to sever the Radical–Socialist alliance as Jaurès, Millerand and Brousse blamed Clemenceau for encouraging demonstrations and then putting them down with force. The Tiger survived this attack, but with his majority reduced to 60. In the cabinet, he postponed the government's bill to abolish court martials claiming that 'if discipline is weakened in the army, then France is finished'. However, when General Langlois, representing the Meurthe-et-Moselle, attacked Clemenceau's military policies in the Senate, pointing out, among other things, that the military budget had been sliced to the bone, the Prime Minister and Picquart brushed aside his charges. As if to give extra force to Langlois' thesis, however, both General Hagron, vice-president of the *conseil supérieur de la guerre*, and General Michel, deputy chief of staff, resigned in protest at the poor state of the army.

The revolt of the 17th provided a much-needed boost for anti-militarists desperately short of success. For the conspiratorial Left, the 17th became a symbol, a prize for perseverance, a myth to dazzle the faithful. But the role of anti-militarists in the mutiny was never established: anti-militarists were conspicuous by their absence in the *Bourses du travail* in Agde and Béziers; soldiers showed no signs of being infected by socialist or anti-militarist doctrines, only expressing worries about their parents, complaints about poor barracks conditions and fears about punishment.[46] What the rebellion did demonstrate was that locally recruited soldiers could not be counted upon to quash civil disturbance.

The debate over local recruitment was an old one in the French army. After the Bourbon Restoration's flirtation with locally recruited units collapsed in a cloud of disorder, the army took steps to see that regiments did not acquire a local flavour. After 1880, republicans introduced recruitment by regions whenever possible, stipulating, however, that no man could serve in his regional subdivision. But Radicals claimed that local recruitment drew garrisons into the mainstream of local life and from 1903 demanded its introduction:[47] 'The Chamber invites the war minister to erase from the instructions given annually to recruitment bureaux anything preventing the incorporation of men in those units which are closest to their homes', read a 7 July 1904 resolution. The Left argued that mobilization would be more rapid and cheaper and regimental cohesion would be improved if young men served with friends and relatives. A 3 October 1904, circular from the war ministry directed that, as far as possible, soldiers were to serve in their local units – except in Paris, Lyon and Marseille.[48]

In the Midi of 1907, where the normal legal and social restraints on excessive behaviour appeared weak, the results of local recruitment were obvious: young men were reluctant to act firmly against demonstrators, the ties of kinship and local loyalty proving stronger than those of military discipline. 'As a result of local recruitment, most of the men took a personal interest in the crisis', wrote Galliéni.[49] Le Blond drew the same conclusion,[50] as did the government which quietly abandoned regional recruitment.

Many officers felt the effects of local recruitment were particularly dangerous in the South, where patriotic sentiments were conspicuous by their absence. 'Far from the dangerous frontier, sheltered from invasion . . . the taste for military things is little developed', wrote General Coupillard, chief of the 33rd division. Despite the fact that some of the army's best officers – Foch, Joffre, Castelnau to name but three – were from the South, southerners, it was believed, did not make good soldiers, at least not while knee-deep in the local environment: 'A captain with some experience put it this way', continued the General:

The civilian population is excessively independent and vain. Badly brought up and undisciplined from infancy, [the recruit is] consequently hostile to military discipline. The youth is wilful, disrespectful, cruel. As a young soldier, he is intelligent, but lazy, critical, argumentative, inclined to see kindness as a mark of weakness. He does not particularly care what his leaders think of him.[51]

The South had long been in the army's bad books, and officers often cited the poor quality of its recruits as one of the strongest arguments against regional recruitment. 'The general commanding the 15th corps (Marseille) notes that some regiments in the 15th corps contain an abnormally large proportion of men with a weak appearance, incomplete physical development, height far below average', read a June 1912 report. 'Nor is the moral quality of the contingent superior to its physical quality . . . The 15th corps covers several large towns – Marseille, Nice, Toulon, Nîmes – where the inhabitants are little inclined to bend to military discipline.'[52] The charges were repeated two years later when units of the 15th corps turned tail before the enemy.

It has not, however, been noted that local recruitment increasingly applied to professional cadres as well as to soldiers, and this was also proved a significant factor in the revolt. In the South and West especially, officers and NCOs looked to settle where they had family connections. This homeward migration had serious consequences for discipline with the introduction of local recruitment. NCOs increasingly re-enlisted to remain in garrisons where they had carved out a comfortable administration job or where their wives had secured a good supplementary income. Officers, especially the less ambitious, tried to settle near their home or that of their wife. The result was a gradual infiltration of local concerns, interests and even politics into regimental life which relaxed the fibres of discipline. General Coupillaud believed that to have southern soldiers led by officers and NCOs from the Midi was a recipe for anarchy: 'If we add that too many officers are from the region and hardly seek to correct their countrymen's defects, we can understand the poverty of military values and the failings of discipline', he wrote. The revolt of the 17th clearly demonstrated that a locally recruited cadre could not be counted on in a crisis. Most officers and NCOs were nowhere to be found when trouble broke out and those who remained only half-heartedly worked to snuff out the mutiny. Galliéni laid the blame squarely on the shoulders of the cadres, blasting

the system of local recruitment, the total absence of precautions by the cadres during the troubles in the Midi and the total failure to recognize their military duties ... Confronted with a difficult situation, officers and NCOs were found wanting, both in devotion and above all in confidence in their ability to control their soldiers, and they showed an apathy which is even more serious as the situation demanded more energy and devotion ... Resistance should have appeared from the first sign of trouble, led by senior officers through the intermediary of NCOs.[53]

The Viticole troubles pointed to a decline in the quality of army cadres. By 1907, many officers had resigned from the army or simply lost interest in their profession. The lower quality of military school graduates did nothing to redress the balance. This general drop in standards was particularly noticeable in southern garrisons, which increasingly attracted officers looking for an easy life. The general commanding the 17th army corps worried that the worst graduates of the military schools aimed to settle in a southern garrison.[54] The NCO situation was hardly better. The two-year service law of 1905 meant that conscripts given stripes were too young or inexperienced to make their authority felt among their comrades. 'The NCOs and corporals do not know what to do', wrote d'Arbeaux. 'They float in a void, and their hesitations are fatal to their prestige and their authority.'[55] Officers claimed that they were forced to name conscript corporals before their qualities were tested: 'Once this corporal is named, the colonel will be obliged in most cases to name his sergeant', read a 1908 report to the *conseil supérieur de la guerre*. 'The length of service is so limited that an NCO who does not re-enlist is useful only for several months at the most.' The report concluded that conscript NCOs would be unlikely to prove effective leaders in combat.[56] 'The attitude of most of the conscript NCOs did not produce a good impression on the general', Galliéni notes of Bazaine-Hayter's 1906 inspection of the 13th corps. 'Too often they lack bearing and correctness of dress.'[57] At Béziers, many conscript corporals tore off their stripes rather than enforce order.

The reluctance of officers and NCOs to intervene forcefully did not stem from their sympathy for the strikers or the goals of the dispute. Rather, they hesitated to act with conviction to curb the excesses of people among whom they now lived permanently. Officers and NCOs were no longer detached figures, outsiders whose habits and rituals were regarded with curious disinterest by the populations among whom they temporarily boarded and whose *métier* was to process conscripts from distant parts. The captain and the adjudant-chef now became permanent local figures, recognizable landmarks like the school teacher and the postmaster. Each class of local recruits drew the garrisons into the easy rhythm of the town, the network of family and personal relationships geared to the business of favour bartering, a petty traffic of weekend leaves exchanged for crates of lettuce or good dinners. Messimy feared that the fighting qualities of the regiments had been compromised: 'It is beyond question that in regiments recruited locally, local questions end up by sabotaging all possibility of a serious military training and education', he declared in his 1907 budget report. 'Officers and NCOs quickly create relationships in garrison towns which can hinder them in the accomplishment of their military duties. Is it possible to deny a leave to the son of an attentive and considerate supplier who delivers first-class merchandise or the amiable host who entertained you the night before? These requests, already troublesome, can become abusive.'[58]

In the South especially, the stronghold of the Radical Party, this black market in military favours contributed to a decline in discipline, for punishments, as well as leaves, became acceptable articles of trade. Pressure brought to bear on officers and NCOs to lift sanctions placed on sons of the influential could prove irresistible. A strict disciplinarian might find that he was not invited to the mayor's annual reception, was cold-shouldered in the café or that his colonel, after the intervention of the local Radical deputy, lifted the punishment he had ordered. Discipline in many units came close to collapse as cadres turned a blind eye to infractions. 'Many NCOs told me that they no longer dared give orders, much less inflict a punishment', General Coupillaud said of the 17th. 'They want to avoid a "fuss", a responsibility. They are motivated almost from fear. This explains the presence of a number of corporals among the mutinous soldiers, several of whom tore off their stripes.'[59] Before giving a controversial order or inflicting punishment, cadres carefully weighed their interests, balancing their military obligations against domestic realities. In time of crisis, such hesitations proved fatal. Colonel Rabier of the 100th infantry noted that, at Narbonne, few soldiers or NCOs could be cajoled into giving evidence, while those who did would certainly face reprisals.

The revolts of the 17th and 100th regiments were isolated events tied to a peculiar set of local circumstances. But while discipline was probably weakest in the South for a variety of reasons – a preponderance of locally recruited soldiers and cadres possibly of inferior quality, many sedentary regiments, the absence of the patriotic tension present in the front line departments of the East and the Radical political hegemony in the South – the military revolts of 1907 pointed to a brewing crisis of leadership and discipline in the army as a whole, of which the Béziers and Narbonne troubles were but extreme examples. For the army had now fallen hostage to politics, and local mayors, deputies and prefects held officers to ransom. These men did not simply purchase favours with bottles of brandy or drinks at the bar, they were prepared to trade in careers backed by powerful Parisian friends ready to make this discontent felt in the rue Saint-Dominique. The Chamber of Deputies became their bazaar, a central stock exchange where politicians swapped favours and retribution for the votes gathered by their local agents. With the Dreyfus affair and the Radical victory, the army became a new frontier for this commercial exploitation, a promised land thrown open to political pedlars, and its inhabitants bent to the service of the new masters.

The vilification of the army as a reactionary institution made itself felt early on in the garrisons. 'Already, in my little town . . . the functionaries who hold the slightest civil authority regard me with a hostile eye', de Civrieux wrote in January 1900. 'My uniform, once respected, is no more than a flunkey's suit.' The consequences of the officer's diminished prestige were soon made evident. A local moneylender attempted to pressure de Civrieux's colonel to get the captain to name his cousin, a regular sergeant, to a position in which he would have control of the squadron's funds. De Civrieux refused and succeeded in convincing the colonel: 'I mention this minor incident, for today such incidents are woven into the fabric of daily military life.'[60]

Relations between local politicians and army officers deteriorated rapidly after 1900. From this time, de Civrieux was constantly to furnish soldiers and horses for the town festivals and even an escort for the mayor in what was probably typical of the growing power of local officials *vis-à-vis* their counterparts in uniform: 'The audacity and the arrogance of the civil servants no longer has any limits', he wrote. 'It seems that the army is made only to give satisfaction to their needs, interests and pleasures. They command; the officers must obey, or watch out.' He claimed that his unpopularity with local politicians earned him a transfer to a remote outpost in the southern Sahara.[61] Whether or not this was true in his case, officers began to attribute enormous power to local officials. Local politicians became agents specialized in obtaining favours for the sons of their constituents – a posting close to home, a good job in the regiment or leave in the middle of autumn manoeuvres. 'One of the causes . . . which must be considered as having exercised a disastrous influence on the moral state of the officers and the troops at Béziers, [is the] constant mixture of the political element in local military affairs', wrote General Bailloud, the 16th corps commander. 'They have paralyzed the command and discredited the authority of military leaders. Even the lightest punishments . . . leaves given to some, refused to others, etc., become the objects of demands, supported by local politicians for electoral reasons.'[62]

Any officer who attempted to punish a soldier, especially if he were the son of someone with influence, did so at his own peril. 'Certainly acts like those which we deplore would not occur if the authors did not believe that they could count on the weakness or indifference of certain leaders', said a colonel in the wake of Etienne's 1906 circular deploring the increase in indiscipline. 'You understand, that now is the great danger. What a colonel fears most is to have that sort of affair in his regiment, and many prefer to silence a scandal rather than provoke a press diatribe whose consequences – the example is unfortunately proved – can harm his career. I tell you: the word almost everywhere is avoid trouble, and this is altogether deplorable. To change this situation, commanders would only need to know that they would be strongly supported by the war minister when they did their duty . . . I promise you that the day that everyone believes this, the disruption caused by a few unfortunates will stop dead.'[63] The forced retirement of the colonels of both the 17th and the 100th and the remark 'present in the 17th infantry, 19 and 20 June 1907, during the mutiny of this regiment' placed in the files of each officer and NCO, served as a stern warning to professionals that a 'fuss' was not pardoned.

While local recruitment strengthened the British and German armies by reinforcing *esprit de corps* with regional pride, in France it opened the barracks door to local politics. Coupled with the army's low status, local recruitment simply bit further into military authority and dragged down discipline. Officers were under no illusion that they would be the losers in any conflict with the natives, and if they were, a flood of Radical rhetoric dispelled doubts. Reformers argued that the authoritarian discipline of the old army reflected a failure of leadership, had alienated the conscript masses and fed the anti-militarists' propaganda mill. Military discipline must be re-established on a new basis of trust and confidence between officers and men.

Radical calls for disciplinary reform trace their origins to conservative experiments of the immediate post-war years. Catholic officers like Captain Albert de Mun preached that army officers were responsible for the moral welfare of their men, obliged to oversee their development as citizens, dampening down class antagonism and forging a sense of national unity and purpose in a divided nation. However, this social ideal died of loneliness, buried under years of peace and dreary garrison routines until revived in 1891 by one of de Mun's disciples, Captain Lyautey. 'The legal obligation of military service also entails the moral obligation of making it give salutary results from a social point of view', Lyautey wrote in a celebrated article in the *Revue des deux mondes*. The administration, inspections and square bashing of army life had created its own logic, obscuring the initial idealism of many young officers, creating a gulf between conscripts and the command. Officers who possessed an intimate knowledge of ballistics or strategy were at a loss how to 'conquer the affection of their men'. Lyautey's cavalry squadron at Saint-Germain became a laboratory for his ideas, where he established communal recreation rooms for his men and generally took their moral education in hand. His experiment attracted the attention of several republican deputies like Jules Charles-Roux and Paul Deschanel who made well-publicized visits to Saint-Germain, earning for Lyautey the undeserved title of the 'socialist captain' and helping to pay his fare to Tonkin.

André revived the social role in 1900: the army must be made to serve the country's social as well as defence needs. In the process, civic spirit would replace authoritarian discipline as the corner-stone of army organization. Saint-Cyr instructor Paul Simon, one of a crop of young republican officers named to reorientate army education, wrote: 'Centralized and authoritarian leadership ... diminishes rather than raises the social worth of young men. Rather than fortify their intelligence and character, it suppresses them. It only deepened in French youth the weaknesses characteristic of our nation – listlessness, lack of initiative, irresoluteness.'[64] André introduced courses on the social role of the officer in every officer cadet school and at the *Ecole polytechnique*, and in 1901 ordered Major Charles Ebener's Saint-Cyr lectures castigating the officer corps for ignoring the democratic and social implications of universal conscription to be printed and distributed to every officer. 'We are the only ones not to realize that together with our role of war preparation, we have to fulfil a social mission of vital importance, and that it is our duty to contribute to the spread of democracy', wrote Ebener. 'This is at the root of the misunderstanding between the intellectual classes and the officer corps.'[65]

Colonel Lavisse, superintendent of Saint-Maixent, and his successor Colonel Sarrail, engaged university professors to lecture to his future infantry officers on economic and social problems while Colonel Sauret at the Artillery and Engineering School called his instructors to 'an ideal of democratic progress that will lead them to consider themselves government delegates for the formation of cadres for a republican army'.[66] Berteaux, war minister in 1905, demanded in a November circular that the army become 'a school of civic duty'.[67] Conscripts would return to civilian life with a high sense of civic duty, order and patriotism. 'The officer is responsible for training his men', stated the provisional infantry regulations for 1902, 'but he is even more their teacher'.[68]

From 1902, the ministry churned out directives and circulars on the numerous innovations designed to heighten civic duty among soldiers of all ranks. Officers were ordered to lecture on economics, history, hygiene, morality and patriotism, agriculture and trades. They were expected to organize trips to local factories. Corners of drill fields were given over to agricultural experimentation. Soldiers' messes were set up in each barracks and the food improved, regimental libraries expanded, recreation rooms established in each regiment and rooms with free notepaper set aside for letter writing.

The reformers also set about eliminating 'immoral' or 'degrading' aspects of garrison life which they believed lowered self-respect and undermined patriotic ideals. They believed drunken, debauched nights in town would become a thing of the past if companies set up cooperative bars to serve 'hygienic drinks'. Soldiers would learn 'the moral and social advantages of social works in general and of cooperatives in particular'. Profits which once went to canteen keepers were now earmarked for regimental self-help societies.[69]

The changes brought about in regimental life were nothing short of revolutionary, according to Henri de Larzelles, a novelist who recaptured the experiences of his 28-day reserve training period in 1905. In a Radical version of Vallery-Radot's *Journal d'un volontaire d'un an*, Larzelles described how officers were now present at training sessions and were generally pleasant with the men. 'Instead of the habitual *rata*[70] which we invariably ate each day during our long months of service,' he noted on his first day:

[I was] brought into the presence of a piece of roast beef on a cushion of potatoes cooked in gravy. I am told that the menu changes every evening ... Each man has his own glass, the tables are covered with linoleum to facilitate cleaning and it is almost comfortable next to the old method where everyone sat uncomfortably at the foot of his bed holding his mess tin as best he could on his knee to the great detriment of the upkeep of the barracks and the uniforms.

In the evening, after the reservist had returned from the local restaurant where he invariably ate his meals, the troops were entertained in regular 'recreation sessions' during which soldiers put on plays, sang or were given a talk on some 'current topic' by officers, always in attendance. The regimental library was well stocked with novels, mainly gifts of officers, and well frequented. Repeating the Radical case that anti-militarism was basically the fault of officers and NCOs, he included the story of an anti-militarist reservist who was won over by the army's new atmosphere of trust and confidence.[71] André too boasted that his programme had transformed the caste mentality of the officer corps and convinced enough ex-servicemen to swing the 1906 elections to the Left.[72]

While army life was not changed at a stroke and officers complained that Radicals had instituted these reforms without backing them up with the required cash, most were long overdue and gradually improved the conscript's lot. In the short term, however, this crash programme on civic spirit did not always have happy results. The 'social role' quickly became a means through which republicans could distinguish and reward their more devoted servants in uniform. With the social role obviously in fashion in high places, officers rushed to apply its basic tenets often to the detriment of military efficiency. Many officers also argued that training now took a back seat to the social role, while the new cooperatives by bringing drunkenness into the barrack walls had helped to undermine discipline.

By 1909, a reaction to the social role began to set in, Gervais, reporter for the parliamentary army committee, told his colleagues that: 'one must not exaggerate the officer's social duty. It is not a question of transforming the commander into a schoolmaster',[73] and he called on the war minister to dampen down the excessive enthusiasm of some reformist officers. Even Messimy admitted that attempts at introducing professional education in the regiments had foundered on the ignorance of the officers called on to organize classes or the sheer diversity of trades and interests among the troops.[74] Galliéni, however, whose colonial career had taught him not to count too heavily on the military administration to supply troop needs, argued that co-operatives at least should be retained, for they taught French soldiers to shift for themselves: 'It is incontestable that the habit of looking after the material needs of his men, above the basics, and to count on something other than the military administration for them . . . is already to accustom oneself to that which will be the rule in war', he wrote to

Millerand in 1912.⁷⁵ A 30 October 1912 Millerand directive complained that co-operatives had overreached their original goal, and he limited them to one per barracks, forbade the sale of alcohol, stipulated that profits must go to regimental aid societies and not be paid back to soldiers as dividends as was a common practice, and that combat troops must not be detailed to run them.⁷⁶

Like many potentially beneficial reforms, the social role was surrounded by a campaign which led many soldiers to believe that discipline had fallen from fashion and that the government was attempting to remove their power to coerce. A September 1904 debate found a strong minority of left-wing deputies in favour of abolishing the 'rabiot' – the power of the regimental council to retain conscripts beyond their statutory service limit for the number of days they had served in the guardhouse. The pressure to abolish court martials also appeared intense: from 1902, deputies introduced bills calling for military cases to be sent directly to civil courts and both Etienne and Picquart announced abolition as part of the government's programme in an effort 'to save money'.⁷⁷ The howls of anguish from officers indicated how much the abolition of a separate military justice touched them in their pride, just the ticket to encourage Clemenceau, who would probably have pushed this measure through had the troubles in the Midi not convinced him that things had gone far enough.⁷⁸ This did not prevent the Chamber from voting to abolish court martials on 11 June 1909. The Senate returned the bill with amendments in February 1913, where it was buried by the war.

In this new atmosphere, punishment had dropped out of vogue and strict disciplinarians wore their ideas like kneebreeches and tricornes. General Pédoya had been among the first to fall in with the new disciplinary line when on 4 November 1901 he announced that no punishment inflicted on a soldier in his first six months of service was to be entered on his record lest it prejudice his subsequent promotion. Pelletan made this the rule in the navy in 1903, while War Minister Berteaux adopted it in 1905: 'One must wait as long as possible to inflict the first punishment', he told corps commanders. 'The first punishment often has an enormous influence on [a soldier's] attitude toward service. It can engender discouragement and lack of enthusiasm in recruits if inflicted before they are familiar with their duties and have an exact idea of the demands of discipline.'⁷⁹ On 31 August 1905, he announced to officers: 'One must attempt to obtain voluntary discipline, based on the elevated sentiment of devotion to the Fatherland and knowledge of duty. One will succeed in this through the judicious development of moral education.'⁸⁰ In response to critics who argued that sergeants and lieutenants were too quick to throw soldiers into the guardhouse, a 1910 decree withdrew their right to do so. Now only captains and senior officers could punish: 'We have deprived [lieutenants and NCOs] of part of their means of action', Messimy wrote in 1911. '[Discipline] has become less easy [to enforce] and many have the humiliation, rather than punishing on the spot, of going begging to a higher authority.' Knowing the reluctance of senior officers to punish, soldiers were less wary of taking a false step.[81]

With a 'humanitarian' concept of discipline obviously in fashion in government circles, and consequently among generals, regimental officers became noticeably reluctant to inflict punishments for which they might be criticized: '"Try to obtain *voluntary discipline*"', General Langlois repeated. 'There it is, the big word spoken officially. And since that time, military leaders no longer dare to serve, and the spirit of discipline melts away like snow in the sun, and melts even faster as each time a serious incident occurs the minister blames the officer.'[82] 'Officers no longer dare to inflict punishment and often the most senior officers erase or attenuate punishments doled out by their subordinates', wrote German General Pellet-Narbonne, commissioned by the Kaiser to write a report on the state of the French army following the 1907 revolts.[83] 'The discipline in the regiment is very benevolent', said Captain Quirot of the 17th. 'We let people off the hook too often and this kindness sometimes could be taken for weakness.'[84]

As if to underline their humanity and their premise that military justice was overly harsh, reformers moved to repair damage already done by court martials by allowing men with disciplinary or criminal records to take their place in line regiments. A 2 May 1902 instruction from André obliged discipline companies to return men to their regular regiments as soon as they showed signs of 'rehabilitation'. This was completed by a 1905 law which obliged line regiments rather than the disciplinary *bataillons d'Afrique* to accept men who had served a maximum of six months in prison before joining the army rather than three months as before. The result was that men with not insignificant civilian criminal records were sent straight into the regiments, while the disciplinary battalions emptied their ranks back into the units: 638 in 1902; 1,951 in 1903; and 1,500 in 1904.[85] In 1906, 6 per cent of conscripts sent to colonial infantry regiments stationed in France had civilian criminal records, which meant between 30 and 90 soldiers per regiment.[86] In November 1909, 13,631 men with civilian criminal records were serving in line regiments.[87] The inevitable result was a rise in disciplinary problems: between 1906 and 1911, the number of soldiers court martialled doubled from 5,917 to over 12,000.[88] General Langlois also complained that rather than discourage the anti-militarist campaign, this 'act of humanity' had proved the anti-militarist point by helping to transform barracks into 'places of crime'.⁸⁹ 'The men from the *bataillons d'Afrique* and the discipline companies incorporated in the regiments in large numbers only too rarely merit the favour shown them to return to France, and are in general a troublesome element of indiscipline and demoralization for the healthy milieu in which they are placed', wrote General Duchesne of the 4th army corps in 1905. 'One must also note that the mixture of alcoholic Bretons and men from the *bataillons d'Afrique* or the worst elements from the Seine, constitute a particularly dangerous assemblage.'⁹⁰

If the Left blamed the growth of anti-militarism on the army, the army could equally lay the responsibility for growing indiscipline at the feet of the Left. The repeated amnesties voted for deserters, the circulars, decrees and parliamentary pronouncements on discipline, the integration of men with criminal records in line regiments, had not created a humanitarian discipline, but had come perilously close to dissolving some regiments into chaos. Even General Pédoya attributed the growth of indiscipline to 'the attacks on the army tolerated by the government, to the insults to superiors which are only weakly punished, to the amnesties which permit deserters to resume their place in the ranks honourably and without losing any of their rights, by this exaggerated kindness toward bad soldiers which is recommended and accepted'.⁹¹

Certainly, few soldiers' revolts had any serious political content: Béziers 1907 was hardly Petrograd ten years later. Poor quarters, bad food and especially lack of leave provided the pretext for revolt in almost all cases.⁹² For instance, after 60 soldiers of Perpignan's 12th infantry sang the *Internationale* in front of the canteen, the colonel invited them to call by his quarters and explain their grievances. Only four did so, to say that they had had no leave for some time.⁹³ General Bailloud also reckoned that lack of leave was behind the revolt of the 100th at Narbonne.⁹⁴ Soldiers of the 17th voiced the same complaints: 'Some of them told me that the food was bad', reported General Lacroisade.⁹⁵ Even in the three-year service riots of 1913, protesting conscripts were upset over being held indefinitely in service, and who could blame them? The point of these demonstrations was not that politics was at their base, but that many protesters obviously believed that they could escape serious punishment. Even the soldiers of the 17th, whose only punishment for some of them was to serve out the remainder of their two years in Tunisia, 'far from realizing the indulgence they have enjoyed, seem to be bewildered by the punishment'.⁹⁶

Pédoya's contention that anti-militarism and indiscipline were encouraged by weak government repression is confirmed by a letter from Private Mazalaique, thrown into the Santé Prison in 1907 for anti-militarist activities, to anti-militarists in Nancy: 'I don't know yet how much time I will be here but I believe that it won't be long because I promise you that it pays off these days to say things against or spread ideas against the army, because our professors are in power.'[97]

For many left-wing politicians, the new disciplinary conventions covered a desire to keep officers off balance and deprive them of confidence in case anyone entertained ideas of marching on the Elysée. Freycinet, while supporting a reflective and intelligent discipline, felt that reformist notions had blunted the sharp edges of authority. 'The evil from which national defence has suffered, and from which it suffers still, is indiscipline', he wrote in 1914. 'We must react against these eminently dangerous tendencies and proclaim that military discipline must be humane and just, but above defiance.'[98]

The Midi revolts pointed to a new and unfortunate change in the attitudes of officers to the demands of service. Many complained that officers spent too much time in administration and knew their troops too little. Humbert warned that discipline was the first casualty:

The anti-militarists of Monsieur Hervé's school have . . . collaborators who are more or less auxiliaries . . . These are the army ministers and the administrators who have done everything necessary to see that our young soldiers are delivered without defence to all the deceiving temptations of indiscipline. One can say that the ministerial circulars and the new model regulations have admirably facilitated the task of the *sans-patries*.

The officer no longer spent time with his men but in administrative chores which made him 'a distant and mysterious person . . . [The soldiers] say that the army is no more than a vast bureau where soldiers are worked while the officers spend their time writing "like idlers".'[99]

Radical reforms, many argued, had transformed officers into petty administrators, so devaluing professional competence. 'Our young officers now do a corporal's job', the *Porte-Voix* complained in September 1907. 'Captains bury themselves in their magazines: they administer!' wrote d'Arbeaux. 'Lieutenants try to get out of training or go simply because they are forced to . . . They have been told they are civil servants and they act like civil servants, mechanically.'[100] Pédoya claimed, along with others, that officers no longer had time for personal study while the President of the parliamentary budget committee, Klotz, spoke of the 'surfeit of work which had made their profession difficult and does not leave them any leisure during the entire year'. In 1909, Gervais complained that the officer had been transformed into 'an honourable civil servant who does exactly what one asks of him, and then works to reduce it to a minimum'.[101]

The impression that indiscipline was a by-product of too much administration was a deceptive one. Rather the reverse was often the case – in the face of growing indiscipline, line officers sought solace in administration: administration became a refuge and an afternoon verifying accounts or stocktaking in the magazine a way of avoiding the increasingly impossible task of command. Troop contact might lead to a delicate situation in which an officer might make his authority felt only with difficulty. Consequently, officers and NCOs sloped off to jobs which would take them away from the regiment and provide an alibi in case of trouble, as happened in the revolts of the 100th and the 17th regiments. 'Perhaps one can attribute the fact that no officer was injured during the mutiny to their absence at the barracks at Agde', wrote General Bailloud.[102] Colonel Meinier complained that NCOs, most of whom quickly abandoned the barracks for the town, had also failed to lend a firm hand.[103] Clemenceau personally ordered the retirement of the colonel of the 100th infantry and threatened to retire other officers for 'illegal absence from the barracks'.[104] 'The impression which one takes away from this affair is that in the 17th regiment, the sentiment of military duty seems very weak', wrote Galliéni. 'Everyone seems to want only to do his job with a minimum of effort and responsibility. . . . The NCOs did not show a strong military education, nor the officers a high moral value and firm character.'[105] Officers and NCOs realized that in any showdown with soldiers, any 'fuss', they often stood to lose: punishments rained down on the heads of officers at Narbonne and Béziers, while Galliéni recommended that 'the soldiers be treated with kindness'.[106] After troubles at Poitiers in January 1905, the *France militaire* recorded what it alleged was a typical soldiers' conversation: 'They've got courage, those boys at Poitiers. We'll see now if they dare punish them. In any case, the captain will be transferred, and that's what they all wanted. In these cases, they pretend to punish the soldiers, but it's always the officers who get it.'[107]

While Radical reforms were aimed to strengthen discipline by rebuilding it on a new foundation of mutual knowledge and trust between officers and men, the result was often the opposite. Principles sound in theory were often abusive in practice, for they omitted essential elements of prestige and perhaps the pinch of coercion needed to make them work, to pull officers and men into a cohesive unit. Discipline survived best in units which managed to preserve a vestige of the old *esprit de corps* – in the cavalry, the *chasseurs alpins*, the *armée d'Afrique* and the colonial army. But under a barrage of petty directives and political interference in the daily life of the regiment, the confidence of line officers slipped away and with it morale and, to varying degrees, discipline in many regiments.

German General Colmar von der Goltz had warned in 1884 of the consequences of a socially insecure officer corps: 'An officer corps which occupies a precarious social position will furnish perfect citizens, but it will be poor in audacious and enterprising soldiers.' Rather than being integrated into society, French soldiers felt disowned by it. If it was no longer possible to do their jobs satisfactorily, officers might at least salvage their careers. The character of the institution declined with the compromises its leaders made with their consciences: 'The civic isolation of officers ... contributes in large measure to the devaluation of their moral worth', declared the *France militaire* on 24 October 1913.

One often speaks of the lack of character in the army ... The causes are multiple, but it is no longer in doubt that the civic isolation of officers is one of the principal ones. Outside the military sphere, the officer is a minor, devoid of confidence, stepping timidly and hesitantly and fearing the smallest obstacle, which he exaggerates tremendously. Our generals are afraid of politicians. We will go further: they are terrified. These men who would stoically, even gaily, face the greatest dangers on the battlefield, tremble before the lowest municipal councillor in their garrison or before a 'pen-pusher' of the 36th order who writes in the local newspaper of the sub-prefecture ... Today, [the officers] are always the designated victims of the politicians' tyrannies and of unstable or arbitrary power.

8

The colonial army

In a dark world of French civil-military relations, the colonial army provided a shaft of light. The suspicion, the hesitation, the latent mistrust which separated republicans and soldiers at home was not transported to the colonies. Soldiers who were distrusted, spied upon and humiliated in France were pampered, promoted and decorated abroad. Overseas, the army was largely immune from close government scrutiny, free to impose its order and ideology upon the native populations which fell under its control and to carve out an area of influence which stretched from Tonkin to Timbuktu, from Pondicherry to the Palais Bourbon. The basic explanation for this lay in the nature of French colonial policy: when forced to choose either peaceful economic penetration of the unorganized world or political domination, the French chose the latter. Military expeditions became the logical corollary of French colonization, and colonial soldiers thrust into the role of conquerors were assigned the task of staking out France's colonial empire. One of the results of 130 years of colonial ramblings was the steady growth of independent habits and attitudes among colonial soldiers, which eventually rebounded on the republic with the soldiers' revolt of 1958.

The French army's modern odyssey began with the siege of Algiers in 1830. What began as a modest punitive expedition mounted for domestic political consumption, a military distraction to carry the Restoration over the difficult days of the July ordinances, in fact kicked off a campaign of conquest which was to last almost 100 years. The July Monarchy found that overseas possessions, once acquired, were difficult to let go. 'After the first landing, the country occupied, it is impossible to withdraw', Jules Harmand, a colonial official, wrote in 1910.

We remain because we are here, because we want to believe it is possible to continue the conquest without great effort, because we do not want to lose the benefits of the sacrifices already made, because we consider the interests of the nation and the natives who immediately attach themselves to this sort of enterprise, and finally because the honour of the army and the prestige of the flag, sometimes the existence of governments, are at stake.[1]

The colonial army

While Paris dithered at the gates of Africa, French soldiers forged ahead – pleading the need to secure their territory against hostile native attacks while delighted at the prospect of a scrap and promotion. Algeria became an army fief, a game preserve where bored and ambitious officers could bag promotion and decorations hard to come by in the France of the citizen-king. Many of the best Saint-Cyr graduates enlisted in the *zouaves*, the *chasseurs d'Afrique* or one of the other exotic regiments mustered for North African service. The classical military science of Jomini and the requirements of European warfare became the first casualty of the French drive into Africa. General de Castellane complained in the 1840s that Algeria was a poor school of war, an opinion proved correct in 1870 when generals who had constructed brilliant careers abroad put on a poor show in Lorraine. The government's ability to control its Algerian commanders became the second casualty: when Paris attempted to curtail military imperialism by forbidding Bugeaud to occupy Kabylia, the General replied: 'I received your note. It is too late. My troops ... have already set out ... If we are successful, the government and France will have the honour ... In the opposite case, the entire responsibility will fall upon me: I claim it.'[2] Algeria was brought under the flag, not as the result of any considered government policy of conquest, but largely because soldiers continued to press outward, already demonstrating a precocious independence which was to characterize colonial expansion elsewhere. This independence was reinforced by administrative control of the colony assured by the *Bureaux Arabes*. Despite the charges of incompetence and corruption levelled at military administration in Algeria, its iron grip on the colony was only broken by the republic in 1871.[3]

While the army digested Algeria, Louis-Napoleon's navy acquired an empire of its own in Senegal and Cochinchina. The consolidation of the scattered coastal outposts and the push into the West African hinterland was largely the work of Senegal Governor-General Louis Faidherbe, using marines and native riflemen staffed by French officers. Acting independently, often against orders from Paris, he edged forward on the argument of security, inflating the dangers and exploiting the weakness of Paris' position and setting an example for a generation of military governors and commanders in the Western Sudan.[4] In Indochina, Admiral de la Grandière seized on a local incident to occupy three provinces with marines, deliberately sabotaging negotiations between the Empire and the court at Hué and presenting France with the beginning of an oriental empire.

Soldiers were by no means the only Frenchmen interested in the acquisition of colonies. Some Bordeaux and Marseilles merchants were happy enough with the colonial trade. Christians looking for conversions and discovery-hungry members of the French Geographical Society – the largest colonial interest group by far – also contributed to pressure for colonial expansion. While often cited to justify expansion, economic factors were at best latent in French colonization. While merchants sometimes requested a colonial concession and colonists straggled abroad, the tone of French expansion remained decidedly military. Businessmen and economists shook their heads at the enormous financial burdens the colonies represented.[5] 'When I consider the terrible expense in men and money which the soldiers in Algeria impose on France, I am increasingly convinced of the need to establish a *civilian* war minister', Tunisian Resident General Paul Cambon wrote in 1884.[6] Liberal economists like Adam Smith had condemned colonies as economic liabilities, leaving the field largely to utopian socialists like Fourier and the Saint-Simonists, men more interested in novel forms of social organization than in macro-economics.[7] Algeria became a testing ground for utopian ideas applied by African converts like General Lamoricière. Bugeaud's military colonies which turned soldiers into farmers, assuring both the colonization and the defence of Algeria, owed much to the disciples of Saint-Simon. But rather than encourage trade and bring economic advantages home to France, maladministration and constant warfare combined to discourage them. Few French colonists were attracted to Algeria and of the 200,000 people of European extraction there in 1870, more than half came from Malta, Italy and Spain[8] and often regretted that they had drifted to North Africa rather than North America.

This situation did not change radically after 1870. Colonial expansion in the Third Republic confirmed the military character of earlier French efforts. Colonies which offered Britons and Belgians interesting opportunities for investment were acquired by France for reasons of glory and maintained largely to keep her turbulent soldiery occupied. In 1885, Jules Ferry distilled three basic elements of French colonialism. The first was economic: 'The foundation of a colony is the creation of a [trade] outlet.' Secondly, he defined 'the humanitarian and civilizing aspect. . . . The superior races have a right . . . a duty to civilize the inferior races.' Lastly, he spoke of a need to break the spell which fixed French eyes on her eastern frontier. France must regain her greatness abroad. 'In the same exalted and shortsighted chauvinism, must we drive French politics into an impasse and, with our eyes fixed on the blue line of the Vosges, allow everything to happen, to be planned, to be resolved without us, around us?' he wrote in *Le Tonkin et la mère patrie in 1890*. 'We are not a great power by digging ourselves in at home.'[9]

Despite the claims made in France as to the vast economic potential of the colonies, they continued to burden the budget without benefiting the homeland. While British expansion moved forward largely on the backs of businessmen like Cecil Rhodes and George Goldie, whose Royal Niger Company tamed Nigeria, the French advanced at the point of a bayonet and the government paid the bill. The budget of the colonial office grew steadily as the pace of colonization quickened – from 42.6 million francs in 1885 to almost 116 million in 1902, four-fifths of which were military costs.[10] North African expansion and the contributions of other ministries pushed the true price of colonial expansion even higher. The luxury goods which were the bread and butter of French industry found few markets outside Europe. Foreign, not French, merchants followed the tricoloured flag: although the percentage of French trade with the colonies grew from 5.71 per cent in 1882–6 to 10.2 per cent in 1909–13, these figures remain insignificant in the volume of total trade. The percentage of France's trade with her empire was proportionally less before 1914 than before the French Revolution. French investors were far more interested in Eastern Europe than in the empire: only 9 per cent of French foreign investment went to the colonies compared with 25 per cent to Russia alone.[11] In 1894, Lyautey found that while Singapore was teeming with businessmen, banks and commercial houses, Saigon offered only soldiers, cafés and administrative buildings, a façade of government rather than a solid building: 'One quickly has the impression . . . that the place would collapse if the administrators, the soldiers and the enormous protective rights were withdrawn', he wrote.[12] In 1892, France's two powerful colonial pressure groups, the *Comité d'Afrique française* and the *Union coloniale*, complained that the ubiquitous military presence in the colonies had proved costly, unproductive and had discouraged trade.[13] 'The "average Frenchman" willingly believes that the colonies exist only to employ civil servants and weigh down the metropolitan budget', concluded a 1927 study.[14] The economic promise of the colonies remained unfulfilled, a carrot which drew Frenchmen on to further conquests, further investment, further disappointments.

France's civilizing mission also failed to live up to its press notices. This was due largely to the fact that most of its ambassadors had acquired their notions of civilization in a barracks. While French soldiers claimed to be bringing peace to a turbulent and barbarous world, imposing stability and encouraging trade, the truth was very often different. In the Western Sudan especially, French soldiers behaved like Claudian emperors, provoking incidents, forcing natives to fight and disrupting established trade patterns. The only trade which flourished in the Western Sudan during almost twenty years of conquest was the slave trade. 'Freed' slaves often found themselves chained together anew, reluctant porters for a French expedition, or, if young and female, distributed as *'épouses libres'* to victorious Senegalese riflemen. In 1894, the future General Mangin, then a lieutenant, was placed in 30 days' detention after buying friends among his servants and interpreters with slave girls.[15] In April 1892, *Le Siècle* attacked military leaders for turning the Western Sudan into 'a slave bazaar'.[16]

The balance sheet of France's civilizing mission was not, however, all red. The arrival of French soldiers more than once ended a local tyranny or state of anarchy which had plunged populations into murderous tribal wars and banditry. Conscientious and humane colonial governors and soldiers ruled in the interests of their charges, respecting native traditions and hierarchies so long as these were not hostile to French rule, building roads, fountains, markets and schools. But the interests of France always came first, which meant that soldiers and administrators, often too few on the ground to mount more than a fragile show of force, allowed local rulers to continue their trade in slaves, their *razzias* against neighbouring tribes in return for a pledge of loyalty.[17] The civilizing mission was not simply a cynical piece of propaganda – in the hands of Galliéni and Lyautey, it became an integral part of the strategy of pacification. But in the final analysis, it offered a moral justification for the race to acquire territory, so that France could console itself that the vast sums poured, apparently vainly, into the colonies were at least keeping natives out of mischief.

The last element, the political one, was the most important and fuelled France's sudden burst of expansive energy after 1880. The colonial idea grew to maturity in the atmosphere of defeat. Although colonial expansion stalled in the 1870s, Gambetta and *La République française* were already beginning to suggest that France could reconquer her place in the first rank of nations by turning outward: 'It is through expansion, through shining outward in the world, through the place they occupy in the general life of humanity that nations persist and endure',[18] he proclaimed in April 1872. A colonial empire would allow France to regain her confidence, speak with authority in the world and turn her attention from the morbid and self-destructive fixation with Alsace-Lorraine.

However, Gambetta never managed to sell his colonial vision beyond a relatively restricted circle of moderate republicans. Politicians from Clemenceau to Déroulède argued that colonial expansion, by diverting French troops and resources abroad, actually weakened France's position in Europe, while the French public remained overwhelmingly indifferent to battles fought between French soldiers and native chiefs. Anti-colonialism became one of the most politically marketable movements of the 1880s: the anti-colonial Right gained over 100 seats in the 1885 elections and two months later the estimates for Tonkin and Madagascar squeezed through Parliament by only three votes. Colonial issues became a favourite meeting ground for Left and Right united to attack the opportunist centre, as Jules Ferry found when his government was toppled in 1885 over Indochina.[19]

The next decade, however, saw a marked change of attitude toward colonial expansion. The reason was simple: the increased European rivalry in Asia and Africa. While most French nationalists were not colonialists, the nationalism of French society made it especially vulnerable to imperialism. For France, unlike most of her European neighbours, the 19th century was a period of relative decline. Perhaps because of this, French public opinion, especially in Paris, was particularly sensitive to any slight on French prestige. The 1893 Siam crisis, Fashoda and the confrontations over Morocco aroused public passion only because French expansion had come up against rival European claims. Although colonialists could not convert public opinion to colonialism, by appealing to French nationalism they could muster widespread support in times of crisis for colonial policies.[20]

As the colonial army was organized and expanded to undertake the colonial campaigns, so the colonial idea became 'militarized', appealing to a Frenchman's patriotism rather than to his purse.[21] 'We soldiers don't understand much about economics', Galliéni wrote to Harry Alis, the Secretary General of the *Comité de l'Afrique française*, in June 1890. 'We only know that there are territories in Africa which should belong to us and that the English and Germans are in the process of tricking us out of them. And we are trying to stop them.'[22] For this reason, French imperialism appeared rushed, almost frantic, pushed by officers eager for prestige and promotion. This sense of urgency was of necessity imposed on competing powers especially in Africa where British, Belgians and Germans had to stake their claims or else see that continent absorbed by France. French imperialism in Africa became one of the principal motors of the 'steeplechase to the unknown'.[23]

The lack of a substantial economic base for colonial expansion and the general absence of public interest in what went on outside the hexagon inevitably meant that, as before 1870, soldiers would once again be assigned the task of colonial conquest. The major burden of colonial expansion fell upon the marines, France's unofficial colonial army until formally organized in 1900, which nearly quadrupled in size from 600 officers and 16,000 men in 1880, to 2,200 officers and 68,000 men by 1900, divided into 19 colonial infantry regiments, 5 artillery regiments, 6 scattered 'groups' and 10 native infantry regiments raised in Indochina, Africa and Madagascar and staffed by French officers. Native troops made up 35 per cent of colonial army personnel.[24] Together with the *armée d'Afrique*, the colonial soldiers transformed the 'Old Empire' – Algeria and a few islands and coastal enclaves – into a vast colonial enterprise. In the process, they often hijacked colonial policy, locking the government into a prison of military whims and initiatives, acting usually without orders, often against orders and defying Paris to discipline them.

The long established independence of Algerian generals spilled over into Tunisia, the first of the Third Republic's colonial adventures. Tunisian Resident General Paul Cambon's most difficult task lay not in dealing with the Arabs but in keeping his own soldiers in check. He complained that for the soldiers, Tunisia represented little more than 'a treasure chest of promotions and decorations'.[25] The frequent complaints of diplomats and colonial officials about unscheduled military initiatives often betrayed a jealous recognition that soldiers had deprived them of their own chances of directing events down avenues not necessarily approved by Paris.[25]

French expansion south of the Sahara paralleled that of North Africa. A series of colonial governors and military commanders led by Brière de l'Isle, Borgnis-Desbordes and Archinard overran the Western Sudan. Paris was forced to bite its tongue as these men edged forward, wasting money in expensive campaigns and embarrassing the government at critical moments, all for a few square kilometres of near worthless bush and a handful of *légions d'honneur*.[26] Archinard's 1891 campaign against Samori was denounced by Colonial Under-secretary Etienne as 'a formal violation of my orders', but nothing was done to curtail military enthusiasm, so that in 1893 soldiers launched attacks on Masina and occupied Timbuktu while Colonial Under-secretary Delcassé and Governor-General Grodet foamed with rage. The Western Sudan, like Algeria in the 1830s and 40s, had become a 'state within a state' where colonial soldiers acted more or less as they pleased.[27] A government which would not have tolerated the slightest show of military indiscipline at home, found its ability to handle headstrong colonial officers limited. This was due in part to the administrative anarchy which presided over colonial expansion. A colonial undersecretariat was created in 1883, but for more than a decade it slipped back and forth between the ministries of commerce and the navy, neither of which was particularly interested in colonial affairs. Even the 1894 creation of a colonial ministry failed to give firm direction to colonial affairs by ending the bickering between the ministries of the navy, war, commerce and foreign affairs over colonial questions.[28]

The lack of clear control in Paris was matched by a haphazard military organization. The marines formed part of the navy. But admirals concentrated their attention on the fleet, leaving the colonial forces in the hands of their inspecting generals, ex-colonial men themselves, and so assuring the colonial troops a great degree of autonomy.[29] The situation was further complicated by the intervention of the war minister, who seconded regular army officers and units of the *armée d'Afrique*, those regiments permanently stationed in North Africa, for colonial duty and who armed and equipped the troops in the colonies. While soldiers in the colonies were nominally responsible to the colonial under-secretary/minister through the colonial governor, the web of control and influence was so complex that colonial officials usually found their ability to discipline overly zealous soldiers circumscribed. Even when Delcassé managed to have Archinard recalled in November 1893 after a series of lightning campaigns which won the republic more territory than it wanted, it was at the expense of the good relations with the navy ministry, which proceeded to promote the 'disgraced' officer to brigadier and install him as director of defence in the colonial ministry.[30] Ten years later, when Delcassé ordered Lyautey out of positions he had occupied on his own initiative in territory claimed by the Sultan of Morocco, the Brigadier managed to mobilize enough support, if not to have the order rescinded, at least to modify it beyond all recognition.[31]

In the battles between soldiers and civilians in the colonies, military men exploited their natural advantages to the full. The agents in the field, the men on the spot, they were best placed to appreciate the exigencies of the local situation. Faidherbe realized early on that Paris' knowledge of Senegal politics was based exclusively on the information he sent home and consequently wrote black reports, inflating the dangers so it appeared as if the French government in Senegal, at the lightest touch of revolt, would topple into the sea. Subsequent colonial governors copied his example, pleading security as an excuse to push just that little bit further to teach some turbulent tribe a lesson.[32] The Quai d'Orsay increasingly denounced these jeremiads as simple manoeuvres to find an excuse for a fight.[33] But this was not always the case. In North Africa and the Western Sudan especially, the fear of a moslem Jihad, a holy war against French rule, troubled the sleep of many commanders. It was an indication perhaps of how vulnerable the French felt in Africa. Each time local marabouts declared a Jihad against the Christians, French soldiers trembled lest the call spark a revolt which would sweep from the Niger to the Magreb. Such 'exaggerations' also revealed a desire for self-preservation in case a setback resulted in a soldier's judgement being seriously questioned. Better to inflate the dangers safely than ignore them at one's peril. 'The situation is worsening seriously', Lyautey wrote to his sister from the Sud Oranais in March 1906. 'But the Quai d'Orsay remains convinced that it is I whom am exaggerating and imagine this attack as an excuse to throw my troops into action . . . If things go badly, it is I who will be the sacrificial lamb.'[34] But this attack, like the great Jihad, proved a phantom fear, for by the 20th century, Islam seldom retained the force to raise its faithful, and tribal chiefs based their military decisions more on an appreciation of the forces present than on the visions of holy men.[35]

Military initiative and indiscipline in the colonies were not entirely of local manufacture: Paris furnished at least the raw materials. Christopher Andrew had noted that the colonial administration was deficient in three ways: it was confused, usually incompetent and it operated outside government control.[36] No one ministry controlled all of Africa: the interior ministry administered Algeria, the Quai d'Orsay was responsible for Tunisia and Morocco while the colonial ministry supervised the rest. The *Pavillon de Flore* housed 'the ashtray of ministries', a ramshackle collection of overlapping departments staffed by functionaries of modest abilities and led by men whose notions of geography were often extremely vague. 'Each department, *organised like a fortress*, deals with the affairs of the colonies which it administers in its own peculiar way', the Deputies budget committee reported in 1917. 'The result is that usually . . . three or four departments deal with them simultaneously and *sometimes offer different solutions* to a problem which demands a single answer.'[37] Ministerial instability led to a constant turnover of personnel at the top which translated into sudden policy shifts and twists, leaving soldiers with an often justified sense of grievance. The problem was not simply that orders from Paris were contradictory; they were often so vague and imprecise as to leave soldiers a wide margin of manoeuvre, a reflection of indecision and often of ignorance in government circles. In 1904, Lyautey complained that he was 'always in a void, without direction, without orders'. Nor had the situation improved two years later when he again noted that calling by the governor general's office to pick up the latest government directives was simply a matter of form, because 'they will be vague, perhaps contradictory, leaving the greatest freedom to local initiative and, above all, they will not, by the nature of things, contain any precise military indications'.[38] In the absence of firm direction, colonial officers concluded that they and they alone gave France's colonial mission force and stability, that Paris was hesitant, timid and ready to act only when forced to by military initiative. Hence the reliance on the *fait accompli*, a lightning campaign justified for reasons of 'security' and to which the *Pavillon de Flore* (colonial ministry) could only shrug its shoulders.

The constant shifting of policies and people in the capital was reflected in the colonies, where colonial administration, too, failed to provide an element of stability. Until 1920, French colonies changed governors on average at least once a year. Constantly rotating between France and various outposts of empire, colonial officials seldom appreciated the needs and problems of their region, much less found time to learn the local language and master the intricacies of native politics; reinforcing the soldiers' conviction that they, the old hands, provided the bedrock of stability abroad. 'The fundamental principle of our administration is its impersonality', wrote Lieutenant Grandmaison in 1898. 'Our colonial administration follows the same system of personnel rotation as in France. From the governor generals to the most humble administrator, all the officials rotate all the time.' This policy wasted money and, worse, disrupted organization. Grandmaison criticized colonial governors for the often premature substitution of civilian for military administrators to prove that a region was 'officially' pacified, to employ officials waiting for the posts, or out of anti-army prejudice. Soldiers might have their failings as administrators, but 'after violent repression, it is necessary to give the country time to discipline itself, to calm-down, to bend to French domination under a stronger and freer authority than that of our civil government ... These are simple people, having more need of justice than legality, who accommodate themselves very well to our summary procedures.'[39] Civilian administrators also suffered from the same absence of direction, the same vagueness of orders as the soldiers. But rather than launch out on their own and seize the initiative, they tended to fall back into bureaucratic slumber, pleading regulations as an excuse for an easy life. This attitude betrayed a difference in temperament which inevitably led to conflicts between hidebound officials and officers who had come to the colonies expressly to throw off the shackles of metropolitan regulations: 'The officer who administers a country is not so deformed by regulations as the bureaucrat', wrote General François Ingold. 'He is happy to escape his own [regulations], those of the army. He feels himself a free spirit.'[40] The absence of stability and flexibility in French colonial policy gave soldiers both the freedom to apply their ideas and the conviction that in doing so they were serving the interests of France, rescuing the colonies, in the words of one soldier, from 'the indecision of central power ... [and] the blunders of civil governors'.[41]

The abysmal quality of French colonial administrators virtually guaranteed that France's colonial 'machine' would only sputter, leaving officers to tear their hair in exasperation. While the British colonial service attracted quality recruits, usually well-educated Oxbridge men, France, with few exceptions, sent out men who, in Senegal Governor General Brière de l'Isle's estimation, 'if not compromised at home were at least incapable of making a livelihood there'.[42] The Frenchman's notorious unwillingness to emigrate meant that the *Pavillon de Flore* had to hire its administrators where it could find them. The colonies thus became a dumping ground for failures, drunks and men who had become a burden or embarrassment to their families; and colonial governors were saddled with subordinates, many of whom would have been rejected even by the Foreign Legion. 'A barber, a peanut vendor, a navvy with the right connections, can be named an administrator of native affairs without the slightest concern for his abilities, his intelligence, his attitudes or his aptitudes', read a pamphlet published in 1911.[43] Poor recruitment meant administrative inefficiency: 'Before us rises the admirable English organisation: large, supple, commanding, directed from top to bottom by gentlemen or men who live and act like gentlemen, whatever their origins, who practise a humane code', Lyautey wrote. 'They have the personnel, we do not.'[44]

Colonial Under-secretary Eugène Etienne made a stab at improving the quality of colonial officials in 1887 by unifying the various colonial services into the Corps of Colonial Administrators and by founding the *Ecole coloniale* in 1888 to provide a corps of trained colonial civil servants. But these reforms did little to lighten the crushing burden of ignorance and maladministration under which the colonial service laboured. By 1914, the *Ecole coloniale* had furnished only 20 per cent of colonial administrators; barely half of the recruits to the colonial administration between 1900 and 1914 had even a secondary education. In 1887, colonial governors rated fully 61 per cent of their subordinates as incompetent. Standards improved over the years, but as late as 1914, 22 per cent of administrators abroad were thought below minimum competence by their immediate superiors.[45] Compared with the elite recruitment of the British service, especially of the Indian Civil Service, the French cut a poor figure on the world stage, as Lyautey, en route to Tonkin in 1894, noted with chagrin.[46] Given the poor quality of colonial officials, it is hardly surprising that officers, two-thirds of whom were graduates of Saint-Cyr or the *Ecole polytechnique*, treated them as social and intellectual inferiors.

Lastly, French officers were allowed great freedom abroad because they were supported by one of the Third Republic's most powerful pressure groups – the 'parti colonial'. The parochialism of French politics, the ignorance of French politicians and indifference of public opinion to colonial affairs, and a sputtering colonial administration meant that French colonial policy was decided to an astonishing degree by a handful of dedicated colonials. If soldiers were given their heads in the Western Sudan, it was because military imperialism suited certain political interests in France. The most important phase of any military operation was fought out in Paris, and no colonial commander would launch a campaign until he was sure that his metropolitan lines of communication were 'covered'. This cover was provided essentially by the men of the *groupe colonial* in the Chamber of Deputies. Founded in 1891 by Eugène Etienne, the *groupe colonial* jumped from 91 members in 1892 to almost 200 ten years later, uniting men of all parties but especially of the old Gambettist centre into a loose association of deputies in defence of colonial expansion. In 1898, Jules Siegfried founded a colonial group in the Senate, whose membership included Freycinet, Constans and Waddington. Outside parliament, colonialism was pushed by powerful pressure groups – the most important being the *Comité de l'Afrique française* founded in 1890 and joined in turn by the *Comité de l'Asie française*, *Comité de Madagascar* and the *Comité du Maroc*, all linked by organization, membership and in an active propaganda campaign for colonial expansion through the organization of conferences and especially through the *Bulletin* of the *Comité de l'Afrique française* with a distribution of 4,000. A separate organization, the *Union coloniale française* created in 1893, grouped 1,219 men with business and commercial interests in the colonies into what was by far the richest of the colonial pressure groups. Its wealth allowed it to broadcast the colonial message on a grand scale, organizing more than 400 conferences between 1893 and 1903, four grand congresses between 1906 and 1911, financing courses at the Sorbonne on the development of the colonies, an annual 20,000 franc prize and a trip to the colonies to university students studying colonial questions. In 1897 it founded both the *Quinzaine coloniale* and the *Ligue coloniale de la jeunesse* which organized colonial conferences in schools. Outside these formal organizations, numerous writers popularized colonial questions, especially in intellectual circles, through such widely read and influential publications as the *Journal des débats* and the *Revue des deux mondes*.[47]

However, colonial propagandists failed to shake the apathy of the French people or of their government. French colonialists never managed to create a mass movement: while the German *Kolonialgesellschaft* counted 45,000 members in 1914, all of the French colonial groups combined barely mustered 5,000 members before the Great War, many of whom were schoolboys. The number of hard core militants never exceeded 500.[48] In 1914, the colonial movement complained that 'the colonial education of Frenchmen remains entirely to be accomplished'.

Politicians, not publicists, remained the most effective protagonists of colonial expansion. For while on the fringe of French politics, colonialists flexed enormous muscle, for several reasons. Firstly, from the beginning colonialism attracted the active participation of a political elite: Jules Ferry, Hanotaux, Delcassé, Etienne and Freycinet among others. This assured not only an active and powerful defence of colonial questions in Parliament, but also gave colonialism a distinctly republican stamp, immunizing it against attacks on ideological grounds from the Left. Colonial soldiers nestled beneath the guns of this parliamentary fortress each time one of their campaigns hit a political snag. Eugène Etienne became their patron saint, 'Our Lady of the Colonials', the man most often turned to in an hour of need. Twice under-secretary for colonial affairs, twice war minister, twice vice-president of the Chamber, and leader of the *Union démocratique* on whose 40 votes rode the survival of more than one government, Etienne's support was worth three divisions. Time and again he intervened to save Archinard, Dodds, Galliéni and Lyautey from the wrath of Delcassé, or to parry the parliamentary attacks of Jaurès or Camille Pelletan when complaining of the brutality or 'independence' of colonial generals.[49] 'The authorities leave me alone because the friendship of Etienne has immunized me', Lyautey wrote in May 1906.

Secondly, these men exerted enormous influence because the apathy and ignorance of the French public in colonial matters was reflected in the government, which allowed itself to be pushed lightly into adventures like Fashoda. The parochialism of French politics in the Third Republic combined with ministerial instability to strengthen the determined colonial lobby far beyond its limited numbers. The colonialists were especially influential when the government was weak, unstable or preoccupied with other matters: the Fashoda crisis sprang from a period of ministerial instability during which successive governments were too preoccupied with their own survival to worry overmuch about a small expedition sent to a place they had never heard of. Moroccan penetration began in earnest while Emile Combes, who cared little for foreign affairs, was busy scourging the Church, and climaxed in 1911 under the Monis ministry, probably the weakest of pre-war governments.[50]

Thirdly, the colonialists were allowed a great margin of manoeuvre because opposition to colonial expansion was weak and unorganized. The strong nationalism of the French Left meant that left-wing politicians were not opposed in principle to colonial expansion. Jaurès inherited Louis Blanc's belief in France's civilizing mission abroad and was prepared 'to support the peaceful expansion of French interests and civilization'.[51]

Lastly, the close links forged between colonialists and soldiers allowed a very effective coordination of conquest. Colonial groups like the *Comité de l'Afrique française* and the *Comité du Maroc* not only included both soldiers and civilians but also combined men of different political views, from the conservative Lyautey to the more radical Archinard, who buried their substantial political differences to work together for colonial expansion.[52] Cooperation was further increased by the rapid intrusion of colonial soldiers into the administrative sphere, which blurred the lines which divided civilians and soldiers. During home leaves, officers lobbied ministers and officials, or were often named to influential positions in the colonial ministry: the *Politique coloniale* complained in 1896 that 'Sudanese affairs are still being run from Paris by the military oligarchy which is daily taking over the *Pavillon de Flore*'.[53] The same overlapping of military and administrative roles occurred in the colonies where officers, especially navy doctors, abandoned the service for the higher pay, rapid promotion and power of colonial administration. In the early decades of colonial expansion especially, many 'civilian' officials were converted officers who shared the tastes and views of their colleagues of yesterday.[54] Many governors were taken from the ranks of the navy or the colonial army – Faidherbe, Jauréguiberry, Brière de l'Isle, Borgnis-Desbordes, Galliéni and Lyautey. Finally, civilian governors and their soldiers often saw eye to eye: Galliéni cooperated closely with Governors Lanessan and Rousseau in Indochina, as did Lyautey with Algerian Governor-General Charles Jonnart who shared his ideas and supported his methods.

As a result, the traditional view of French soldiers 'slipping the leash', rushing to fill in the blank spaces on the map without orders, against orders, must be qualified. The most important colonial campaigns were carefully mapped out by colonialists. Their tactic was simple and effective: colonial soldiers edged forward, their path often smoothed by bribes paid to native chiefs from funds supplied by one of the colonial groups like the *Comité du Maroc*. Once the flag was committed, colonialists could count on the hair-trigger nationalism of the French public and Parliament to rally the nation to the colonialist cause. The effectiveness of this tactic was demonstrated at Fashoda. When Marchand proclaimed that he was 'firmly asserting our rights on the Nile against the English', the Deputies voted the credits for the expedition by 471 votes to 18. Opposition came not from the Socialists but from a handful of dissident colonialists who realized the futility and potential dangers of the expedition. Their leader, Camille Bazille, was silenced by none other than Jaurès: 'This is not a political vote we are called upon to make,' he told deputies, 'it is a national vote.'[55]

The takeover of Morocco, too, demonstrated the effectiveness of close cooperation among colonialists in and out of uniform. It also signalled that the freedom of colonial soldiers, so great in the Western Sudan, must be modified to meet new circumstances. Germany's interest in North Africa accelerated the process which since the 1893 Siam crisis increasingly brought colonial issues into the sphere of European diplomacy. Colonial acquisition was no longer simply a question of dealing with native chiefs, an affair of officers and colonial officials, but was now drawn into the realm of international relations, the province of the Quai d'Orsay. A French invasion might touch off a European war, and to drive this point home, in 1905 the Kaiser stepped off his yacht in Tangiers to proclaim that Germany recognized Morocco as an independent state. While successive French governments remained determined to acquire Morocco, their tactics had to be adapted to the new situation. Morocco could not simply be handed over to colonial soldiers like the Western Sudan. French penetration must be prepared by the diplomats, and their cautious diplomacy inevitably provoked the wrath of soldiers who argued that it was out of place in a colonial situation. Moroccan penetration sharpened the conflict between the colonialists and the diplomats.

Morocco provided Lyautey with a springboard to prominence. A colonial soldier who had won his spurs serving under Galliéni in Tonkin and Madagascar, Lyautey was placed in command of the Sud Oranais in 1903 with the task of stopping attacks by marauding tribes out of Morocco into Western Algeria. Lyautey's methods soon irritated the Quai d'Orsay and its diplomatic mission in Tangiers. Diplomats at the time, and historians since, have seen Lyautey's conduct at Ain -Sefra as typical of that of a colonial soldier – independence bordering on insubordination, inflating minor incidents and inventing threats to undermine Delcassé's cautious diplomacy and push for a military solution to the Moroccan crisis.[56]

But to accept such a verdict without qualification would be to ignore the subtle changes, the new note of caution which surrounded military action in the Sud Oranais. Lyautey certainly used all of the tricks of a colonial commander, occupying positions without authority and changing their names to throw the Quai d'Orsay off the scent. 'It is understood that to spare diplomatic susceptibilities, Béchar will no longer be called Béchar but Colomb, if you get my meaning', he wrote to Galliéni.[57] But the conflict between the soldiers at Ain-Sefra and the diplomats at Tangiers masked a more fundamental struggle over Moroccan policy in Paris between Etienne and Delcassé, and one which strengthened the links between the colonial army and its Paris patrons. Lyautey was allowed more leeway than was traditionally accorded a metropolitan commander; the right to correspond directly with the governor general and to order military operations without first clearing them with division command in Oran. This 'independence' was sharply attacked by Jaurès in the Chamber. But Lyautey's relative autonomy in no way challenged the principle of civilian control over the army in the colonies. On the contrary, it illustrated forcefully that the 'independence' of colonial commanders was directly dependent on the strength of the politicians who 'covered' for them. It was an independence which imposed discretion and restraints and required a man prepared to nibble away at Morocco rather than devour it in great mouthfuls: 'Here I believe only in blows struck on the sly and ground gained quietly', he wrote to his friend, the Viscount de Vogüé.[58]

Morocco marked a new phase in this traditional alliance between the colonial army and the *groupe colonial*: whereas before the colonial army and colonial interests had worked largely in tandem toward similar goals, now they are integrated into a colonial machine which turned on the beat of the same motor. Lyautey, because of his sensibilities, his social background and professional experience, his letters which found their way into influential political and literary salons in the capital, was certainly the colonial officer best suited to a delicate command. Lyautey's action in the Sud Oranais was not a re-run of the Western Sudan, soldiers let loose for promotion and glory. Lyautey became the agent to undermine Delcassé's political position used both by the colonial politicians and eventually even by Combes and André out to get even with the foreign minister for his opposition to many of their domestic policies. When Delcassé ordered Lyautey off Ras-el-Ain, occupied without orders and renamed Berguet to escape notice in Paris, not only Jonnart and Etienne jumped to Lyautey's defence, but also the chief of the French general staff Pendezec, and Combes and André intervened to contradict the foreign minister.[59] By the Tangiers crisis of 1905, Delcassé was completely stripped of support.[60] Lyautey was not particularly happy with this colonial–foreign office confrontation, in part because he believed that it restricted rather than augmented his freedom, but basically because he realized that Morocco was not just a side-show mounted to keep soldiers in a good humour, but required a collective effort involving all aspects of French policy-making machinery.

The Lyautey–Delcassé battle demonstrated that Lyautey, like Galliéni in Indochina, sought a comfortable working relationship with civilians rather than head-on collisions which, in the long run, only complicated his task. It also demonstrated that in confrontations with popular and successful colonial soldiers, politicians, even the most skilled, were never absolutely sure of finishing in the first place. Delcassé's 1893 show-down with Archinard had ended in a stand-off while that with Lyautey left him a poor second, for he found that his colleagues preferred his resignation to that of the Brigadier. This phenomenon was not confined to France. In India, following the South African war, the redoubtable Lord Curzon was bested by Kitchener after the two quarrelled over military policy. When it came to choosing between the Viceroy and the Commander-in-Chief, the government chose the latter.[61]

While the question of overall civilian control of military operations in the colonies was never challenged by the soldiers, the degree to which this control was applied was a bone of contention. The nature of government policy and Paris' limited means of control gave soldiers great autonomy within the overall framework of colonial expansion. The growing strength of the Colonial Party also gave colonial generals added clout. The Colonial Party dragged military commanders into the political squabbles in Paris, using them to counter the opinions of experienced politicians like Delcassé, blocking attacks from the parliamentary Left and encouraging the already well-developed tradition of political awareness in the ranks of the colonial forces which was not duplicated at home. The colonial army, unlike its metropolitan counterpart, was protected from political reprisals. This was assured when Etienne shielded Lyautey from Jaurès' attack on his 'independence', effectively ending left-wing hopes of enlisting moderate republican support for a significant critique of the colonial army.[62] The Colonial Party allowed the establishment of a political tradition in the colonial army, not political freedom, but a belief widespread among colonial officers that they had an active part to play in all decisions affecting the colonies.

While the much remarked independence of colonial commanders was certainly a factor in the politicization of the colonial army, more important to this process was the evolution of a distinct colonial personality. The colonial army was not simply the metropolitan army in short trousers, but a force whose officers were distinguished from their colleagues and compatriots by their separate roles and attitudes.

From the beginning, the colonial army was the step-child of the armed forces, virtually ignored by the navy to which it belonged and regarded with condescension by the army. Colonial service offered few professional attractions – the bulk of money and promotion went to the navy while colonial soldiers essentially provided security for distant anchorages. Despite their well-deserved reputation for heroism – the colonial infantry was virtually annihilated at Bazeilles in 1870 – the colonial services remained low in the military pecking order throughout the 1870s, a largely demoralized force, ranked socially and professionally only a notch above the transportation corps. As a result, the marines had scraped together an officer corps largely from men who had graduated near the bottom of their classes at Saint-Cyr and occasionally the *Ecole polytechnique*: between 1874 and 1880, for example, between fifty and ninety per cent of Saint-Cyr cadets who chose colonial service had graduated in the bottom quarter of their class.[63]

However, 1880 saw a change of fortune. Over the next 32 years, the colonial army was expanded to provide garrisons for Indochina, Madagascar, the Western Sudan and eventually Morocco in 1912. From 1878, Saint-Cyr classes took names inspired by colonial victories – Zoulous, Kroumirs, Soudan – until by 1914 fully nineteen classes, or fifty per cent, registered colonial names.[64] The colonial army's newly acquired prestige together with double pay and seniority offered abroad soon told in officer recruitment. In 1881, eight of thirty-five Saint-Cyr cadets who chose colonial service were ranked in the top quarter of their class and in 1884, twenty-five students in the top quarter of their class chose the marines. In 1884, for the first time, the average class rank of cadets choosing the marines was slightly superior to that of cadets who had selected line infantry regiments. In 1886, 18 of 40 cadets choosing the colonial infantry were in the top third of their class and the average class rank of marine second lieutenants was 155 compared with 198 for line regiments. Only one man in the last quarter of the class volunteered for the marines.[65] While the average class rank depended on the publicity given to a colonial campaign in a given year, one can conclude that by 1886 the quality of recruitment to the colonial army had at least drawn level with that of line regiments. To the improved recruitment from Saint-Cyr was added the number of talented regular officers seconded to the colonies for the duration of a campaign – men like Galliéni and Lyautey – who made valuable contributions to the spread of the French empire. While the colonial officer corps in no way constituted an elite, the tough conditions and constant combat of the colonies tended to operate a natural selection, pushing the best officers to the top and consigning the rest to quiet oblivion.

Expansion, active service and improved recruitment did not solve the colonial army's problem of prestige. It rather increased the friction and resentment between colleagues at home and abroad. The barriers which separated colonial and metropolitan soldiers were both social and professional. Louis Baron calculated that forty-six per cent of Saint-Cyr cadets who chose the colonial army between 1872 and 1891 were drawn from the 'popular classes', while the remaining fifty-four per cent he classed as 'bourgeois'. Only six per cent of colonial officers bore aristocratic *noms à particule*; many of them were officers' sons, minor civil servants and one even a shopkeeper. In 1883, for instance, fully twenty-one per cent of Saint-Cyr cadets bore a *nom à particule*.[66] Perhaps more significant than these imprecise class categories is the fact that sixty-eight per cent of men who chose a colonial career were scholarship students at a time when only one-third of Saint-Cyr cadets could not pay their own way.[67] While the solid middle-class character of the metropolitan army precluded its putting on social airs, the lower social recruitment of the colonial officer corps placed a certain distance between the two officer camps. Colonial service fell largely to poorer officers who lacked the education or connections to stake out a career in France and to those who wanted to see some real 'active' service. To these were added difficult or restive men like Lyautey, so that colonial service became a punishment, an exile for men with little future who trailed behind their classmates at Saint-Cyr like Archinard, or who like Faidherbe were bored at home. For line officers, colonial men were little more than a 'collection of hooligans', exiles fleeing debts and paternity suits.[68]

Professional barriers between home and colonies were more important still. Colonial soldiers were regarded by their metropolitan colleagues as little better than adventurers, men forced abroad because of poor professional prospects or social ostracism, 'bachi-bouzouks' playing out a parody of military life rather than engaged in serious soldiering. This prejudice stemmed in great part from 1870, when men who had earned brilliant reputations in Algeria, Mexico and other far-flung battlefields proved inept when faced with a serious European enemy. The feeling persisted in the metropolitan army that colonial skirmishes provided poor preparation for European warfare and soldiers who chose exile abroad were lost to the serious business of preparation for war with Germany. Captain Emile Mayer noted that Galliéni had lived 'far from the army' while Lyautey met a wall of prejudice when he returned to France in 1902 after nine years under Galliéni in Tonkin and Madagascar.

The tensions between colonial and home soldiers passed beyond simple squabbles over funds or decorations, both of which colonial men believed in short supply,[69] or sterile snobbery based on differences in education or function, all too common in the army before 1870. The divisions between the two military camps reflected different temperaments, different outlooks on life. The professional advantages or the prospect of adventure drew some to the colonies. A few volunteered out of family tradition, but barely ten percent of Saint-Cyr cadets who selected colonial service were sons of naval or colonial army officers, petty officers and NCOs or of merchant marine officers.[70] Although the Finistère, where two colonial army regiments were based, sent a sizeable contingent of officer volunteers, the North and the East were also well represented and virtually all areas of France furnished colonial officers. While the professional advantages, the prospects of battle and glory, family tradition and geography played a part in the recruitment of colonial army officers, one cannot escape the feeling that many, perhaps most, officers, in the 1880s at least, went to the colonies either because they had no choice or by accident. Except in 1886, the bottom quarter of each Saint-Cyr class continued to send a sizeable contingent into the marines.[71] Many of the best men wandered out by chance – Joffre to forget the death of his wife and Lyautey because of his homosexuality and his circle of literary and political friends. Lyautey's 'Rôle social de l'officier', published by the *Revue des deux mondes* in 1891, with its attendant political publicity, had become an embarrassment for the high command, and helped to pay his fare out.

Whether colonial officers climbed on the boat by choice, accident or by force, they felt the trip outward like going from a small room into the open air. Away from the tedium of garrison life with its dreary routine of square-bashing, filing reports, preparing professional examinations and endless evenings passed in cards, drink or idle conversation awaiting promotion, colonial officers stumbled upon a vocation. For Lyautey, like so many others, the colonies offered a road to Damascus, rescuing him from the 'sterility, the deadness and above all the military academicians' of the metropolitan army. Colonial soldiers saw themselves as 'men of action', involved in the great work of empire-building, a 'struggle with fists bared' and decried the talent, energy and spirit which mouldered away in French garrisons. Lyautey pitied 'the poor devils in Paris who believe that they are living because they dine at Durand's, applaud the latest play, spend the evening at the café de Paris in the company of fast women or else remain tied to the petticoats of their wives, discussing for hours on end the colour of their trousers or the cut of their shoes, etc.'[72] He praised those who had rejected 'the comfortable life in the garrisons of France' to join the 'patriotic task ... in the front lines'. Only in the colonies were the best French traditions kept alive: 'It is the colonial idea which pays', he wrote. 'One refuses to understand that it is there and there alone that, for the past twenty years, the tradition of French energy has been maintained.'[73]

Colonial men decried the 'Prussification' of the metropolitan army and with it the yardsticks devised to measure the ability of metropolitan soldiers. And well they might. Men who had been uninspiring in the classroom or led undistinguished careers in France, the Faidherbes and Archinards, caught fire in the colonies. For the first time their imagination was stimulated and their abilities taxed, as they confronted an enemy and not an exam sheet. Even officers like Galliéni and Lyautey who had passed through the *Ecole de guerre* turned their backs on the rules, the rote learning, the 'formalisme métropolitain',[74] which stymied initiative and paralyzed imagination.

Colonial soldiers quickly developed a contempt for their metropolitan colleagues, the contempt of the man of action for the idle or the academic. The future General Mangin spoke condescendingly of his Saint-Cyr classmates who collected their promotions 'without having done more than organize an arms depot at Toulon or Brest' while he had been wounded in battle.[75] Colonial service, not the *Ecole de guerre*, was the true school of war. This was graphically illustrated during the 1885 retreat from Lang Son. When General Négrier was wounded in the initial ambush, the command passed to Colonel Herbinger, one time instructor at the *Ecole de guerre*, who immediately ordered a retreat. The retreat from Lang Son, Borgnis-Desbordes wrote to Félix Faure in May 1885,

was, after all, the unorganized flight of a brigade left in the hands of a very knowledgeable man, an ex-professor at the *Ecole de guerre*, certainly intelligent, with a laudable theoretical knowledge of his profession, but absolutely losing his head on the spot in practical war conditions which are not books ... When General Brière told me on the evening of the 28th that the brigade was retreating under the command of Colonel Herbinger ... an ex-professor at the *Ecole de guerre*, I told him: 'Then we are buggered' and I was right.[76]

Colonial officers argued that their task demanded imagination, judgement and special skills not required in the stiff obedience of home service. Colonial soldiers were forced to adapt their tactics and methods to each new situation rather than apply a pat formula pushed up by the *Ecole de guerre*. The 1881 invasion of Tunisia demonstrated that traditional military tactics which relied on the invading column, the pitched battle with the enemy routed and the country pacified had to be rethought. French forces invading from Algeria met little resistance, allowing the French to make their political arrangements in Tunis and the Chamber to breathe a sigh of relief at the relative ease and cheapness of the operation. However, as soon as French troops vanished to garrisons in France and Algeria, the southern tribes revolted requiring another French invasion, this time permanent. In the face of overwhelming forces, natives melted into the hills, either avoiding skirmishes or contenting themselves with small guerrilla raids around the fringes of the column. Once the French disappeared behind a sand dune they revolted anew. The Tunisia expedition set the pattern of invasion, withdrawal, rebellion and occupation which was to be repeated elsewhere.[77] The long French experience fighting guerrilla wars should have shown up the shortcomings of the column. However, one of the characteristics of the French experience abroad was that this lesson had to be relearned with each new campaign and with each new area of conquest. In Senegal, Faidherbe, too, found that an expedition without an occupation was virtually worthless and had to be accompanied by a programme of economic development to convince the natives that French rule was beneficial.[78] These ideas were absorbed and developed by Galliéni in Tonkin and Madagascar and by Lyautey in Morocco.

The obvious disadvantages of the column in colonial warfare did not mean that it was immediately dropped from the repertoire of colonial expeditions. In part this resulted from the fact that the column was sometimes necessary to move large numbers of troops against native concentrations or fortified towns. But in general, the massive invasion was an unsatisfactory and sometimes dangerous way to subdue a hostile territory, as General Négrier discovered when his column was ambushed and forced to retreat with heavy losses from Lang Son in 1885. Lyautey, too, objected that the massive mobilization, funding and publicity given to large scale operations often created political difficulties at home.[79] The survival of the column in the colonies beyond what should have been its natural lifetime was due to two factors: firstly, the lessons and methods of colonial warfare not passed on from generation to generation of soldiers. If colonial conquests absorbed, however temporarily, the public imagination, they made little impact on the bulk of the army which had not participated in them. Colonial soldiers were glorious but relatively few, and their doctrines did not become part of the stock-in-trade of the profession. Only a small percentage of military energies and personnel was absorbed in colonial expeditions, the army remained geared to European war and faithful to its Napoleonic concepts. Once the conquest was complete, and the commander passed on, his ideas were relegated to the archives and the light mobile units created to answer the special difficulties of colonial warfare were gradually absorbed into the military structure, acquiring more equipment and consequently losing their original mobility, transformed into decorative and exotic versions of line infantry. When Lyautey arrived at Ain-Sefra in 1904 to be shown a 'mobile column' bulging with impedimenta by officers of the *armée d'Afrique*, he asked: 'What do you in this country call a heavy column?'[80] Each new military generation had to start from scratch, applying the traditional tactics and meeting the same failure. Doctrines and techniques of colonial warfare were not taught at Saint-Cyr or the *Ecole de guerre*, but were acquired by necessity by imaginative colonial men like Faidherbe and Galliéni who each time returned to the source – 'C'est du meilleur Bugeaud', Lyautey said of Galliéni. Secondly, the column floated on the personal ambition of soldiers eager for a scrap, *la casse*, which brought with it honours and promotion, the only way to break the strait-jacket of seniority, and to whom the prospect of measured penetration using force as a last resort appeared dull.[81]

These attitudes, if not transformed, were at least superseded by those of a new generation of soldiers led by Galliéni. Indochina had become the running sore of the French empire where outmoded military tactics and civil-military friction combined to sabotage pacification. Galliéni, backed by Governor General Lanessan, launched a new tactic based on his experiences in the Western Sudan where, unlike most of his military contemporaries, he had combined conquest with economic development. Supported by men like Pennequin and Lyautey, he turned his back on the traditional military expedition. 'This method has only given illusory results', he wrote to Lanessan, 'because it does not destroy the [pirate] bands, [but] simply pushes them back to the exterior, from where they return, they have not been pushed into neighbouring territory already pacified, thus the work has always to begin again. . . . The surest method is to make the terrain inhospitable. . . . Soldiers thrown into a new territory must remain there, live there, colonize it.'[82] Galliéni divided the turbulent border region with China into four military districts, each subdivided into 'circles' ruled by officers from French posts planted at 25-kilometre intervals from which French forces gradually extended their influence into the countryside – a '*tache d'huile*' or oil spot growing larger until it covered the entire territory. Lyautey adapted the *tache d'huile* to Morocco, organizing a three-tiered defence system which made the best use of the natural qualities of his troops. The Foreign Legion and the *bataillons d'Afrique* occupied towns and oases. Mounted legionaries assured the security of the surrounding countryside and provided support for lightly armed native riflemen who roamed further afield.[83] Beneath this umbrella of security, French soldiers constructed markets and roads to convince the native populations that French rule brought peace and prosperity. In Galliéni's system, the military and administrative functions were combined, stretching the traditional military virtues to include diplomacy and administration. This required men with special talents, 'the recruitment of an elite'. Not every soldier was suitable for colonial service which required 'the right man in the right place'. While Galliéni's system owed much to Lamoricière's Arab bureau developed in the 1830s, it rejected the distinction drawn in North Africa between the administrative role and the troop command. 'A colonial expedition must always be directed by the leader designated to be the first administrator of the country after the conquest', Lyautey noted.

These administrative functions seem incompatible at first with the idea which one has of a soldier in certain milieux. It is there, however, that the colonial officer finds his true role ... It is also the most delicate, for it demands more application and effort, showing up his personal qualities. For to destroy is nothing, to reconstruct is more difficult.

Therefore, colonial soldiers, even young lieutenants, were given administrative responsibility and the distinction between officer and official melted away.[84] The primary role of the army in the colonies was not to fight, but to administer – the real contribution of colonial generals like Galliéni and Lyautey was in government, not warfare.

A colonial soldier was not simply a metropolitan officer banished to the bush. Colonial service demanded a suppleness and skill not usually found in the rigid specialization and classical divisions of continental armies. Lyautey complained incessantly of officers abroad who attempted to re-create the comfortable routines and habits of France, sidestepping responsibilities and sinking steadily into red tape, regulations and restrictions. The future General Gouraud blasted officers more concerned with form than results.[85]

Anti-militarism, then, emerged as a strong theme in the attitudes of colonial soldiers – one could almost believe that certain of Lyautey's letters had been written by Hervé, had not Lyautey's literary style been vastly superior to the frantic rhetoric of the left-wing journalist. 'The army must be rejuvenated with a vengeance', he wrote in 1905. 'It is the citadel of every routine, of every stupidity.'[86]

The anti-metropolitan attitudes of colonial soldiers and their parliamentary patrons and the belief that colonial conditions required special men and methods were mirrored in the 1900 colonial army law. A law organizing the colonial army had been on the cards since colonial expansion had demonstrated the navy's inability or unwillingness to administer efficiently its colonial forces. Between 1881 and 1885, no less than sixteen bills reorganizing the colonial army were submitted to parliament. Opposition to the organization of a colonial army was concentrated on political extremes. The Left protested that a colonial army would facilitate imperialism, and unofficially expressed its fears that black troops might be used as strike-breakers. Some deputies on the Right argued that to transfer the marines to the army would undermine its 'traditions'. The navy ministry attempted to renounce responsibility for colonial defence in February 1890, but in 1893 the Senate rejected the government's request for the creation of a separate colonial force. The separate organization of the colonial army was delayed by ministerial instability, the question of recruitment and the simple fact that it was not an issue which demanded immediate attention. Even politicians with strong colonial interests were divided on the question of the best home for the colonial army. Etienne, for instance, argued that the colonial army should go to the colonial ministry[87] but most of his colleagues opposed a third military ministry.[88]

The question of colonial army organization lingered, of interest to the navy and war ministries and to colonial officers themselves, until the Fashoda crisis and the arrival of General Galliffet in the war ministry prodded parliament into action by exposing the gaping holes in colonial defence. Colonial interests seized upon the crisis to push home a separate colonial army organization. 'The fleet has not one point of support which would allow it to save the honour of our arms, much less to fulfill its assigned role', Borgnis-Desbordes wrote after an 1898 colonial inspection tour whose findings were published by the *Comité de l'Afrique française*. 'Everything is lacking: personnel, *matériel*, organization.'[89]

Partisans of the colonial army argued that colonial soldiers must be transferred from the navy to the war ministry and that within the war ministry they must remain autonomous. The deputy Lannes de Montebello believed that the attachment of colonial troops to the rue Saint-Dominique was simply common sense. Only this way could the war ministry play efficiently to meet defence needs, both at home and abroad. A colonial force under the war ministry would also iron out difficulties in the colonies. Colonial army partisans, however, were adamant that the colonial army, while under the war ministry's jurisdiction, should retain a command structure distinct from that of the metropolitan forces. Promotion figured most prominently in this demand: colonial officers feared that amalgamation with the metropolitan army corps would slow promotion to the French rates. They also argued that amalgamation would result in abuses, with well-connected metropolitan officers being sent to the colonies for brief periods to pick up quick promotion at the expense of the long-serving colonials. Lyautey also feared an influx of 'mandarins armed with all the academic qualifications who only lack a quick, easy campaign to jump a rank more rapidly. One must be wary of the men who come to the colonies to refight Austerlitz', he continued. 'They are badly prepared for the patient, thankless and obscure tasks which make up the daily duties – the only useful ones – of the colonial officer.' Only colonial superiors were in a position to appreciate that pacification was more important than the *'action d'éclat'* in colonial service. 'Does one not realize that it requires more authority, composure, judgement, tenacity, to maintain a hostile and turbulent population in a state of submission without firing a shot than to suppress them with cannon once they have revolted?'[90]

Lyautey's contrast between colonial soldiers out to pacify by peaceful means and metropolitan officers looking for sharp action and subsequent promotion was more an attempt at good relations than a stab at the truth. The image of an army imposing peace on warring tribes, sharing its skills with the natives and investing its labour in the improvement of the colonies bought support and votes for colonial expansion. But more than a fiction staged to gouge money from Parliament, it represented an ideal to which he and Galliéni subscribed. Their subordinates, unfortunately, did not always share these views. If Paris sometimes found it difficult to control its soldiers in the colonies, colonial commanders were not always any more successful. Paul Cambon complained in 1883 that the commanding general in Tunisia 'cannot restrain his personnel and maintain them within the limits of a provisional administration'.[91] Some even claimed that Joffre's march on Timbuktu resulted from the insubordination of Captain Laperrine, who threatened to march alone with his native Saharians if Joffre did not act.[92] Even Lyautey sometimes failed to curb Laperrine's appetite for adventure: when the Lieutenant colonel crossed the Sahara with his Saharians in 1906, leaving the vital oases unguarded, Lyautey wrote: 'Experience proves to my great regret that my authority over Lieutenant colonel Laperrine is insufficient to prevent such acts.' However, rather than discipline him Lyautey praised his initiative and asked only that the oases be placed under a separate command.[93]

To a certain degree, insubordination was built into the colonial army system, as long as it guaranteed the rapid acquisition of territory and demonstrated the spirit of initiative upon which colonial soldiers prided themselves. Insubordinate soldiers had little to fear either from politicians or military commanders, or from poorly armed natives. Occasionally, however, French officers carried their initiatives too far, sometimes with disastrous results. Bonnier paid dearly for his over-confidence at Timbuktu. In Morocco, too, colonial soldiers on at least one occasion underestimated the opposition.

In December 1914, a French force without Lyautey's orders launched an offensive to subjugate the unpacified mountain tribes around Khenifra in central Morocco, where they were cut off and virtually annihilated. Lyautey blamed the disaster on a current of officer opinion which condemned his ideas as:

a method of passive occupation, inert, timorous, disguising its impotence under the label of 'tache d'huile', 'progressive penetration', 'combination of politics with force' and other twaddle which are but the mask of men lacking audacity, avoiding responsibilities, fearful of war ... Such theories could only be believed by young officers who, naturally, only want a fight or to certain commanders who ... are always ready to sacrifice the general interest to look for a local success.[94]

Khenifra demonstrated that the contradiction between persuasion and bloodshed and the problem of imposing discipline on headstrong commanders had not been resolved. It also pointed out the difficulties of attempting to apply a doctrine of persuasion and good works with a force which had a strong interest in picking a fight. Lyautey criticized the metropolitan promotion system which rewarded only grey hair and bravery. '[Colonel Laverdure, the Khenifra commander] was convinced that he would succeed with audacious acts', Lyautey continued.

And this is once again the result of a state of things to which I have often called attention and more than ever since the war. It is certain that the school [of thought] of which I have just spoken has found much more support as it is exclusively the 'feat of war' which is rewarded. . . . *The point upon which I insist is the absolute necessity* in colonial war in general and in particular in the conditions which we now find ourselves in here *not to take account exclusively* of 'feats of war', but to understand at all costs that peaceful results obtained with other difficulties and other merits must be appreciated.

Unless this was done, he warned, unless his promotion requests for officers were honoured, then discipline in Morocco would be compromised.[95]

Kanya-Forstner, contrasting French and British army attitudes to colonization in West Africa, defined them as the difference between the warrior and the administrator: the French promotion system gave its officers an interest in provoking conflicts, grabbing territory, shunning an administrative role as a poor substitute for conquest. The British in Nigeria, on the other hand, looked upon war as a simple prelude to administration. Political rather than military posts were the more attractive, and officers like British Colonel Lugard sought to make their reputations as governors rather than as military commanders.[96] While this assertion is no doubt correct for the Western Sudan, there were clearly two schools of thought in the French colonial army – that of Archinard and Borgnis-Desbordes in the Western Sudan which relied basically on the sword, and that of Galliéni and Lyautey in Indochina, Madagascar and Morocco which preferred persuasion. Obviously, the differences were not as clear-cut as this – colonial officers in Africa found that administration followed inevitably on the heels of conquest, while Galliéni and Lyautey never hesitated to keep natives in line with the crack of a whip, firm believers in combining politics with force. Although the Galliéni–Lyautey school never succeeded in laying the ghost of the 'feat of arms', it is certainly they who made the most lasting contribution to theories of colonial warfare, both because their methods were politically more marketable and because in the final analysis they proved more successful. They argued convincingly that no basic contradiction existed between the military and administrative roles demanded of colonial officers.

The differences which separated French and British soldiers were not always those of the warrior and the administrator, but rather betrayed different attitudes toward ambition. This stemmed in part from the social differences between French and British colonialism. British colonialism had class, and Her Majesty's officers were expected to conform to a strict social code. The Indian army, especially, reflected that obsession with regimental respectability which characterized the British army at home, transforming British messes into militarized if slightly rowdy versions of London clubs. No such atmosphere was to be found in the French army. If the Foreign Legion lent a certain romantic panache to French colonialism, this did not alter the fact that it was composed largely of runaways, criminals and lunatics for whom an evening out was incomplete without a brawl. Many British officers were ambitious, but social convention took the hard edge off their desire to succeed. British officers had to get on in the mess, and this meant being a good all-rounder – good at sport, at drink and jolly pleasant company. They, too, welcomed the prospect of action which brought distinction and promotion. When campaigning was announced in an Indian army mess, Kipling wrote that the men 'cheered lustily... the majors smiled with sober joy and the subalterns waltzed in pairs down the mess-room'. Colonial wars found no shortage of volunteers in the British army any more than in the French. But while success in the British army required discretion and ambition cushioned by the social virtues expected of gentlemen,[97] no such social inhibitions existed in the French colonial army where officers wore their ambition on their sleeves. 'This life in the marines is superb, but it sharpens ambitions to an unimaginable degree and makes competition ferocious', Lyautey wrote from Tonkin.[98] The result was that French colonial officers were prepared to push hard to get to the top. 'I am condemned to succeed or to break my neck', Lyautey wrote to Galliéni when he took over the command of the Sud Oranais. 'But you taught me a long time ago that the colonial career swung between these two alternatives and that one should consider it dispassionately. This is what I am doing, playing double or nothing.'[99] The operations mounted for no other reason than to get on the promotion list, the petulant threats of resignation, the intrigue, the crass careerism had no place in the gentlemanly atmosphere of a British mess – not because British officers lacked ambition, but because these French practices were so *arriviste*.

The final, if unofficial, reason put forward by French colonial men for a separate military organization was the political one. Colonial officers always claimed that their army would remain aloof from the 'squabbles and bickering' of French politics. In a sense, nothing could have been further from the truth. If Galliéni and Lyautey wrote letters with a frequency which made Madame de Sévigné look lazy, it was precisely because they had to build up and exploit political contacts to keep colonial expansion well-oiled. French ministerial instability which provoked swings and shifts in colonial policy, the eccentricities of colonial administration and the need to secure generous government funding forced colonial officers to spin a web of relations with Parliament and pressure groups. Both Galliéni and Lyautey were able PR men, careful to avoid statements which would compromise relations with the moderate republican leadership which provided the foundation of colonial support. They needed all of their skills at the turn of the century when Fashoda and the Dreyfus affair threatened to drag the colonial army into the political arena.

The refusal of leading colonial soldiers to step directly into French politics, however, and the geographical isolation of the colonial army did little to deaden the extreme sensitivity which its officers displayed for political events at home. The scandals, the selfishness and incompetence of republican politicians and the listlessness of a society which tolerated them, frayed the nerves of officers charged with showing the flag, offending their obsession with national prestige which fuelled the French colonial enterprise. Colonial men with time on their hands took an active interest in French politics. The letters of Galliéni and Lyautey are full of requests for books on the latest political subjects; the knowledge that they were protected from political reprisals by powerful Paris patrons encouraged them to state their views with a vigour which would have endangered the careers of metropolitan officers. While criticism of republican government and of the timidity and 'stagnation' of French society was not confined to the colonial army, it found forceful expression among men on the outside looking in. For the first time, French officers saw France through the eyes of foreigners, and the image was less than flattering. Government instability and the petty political quarrels in Paris were condemned for causing regrettable shifts of colonial policy, but even more for pillorying the image of France abroad. Lyautey condemned 'this incompetent, omnipotent, unstable and irresponsible parliamentarianism',[100] while Colonel Peroz blasted 'these leaders who, for the most part, do not know what they want or, if they do, do not dare to act on it'.[101] For colonial officers, the failings of republican government were not simply a technical question which could be regulated by a *coup d'état*, even had they been so inclined, but a more fundamental reflection of a people which had lost heart, of a country bled white by its own quarrels, whose moral anaemia expressed itself in bureaucratic centralization and institutional paralysis in which caution crowned the pyramid of social virtues. 'A career carefully regulated and secured by the state has become parents' ideal for their children, whose number they carefully limit to protect them from the uncertainties and dangers of a struggle for life which becomes harsher every day', wrote Captain Grandmaison.[102] Lyautey believed that he had a 'social duty to tear this country away from decomposition and ruin. Not by a change of government, an empirical and impermanent remedy, but by a violent reaction against habits, inertia and worries. . . . France is dying less from '70 and its regime than from internal contradiction and atrophy in which everyone grows complacent amid material comfort', he wrote.[103] He failed to understand why investment had not followed the flag, and blamed it in part on the timidity and even dishonesty of businessmen who preferred quick fortunes gained in shady speculation to money placed in the colonies.[104] He contrasted the prosperity of English colonies with the stagnation of France overseas: 'What do you expect! The English have initiative in the blood.'[105] The image of France retained by these men buried in the bush was one of political dissension and bourgeois decadence, of countrymen obsessed with their own personal comfort, of Frenchmen unworthy of France.

The 1900 law acknowledged the separate requirements of the colonial army, but, more important, placed the official seal on a set of habits and attitudes which could only encourage the growing personality split within the army and ultimately between colonial soldiers and France. An 1893 law restricted conscripts to colonial units stationed in France, leaving foreign service to professional volunteers. Colonial commanders argued that they could concentrate on recruiting an 'elite' cadre with the 'aptitudes' required for colonial service not always to be found in the annual contingent.[106] The elimination of conscripts from colonial duty also removed one potential hold which deputies with sons of influential constituents in uniform might have on colonial commanders, while service with colonial regiments in France often fell to keen conscript volunteers, men unlikely to create the sort of discipline problems experienced by some home units: 'The increase in the number of requests [by conscripts] to serve in the colonial troops indicates that they are considered with favour by a great many young men', read a 1907 report.[107] The 1900 law increased the independence of the colonial army, ending its competition with the navy and insulating it against a takeover bid by the rue Saint-Dominique. The colonial army was answerable to the war minister, but its separate general staff placed it largely beyond the reach of a military hierarchy dominated by often hostile metropolitan officers.[108] While contact between the colonial and metropolitan armies was frequent, it usually worked in favour of the former. Article 9 of the 1900 law reserved colonial commands exclusively for men with colonial experience; colonial generals like Galliéni, Joffre and Lyautey often returned to top commands in France. The law sought to slam the door to colonial service on metropolitan officers. But rather than import their metropolitan 'rites' to the bush as deputies feared, metropolitan officers like Lyautey and Grandmaison who were seconded abroad fell quick converts to the views and habits of their colonial counterparts. With the first hint of a new campaign, colonial men on rotation home rushed for the boat out, as Colonel Frey noted in 1888.[109]

Nor could the 1900 law stunt the growth of colonial dissatisfaction with the Third Republic. The law required colonial officers to return home every two years and, after a tour in France, to be reassigned to an entirely different colony. Legislators clearly hoped to prevent the development of a strong separatist spirit, with soldiers throwing down roots in the colonies. However, a tour home, rather than renew contact with France, often had the opposite effect, especially after 1900, when a few months in France could be a depressing experience: 'It is only on return to France that a man realizes that his tastes, his habits, his customs are no longer those of his country and he too often hastens to return to the colony which has become his fatherland', wrote General Trentinian in 1911.[110]

Thirty odd years of military apartheid resulted in the development of separate ambitions and attitudes among colonial soldiers, men who had rejected safe careers in France, the deadly routine of provincial garrisons or the narrow caste pride of staff officers, the instinctive fear of politicians, responsibilities or the false step which could shatter a carefully constructed career. Jean de Pierrefeu, a reserve lieutenant who spent most of the Great War at General Headquarters, found colonial officers better read, more imaginative and better company than the bureaucrats who peopled the staff. The war returned many colonial commanders to France to replace generals adept at negotiating the labyrinth of *kriegspiels* and political connections. Galliéni, Mangin, Gouraud, Henrys and Franchet d'Espérey were only a few of the officers who provided irrefutable proof of the solidity of the colonial school and the quality of its officers.

The creeping disillusionment with France and her politics was soon wired home. After a few years of Radical rule had served to accentuate the confusion and divisions of Frenchmen and to wear down the morale and, most officers agreed, the fighting qualities of the army, colonial soldiers began to suggest that the salvation of France and her army depended upon a strong injection of colonial spirit. Colonial soldiers offered their example as an antidote for the ills which poisoned the French body politic: men of action, spirit and imagination, risk-takers whose patriotic sacrifices and unselfish existence should serve as an example to a timorous people. As the missionaries of France abroad, they returned home to unite a divided people. Lyautey preached the colonial greatness of France with evangelical fervour, foreseeing 'an increasing number of innovators, formed by the colonies, strong, removed from every-day demands, far-seeing. This group will react upon metropolitan inertia to establish a continuing and regenerating current of life between France without and France within.'[111] Captain Grandmaison, too, believed that the 'moral forces' unleashed in the colonies could be harnessed to transform French decadence.[112]

Colonial soldiers argued that their spirit of initiative and sacrifice would lend fibre to French life, helping France to face up to the challenge Germany posed to national security. By 1905, colonial soldiers began to turn their attention from the colonies to the continent. This evolution was aided by several factors. In the first place, the colonial army's very success in the colonies appeared to many to have eliminated its *raison d'être*. Politicians who had been claiming at least since 1890 that the era of colonial conquests was over, seemed at last to be speaking the truth. 'The heroic period of our colonial history is finished', declared Paul Deschanel in 1906. 'The time of conquests is passed. Now we must develop our acquired positions and improve our present domain. Today, economic questions are of the first order.'[113] Officers who had given birth to France's vast empire, now slumped into a state of post-natal depression, many unaware that Morocco would soon be thrown open to military imperialism. Once the great feast of conquest had been reduced to a few bones and scraps, colonial officers were confronted with the same problems as their colleagues at home: the grim reality of slow promotion, low pay, sinking prestige and sheer boredom. Recruitment tailed off: the 100 Saint-Cyr cadets who chose the colonial army in 1902 dropped to 25 by 1911, leaving one-third of colonial officer vacancies to be filled by men promoted directly from the ranks.[114] Soldiers, too, were more interested in 'the five-franc piece which represents a day's work' than in colonial service.[115] The general crisis which had struck the army was thought 'more accentuated' in the colonial forces.[116]

Ironically, the crisis which had prompted the colonial army's definitive organization, Fashoda, had also ended the British threat to the colonies. France and Britain amicably sliced the remainder of the colonial cake and, in doing so, temporarily put the colonial army out of a job. The colonial army's new vocation for home defence was in part a search for work, an attempt to find a new role to snap it from its torpor. In this search for employment, the Kaiser offered a helping hand. The French attempts to absorb Morocco produced a series of confrontations with Germany which dragged colonial questions into the scope of European diplomacy. Increasingly, colonial officers began to realize that Germany, not Great Britain, posed the greatest threat to the empire. But while a conflict with Britain in 1898 would have been fought out in the colonies, that with Germany would be decided at home. Colonial soldiers had never expected to sit idly in the colonies during a European war, leaving the metropolitan army to duel alone with Germany: even in 1870 the marines had contributed their share of futile heroism to the war effort. But the defence of France now appeared the prime mission.

The entry of the colonial army into France's defence calculations was encouraged by her very weakness compared with Germany. This was forcefully brought home in 1905 when General Pendezec warned the government that the army was in no state to repel an invasion. Six years later the situation was little improved: Joffre told Prime Minister Caillaux at the height of the Agadir crisis that the chances for French arms in a show-down were no better than 70 per cent. Colonial officers argued that the colonial army would add both quantity and quality to French defence. Colonel Mangin's 1910 book, *La Force noire*, pointed out that the colonies contained an inexhaustible supply of manpower to fill France's defence needs. The creation of new units of heavy artillery, automobile transportation and the air corps had strained France's manpower reserves to the breaking point. French defence could only be assured by the massive expansion of native units. Mangin lamented the fact that Algerian colonists afraid to arm mutiny and the Left had combined to sabotage expansion.[117] 'It is no secret that we shall soon lack 50,000 men on the eastern frontier', Colonel Peroz repeated. 'If not upon the colonial army then upon whom can we count to plug this gaping hole?'[118] General Gouraud looked to extract at least two army corps from Africa: 'That will count in the balance on the day – for it will certainly come – when the old score is settled.'[119]

Secondly, colonial apologists argued that their army offered a solid corps of officers and NCOs with battlefield experience not found in France, an echo of colonial-metropolitan tensions within the army. The colonial army had escaped the shock waves of the Dreyfus affair, the shabby treatment of professional soldiers and the degradation of the military ideal through the application of left-wing theories of the 'nation-in-arms'. 'In France, the military spirit is losing ground', Colonel Peroz claimed in 1909.[120] French defence was in the hands of half-trained and perhaps pacifist conscripts: 'What one can see quite clearly is that in the near future this national army [will be] totally unable to guarantee our territorial integrity because it is socially unreliable.'[121] Colonial men believed that their army provided an elite force whose numbers, competence and military spirit would prove the salvation of France. Behind these arguments also lay a desire to justify colonial expansion, increasingly under attack from the Left. Jaurès seized the three-year law debates of 1913 as an excuse to launch an all-out attack on the French take-over of Morocco, arguing that colonial expansion absorbed troops vital for home defence.

While for Lord Salisbury, at least, India was 'a barracks in an oriental sea', French colonialists never succeeded in convincing their countrymen of the empire's potential contribution to French defence before 1914. Despite the obvious military qualities of Algerian troops in the Crimea and in the Franco-Prussian War, Messimy's call for an Algerian army of 100,000 men and Mangin's for an even larger *force noire* fell on deaf ears. In August 1914, only 35,000 Algerians and 30,000 *tirailleurs sénégalais* were under arms.[122] The full exploitation of the empire's manpower resources before and during the Great War was hampered by three factors: doubts expressed by the high command about the solidity of native recruits; fears that conscription would provoke a colonial rebellion; and, lastly, the unwillingness of French settlers to accept the political reforms which must necessarily accompany conscription. French generals were gradually won over by the Algerians and were especially impressed by the Moroccans: the most decorated unit in the French army in the 1914–18 War was a Moroccan unit, but only 23,000 Moroccans fought in the trenches because pacification of their country was not yet complete. However, the high command was less enthusiastic about recruits from south of the Sahara. Black troops were used at Gallipoli, but did not appear on the Western Front in large numbers until 1916, where many suffered horribly from the cold. Despite their valour at Verdun, poor training and leadership caused some black units to falter during the 1917 Nivelle offensive. The application of conscription in Algeria provoked the Batna rebellion toward the end of 1916, which cooled the enthusiasm of colonial officials for the conscription of their wards.

Ironically, it was Clemenceau, by his own reckoning 'the least colonialist of Frenchmen', who breached the barriers to colonial recruitment, not as an act of faith in the empire but as one of desperation. In the bleak days of 1917, the prime minister allowed himself to be convinced by Mangin that the manpower resources of black Africa must be tapped, while Charles Jonnart, president of the *Comité de l'Afrique française*, and Pierre Flandin, chairman of the

Réunion des études Algériennes, told him that Algerian conscription was possible if coupled with reforms guaranteeing the basic political rights of Moslems. 'Better to run risks in Africa than on the front', Clemenceau concluded.[123] The 1918 call-up placed 72,000 blacks and 50,000 Algerians in French uniform without a serious hitch. In all, the French empire provided 518,000 troops and 200,000 war workers for French factories. While this was by any standard a substantial contribution to the French war effort, Mangin claimed that these figures could have been 'easily trebled or quadrupled' if African recruitment had been planned before 1914.[124]

The Great War accomplished for the colonial army what several decades of colonialist propaganda never achieved. The recruitment of French Africa's first great conscript army reassured Frenchmen in the inter-war years that 'La France de 110 millions d'habitants' could stand up to the demographic and economic superiority of Germany.[125] The war also raised the prestige of the colonial army, many of whose officers had climbed to high rank in the war, proof that modern war was the realm of men of character and practical experience rather than of theorists.[126] But perhaps the most important contribution made by colonial soldiers in 1914 was to the nation's psychological preparation for war. Colonial soldiers threw themselves into the task of preparing a generation of Frenchmen for the gruelling test of European war and kindling an offensive spirit in an army anaemic with distrust. The colonies had come home to rejuvenate France.

9

The army and the Nationalist Revival

In the history of the French army before the Great War, 1911 marked a turning point. The Moroccan crisis of that year introduced a new note of urgency into military debates. Beneath the threat of war, politicians like Poincaré, Messimy and Millerand set out to rehabilitate a war machine which had grown rusty from over a decade of neglect and restore the army as the focal point of French patriotism and national pride.

The Nationalist Revival, as the period between the Agadir crisis of 1911 and the outbreak of war has come to be called, was the product of a serious deterioration in Franco-German relations which began with the first Moroccan crisis of 1905. While no threat of war existed, Frenchmen could indulge in a witch-hunt against soldiers, priests and other enemies of the republic. When Germany suddenly appeared as a serious threat to peace, public complacency was shaken. By 1911, when Germany again challenged France over Morocco, French public opinion had hardened – in 1905, few wanted to fight. By 1911, a significant number of people were prepared for a show-down with the Kaiser. This change of attitude had first become apparent at the top. In 1905, the high command had informed the government that the French army had no chance of winning a war with Germany. Two years later, the chief of the general staff, General Hagron, resigned, giving as his reason France's abysmal state of military preparedness which the government seemed in no haste to repair. However, from the 1908 affair of the Casablanca deserters which again strained relations between the two countries, the attitude of leading Radicals toward the army began to mellow: Clemenceau named Foch to command the *Ecole de guerre*, despite his Catholic background, while reports of the annual military budget began to suggest improving the conditions of service for professional soldiers as a means of reviving sagging army morale. With the second Moroccan crisis of 1911, the restoration of military strength had become a first priority among Radical politicians. While one must not exaggerate the scope of the Nationalist Revival which especially influenced the young, the intelligent and the Parisian, by 1911 nationalism had become a significant factor in French politics responsible for the election of Poincaré as president in 1913 and for the passage in that year of the three-year service law.

For the reformist historians of the inter-war years, whose views have never been fundamentally challenged, the Nationalist Revival issued in a catastrophic period of reaction which bolstered the prestige of professional soldiers and, in the words of left-wing historian Georges Michon, 'returned the army to its pre-Dreyfus affair state'.[1] Monteilhet, who sees the history of French military institutions from 1875 to 1914 as 'basically the struggle for survival by the professional army . . . against the nation-in-arms', believed that these three years saw a fundamental shift in the balance of power in favour of the former.[2] The history of the army in the Third Republic is seen as one of a conflict between two systems. The Nationalist Revival announced a reversal of policy which, by pandering to the professional interests of the army, led inexorably to three-year service, the offensive *à outrance*, 'the disdain of heavy artillery, machine guns, field fortifications as well as the worth of reserves'.[3] In short, the politicians of the Nationalist Revival had relinquished the political control over the army conquered so painfully during the Dreyfus affair, and thus condemned Frenchmen in uniform to suffer all of the idiocies, blind prejudices, lack of foresight and slaughter of the war's opening months.

How true a picture is this of military policy in the three years before the war? The politicians in power after 1911, and particularly Alexandre Millerand, war minister for most of 1912, certainly set out to modify many of the policies inaugurated under the André ministry. Conscious that war loomed large, they set themselves the task of restoring the tumbled-down authority of military leaders and rekindling enthusiasm for French defence in a population grown apathetic during decades of peace, while bolstering the badly shaken morale of officers and NCOs. The question of how far they succeeded in restoring patriotism as a fashionable sentiment in the nation at large is answered by other authors. But what of the effect of the Nationalist Revival on the authority of the high command and the morale of the forces?

The reforms of the high command pushed through by Galliffet and André had strengthened the position of the war minister and reduced that of the generals. The chief of the general staff, chosen from among rather junior major generals, was from this period simply a senior ministry functionary without power to command service directors. The vice-president of the *conseil supérieur de la guerre*, who was to command the armies in the field, had no organized staff in peacetime. Nor were the designated corps commanders allowed to organize and train their staffs or to inspect the troops who would make up their wartime commands. This was a system which sprang from the fear of a *coup d'état* rather than one designed to ensure military efficiency.

The obvious weaknesses of this arrangement were exposed in 1911 when the war minister, General Goiran, was questioned in the Senate on the role of the generalissimo. 'There is no generalissimo, there is only a vice-president of the *conseil supérieur de la guerre*', Goiran replied. On the outbreak of war, the vice-president would take command of the principal north-east army group while the chief of the general staff would remain with the war minister in Paris. 'The government must control the overall wartime operations. The war minister is its executor. There are army group commanders, each of whom has a mission.'[4] Senators, deputies and public opinion, shaken by the Moroccan crisis and aware that the French army might not be capable of repelling an invasion, failed to find this answer satisfactory. Goiran's reply brought down the Monis government.

The major task of re-structuring the high command fell to Adolphe Messimy, who replaced Goiran on 27 July 1911, and his successor of 15 January 1912, Alexandre Millerand. Both men sought to make the chief of the general staff the undisputed military chief, answerable to the government through the war minister, and to bolster the power of the *csg* as a central organ of policy making, direction and standardization in the forces. André, in his 1903 reform of the high command, had failed to define the relationship between the vice-president of the *csg* and the chief of the general staff, and resulting constant friction between them sabotaged war planning. The 1911 decree abolishing the vice-presidency noted the defects of the old system: 'The presence of a vice-president isolated and without constant contact with the chief of the army general staff has resulted in an unfortunate overlapping of duties. The chief of the army general staff, who must prepare for war, works independently and without direct contact with the general officer destined to command the principal army group.'[5]

In 1911, Messimy overcame republican fears of strong army leadership and appointed Joffre chief of the general staff. The following year, War Minister Millerand abolished the post of chief of the army general staff to end the bickering between Dubail and Castelnau over their relative functions, leaving Joffre in undisputed command. But how extensive were Joffre's powers? Very extensive indeed, according to Professor David Ralston who argues that Joffre was now even more powerful than his German counterpart: 'The military situation created for Joffre by the 1911 decree in the democratic and republican state of France was actually stronger than that of his counterpart in aristocratic, militaristic Germany, the younger Moltke', Ralston writes. 'Joffre had virtually unlimited power with regard to the army', but even more: 'These . . . steps . . . gave to the army almost complete autonomy within the state.'[6]

The power of the chief of the general staff over the army and the degree of autonomy which the 1911 decree gave the army within the republic, however, was more than a simple question of legal phrasing. These depended ultimately on the personality of the new chief and on the habits and traditions of the forces. Had Messimy's first choice, General Galliéni, not declined the post, the history of the army might possibly have been different. A colonial man who possessed a lively and imaginative mind, Galliéni was well known for his intolerance of the bureaucratic and timorous ways of the metropolitan army. Whether he possessed the ruthlessness to sweep out the Augean Stables which the war ministry had become and to establish the chief of the army as a real power in the republic will never be known, for he reminded Messimy that he was too near retirement to take up a task which would require some years to complete. 'I see two men,' Galliéni told Messimy, 'Pau and Joffre'.

General Pau was the army's candidate. An austere Catholic whose loyal and frank character had won the respect of his fellow officers, he was an excellent administrator. However, his interview with Messimy did not go well. Pau told him that, were he appointed chief of the general staff, he would insist upon taking over the prerogative reserved for the war minister of selecting generals. This was clearly not the man in whom to confide the delicate and sensitive task of leading the army.

The mantle of army leadership fell therefore by default on Joffre. Joffre seems to have been somewhat surprised by Messimy's offer, and well he might have been, for there was little in his background or career which had singled him out for the post of commander-in-chief. A graduate of the *Ecole polytechnique* with a mediocre school record, he owed his rapid promotion to the expansion of the army after 1871 and his colonial service. He was a competent technician, but he frankly acknowledged that he knew nothing of staff work.[7] And this was the man whom Messimy chose as chief of the general staff!

Joffre's ability to impose a coherent tactical doctrine and armaments policy, his 'virtually unlimited power with regard to the army', will be discussed elsewhere. But what of the charge that the Messimy–Millerand reforms 'gave to the army almost complete autonomy within the state'? Even a superficial acquaintance with Joffre's character reveals that he was hardly an empire builder. The traits which had made him a successful and popular soldier – forthrightness, honesty, consideration for subordinates – were positive liabilities in the new world which he now entered, a jungle of parliamentary manoeuvre and clever debate. He could be ruthless, as his axeing of commanders found wanting in 1914 demonstrates. But this soft-spoken, unimaginative and somewhat feckless man was utterly devoid of the ambition and deviousness required to carve out a position of power within the state. Instead, that power was thrust upon him in the crucible of war in 1914.

Nor was it the intention of the leaders of the Nationalist Revival that the army should ever escape their political control. Pau was rejected, Messimy states quite categorically, because the war minister had no intention of relinquishing control over officer promotion. Millerand's critics argue that he deferred too much to the advice of his service chiefs and allowed the conservative officer corps to regain control of military policy. Millerand believed that the role of the war minister was to act as the army's political chief, its defender against attack and arbiter in controversial issues. He had no knowledge of strategy and tactics, nor was he competent to deal with questions of *matériel*. But then few politicians were. The decrees reorganizing the high command simply recognized that the war minister could not be the administrative, technical *and* the political head of the army.

At least, not in the Third Republic, where the war ministry was plagued by instability and inexperience. Appointments often fell to generals and specialists, 27 per cent of whom served only one term of office then quit government altogether. Twelve per cent of foreign ministers and only ten per cent of those who served in the finance and interior ministries had such a brief passage in power.[8] The Dreyfus affair had done nothing to increase the desire among senior army officers to swap a stable command for the rough and tumble of parliamentary debate. Consequently, as before 1899, rather junior divisional commanders were most often named, as was the case with André, Picquart and Goiran. Messimy was scathing in his criticism of the phlegmatic General Brun, war minister in 1910,[9] a view shared by Emile Mayer: 'The man was a real sceptic', he wrote. 'He did not believe that war would break out, so he did as little as possible to prepare for it.'[10] Civilians named to the rue Saint-Dominique were usually selected from among second rank politicians like Messimy, Lebrun and Noulens. Berteaux, a man who had fixed his ambitions on the presidency until a tragic accident cut short his career in 1910, paid little attention to the needs of the army during his two terms as war minister. The main concerns of Etienne, who served six terms as war minister, were colonial, not military: 'No man more ignorant of military affairs has ever occupied the rue Saint-Dominique', Monteilhet said of him.[11] Millerand was the only class politician to sit in the war ministry after Freycinet's resignation.

Politicians in the rue Saint-Dominique often placed the direction of the army low on their list of priorities. Parliamentary sessions, committee meetings, dealing with favour seekers, party or constituency business left ministers little time for the nuts and bolts of ministry business. When in 1905 Jonnart, the governor general of Algeria, attempted to see War Minister Berteaux, he was told that the minister was busy on a speech for a dedication at Mauberge: 'and his private secretary told me how difficult it is to speak in a town where the municipal council is divided in two, where the deputy is a socialist and the councillors are centre–left', Jonnart wrote to Lyautey.

I profoundly shocked him when I timidly suggested that perhaps (I said perhaps!) the Minister should not have accepted to speak at the Mauberge dedication. I am told that between now and 15 October, this extraordinary man must attend *nine* dedications. He obviously has the primary quality of a military leader: endurance. But for me he is invisible when it is a simple question of service matters.[12]

The absence of firm ministerial direction told in the rickety organization of the war ministry and the high command. The ministry's 14 services and 'directions' worked independently, while the high command counted 11 technical committees and 100 temporary ones, often with identical functions and little inclination to leave the stage. Between them the ministry and the high command employed nearly one-third of France's 330 generals in 1909 in purely administrative jobs.[13] 'It is materially impossible for even a talented and diligent minister to coordinate and direct so many different sections', Gervais, a member of the parliamentary army committee, wrote in the *France militaire* on 15 February 1914. 'With only the minister to coordinate them, they work independently.'

The reorganization of the high command ended the fiction that the war minister could act as a substitute for a chief of the general staff. What it did not do was to make Joffre more independent than Moltke. The difference in the positions of the two men remained fundamental: Joffre was the soldier of a republic answerable to parliament through the war minister, while von Moltke commanded in a garrison state where military considerations increasingly gained the high ground in important policy decisions, owing explanation only to the Kaiser. Millerand and his immediate successors believed it their duty to protect the commander-in-chief from undue political interference, but civilian legal restraints remained and only awaited a Clemenceau to tighten them in the dark days of 1917. In contrast, the German commanders went from strength to strength and ended by ruling their country behind the thinnest trappings of civilian power. While Joffre no doubt had a powerful say in the nominations for top army positions, he found his ability to influence many aspects of military policy, especially concerning armaments, severely limited.[14] Although on paper, the new generalissimo might have extensive powers, in practice war ministers often took decisions without consulting him, while entrenched service directors refused to recognize his authority to dictate an overall scheme of army needs. And, of course, Joffre *always* deferred to the government in questions of strategic planning and the declaration of war, insisting upon a clear directive before he undertook the invasion of Belgium.[15] Schlieffen and his successors hardly worried about such diplomatic niceties, giving assurances to Austrian Chief of Staff Conrad of German support in any war with Serbia, openly pressing for war with France, demanding the invasion of Belgium as a military necessity and slamming the door in the face of the last bids for peace in 1914. In Germany, the influence of soldiers in policy decisions was immense; in France, the republic left them in no doubt about who was in charge. The republic did not forfeit control of its soldiers in 1912, as Ralston and others have argued. Joffre's relative independence from government control dated from his victory on the Marne, which transformed him overnight into a national hero.

In 1912 Millerand stated categorically that, in a war, the government directed the overall strategy while the soldiers conducted operations designed to achieve the goals of that plan: 'In short, one can say that the government *directs the war*, leaving the *conduct of operations* to the supreme command.'[16] This hardly spells a doctrine of independence from civilian control. On the contrary, the Nationalist Revival strengthened government control over the conduct of military policy: the *comité supérieur de la défense nationale* was re-constituted in July 1911 to include the ministers most concerned with defence and mobilization as well as top generals, admirals and civil servants with the goal of unifying and rationalizing defence policy. Millerand also divided the great general staff and ministry bureaux into a mobile section to leave with the generalissimo on the outbreak of war and a sedentary group to remain in Paris with the war minister:

The sedentary section which will remain with the Minister is aware of all of the questions of organization, mobilization, concentration and preparation and is able to furnish all the useful information as well as, of course, the deputy chiefs of the general staff . . . [two of which] aware of all of the questions considered at the general staff remain in Paris next to the Minister.[17]

Millerand failed to realize, however, that the conduct of operations themselves was bound to have political consequences. His refusal to check the bloody futility of Joffre's 'nibbling' strategy in the war's first two years gradually built up resentment which tumbled the commander-in-chief and brought Père-la-Victoire to power on the crest of a growing belief that 'war is too important to be left to the generals'.[18]

A revitalized and strengthened *conseil supérieur de la guerre* set out to coordinate vital military reforms. 'The great merit of the 28 July 1911 decree', Millerand told the Chamber on 22 March 1912, '... is precisely to have united, tied together, these two indispensable organs of war preparation which for twenty years were isolated: the *conseil supérieur de la guerre* and the general staff.'[19] Virtually moribund since its creation in 1872, the *conseil supérieur de la guerre* was revived by Freycinet in 1888, 'to coordinate and centralise the work undertaken to strengthen the army and national defence'.[20] The task proved a difficult one. 'They do not train the high command seriously', Messimy wrote in 1907.[21] Among its twelve members were the designated army commanders, although neither the armies nor the army staffs existed in peace time. On 27 February 1901, André abolished their right to inspect the corps which could make up their wartime commands in the conviction that local commanders could best judge their own troops, so eliminating an important element of central control and standardization.[22] Army commanders were named only provisionally and army organization was limited to an annual meeting between the designated army leader and his staff chief for a map exercise.[23] Messimy's 28 July 1911 decree reinstated inspections by members of the *conseil supérieur de la guerre*, strengthening their powers over the troops who would make up their wartime command, bolstering the authority of the future army commanders, so vital in an army which admitted no rank above that of major general. The nuclei of the army staffs were also created.[24] When the Left complained that these reforms blessed the army with too much potentially dangerous independence, Millerand replied that army discipline and loyalty were beyond question and that military efficiency, not politics, should dictate military reform. He brushed aside charges that he had reinstalled a covey of pro-clerical generals in the rue Saint-Dominique and told the *Radical* on 21 September 1912:

> General Castelnau has never been involved in any placement of personnel: his sole mission is the preparation of the army for its great tasks, and it is impossible not to recognize the great technical abilities which he exercises in carrying out his task. General Joffre is responsible for controlling nominations and General Legrand, chief of the general staff on an equal footing with General Castelnau, prepares with the generalissimo all of the promotion lists and personnel movement. Now, General Legrand is not, I imagine, suspect by the republicans; nor General Joffre.

Political leaders looking over their shoulders at the time of the Agadir crisis feared that a decade's obsession with political loyalty had compromised the quality of the high command. As influence had replaced ability in the promotion stakes under the André ministry, the quality of leadership had declined. Candidates for high office had to please in high places, whether this meant putting on a republican face or simply avoiding causing their patrons embarrassment. Joffre had been named generalissimo not because he was the best candidate but because he was a 'Republican' officer. Senior army positions were soon occupied by officers who had staked out careers in the ministry or in the corridors of parliament.

The sorry state of French military leadership was a matter of open discussion. Already in 1904 Lyautey had noticed that Radical attacks upon the army had undermined the confidence of commanders.[25] The conservative *Porte-Voix* noted on 11 February 1912:

When you compare the generals of 15 or 20 years ago to those of today, you are struck by the inferiority of the latter . . . line officers are frequently amazed by the feebleness of their appointed leaders. Ill-at-ease in the field, they are utterly incompetent and at sea in regimental service . . . In short . . . the products of the presidential and ministerial ante-chambers do not exactly shine.[26]

An inspection report by General Dubail in November 1913, just months before the outbreak of war, said that top officers were 'timid and indecisive . . . Nowhere do they act with resolution. We must develop character, a taste for risk and responsibility.'[27]

French generals, with an average age of 61 in 1903 against 54 in Germany,[28] were often too old or too ill to campaign. But officers refused to denounce them and they stayed on . . . and on. On 1 November 1910, the *Porte-Voix* estimated that at least 30 generals, 20 colonels, 25 lieutenant colonels, 80 majors and 100 captains were physically unfit to campaign. But a stern letter from War Minister Brun before the 1910 manoeuvres had resulted in the retirement of only two colonels, two lieutenant colonels, sixteen majors and six captains. Messimy complained on 27 July 1911 that 'ministerial orders have for too long remained a dead letter', and ordered into retirement any officer unable to ride a horse. He met with no more success than did Brun. Emile Mayer reckoned that had this measure been strictly applied, the corpulent Joffre, whose efforts to mount a horse provided an early morning pick-up for his neighbours, would have been among the first to collect his pension. The *Cri de Paris* published a cartoon of a general ordering a captain to list officers unable to campaign: 'Of course, general', the captain replied. 'Shall I place you on the list?'[29]

Manoeuvres provided sad testimony to the declining quality of French leadership. After viewing those of 1905, Gervais, a member of the Parliamentary army committee, wrote: 'Our leaders were obviously poorly trained . . . in practice, many generals, caught unprepared, lacked composure, judgement and common sense . . . I have no wish to enumerate all the mistakes I have seen . . . some of them worse than absurd.'[30]

One of the two generals chosen to lead a manoeuvre army each year between 1909 and 1914 had reached the retirement age.[31] Autumn manoeuvres, a dry run for war, were thus transformed into an elaborate retirement ceremony. In 1912 manoeuvres climaxed on the third day when army commander General Galliéni captured his opposite number, General Marion, his entire staff, one of his corps commanders and his staff, the corps artillery and four aeroplanes.[32] In 1913, both commanders retired soon after manoeuvres finished. Jaurès complained in 1910:

The grand manoeuvres are nothing but a parade where military leaders hope to be noticed, not through good planning and organisation, but by the press and politicians. The point is not who best directs his forces to achieve precise goals, but who will have the most influential newspaper editor in his car . . . The best part of their strategy goes into press campaigns against their rivals, while battalions, regiment and brigades move in a void, without firm direction or goal.[33]

In 1911, Messimy found the top positions at the rue Saint-Dominique in poor hands: 'There now was no-one at the top of this hierarchy. Deprived of real leaders, general staff officers had divided into factions, primarily according to doctrine. Little "sects" had been established.'[34] The generalissimo designate in wartime, General Michel, a product of the ministries and favoured aide-de-camp assignments, was 'terrified of responsibility'. The chief of the army general staff, Laffon de Ladébat, was 'a perfect bureaucrat'.[35]

Messimy and Millerand sought to recast the high command, but found their ability to dismiss incompetent generals limited. Joffre pointed out that once a general was named, it was virtually impossible to sack him: 'When it is a question of eliminating a general for professional incompetence, the war minister is almost entirely disarmed in the present state of our legislation', he wrote to the war minister in October 1911.[36] Consequently, Messimy was forced to fall back upon the inadequate expedient of premature retirement for the grey and the unfit.

Although, before the wholesale purges of August–September 1914, Messimy, Millerand and Joffre could do little to eliminate incompetent leaders, they sought to bolster the military competence of the army's next generation of generals. On 9 January 1912, Messimy told members of the *conseil supérieur de la guerre* that he expected a frank appreciation of officers whom they were to inspect: 'In spite of the observations and the repeated orders of the minister, the reports on officers still do not give an exact idea of their true worth', he wrote.

Usually written in terms marked by a vague and unenlightening kindness, generally silent on the defects of the officers and on their physical and intellectual shortcomings, sometimes manifestly exaggerating their qualities, they do not supply the minister with sufficient information which permits him to single out meritorious officers from those whose career has gone far enough or even who should be eliminated. This situation is particularly serious where the promotion of colonels and generals is concerned.[37]

Millerand set out to correct the abuses in the promotion system introduced by the Radicals, which he believed had pushed the wrong men to the top: 'The goal is to assure the recruitment of generals who are competent', he noted after a conversation with General Pau. 'It is a question of 500 officers. Ten years ago, we could have found competent men by the hundreds. For promotion, the only rule must be absolute order of merit; all questions of age, seniority, campaigns are abstract.'[38]

On 25 January 1912, Millerand abolished prefectorial notes on the political opinions of officers, to limit the influence of politics in promotion calculations. He then withdrew, except in exceptional circumstances, an officer's right, accorded in 1905, to see the efficiency report on him drawn up by his superior. In this way, he hoped that banal reports would give way to a more candid appreciation of an officer's qualities.[39] He re-established promotion committees at various points in the hierarchy, capped in each army and service by a council containing generals from outside the Paris garrison to break the hold of the capital and ministry on officers promotion. He vowed to stick closely to their recommendations.[40] An 11 January 1913 circular encouraged corps commanders to discuss their promotion recommendations with their subordinate commanders rather than simply gather them together to read them out.[41]

Promotion chances were also affected by garrison assignments. Officers in and near Paris enjoyed a higher promotion rate, while the crack sixth corps on the German frontier ironically had the lowest rate.[42] 'The Paris garrison and the large cities are reserved for those protected by the powers of the day', the *Porte-Voix* complained on 11 March 1912. Millerand ordered a more frequent turnover of Paris personnel, but like the orders of so many of his predecessors these too fell on deaf ears at the war ministry. Charles Humbert complained in the *France militaire* on 1 February 1912 that the worst graduates of the officer schools were packed off to eastern garrisons, while generals regarded an eastern command as a punishment, a statement which was only partially true. Millerand also promised to favour eastern garrisons for promotion and decorations.[43] However, this did little to loosen the iron grip staff officers held upon promotion. In 1910, 9.6 per cent of brevet staff captains serving infantry regiments were promoted to major, against 1.3 per cent of non-brevet captains. The figures were 9.3 per cent against 1.5 per cent in 1911 and 11.75 per cent against 1.2 per cent in 1912.[44] The surest tickets to promotion were those of an aide-de-camp or a ministerial assignment. Of 130 infantry captains promoted to major in 1906, 23 were aides-de-camp. In the same year, eighteen per cent of all infantry captains who were aides-de-camp were promoted while barely two per cent of infantry captains otherwise employed moved up.[45] In 1910, 34.5 per cent of the captains serving in the infantry department of the war ministry received discretional promotions to major; in 1911, the figure shot up to 62.5 per cent.[46] These figures went down slightly under Millerand,[47] but favoured positions in the ministry, military schools and other special assignments were well rewarded.

The men who felt the warm breath of war in 1911 feared that they might be forced to fight it with an army whose morale had bottomed out. Millerand capitalized on the mood of public resentment over German bullying at Agadir in July 1911 and over the November signing of the Franco-German agreement on Morocco, the Congo and the Cameroons to encourage a martial spirit in the nation with weekly military parades in garrison towns. A 2 March 1912 military retreat in Paris drew an estimated 10,000 spectators. Those in Nancy, Lyon and other towns were equally spectacular, only occasionally marred by anti-militarist counter-demonstrations.[48] 'Do not think that the restored tattoo is mere child's play, it is the sign of a revival', the *Echo de Paris* wrote.[49] From June 1912, drums and bugles, abolished by Picquart in 1906, once more punctuated daily regimental routine 'in order to give barrack life a gaiety and an animation desirable from all points of view'.[50]

But the politicians of the Nationalist Revival realized that it would take far more than noise to raise the morale of the armed forces. Historians have noted that army morale hit its nadir during Clemenceau's first ministry, but they have not pointed out that it continued to bump along rock bottom until August 1914 and that one of the major results was the first tentative steps toward unionization of professional soldiers.

A fierce battle to unionize teachers and civil servants had been fought during Clemeneau's first ministry, and soldiers could hardly be blamed if they began to move toward the sound of the guns, especially after the *Vincennoise* had pressed so effectively for a new deal for administration officers. 'The administration officers have obtained . . . some very substantial advantages in the last few years, and no one can blame them: they have triumphed because of the cohesion of their assault upon governmental favours', the *France militaire* wrote on 11 October 1905. 'Encouraged by their success . . . now perhaps they are going too far, or too fast, in their claims.' In 1904, André stifled an attempt to form a 'union of officers promoted from the ranks', while in 1907, Picquart forbade the *'Union des sociétés des officiers'*, an umbrella organization grouping the military school mutualist societies, fearing that it might actively fight for military reforms.[51] In 1909, the war ministry founded a *'Société nationale de secours mutuels'*[52] probably hoping to undercut the *Saint-Cyrienne*, *Versaillaise* and other mutualist officer societies which were beginning to act as vehicles for officer discontent.

By 1909, officer grumblings began to take on more serious manifestations. Not surprisingly, the first shock waves came from the colonial army where the traditional complaints against Radical military policies combined with slow promotion to produce a crisis in a force where career expectations were high. Discontent was directed both at politicians and at generals, who, it was felt, had done little to protect the interests of their subordinates. In the atmosphere of the post-Dreyfus affair army, only conscripts, not professionals, were worthy of the attentions of generals.[53] Promotion, they claimed, went almost exclusively to staff officers, aides-de-camp, and the well-connected: 'One can say that favouritism counts for five tenths, nepotism four tenths and merit one tenth.' An attempt by colonial officers at Toulon to set up 'study centres' in each colonial regiment to send delegates to a Paris conference crumbled when General Archinard persuaded officers that they must look to their military superiors to protect their interests. However, Toulon police reported that officer discontent again raised its head in 1911 with the Raiberti bill to fuse the colonial and metropolitan armies.[54] Attempts to direct discontent in colonial regiments never got off the ground, but they did cause the government some concern: 'Since [1909], many southern garrisons, particularly Toulon and Perpignan, have been the scene of the same sort of agitation', the war minister wrote to the prime minister in 1911. 'In any case, this agitation was never so serious that the military authorities had to intervene . . . It is also true that the turnover of personnel in colonial regiments makes the creation of permanent associations more difficult.'[55]

The organization of metropolitan officers presented a more serious threat: 'It is hardly surprising that the soldiers, who feel abandoned, who are not organized . . . feel tempted to give themselves the same power as other servants of the nation', wrote Paul Boncour, deputy for the Loire-et-Cher, in 1909.[56] Demands to organize officers reached a peak in 1911–12. In February 1911, a group of officers promoted through the ranks claimed that unionization was the only way to force the gates of the army's senior grades: 'We demand not to be systematically sacrificed and shoved aside in the promotion lists', read their manifesto. 'There is but one way, dear comrades, to be heard, and this consists, without prejudicing our professional duties, that is remaining respectful and disciplined, in having but one unified leadership, one unified tactic . . . Dispersed, we are ineffective, without cohesion, consequently powerless. Think what authority a group like ours could have.'[57] Messimy broke up the *Union centrale* in 1911 by scattering its organizers to the four winds[58] while an attempt by the editor of the socialist *Petit-Var* at Toulon to form a naval officers' union was crushed by police who surrounded the café where officers had been invited to an 'apéritif de solidarité'.[59] In March 1911, Radical General Pédoya attacked retired right-wing Major Driant's *ligue militaire*, which claimed a membership of 635 officers and 63 generals, focusing parliamentary attention on the growing dissatisfaction in the officer corps.

The 14 March debate woke up many to the new mood of militancy in the forces: 'Despite the government, one can fear that soon there will be powerful associations in the forces with which one must negotiate', *Le Temps* wrote on 20 March 1911. Although officer associations like the *ligue militaire* generally grouped retired officers to place them beyond the reach of the government:

their influence can be exerted over young serving officers. But what is disturbing in the army . . . is that the attitudes of officers have changed entirely over the past few years. It is not the attitudes of generals or of men serving in high military positions which have been modified, but those of subalterns, lieutenants and captains. Whether they come from Saint-Cyr or through the ranks, they are unanimous in declaring that the hour for associations and groups has arrived for them. What is the origin of this change? From several causes, first of which is incontestably that the prestige of the uniform is much diminished in France. Have we not also for the last few years debased too much the merit and the mission of officers? . . . If the prestige of the officer has disappeared little by little in the nation, it is even more evident that his authority in the barracks has become more and more precarious.

It was this new mood of militancy in the armed forces, the feeling among professional soldiers that they had for too long been treated unfairly by the government and by their own leaders, which worried many politicians. The Leroy committee formed to investigate the growth of NCO 'friendly societies' in Paris and other garrisons in 1911 concluded in October 1912 that the forces had only narrowly escaped unionization.[60] Ajam, deputy for the Sarthe and a member of the parliamentary army committee, also reckoned that unless the government took steps to rectify fundamental professional grievances, unionization for the forces was certain.

As if to underline his point, newspapers specializing in military affairs buried their substantial political differences to co-ordinate a campaign for political rights for officers. A poll carried out by the left-wing *Armée et Démocratie* in 1911 revealed that the overwhelming mass of officers called for the same political rights as other citizens: 8,589 officers wanted to be given the vote, against only 221 who did not. 6,541 called for officers to be allowed to run for office against 2,728 who thought it a bad idea.[61] 'Professional soldiers have no way to defend their material and moral interests', the newspaper wrote. 'They constitute a group of untouchables in the nation.'[62] Captain d'Arbeaux pointed out the inconsistency of calling upon officers to lead the moral regeneration of the country and then refusing them basic political rights, an attitude which made the question asked in 1910 of prospective Saint-Cyr cadets, 'describe the different voting methods in France since 1789', something of a joke.[63] Jaurès, too, complained in the *Armée nouvelle* published in 1910 that the refusal to give professional soldiers the right to vote had entrenched a 'spirit of clan, routine and intrigue' in the forces.[64]

Radicals hotly opposed political rights for officers: 'If by some misfortune they acquire any political influence . . . the era of pronunciamentos will be open', Ajam told parliament.[65] However, pressure continued to mount, even from the Left, to give all soldiers the right to vote: 'The exercise of civic rights abolished by the accomplishment of the first of civic rights, that of defending the city of the Fatherland!' cried Guesde. 'What a contradiction not to say aberration.'[66] The *France militaire* claimed that deputies would only wake up to the needs of the army and soldiers recover their confidence once the officers conquered the vote.[67]

Unions never really threatened to take root in the officer corps: a strong middle-class aversion to unions, respect for the traditional military hierarchy and, above all, government repression combined to weigh against the campaign for unionization. On 4 September 1912, Millerand simply forbade soldiers to join Driant's *ligue militaire*. But professional grievances continued, a smouldering revolt which could only be quenched by reforms to prove to officers that the army was back in favour with the power elite.

The unionization debate was important, not because unions threatened to sweep the officer corps but because they forced the government toward reforms destined to raise the prestige and the morale of professional soldiers, to demonstrate to officers that the government and the military chiefs, not union organizers, were their real patrons.

Millerand's 24 July 1912 decree abolishing many of the advantages won by administration officers was designed to deflate the influence of the *Vincennoise*, demonstrating to combat officers that organized pressure group activities no longer influenced government military policy. 'I decided to use all my powers to finish with a practice which threatened to destroy the army', he said of this decree.[68] His 2 January 1913 order forbidding officers to contribute to any fund destined to further professional military interests tried to dry up money paid by administration officers to support pressure group activities.[69]

'The Millerand reforms soon appeared to be sops to the General Staff who were seeking revenge for the Dreyfus affair and the republican military reforms carried out since 1899', wrote George Michon.[70] But Millerand's substantial programme of military reform was not a gift from conservative politicians to professional soldiers, an attempt to tip the scales against the 'nation-in-arms', but was forced upon them by the realization that unless steps were taken to rectify basic professional grievances, the government might face a trauma of unionization in the forces which would make those of teachers and postal workers look trivial in comparison.

Millerand's reforms set out to remedy many of the basic grievances which fed the army's morale crisis and to hoist army prestige back onto the pedestal from which it had been tipped in 1899. The uniform provided a visible symbol of this determination. He reinstated the infantry epaulette abolished by Messimy and strictly curtailed the wearing of civilian dress, especially for NCOs and soldiers: 'Civilian dress can expose NCOs to unfortunate temptations and push them to expenses which they cannot afford', he wrote. 'These temptations are especially troublesome for young NCOs.'[71]

This coupling of the uniform with military prestige had unfortunate consequences, for it undercut attempts to introduce a camouflaged battledress adopted by most other European armies before 1914. The question had been under study since 1899, and in 1911 three regiments were kitted out with a less target-worthy green for the autumn manoeuvres. The Right, however, denounced any attempt to put the traditional red trousers in storage as a deliberate coup against military panache. The *Echo de Paris* typically believed the dull colours to be the fruits of a masonic plot: 'The camouflaged uniform ... seems calculated to diminish [the army's] already compromised prestige', it complained on 2 October 1911. 'Thus the goals of the masonic covens are achieved.' The green uniform was discarded in December 1911 after Clémentel, the budget reporter, complained that the camouflaged uniform 'went against both French taste and against the needs of the army ... The red trousers have something national about them.' War Minister

Etienne was more categorical: 'Abolish red trousers?' he asked the parliamentary army committee in 1913. 'No! Red trousers, c'est la France!' Credits for camouflaged uniforms were voted only 15 days before the outbreak of war.[72]

Millerand turned his attention to rebuilding officer corps solidarity badly shaken since 1899. In July 1912 he re-established the obligatory mess for bachelor lieutenants, abolished by André in 1903 after a poll of corps commanders found only one who opposed it. He also attempted to tighten army discipline. Radicals had set their sights on a root and branch reform of the court martial since the Dreyfus affair. In November 1912, Millerand intervened in the Senate to modify reforms proposed by the Chamber to send many military cases to civil tribunals and considerably soften the penalties. 'Even Switzerland has court martials', he told senators.[73] Court martials were reprieved by the German attack of 1914. Millerand also upset a 1905 law which had dumped many men convicted of civilian crimes straight into the regiments rather than into the disciplinary *bataillons d'Afrique*, leading many to associate the increasing indiscipline in the forces with the influx of men with prison records.[74] Discipline companies attached to each regiment to take men who bent unwillingly to military life were reorganized in areas away from the civilian population and more suitable for training.[75] Corporals, sergeants and lieutenants had the right to punish soldiers, removed in May 1910, restored on the condition that each punishment was confirmed by the company commander after hearing the soldier: 'The right to punish is a corollary ... which must be considered one of the prerogatives inseparable from authority', read the 13 May 1912 decree. However, officers were required to keep some of their number on duty in the barracks at all times.[76]

The abusive application of other Radical reforms was also brought to heel. Co-operatives set up by André both to keep soldiers off the streets and to teach them the value of common enterprise had, Millerand complained, 'exceeded little by little the precise and limited goals established by ... my predecessors'. Once officers realized the enormous profits to be made, co-operatives spread like wildfire and with them incidents of drunkenness and, to a lesser degree, graft. Charles Humbert complained that the co-operatives, originally meant to be morally uplifting, had degenerated into low cabarets 'where the soidiers stroll from one to another in a sort of Grand Duke's round with the corporals leading the dance. The cases of drunkenness are numerous and ... alcoholism replaces the games of cards, backgammon and billiards which we thought we were encouraging.'[77] Humbert also complained that they creamed off men, especially NCOs, who would be more usefully employed in training.[78] Millerand limited each regiment to one co-operative, forbade the sale of alcoholic drinks formerly permitted mainly to boost the receipts of depressed south-western wine growers and ordered profits to be paid into regimental funds or beneficial activities rather than into soldiers' pockets.[79] He also gave the right to permit leave, especially for agricultural work, back to regimental commanders. A 23 August 1910 circular had required prefects to determine which soldiers would be permitted home for the harvests. On 28 June 1912, several deputies claimed that this system had led to abuse, with the best-connected rather than the most needy allowed home.[80]

Millerand was forced to resign on 12 January 1913 after the reintegration into the territorial army railway troops of Lieutenant colonel du Paty de Clam, a prominent anti-Dreyfusard retired from the army in 1906, provoked a political storm among deputies who claimed that Millerand was handing the army to the forces of reaction. In his defence, Millerand pointed out that he was simply honouring a promise made by his two immediate predecessors to admit du Paty de Clam into the territorials if he dropped a standing complaint against the war ministry. Millerand stuck on a 'question of honour' and so forfeited his portfolio.[81] Paléologue blamed Poincaré's 'inexcusable weakness' for Millerand's departure: 'The effect abroad of Millerand's brusque resignation is deplorable', he told Briand. 'They will be dancing in Berlin.'[82]

Historians have claimed that the passage of Messimy and Millerand through the rue Saint-Dominique had a 'tonic effect' upon army morale.[83] Certainly, the *Porte-Voix* noticed a revival of morale in the army in 1912, stimulated by fears of war in the population and by a renewed interest in military reform in government circles.[84] But while ministry officers and generals close to power perhaps appreciated a new determination to bolster national defence, it is unlikely that this filtered through to provincial garrisons. Eugen Weber noted that the Nationalist Revival was a Parisian phenomenon which only occasionally touched the provinces.[85] Military newspapers, even the pro-government *France militaire*, continued to point out that military life had retained all its servitudes but little of its grandeur.[86] While Messimy's reform of the high command did something to prepare the army to counter the Schlieffen plan, officers could not be expected to take to their bosom a man who had pitched his political appeal on the defiance of his military superiors: 'Jealous of their stars, this ex-captain of *chasseurs à pied* treated our generals as underlings without importance', the *Porte-Voix* complained after the fall of Messimy's ministry.[87] He was remembered not for his reorganization of the high command but for his request for prefectorial reports on the political opinions of officers and even the religious habits of their wives: '[The officer] is fed up with knowing that his career, already difficult enough, is at the mercy of information taken from unknown sources', the *Porte-Voix* wrote on 12 January 1912. Emile Mayer thought Messimy: 'a light-weight politician, inconsistent, who believed that his time spent in the army and the two years at the *Ecole de guerre* should be taken seriously and who took himself for a real soldier'.[88] According to his son Jacques, Alexandre Millerand believed Messimy to be 'un agité, un peu fou', an opinion given substance by Messimy's repeated letters to Joffre during 1914, demanding that officers found wanting be dragged before a firing squad.[89] Historians have claimed that Millerand courted army popularity by acting as the agent for the desires of the high command. However, Joffre argued that Millerand did not consult his generals enough: one of his first acts in January 1912 was to slash a promised 240 million francs in extra credits, earmarked for vital improvements in artillery and training camps painfully squeezed out of Messimy, to 50 million after a single tête-à-tête with Finance Minister Krantz.[90]

Nor were many of Millerand's reforms popular in the forces, however well intentioned or useful they might have been. The obligation to remain in barracks at night, the restrictions placed upon the wearing of civilian clothes, garrison rotations which hit the pockets of married officers and NCOs, the abolition of the right to see personal files and charges of promotional favouritism which were thought especially bad under Messimy, caused the *Porte-Voix* to lump Millerand with the worst war ministers: 'Millerand's work can be summed up in a few lines', it wrote on 20 January 1913. 'He looked to terrorize officers by every means. Did he succeed? Yes!'

Raoul Girardet believed that the army recovered quickly from a 'brief' crisis at the beginning of the century.[91] Rather, the Dreyfus affair can be seen as the beginning of a long crisis of morale which continues even today, a period only briefly punctuated by the Great War. After a very short victory celebration in 1918, the army again fell from fashion, attacked from the Left, held in low esteem by the middle class and stumbling from defeat to defeat.

'Millerand, at the ministry of war, was doing his best to save the confidence of the people in its army and of the army in itself', wrote Weber.[92] But the confidence of many professional soldiers in the government remained low. The three-year-law riots of 1913 demonstrated that officers had yet to shake out the wrinkles of the morale crisis and that their authority over their troops wobbled even in the patriotic eastern garrisons. Coming on the heels of a year of intense agitation surrounding the Aenoult affair, which saw over 100,000 people attend the dead soldier's funeral, the three-year-law riots revealed an army whose nerves were still frayed. On 29 March 1913, meetings were held throughout France to protest against the government's proposed additional service year.[93] When the cabinet announced in May that conscripts would be retained in the forces beyond their statutory two years' service, several garrisons erupted with discontent. In Toul, 200 soldiers shouted 'Hou! Hou! les trois ans!' and dispersed only after 25 were arrested. Soldiers at Belfort and Nancy sang the *Internationale*. Both Rodez and Mâcon witnessed demonstrations by up to 300 soldiers.[94] Twenty garrisons reported serious trouble[95] while many others recorded a 'restlessness' which threatened to break into open revolt.[96]

Noting the presence in many infected eastern garrisons of large contingents of Parisians, officials suspected that anti-militarists had carefully prepared the ground for these revolts. 'We are not faced with a military mutiny, but with a political movement', General Pau, sent to investigate the disorders, reported.[97] Pichon told Paléologue that the *CGT* had stirred the conscripts' revolt[98] while the police reckoned that 'the incidents at Toul and Belfort, which will probably occur in other garrisons, are nothing but the logical outcome of propaganda'.[99] Many Paris newspapers also bought and sold an anti-militarist conspiracy.

On 25 May, the minister of the interior asked prefects to forward the names of known anti-militarists serving in the troubled regiments and lists of *Bourses du travail* or *Unions des syndicats* in garrison towns. One Paris regiment claimed to have 17 syndicalists in its ranks. Otherwise only one of 28 regiments which had experienced trouble listed as many as two known anti-militarists; four regiments had one each. Of 20 garrison towns reporting trouble, only five had a *Bourse du travail* and six a *Union des syndicats*. Toul and Rodez, where the worst disorders had been reported, listed no militant anti-militarists either in the regiments or in the civilian population.[100] The trial of five soldiers accused of leading the demonstrations at Toul revealed that they had no anti-militarist nor trade union connections but were exemplary soldiers.[101] The riots appear to have been a spontaneous eruption of discontent against the announcement of extended service.

Officials, however, remained on their guard, convinced that anti-militarists stood behind the troubles. Paris police raided anti-militarist haunts on 6 June, and when the Left announced plans for large 1 October demonstrations to coincide with the normal departure date of the class of 1910, the war minister, acting on rumours that a large demonstration was being prepared in the 162nd infantry at Verdun, ordered an enquiry into the morale of the eastern garrisons. Police reported that army morale was good, but urged the government to set a definite liberation date for the 1910 class.[102] Poincaré predicted mass desertions on the day the conscript class should be liberated.[103] On 2 October, the day after the class should have been sent home, the prefect of the

Haute-Sâone reported that no CGT agents had turned up to incite soldiers and that garrisons had remained calm.[104]

Historians have tended to skip over the 1913 riots, ignoring them as slight ripples in the mounting tide of the Nationalist Revival. But while the riots were undoubtedly isolated events springing from a very understandable disinclination on the part of many conscripts to remain under the colours indefinitely, many at the time saw the riots as cast-iron proof of the progress of anti-militarism in the French ranks and of the basic lack of patriotism in the country: 'Incidents of collective insubordination are multiplying to a terrifying degree', one German newspaper reported to its readers. 'This wave of anti-militarism demonstrates how much patriotic sentiment has declined in France.'[105] The Kaiser was delighted that a measure so obviously calculated to show French resolve in the face of German military expansion had backfired: 'How can you ally with the French?' he asked the Czar, on a visit to Berlin in May 1913. 'Don't you see that the Frenchman is no longer capable of becoming a soldier?'[106] Poincaré was thrown into a depression so black that he even threatened to ask his arch-enemy Clemenceau, 'as patriotic as the Jacobins of 1793', to form a government if Barthou were overthrown on the three-year-law.[107]

The riots also revealed an officer corps whose faith in itself and in its leaders had not been strengthened by the Nationalist Revival. For many, 1913 was simply 1907 six years on: 'I was saddened and struck during the recent mutinies less by the anger of the soldiers than by the reserve of the officers', wrote Edmond de Mesnil. 'They seemed to me to lack initiative and decisiveness . . . I believe that their failure to act and their resignation revealed a fear of responsibilities which betrays a crisis of morale.'[108]

Typically, the government blamed the officers for failing to snuff out the mutiny rather than their own ill-advised decision to retain the 1910 conscript class indefinitely. War Minister Etienne demanded a list of officers 'remote' from their men and tightened surveillance in barracks: more officers were kept on duty at night, leave was suspended and restrictions placed upon the wearing of civilian clothes. Several regiments were transferred to Algeria and Corsica and a double dose of training was ordered for others. 'In some places, the life of officers and NCOs has become hell', the *Porte-Voix* complained on 1 July.

In the final analysis, the Nationalist Revival, far from restoring the army's confidence, appeared only to emphasize how far army morale had slipped: military unions, continued resignations of well-qualified officers, especially polytechnicians, low pay, slow promotion, a shortfall in NCO recruitment and the widely held belief that many regiments were rotten with anti-militarism as shown by the 1913 riots all demonstrated that morale had not crawled from the abyss into which it had fallen after 1900. Had politicians really looked to conquer military affection, they should have rewritten Clemenceau's deeply resented precedence decree of 1907. But even Millerand did not alter that. Professional soldiers might be forgiven for failing to distinguish the Messimys and Millerands, who for years carried the torch of antimilitarism, from those who now claimed to be stoking the flames of French patriotism.

Nor did the Nationalist Revival restore the authority of the high command. It is simply ludicrous to suggest, as does Ralston, that Joffre was more powerful than Moltke. The government may have become reconciled in the face of the growing German threat to name a chief of the general staff. But Joffre's authority was hedged by so many safeguards – not the least of which was his personality and lack of experience – that the army continued to function, or not to function, largely as before. War ministers and ministry officials often simply ignored him. For his part Joffre considered himself simply as 'a direction equal to other directions', who could request and supplicate, but whose ability to command was circumscribed.

10

The three-year law

A second generally held misconception about the Nationalist Revival is that it built up the professional army to the detriment of the 'nation-in-arms'. Nowhere was this more apparent than in the three-year service law of 1913. By boosting the number of men on active service, soldiers showed their disdain for the fighting qualities of reservists and their preference for an offensive led by highly trained professional troops. 'After the three-year law, [the reserves'] role would become absolutely secondary', wrote Monteilhet, who claimed that 'the reserves declined with the abusive extension of the regular army'.[1] For Michon, too, the law testified to 'the disdain ... of the worth of reserves'.[2]

But the 1913 law again demonstrated the essentially pragmatic approach to military reform of the immediate pre-war years. The three-year service law was a serious if hastily improvised and somewhat mismanaged attempt to remedy many of the glaring defects of French army organization. Far from strengthening the professional cadres to the detriment of the reserves, as historians like Monteilhet and Michon have claimed, the law recognized the reserves as an essential component of French defence and sought to put muscle into that dangerously weak force.

Politicians of the Nationalist Revival argued that a strong professional cadre was the first requirement of a useful reserve. The 1912 infantry cadre law, the three-year service law and the improvement of the railway network all aimed at a more efficient use of the reserves.[3] '[The reserves'] importance is linked to the number of regular units, for it depends upon the number of regular cadres able to lead them', wrote Joffre. 'The reorganization of our reserve formations aimed to make them more supple and improve their cadres, allowing us to utilize them earlier alongside our regular troops ... The cadre laws ... in particular that concerning the infantry, aimed essentially to organize more solidly the cadres and leadership of reservists and permitted us to use several reserve divisions in the front lines.'[4] Plan XVII approved in May 1913 boosted the number of reserve divisions employed in the front lines from 22 to 25.[5]

Millerand readily admitted that his 1912 cadre law, which created ten new infantry regiments and a complementary cadre of officers destined to staff reserve units on mobilization, was calculated to boost promotion and to raise the quality of the officer corps. But he saw no contradiction in taking steps to end the serious officer 'recruitment crisis . . . assuring the command from a moral point of view the maximum force and prestige from the bottom to the top [of the hierarchy]' and strengthening the reserves. 'The principal object of the bill . . . is the definitive, complete organization of the reserves', he told parliament. 'To do this, to give to the reserve regiments the cadres which are vital, we had to go to the regular army and resurrect the organization of complementary cadres.'[6] The law placed reserve regiments under a regular lieutenant-colonel, gave each reserve battalion a professional major and most companies career captains and six regular NCOs.

The three-year law, like that on infantry cadres, also looked to boost the value of French reserve troops: 'The three-year law provides . . . a marvellous tool to raise the worth of our reserves which the two-year law weakened by destroying the lower cadres', the *France militaire* wrote on 14 July 1914. Even the conservative *Porte-Voix* admitted in the heat of the parliamentary debates that: 'Parliament is above all preoccupied by one idea: the staffing of the reserves.'[7] In April 1913, War Minister Etienne told a Rouen audience:

> As things now stand, we are obliged to mobilize our armies behind inadequate cover forces . . . People also claim that our bill undervalues the utilization and the capital role of the reserves. I reject this claim . . . we want our reserves, which are a very great force, to melt into a well prepared regular army. If the regular army melts into our reserves, the situation changes and our power is diminished. In the conditions created by foreign rearmament, it is essential to create an active, strongly organized cadre for these reserves.[8]

Deputies were unanimous that French reserve forces were potentially excellent, but lacked the firm hand of a trained cadre. In a 2 December 1912 report to the Deputies, Treignier, citing German General Faulkenhausen, pointed out that Germany's increased dependence on her Landwehr meant that France must strengthen her reserve organization. Quoting from the ex-vice-president of the csg, General Lacroix, he said: 'Since 1905, all the reserve regiments brought to the training camps have proved that, without regular cadres, they had only a very limited usefulness . . . the less a force is trained, the more it needs a solid cadre. This is why we need a complementary cadre, earmarked for staffing reserve formations.'[9]

The two-year service law of 1905 had placed France's defence burden squarely upon the shoulders of the reserves. The regular army's primary mission was to train the nation's citizens for war: 'What is the army of today if not a school for reservists?' Senator Rolland, author of the two-year bill, told the Senate in 1902. 'And how can we hope to establish a school for reservists if our regular army is not sufficiently prepared in the skills of war?'[10] Yet it was the very malfunctioning of the military machine under two-year service which weakened the reserves and undermined France's military potential. By improving the quality of the regular army, the government hoped to beef up its reserves.

The 1905 law had stripped the cavalry and the 'special arms' of a third of their combat strength. Because no attempt had been made to adapt a rigid and wasteful army organization to the needs of two-year service, training had been the first casualty. This was especially acute during the winter months when more than half of the army was made up of partially trained conscripts: 'Infantry companies can barely muster 40 men. In the cavalry regiments there are hardly enough men to groom the horses and do the daily chores', Herissé reported to the deputies on 2 June 1913. 'Exercising the horses can barely be carried out under normal conditions in the artillery. Without exaggerating, one can say that each year the French army is disorganized until the day that the new recruits ... can be mobilized, that is until March or April. Until then, the infantry barely exists and the mounted arms do not exist at all.'[11]

Training personnel were in short supply. Problems of NCO re-enlistment, already acute before 1905, were aggravated by the two-year service law. Many believed the temporary soldiers of the two-year law were eager to return to civilian life and forgo an army career. Furthermore, soldiers were now encouraged to join the reserves as NCOs or subalterns rather than re-enlist. Reservists, not regulars, were regarded as the country's principal defence force. Old soldiers found fewer re-enlistment places held for them while young, short-service conscripts were promoted over their heads to fill, inexpertly, the many NCO vacancies ... and to leave after six months or so.[12]

These problems could prove disastrous upon mobilization, especially if war broke out in the winter months when one class only was fully trained. Reservists, especially reserve officers and NCOs, would not be battle-ready, while the regular army could not provide a solid mould into which reservists could be poured. Under the 1905 law, a line infantry company would swell from 113 to 250 men upon mobilization. Herissé pointed out that as most line companies had only 80 or 90 men present for duty, front-line units would be swamped with half-trained reservists. Even Jaurès, who supported a national militia, admitted that some infantry companies could have as few as 40 trained soldiers on mobilization.[13] A mobilized French infantry regiment counted only 95 career sergeants, many of whom filled administrative posts, while all of the 215 NCOs in a German infantry regiment were professionals.[14] 'What distinguishes the reservist from the regular above all is that manoeuvre, war, is not his natural milieu', read the 1913 Paté report.

He has lost all his fitness, he has forgotten with a certain satisfaction the habits of discipline. He must therefore be acclimatized. The reservist will not march like the other men unless he is well led, and by this one means not just by NCOs but by a certain number of soldiers in good moral and physical training. If the cadre is lacking, it is the reservist who could have a bad influence upon the leadership.[15]

French politicians and soldiers were forced to look closely at the deficiencies of the 1905 law after Germany began to shift the emphasis of its defence expenditure away from the navy to the army. Encouraged by the Krupp-financed 'Wehrverein', the Reichstag in 1911, 1912, and 1913 pushed through laws which raised the peacetime strength of the German army from 653,000 to 863,000 men and gave it 42,000 career officers and 112,000 NCOs to 29,000 officers and 48,000 NCOs in France.[16] Joffre calculated that this strengthened both the training in the German army and its ability to utilize German reservists. 'We quickly realized that we could not carry through serious reforms without modifying the 1905 law', he concluded.[17] The parliamentary army committee agreed that three years' service was 'necessary for the security of our territory and the future of our country. We voted for it because the present state of Europe requires that we be prepared if we are to survive.'[18] The problematic nature of the Russian alliance and the poor state of the Russian army meant that no one on the Left or the Right suggested Russian manpower as a remedy for French numerical weakness.

Felix Chautemps led a chorus of left-wing deputies who argued that the 1905 law had been sabotaged by a hostile high command who refused to apply it. The three-year bill 'is a justification of the failure to apply the provisions of the 1905 law, as well as the absence of training camps, lack of organization and activity of the military preparation societies, the reserves and the complementary cadres. It is, into the bargain, the army brutalized, passive and ready to do the bidding of its chiefs, the decided enemies of the Republic', he concluded.[19] Jaurès, too, blamed generals for not simplifying training methods to deal with short service conscripts: 'If several generals hold the spirit of the law at bay, they do it in an oblique and almost occult manner', he wrote in 1910. 'They do not introduce simplifications in manoeuvres and adopt more liberal and direct methods of education implied in the reduction of service time. But they do not dare speak out against the law.'[20]

Chautemps also blasted military leaders for wasting 80,000 soldiers in non-combatant jobs. The running sore of the French army was the 'shirker' – a man assigned to non-combat duties after his first year of service. Fully 60,000 soldiers were employed in this way after 1905, many as batmen,[21] while 20,000 others were taken for administration and support jobs, compared with only 7,000 in Germany's larger army. In 1903, an infantry company of 105 men counted 41 in non-combat positions.[22] Messimy complained that the 3,000 musicians in the 1913 army would fill four chasseur battalions and suggested that civilians take over certain non-military army jobs, as in Germany.[23] Chautemps argued that, if these 'shirkers' were returned to training, the army would not need an extra year's service to make up its manpower deficit. 'We can still scrape the bottom of the barrel', he told deputies.[24]

Authors of the 1905 bill realized that the army must be reorganized if two-year service were to prove effective. In his 1904 report, future Radical War Minister Berteaux claimed that the length of service should be determined by training requirements and recruitment of NCOs and reserve officers.[25] Increased literacy and less emphasis on traditional drill, it was suggested, had speeded up training and formation of cadres.[26] 'One year of service is enough to train a man. During the second year he confirms his training, perfects it, makes it durable ... During the third year, in effect, the soldier, almost always employed elsewhere than in his unit ... trains only intermittently, generally forgetting more than he learns.'[27] Conscripts familiar with horses would be sent to the cavalry and field artillery while artillerymen and engineers would concentrate on mastering only one speciality.

The training of reserve cadres was to be facilitated by the extension of locally organized military preparation societies which initiated young men into the fundamentals of soldiering before they reported for military service. Conscripts with a certificate of aptitude from a preparation society could be promoted to corporal within four months of joining the army and would be encouraged to take a reserve officer examination. This allowed a successful applicant to serve his last six months as a reserve second lieutenant. Berteaux boasted that this would eliminate the reserve officer deficit and allow the government to axe idle line officers, leaving just enough regular officers to 'act as instructors and teachers'.[28] In this way, reserves would be assured a steady stream of competent officers and NCOs.

The second touchstone of the two-year reform was the replacement of soldiers in the army's many non-combatant jobs by civilians or conscript 'rejects' – men declared unfit for military service under the 1889 law who were thought perfectly capable of holding down a sedentary job – an estimated 35,000 men each year.[29] Decorative units like bands or the many ceremonial guard details which festooned Paris and other cities were to be abolished and their troops poured into line regiments.

Pre-1905 opponents of two-year service had pointed out the dangers of basing military reform on a reorganization which had yet to take place, but their warnings had fallen on deaf ears.[30] In 1913, the charge that the high command had sabotaged the two-year law was adopted by the Left as an article of faith. However, the shortcomings of the French army were more serious than those which a conspiracy of disgruntled generals could have produced. The 1913 law aimed to remedy the army's two major weaknesses – the shortage of NCOs and poor training of reservists and regulars. A close examination of the army's state in 1913 reveals that the high command found its ability to cure either of these maladies strictly limited.

The 1905 law had counted upon the recruitment of solid cores of professional NCOs to staff inexperienced conscripts. Their failure to materialize was due both to institutional factors peculiar to the French army and to a recruitment crisis tied to a general decline in army morale after 1900. The Napoleonic tradition of promotion through the ranks meant a constant haemorrhage of qualified NCOs into the officer corps, so that the French army had no stable NCO 'class'. In Britain and Germany, the sergeant-major commanded respect and authority and the men who achieved this rank, blocked by their social origins and closed system of officer recruitment from breaking into the officer corps, counted themselves successes. In France, the modest social origins of many officers combined with the tradition of promotion through the ranks to deflate NCO status. The best sergeants were creamed off, leaving young inexperienced conscript NCOs and professionals who lacked the qualities to become officers. For instance, 74 per cent of artillery second lieutenants in 1910 were ex-NCOs.[31] This, combined with a shortfall of re-enlistments in the years immediately preceding the war, led to an NCO crisis. 'The quality of our professional NCOs has dropped in the last few years', wrote General Durand in 1911. 'Everyone agrees with this fact . . . today the cadres are stuffed with too many NCOs who are old, tired, who have lost their enthusiasm but who do not want to retire and so stop promotion.'[32] 'We were obliged to re-enlist second-rate men to fill the places', General Alexandre, one of Joffre's staff officers, said of pre-1914 NCOs. 'Generally speaking . . . in this respect we were vastly inferior to the German army.'[33]

To poor quality was added the fact that many re-enlisted NCOs occupied administrative, not combat, posts and so put little stuffing into fighting units: 'It is not in the combat troops that the largest number of re-enlisted NCOs can be counted, but rather in the accessory services, administrative sections, recruitment bureaux, military justice, etc. Our eastern neighbours have for a long time used civilians for most of these jobs which have nothing military about them but the name', Charles Humbert wrote.[34] The lack of experienced NCOs struck Joffre forcibly in August 1914 when he saw roads strewn with abandoned equipment: 'cadres, not yet in control of the situation, did not always appear to be very energetic'.[35] Nor could the high command do much to alleviate the growing morale crisis among NCOs. Poor pay and re-enlistment bonuses discouraged professional NCOs. Nor did promised civil service jobs always materialize on retirement. Government bureaux continued to set age limits too low, did not publicize vacancies or, often under political pressure, filled jobs slated for ex-NCOs with civilians.[36] Career sergeants and corporals also faced prejudice from conscripts who, comparing them to prostitutes, called them 'les vendus'. The future General Veron, who volunteered in 1908 to finish his service early, was frequently told: 'Then you didn't have anything to eat, so you signed up.'[37] 'The jeers and jokes of conscripts of which re-enlisted soldiers are the butt, especially in the infantry and the artillery', had discouraged re-enlistment, a May 1912 report concluded. 'This results from a prejudice which has dire consequences and which unfortunately is difficult to overcome.'[38] This state of affairs had certainly been exacerbated by attacks on the army from the Left, which characterized NCOs as men too poor and ignorant to make a living elsewhere. The result was a shortage of NCOs. Messimy reported in 1907 that 2,500 places for experienced NCOs remained vacant.[39] By 1912, the re-enlistment crisis had spread even to the popular Paris garrison.[40] A parliamentary report of December 1913 estimated that the army was short by 6,000 career sergeants.[41] Humbert complained that of 23,000 places for re-enlisted corporals, only 8,000 had been filled. Re-enlisted soldiers were to fill eight per cent of the infantry and 15 per cent of the cavalry ranks, according to the authors of the 1905 law. On 1 October 1907, however, the army counted only 1,157 re-enlisted soldiers.[42]

The 1905 legislation which discouraged re-enlistment, low pay, lack of promised civil employment and low prestige which resulted in part from a concerted campaign on the Left to pull down army status were responsible for the shortfall in NCO re-enlistment which was one of the major arguments behind the extra service year. 'The falling off ... of long-term volunteers and re-enlistments is worrying for every arm', General Meunier wrote after a 1912 inspection tour in the 14th and 15th army corps.

The cavalry is especially hard hit . . . Re-enlisted corporals and brigadiers are sick at heart and discouraged. This stems from moral causes: because their standing is the same as that of a conscript with a few months service and his stripes. Secondly, because their position seems hopeless . . . a re-enlisted corporal . . . cannot be promoted to sergeant until there is a re-enlistment vacancy . . . In the cavalry especially, corporals see yesterday's recruits become tomorrow's superiors, promoted to a non-regular position. . . . Volunteers, often from their arrival in the regiment, are the object of the hostility of cavalrymen and even conscript NCOs. They are spared no insult, not even the most humiliating of all, which consists of throwing in their face the well-known taunt: 'You have no bread at home'.[43]

The re-enlistment crisis had pushed commanders to sign up men of doubtful quality: 'One can say that two-thirds (of volunteers) signed on for the enlistment bonus, and as soon as they join up they commit a grave error which allows them to spend their time in prison', General Abonneau said after a 1913 inspection in the cavalry. Discipline problems had caused commanders to become more selective, but this had driven enlistment and re-enlistment down still further. 'A large number of punishments and reductions to the ranks are inflicted on [re-enlisted] NCOs', he wrote. 'Today, forewarned, regimental councils are more selective, which accounts for the shortfall of enlistments which are now examined with more caution.'[44] One of the major arguments in favour of three years' service was that it would give the army a better and more experienced conscript NCO: 'From now on, we shall no longer be obliged, to replace departing NCOs, to promote corporals at the end of their first year of service before their individual aptitudes are developed . . . We will be in a position to constitute a solid core of sergeants', the war minister wrote to corps commanders on 12 September 1913.[45] However, the war intervened before the reform could take effect.

The 1913 law was designed to give the army a better conscript NCO, not to bolster the professional army. Given the trough into which the morale of career NCOs had fallen after 1905, reformers realized that the army could no longer count almost exclusively upon their career sergeants and corporals to stiffen the ranks. While NCO discontent was also apparent in Germany,[46] in France it took a particularly cancerous form.

Discontent among French NCOs bubbled to the surface in 1908. Taking their cue from public service employees, some NCOs threatened to report sick if Parliament failed to pass pension legislation for widows and orphans of NCOs. The government blamed this unprecedented strike threat in the army on militant NCOs in the *solidarité militaire*, an NCO mutualist society. Founded by General Pédoya in 1902 for career NCOs, the *solidarité militaire* counted 4,828 members in January 1908,[47] when militants threatened strike action. This move for strike action dissolved however, after the war minister, in a September 1908 decree, forbade NCOs to join the association.[48] In April 1909, the central office of the *solidarité militaire* told its branches that the association could neither seek to change ministry decisions nor lobby for reforms of service conditions. But the threat of militant action clearly paid off in terms of membership – when the war minister lifted the ban in November 1909, the *solidarité militaire* saw its membership double to 10,000 or a third of career NCOs.[49]

Smouldering resentment among NCOs flared up again barely two years later with attempts to organize NCO 'friendly societies' in virtually every French garrison. The government feared that this move was closely tied up with pacifist attempts to infiltrate the army, especially after Sergeant Bonnefous of the 83rd infantry regiment and a member of the *solidarité militaire* was arrested at Toulon allegedly for sabotaging railroads. Toulon police wrote on 25 July 1911, that the *solidarité militaire* was 'a centre of syndicalist action in the army ... while not claiming that the sabotage was ordered by the *solidarité militaire*, the facts point to a link'.[50]

Paris police, investigating attempts to set up NCO friendly societies in the 46th and 89th infantry regiments, feared that the *solidarité militaire* harboured a militant element which might stop at nothing to sabotage mobilization: 'Young NCOs are ready to take energetic action when the time comes. By this they mean a military strike in a revolutionary situation.' But a 27 January 1913 report found police 'too pessimistic'.[51] Rising NCO discontent which was supported by several Paris newspapers, including the *Figaro* and *Le Temps*, pushed parliament to investigate. The Leroy committee reported on 24 October 1912, that the NCO morale crisis was serious: 'If the founders of this society had been less divided, the NCO friendly society would now be in existence', the report read. 'And one can say with certainty that almost all NCOs would belong, as none oppose their own interests. We are told that unless NCOs are better treated, they will again take up more seriously than ever their approaches to politicians and the press and renew their attempts to form a friendly society to raise the moral and material level of their existence.'[52] 'Officers take care of the soldier because he has in his family political connections,' NCOs complained, 'while the NCO is without defence until after he retires.'[53] The committee found that militant NCOs pressured and even intimidated colleagues to drive down re-enlistments and so stoke the NCO crisis.

The army clearly did not need to fear an NCO-led revolt on mobilization. But the dangers of the NCO crisis to army efficiency were spelled out by Leroy: 'Those who believe themselves poorly treated and who can find a civilian job leave the army, these are generally the most intelligent', his report stated.

What is left are mediocre instructors who can do absolutely nothing else. . . . The lower cadres lose little by little their best elements, their elite men and slowly but surely the corps of NCOs will become what it was 20 years ago, that is, it will contain only NCOs of limited intelligence without education and incapable of being good instructors. The NCOs say that they leave the army with regret and if the pay were sufficient and promotion given on merit and impartially, they would not dream of leaving the army.[54]

A shortage of NCOs and a sharp drop in their quality after 1905 undermined training. On 26 June 1913, the *France militaire* criticized deputies for concentrating debate on the reserves while shoving into the background the point that the 1905 law had deprived the army of cadres. Those who voted for the 1905 law had realized that training time would be cut down. But Berteaux had told deputies in 1904 that as over three-quarters of each conscript class was now literate, compared with slightly over half in 1889, and as drill and close order tactics had become a relic of the past, training and the formation of cadres would be speeded up.[55] The elimination of 'shirkers' and their replacement by soldiers unfit for combat and civilian workers would send more men to training.[56]

In 1913, Jaurès and others on the Left criticized officers for not simplifying training methods and for relying upon the traditional drill rather than on field exercises. However, a shortage of training personnel and of training areas combined to sabotage military preparation. City garrisons had no training grounds. Other regiments, especially in the cavalry, found their grounds unusable in the winter months when troops were expected to acquire the fundamentals of soldiering. Major de Civrieux complained in 1908 that his cavalry regiment's training field was nothing but clay, water-logged for eight months of the year.[57] The future General Weygand remembered that his regiment at Saint-Etienne was forbidden to gallop or to practise mass manoeuvres for fear of collapsing the mine shafts which ran under their drill field. In November 1906, General Bazaine-Hayter deplored the lack of firing ranges for the infantry and artillery: 'The result is that the standards of marksmanship leave much to be desired in the French army and that the units are not supple enough, do not manoeuvre well, despite the efforts of the cadres, the good will and the intelligence of the troops.'[58] Autumn manoeuvres were also accused of neglecting troop training.[59]

Training camps were few and inadequate. While Germany counted 26 camps in 1912, of at least 5,625 hectares each, France had only seven, the four largest – Châlons, Coëtquidan, Courtine and Mailly – ranging from 2,000 to 3,000 hectares. Châlons was badly organized and in need of renovation after 1910, and Mailly was considered virtually unusable. The remaining three were only brigade-size. French spending on these camps increased from 2,995,000 francs to 4,600,000 annually between 1908 and 1911, but still fell far short of the German investment. In 1911 alone, Germany spent the equivalent of 14,346,000 francs on training camps. Only one-third of regular French troops and a quarter of reservists on the second of their two training periods could hope to visit a training camp each year.[60] Officers and NCOs often had no alternative but to fill training hours with traditional drill.

Training often took a back seat to the petty demands of garrison life. After accounting for inspections, sickness and duties, Major de Civrieux estimated that his cavalrymen averaged twelve hours – twelve unsteady hours – a month on horseback.[61] A soldier's second year had very little to do with training, and left-wing deputies blamed officers for squandering front-line soldiers in frivolous and unnecessary tasks. 'It was not enough to have them look like Epinal Prints, with lots of NCOs, drummers, musicians, flag-bearers, canteen keepers, and very few privates', War Minister Picquart wrote in the *Aurore* in 1907.[62]

Republicans looked for ways to overcome the training handicap. Grandmaison urged officers to: '1. Mingle and talk with the soldier, advise him and express opinions on current affairs. 2. Give classes on moral theory.' He developed a training scheme which allowed soldiers to train themselves in large measure by drilling individually under minimum supervision: 'We cannot ask a young and inexperienced corporal to decide what [training] methods to employ.'[63]

Critics argued that the social role demanded of officers cut further into training time. Senior officers were more concerned with administrative detail, especially the functioning of co-operatives, than with training. Humbert claimed that emphasis on moral education had made the first line of the training regulations – 'War preparation is the unique goal of troop training' – something of a joke.[64] De Civrieux remarked bitterly that inspectors were concerned with moral and professional training not for soldiers, but for civilians.[65] 'For several years, our soldiers have learned everything in the army but what they should learn – soldiering', *Le Temps* wrote in 1912.

> They are taught beekeeping, mushroom growing, tree farming. They are lectured on mutual associations, civic duty, co-operatives, steel-making, and all at the expense of serious war preparation ... The officers with the best reports in the general inspections are not always those whose troops have performed well in manoeuvres, but those who gave the most lectures on civics and morals, and who have the smartest or the richest co-operative.[66]

Captain d'Arbeaux also complained that military science took a back seat to an officer's social mission.[67]

The 1911 manoeuvres bore testimony to the army's poor training: 'The infantry was not supple and revealed its lack of training; the fronts of attack bore no relation to the available means, terrain was badly utilized', Joffre remembered. 'The artillery and the infantry never tried to link their efforts. The most elementary notions of cover were disregarded. The different arms demonstrated a profound ignorance of each others' needs and possibilities.'[68] A circular from Millerand, dated 20 January 1912, said that training was not being properly carried out and ordered generals to ensure that it was.[69] Later that year, however, British observers reported of the French manoeuvres: 'Once they were deployed, the French infantry displayed marked inferiority to our own in minor tactics. There was not the same dash or anything like the same efficiency in fire direction and control. The infantry, like the cavalry, did not seem to realize what modern rifle fire was like.'[70]

In 1913, the Left argued that the army's misuse of manpower, not the 1905 law, was responsible for poor training. The bad utilization of manpower sprang in part from cumbersome army organization. Strong measures on the part of officers could no doubt have eliminated some unnecessary sinecures. But weak leadership at the top hardly encouraged efficiency at the regimental level. 'The incredible and destructive number of "shirkers" is the logical result of the weak leadership springing from our political and social organization', the Count de Goulaine had told the Senate in 1902.[71] Officers claimed that batmen were still required to train, but one may doubt that this was always enforced.

Politicians, not soldiers, were responsible for much military inefficiency. To make up the numbers after 1905, conscription boards were directed to take men who previously had been rejected as unfit, an estimated 35,000 in 1907.[72] Many of these men lacked the skills to fill sedentary jobs while their physical incapacity disqualified them for anything more strenuous, so that they were often sent straight home by the regiments, although, according to some reports, they continued to be counted in army strength.[73] Attempts to abolish military bands, destined according to Messimy to give the army four chasseur battalions, had to be abandoned after they provoked howls of protest from local mayors who thought them an indispensable accoutrement to the annual 'fête du village'. Likewise, the ceremonial guard details which devoured 10,000 men daily in Paris and other cities, according to Humbert, were maintained on the insistence of civilians, not soldiers.[74] The extension of co-operatives, canteens and libraries after 1900, while perhaps laudable reforms, required soldiers to run them and so deflected more men from training. Millerand's 24 July 1912 decree limiting co-operatives to one per regiment aimed to return more men to training.

Shortages in combat troops also resulted from bad distribution of soldiers. The 1889 law had provided many legal loopholes used by soldiers to postpone or mitigate military service. The 1905 law aimed to make 'service equal for all' and abolished the 'special assignments' which allowed young men to serve near home. With the legal escape hatches bolted shut, families used influence to ease the military passage of their sons. Barely a year after the passage of the two-year service law, commanders began to complain that soldiers with influence were managing to avoid unpopular garrisons, creating manning problems.[75] A September 1910 report complained that as a result of the *piston* – an influential friend – many combat regiments, especially in the East, lacked troops while regiments in desirable garrisons and auxiliary services were stuffed, 'the desire to keep her son close to home being unfortunately one of the characteristic traits of the French mother, especially in the upper classes'.[76] But nothing was done, indeed nothing could be done under a regime in which favouritism served as the small change of politics, and the complaints continued.[77]

The real success of the law depended upon the substitution of civilians for soldiers in many non-combatant jobs, as in Germany. But this was not done for two reasons. In the first place, it was too expensive. An April 1913 report estimated that the substitution of civilian for military manpower would mean that 31,000 troops could be returned to combat posts ... at the cost of 32 million francs annually.[78] Henri Paté pointed out that of 700,000 francs requested in the 1913 budget intended to replace 7,000 soldiers in the artillery and the medical corps with civilians, Parliament allowed only 200,000 francs for nurses.[79] Secondly, the government feared that dependence upon civilian workers might soon mean that trade unions would have a strangle-hold on French defence. The militant anti-militarism of some workers in the Brest and Toulon arsenals led to government purges there in November 1908.[80] The *CGT*'s campaign to unionize war department workers climaxed with a 16 December 1912 demonstration in Paris. In a 7 December circular, Millerand told employees that they were forbidden by law to strike and threatened to deal harshly with any unexcused absences on that day.[81] He also reminded directors of war establishments of the 1905 circular which obliged them to keep an eye on militant workers and to see that they were given no important jobs. Published in several Paris newspapers, this circular produced a storm of protest on the Left. In Parliament, Lucien Violin demanded that Millerand abolish secret notes on workers in war establishments, which he refused to do.[82] Politicians were reluctant to increase the number of civilian workers in the army, thereby perhaps giving anti-militarists yet other bridgeheads into the forces.

Two-year service might also have been salvaged had the French been prepared to alter radically their system of induction and training. The French army lived by a rigid military calendar. All conscripts arrived in October for four months basic training, leaving the end of the year very thin on military skill. They then graduated to section training, regimental training in the spring and summer, and finally autumn manoeuvres. A system whereby a fraction of each contingent would be incorporated at various times in the year and trained in special training sections or camps, sending the regiments a steady stream of trained men, would no doubt have helped. But when this was suggested during the 1913 debates, Joffre pointed out that this would not solve the basic problem of manpower shortage. This also flew in the face of army practice. In an era before cost-efficient techniques had influenced military organizations, the regiment was the central unit of army organization responsible for training its own soldiers, the military calendar sacrosanct and the annual social ritual of the conscript call-up ingrained in the country, binding successive generations of young men together and solidifying respect for civic duty and the national ideal.

Many blamed the shortcomings of the reserves on the inefficiency of the barracks army and the distaste of regular soldiers for the citizen soldier. No doubt, some regulars might have felt that the arrival of reservists disrupted the comfortable regimental routine. But the roots of poor reserve training ran deeper than professional prejudice. In 1908, Parliament cut the time reservists spent in training periods, from 69 to 49 days and that of territorials from 13 to 9 days, complaining that they simply wasted time in barracks. Picquart ordered commanders to train reservists and the government cut the number of reservists allowed to skip training altogether: in 1910, 82 per cent of reservists eligible for training that year accomplished their reserve period, compared with 68 per cent in 1906.[83] Nevertheless, this meant that 40,000 reservists managed to avoid training.[84]

Historians have made much of Picquart's 1908 order forcing reservists out of the barracks and into training camps as proof of the Radicals' desire to intensify reserve training.[85] However, the lack of training camps meant that seldom more than one-quarter of reservists on the second of their two training periods could visit a training camp each year, so that the situation was often little changed.[86]

The reservists themselves often proved reluctant soldiers. The war minister complained in 1910 that up to 40 per cent of reservists had been left behind in barracks in some units, claiming to be unfit for training,[87] and ordered commanders to check their claims closely. But attempts to make reservists bend to a strict military regime often boomeranged on officers. Incidents of collective indiscipline among reservists during field exercises were not infrequent after 1905. De Civrieux noted in 1908 that officers had trouble keeping discipline in his reserve unit when the town turned out to see reservists off in the North. The Colonel limited afternoon exercises to one hour after 18 per cent of men dropped out on the first day. Several days later, the 'official' drop-out was almost one-third, and he reckoned that it would have gone as high as 40 per cent had the full training schedule been followed: 'The Imperial national guard was as worthy an organization as this reserve army which exists only on paper, unable to leave the barracks even if they can get there', he wrote, perhaps too pessimistically. '[It is] empty of all endurance, all discipline, all enthusiasm.'[88]

The real weakness of the reserves, however, lay with the reserve cadres, for if the Radicals at least paid lip service to the training of reservists, cadres were sadly neglected. One of the paradoxes of reserve reform had always been that attempts to train reserve officers and NCOs to acceptable standards often discouraged improvements, for governments fell back on patriotism rather than pay and other advantages as the main incentive for extra reserve duties. Attempts in the 1890s to set up supplementary training periods for reserve officers foundered on apathy, expense and sheer inconvenience.[89] Despite claims that the strength of French defence resided in her reserves, governments did little to encourage reserve officers beyond throwing a handful of devalued decorations at them each year. After the 1889 abolition of the one-year volunteers had removed the last serious inducement to join the reserves as an officer, convincing qualified young men to accept the extra burden proved difficult: in 1910, the war minister complained that reserve officers were resigning after completing their conscript classes' second training period rather than face the required five training periods.[90] Budget reporter Klotz observed complacently in 1906 that 7,451 vacancies for reserve lieutenants could be filled with NCOs if war broke out,[91] but this did little to calm fears for the solidity of reserve cadres. The 1905 law allowed qualified conscripts to spend their last six months as reserve second lieutenants, but de Civrieux, at least, thought the experiment a failure: 'These gentlemen increasingly show less and less enthusiasm and worth', he wrote.

This year we received the first group of young men doing their last six months of service as officers... what rubbish! My God! One feels that these boys believe that they are on a six-month holiday, amusing themselves by strolling in town or around the barracks, incapable of leading a squad. I am only speaking of what I have seen. Perhaps it is better elsewhere, but I doubt it.[92]

When General Cools criticized low reserve officer standards in 1904, he was officially rebuked, 'but his opinions are shared by everyone in the milieux', military critic Jacques Haroué wrote.[93]

Reserve NCOs were little better. Conscript NCOs were short of training and authority. This was especially true when they commanded men whom they knew or worked with in civilian life. Career NCOs who had left the army often could not be mobilized because they occupied critical civilian jobs, like postmen. France counted almost 40,000 NCOs in this category and efforts to persuade the various ministries to scratch them from the exemption list met with a flat refusal.[94]

Many blamed reserve officer resignations on the superior disdain with which career officers treated their reserve colleagues.[95] General Legrand-Girard, however, countered that it was not military prejudice against civilians but rather the low prestige of the army resulting from the Dreyfus affair which had provoked the many vacancies in reserve officer ranks. 'One must not forget that the unfortunate crisis which France went through after 1898 provoked many resignations among reserve officers, together with purges, and this above all produced a pronounced disinclination in the leading classes to occupy military posts', he wrote. 'All infantry and artillery regiments had numerous vacancies in their reserve officer positions . . . As for the lower cadres, NCOs and corporals, the experience of annual training demonstrated how little authority they had over their men, so that they had to undergo a further training period before they could be relied upon.'[96] Messimy admitted in 1906 that 'the real ostracism which reserve officers faced for so long has now completely vanished and is only a bad memory'.[97] The future General Veron noted that when he was completing his last six months' service as a reserve second lieutenant in 1909, he had been cordially received by career officers.[98] While professional officers believed that their knowledge of soldiering outstripped that of the amateurs, there is little evidence to suggest that reserve officers met a discouraging wall of hostility when they joined their regiments or that professional prejudice against conscript temporary gentlemen counted as a significant factor in the resignations of reserve officers after 1900.

1905 reformers had pinned their hopes on France's 5,065 military preparation societies to remedy the problems posed by shorter service and the absence of reserve lieutenants and sergeants. An 8 April 1903 law allowed conscripts with a *brevet d'aptitude militaire* to be named corporals within four months of induction, after which they could easily conquer positions as sergeants and, hopefully, reserve second lieutenants. In December 1904, a committee formed of representatives from the war, education and interior ministries met 'to unify [training] methods for the schoolboy, the gymnast and the soldier', while article 94 of the two-year service law stipulated that physical education and military training would be carried out in lycées.[99]

Neglect of these groups was yet another charge levelled by the Left against the government, but it is unlikely that they could have rescued the two-year law. Like many reforms, poor financing proved a major stumbling-block to their effective organization. While Switzerland's 4,000 societies received the equivalent of two million French francs in government subsidies, Germany's 7,000 societies the equivalent of 1,500,000 francs and Britain's shooting societies the generous gift of between 12 and 13 million francs annually, France's 5,065 societies of 869,000 people received a paltry 167,000 francs to which was added 223,000 francs worth of free ammunition handed out to territorial army shooting societies.[100] Attempts to spread physical education classes in lycées also tripped on the lack of capital: by 1908, France's 107 lycées counted only 134 physical education instructors, or one for every 425 students.[101]

To problems of poor financing were added those of inaccessibility. A 1908 report complained that military preparation societies were almost unknown outside of the larger cities and towns and so did not benefit rural recruits.[102] An April 1910 circular from the interior minister ordered police to organize them in rural areas, but to little effect:[103] in 1912, Millerand noted that only 4,000 of France's 36,000 communes boasted a society and he ordered officers to take an interest in local groups.[104]

Nor did the societies themselves always prepare conscripts for the rigours of military service. Only 320 societies were dedicated to 'military training and preparation' with the rest reserved for cycling, boxing, swimming, fencing, gymnastics, athletics, shooting and horseback riding – and so did not prepare young men to pass the *brevet d'aptitude militaire*. The number of young men awarded the *brevet* jumped from 3,092 in 1908 to 5,686 in 1910, but critics found standards still too low.[105] 'As far as the raw material, the soldier, is concerned, we have published ... in-depth studies which ... have demonstrated the shortcomings of the test for the *brevet d'aptitude militaire*', the *France militaire* wrote on 7 January 1914. But when the war minister answered his critics in 1914 by raising the points required for a *brevet* from 450 to 700, the failure rate was 75 per cent, which, the *France militaire* complained on 20 June 1914, had discouraged young men from applying.

The greatest barriers to the effective spread of military preparation societies, however, were political: 'These societies have the disadvantage of resembling too closely the *bataillons scolaires*', the 1908 army committee report read. 'The committee insists especially on that point.'[106] From the beginning, military preparation for youth formed an important element in republican plans to prepare the nation for national service. In 1882, Education Minister Paul Bert set up a committee of military education to draw up a programme of military and patriotic education in French schools. One of its members, Paul Déroulède, wrote:

> Its job was nothing less than to transform the youth of our schools into a legion of brave Frenchmen, to arm them from youth with male sentiments and virile habits which make the true soldier: this was first the cult of the flag which would fortify the love of country; a taste for arms . . . the respect for discipline which unified our efforts and made everyone equal in the face of duty; pride in the name of Frenchmen . . . this was the proposed task.

The committee set itself the task of organizing the student drill companies which had sprung up in several cities, the most famous being in Paris' fifth arrondissement, to choose books, songs and pictures and standardize drill and exercises.[107] Paris Municipal Councillor Aristide Rey led the organization of these *bataillons scolaires*, which soon spread to other French cities and towns, with twelve-year-old boys, mostly sons of workers and merchants, being drilled twice weekly and receiving basic gymnastic and boxing instruction. Following the *bataillon scolaire's* first parade on 13 July 1882, watched by a huge crowd in front of the *Hôtel de Ville*, the Paris municipal council voted to set up 24 battalions in Paris under the command of a major and four captains paid by the city. Poorer families would be furnished with uniforms.[108]

However, the spectacle of uniformed and armed soldiers commanded and paid by municipal councils raised fears of a national guard revival, especially after Paris politicians increasingly talked of opening the *bataillons scolaires* to eighteen-year-olds, and officials discouraged the *bataillons scolaires* in favour of gymnastic societies, especially after the arrival in 1881 of Jules Ferry in the education ministry: 'It took only three meetings to transform the military education committee into a simple gymnastic committee', Déroulède complained, blaming 'a completely incurable lack of sympathy for the army among most republicans'.[109] But it was fear of a resurrected national guard, not anti-military sentiments, that provoked the reaction against the *bataillons scolaires*. 'We differ in our choice of means, but our goal is the same', Ferry said. 'An army does not exist without military spirit.'[110] General Chanzy spoke for the army when he told a gymnastic meeting at Rheims in 1882 that its job was to build strong bodies and dedication, the army would train the soldiers.[111] Government subsidies encouraged the growing number of sporting societies declared '*d'utilité publique*', especially after many generals objected to these *ad hoc* military companies.[112] On 14 July 1884, the Paris *bataillons scolaires* held a parade to rival the official ceremony, and in the 1885 elections, 47 candidates, mainly Parisian, called for preparatory military training for youth.[113] But on 5 October 1888, the *Avenir militaire* reckoned that they were in serious decline: 'The military training given in the *bataillons scolaires* is altogether unsatisfactory, and the drill to which the children are subjected has no other result than to disrupt their studies and encourage a most dangerous spirit of indiscipline.' The following year the unhappy experiment ended.

For many nervous local officials, military preparation societies bore the all too familiar stamp of the national guard, an image which the inclination of many gymnastic societies to spend Sunday afternoons practising drill did little to dissipate. In July 1911, for instance, the Mayor of Nouzon, near Mézières, refused to permit a parade of the local gymnastic society because it smacked of a militia.[114] Reformers constantly appealed to societies to stop 'playing soldiers' and concentrate on preparing physically strong, disciplined recruits.[115]

Political differences of opinion on the national level were often reflected in the societies, driving away many potential members. In many communes, the priest and the school teacher ran competing societies. Messimy complained in 1907 that 'all the societies are far from reflecting principles compatible with those followed for the last seven years by the Republican party',[116] and demanded that they 'abide by secular and republican principles'. 'L'Union des patronages de la France', which provided a central office for Catholic societies, scandalized Radicals by taking 500 young Frenchmen to Rome for a gymnastic competition.[117] 'Many of the societies . . . adopt a well-defined political line and, if they persist, always end up by affiliating to a group whose label discourages many [potential] members who do not want to be compromised', the *Porte-Voix* noted on 20 February 1911. Politics proved the greatest handicap to the spread of the societies: 'If the military preparation societies have not spread, it is because the prefects, for political reasons, refuse to authorise them', Emile Laurent told the deputies on 2 July 1913.[118] Millerand deplored the squabbling for control of the military preparation societies and, after the minister of the interior had refused to authorize several societies on political grounds, he demanded that the control of the societies be turned over to the war ministry. 'It is now more important than ever that, behind the mask of military preparation societies, other goals are not pursued and that politics do not mix with the military training of French youth', he told the *Fédération nationale des sociétés de préparation militaire de France* on 15 June 1912. On 26 October, he told Paris societies: 'I understood that in some places, rather than one society grouping all young men, there were two: that of the teacher and that of the priest ... the army is France.'[119]

In its final form, the 1913 law raised regular infantry companies from 113 to 140 men so that slightly more than one-third of their strength would be furnished by reservists on mobilization. Opponents of the bill hailed this as the triumph of the professional army and a step backward in the struggle for a 'nation-in-arms'. 'The Chambre was faced with two possible military organizations, one which standardized a routine, and another modern concept which limited military service to the time necessary for training', wrote Michon.[120]

The three-year law was undoubtedly a simplistic and unsatisfactory solution to France's military problems. Thorough reform, not an extra year's service, was needed. But in the face of these problems, the Socialists could only complain that reforms had not been carried out and suggest that France move instead to a militia. The idea of a militia found its most articulate champion in Jaurès. He called for the establishment of an army on the Swiss model, with soldiers doing only six months' service and returning periodically for training sessions. A small core of career officers and NCOs would be maintained to keep the forces ticking over but the bulk of the cadre would be provided by the reserves.[121]

The militia system, however, offered a solution to France's defence problems which was as simplistic as the extra service year. Jaurès argued that France should assume a defensive posture, making the best model for the French army that of Switzerland: 'Basically, what is the Swiss army?' asked Henri Paté. 'A fortress army which represents the admirable effort of a population no greater than that of London. We need a field army, that is to say, one better in quantity and quality than the Swiss army.' Paté claimed it was to Germany not Switzerland that France had to look for a model. Lastly, he dismissed Jaurès' call for a militia as unrealistic, for, by the Socialist leader's own admission, it depended for its success on the same institutions as the two-year law: military preparation societies and reserve troops and cadres willing to make sacrifices for military training. André Hess agreed that six months was enough time to train a soldier, but not the cadres.[122]

Jaurès does not appear to be the military prophet which many see in him. Henri Contamine speculated that a Jaurèsian militia would have found it hard to break the well-disciplined German army in 1914. Jaurès' militia recalled the Spanish Republican armies of 1936 rather than the Swiss militia, 'whose traditional character rests on a sense of civic duty which has never been associated with the French Left'.[123]

The 1905 law, too, had depended for its success on a spirit of sacrifice and civic responsibility, as well as a strengthened and efficient army organization. But the inherent contradiction of Radical policy lay in its denigration of the professional army as militaristic and anti-republican while at the same time expecting young men to step forward to perform their patriotic duty – first in military preparation societies, then perhaps as volunteers or re-enlisted NCOs, and finally as reserve officers and NCOs.

Reservists proved excellent when trained, but military chiefs might be forgiven their reluctance to throw reservists into the fray from the first hour. Even General Michel, hailed by the Left as a champion of the reserves after his 1911 plan to use them in the front lines was rejected by the *conseil supérieur de la guerre*, had few illusions about the solidity of reserve units without a strong cadre. Few could blame his colleagues for being cautious about using the reserves on the outbreak of war, after Michel had written on 15 June 1911: 'These reserve divisions exist on paper, but who can guarantee their solidity?'[124]

The poor performance of some reservist units in the opening weeks of war was due to a combination of poor training, which affected the entire army, poor cadres and unimaginative leadership from regular officers. Reservists proved able fighters once acclimatized to war, as many soldiers had predicted, but their solidity in the first days was shaky: 'We are very disillusioned with the reservists', the commander of the 14th corps reported on 22 August 1914, 'for the moment, they are employed as workers and as trench guards in the hope that they will be in a better state in a few days.'[125] 'Reservists have run away wherever we have sent them', he wrote the following day. 'Their commander has declared them more or less useless. I am obliged to act as if I did not have them. It has become dangerous to count upon them for even the smallest operation.'[126] By far the biggest disappointment proved to be reservists from the 16th corps who broke and ran in the face of the enemy, confirming the poor opinion of many officers for Southern soldiers.

Officers must also shoulder some of the burden for the poor performance of reservists. Emile Mayer admitted that his territorial regiment contained many 'mediocre' elements, but, rather than whip it into fighting form, the high command simply shunted it to Rouen where it vegetated in enforced idleness.[127] The future General Weygand, Foch's chief of staff in 1914, wrote that his commander was also forced to withdraw reservists from the front lines 'because of the disorder created by their lack of cohesion and solidity'. He noted, however, that the substitution of a more energetic reserve chief did wonders for their fighting qualities.[128]

In the final analysis, the failings of the reserves were those of the entire army: poor training and poor leadership. Both of these shortcomings had been accentuated, to say the least, since 1900, and the 1913 law aimed to correct them for the entire army, not just the professional branch of it. The three-year law marked another step in the re-entry of the reserves into official army favour. The stronger the regular army, the more faith officers placed in the usefulness of reservists. Plan XIII drawn up by Boisdeffre and Miribel in 1895 called for the immediate use of 33 reserve divisions.[129] With the decline of overall military efficiency after 1900 went a decline in the role of reservists to 22 divisions in 1910. Joffre's plan XVII bumped reserve divisions in the front lines back up to 25.[130] If the Germans proved more willing than the French to throw their reserve units in from the first hours of battle, it was in part due to the fact that Joffre expected to feed them piecemeal into the battle,[131] but also because the German reserve units were better than their French counterparts – better trained and better staffed by professional officers and NCOs and keen reserve cadres.[132] The 1913 law sought to bring the entire French army, reservists included, up to the standards of its German rival.

Was this, then, the crowning victory of Monteilhet's 'professional army'? A law which sought to give the army good conscript NCOs to replace mediocre professional ones, to stiffen the reserves, to provide more men for the expansion of vital arms like the air corps and the heavy artillery, and to replace platitudes about civic spirit and military preparation which did service for military reform among the radicals with more solid organization and training, all this was more pragmatic than 'professional'. It was proof that a new spirit of realism was beginning to take hold in the army. Alas, it came too late for the forces fully to come to grips with their inadequacies. For the army had fallen into a dream world where the study of war bore little relation to reality.

11

The spirit of the offensive

For historians of the nation-in-arms school, the Nationalist Revival marked a turning point in the history of the pre-war army, when a group of right-wing politicians allowed a conservative military elite to re-establish their hegemony over the forces. The result was the implementation of a military system which turned its back on reservists and defensive tactics in vogue before 1912 to take the offensive with its barracks troops. But military systems are seldom changed at a stroke. If we have insisted on the failure of the Nationalist Revival to lift the army's crisis of morale, to do little more than begin to tackle the serious defects in army organization and training, the shortcomings in the high command and the continued confusion and debate over tactics, it is not, as in the style of novelists who concentrate on the less attractive aspects of their characters, to conjure up the picture of an army incapable of effective action. The French army's stand on the Marne in September 1914 demonstrated that it contained enough competent generals, a skilled general staff and a complement of soldiers fired by patriotism and a spirit of sacrifice to stem the German advance. Our purpose is to challenge the notion that the army was unified by a set of rules, guided by any logical system. Confusion and divisions persisted. Nowhere is this more true than in the theory of the offensive.

French casualties in the first 15 months of the Great War virtually equalled those of the next three years. Desperate attacks left 995,000 French casualties in 1914 and 1,430,000 in 1915, compared with 2,541,000 in 1916–18, and shattered French faith in the offensive.[1] 'It was obvious that the principles of the offensive which we tried to inculcate in the army before the war were too often misunderstood and misapplied', wrote Marshal Joffre.[2]

Responsibility for the ill-fated offensive had been laid at the door of a soldier elite led by Foch, Langlois and Grandmaison, working from the ideas of Clausewitz and Ardant du Picq.[3] Historians from the conservative British General Fuller to Monteilhet, a left-wing republican, have seen the French offensive as the product of the *Ecole supérieure de la guerre*, accepted by the high command and the general staff and diffused in training and manoeuvres. 'When we look back on Foch's offensive *à outrance*, we see Clausewitz throughout', wrote Major-General Fuller. 'His offensives *à outrance* and his battles *aux allures déchainées* became the doctrine of the French army.'[4] Monteilhet, too, viewed the 1914 offensive as the product of the military hierarchy. 'The professional army implies the premature offensive of 1914, and this springs fatally from its very nature', he wrote.[5] He saw the offensive as 'a theory linked in origin and in object to the destiny of the professional army', and attributed its revival to the *Ecole de guerre*'s historical approach to military science and fascination with Napoleonic campaigns.[6]

But an army as riven by political and social strife and internal doubt as the post-1900 French army was simply not capable of formulating or applying a tactical doctrine. The tactical offensive was a product of something other than professional miscalculation and the army's increasing 'confidence in itself in the years after 1910'.[7] Rather it sprang from the army's very lack of confidence, its poor organization and material weakness. To understand the genesis of the offensive, we must look more closely at the state of the army.

The offensive had for a century been part of the ideological baggage of the ultimately victorious republicans, and held sway after 1900 as the army came increasingly under their thumb and under the influence of the 'nation-in-arms' theory. It rested on a sentimental adherence to the offensive tactics of the Revolutionary armies with no attempt to adapt the theory to modern warfare. At this point in their history, however, the offensive was also a vindication of many current military weaknesses. The theory of the offensive nicely papered over serious army cracks.

The French army had no standard doctrine, only a few officers who wrote about tactics. Joffre recognized this on his appointment in 1911 as chief of the general staff: 'The mass of the army, so long a defensive body, had no doctrine and no training. Not knowing what path to follow, it ceased to transmit the rough doctrine of the offensive.... To create a coherent doctrine, to impose it on officers and men alike, to create an instrument to apply what I considered the right doctrine – that I held to be my urgent duty.'[8] In 1906, Major Driant noted that officers were free to choose among the various tactical theories of several generals,[9] and British officers watching the 1912 manoeuvres were unable to fathom the 'system' underlying them.[10] The 1912 infantry regulations, the *Porte-Voix* complained, were unclear on tactical questions and reflected 'the intellectual anarchy of the army's so-called elite'.[11]

This absence of doctrine was in part the intention of General André, who believed that any doctrine stifled individual initiative: 'Everyone could select a system in harmony with his own character, energy, temperament, aptitudes . . .', he said of his new infantry manual. 'Hoping to develop the initiative of subordinate commanders, it would have been absurd to limit the freedom of our army's elite with formulae.'[12] On 27 February 1901, he abolished general inspections, so eliminating an important element of central control and standardization, in the conviction that local commanders could best judge their own troops.[13]

The doctrine of the offensive was also bound up with the 'social role' pushed by Radicals after 1900. Radical reforms aimed to break down traditional notions of authoritarian discipline and produce an army of highly individualistic and patriotic soldiers, where individual initiative and a sense of duty replaced the automatic response. By re-forging the links between soldiers and the command, by raising the moral tone of barracks life and reinforcing the patriotic sentiments of conscripts, republican reformers believed that they had found a formula which would pay dividends on the battlefield. Only patriotic soldiers could be counted on to act bravely under fire. This conviction dated from 1793 when patriotic French troops had overwhelmed the choreographed armies of despotic states. 'The factors which push a group of men to attack the enemy despite impending death are unquestionably moral and psychological factors', wrote Saint-Cyr instructor Paul Simon. 'They are the patriotic personal will to conquer and a hatred for the enemy who threatens his home . . . The desire to conquer, patriotism and devotion are personal things. They must be rooted in each man's heart by inheritance or through education.'[14] Major Grandmaison, high priest of the offensive and a future general, commented: 'We are rightly told that psychological factors are paramount in combat. But this is not all: properly speaking, there are no other factors, for all others – weaponry, manoeuvrability – influence only indirectly by provoking moral reactions. . . . The human heart is the starting point in all questions of war.'[15]

The only tactic suited to an army of highly motivated patriots was the offensive, Grandmaison proclaimed. 'A well-spring of individual initiative is a valuable acquisition which we must never again abandon. But to bear fruit, this initiative must be applied to a positive doctrine. The study of the offensive is the only solid base for infantry training.'[16] Messimy also tried to link democratic idealism to offensive warfare: 'To conquer is to advance', he declared in his 1907 budget report. 'They must acquire the will to advance and to conquer.'[17]

The theory of the offensive, supported by the republicans for a hundred years, triumphed with the Radical regime. The reckless attacks of 1914 were not the result of a rational doctrine but of a 'mystique', an irrational cult[18] imposed not from the top of the military hierarchy, read out like the Bishop's pastoral letter from the pulpit, but evolved closer to its base under a flabby high command. A decade of warfare waged against the political loyalty and the moral authority of the service chiefs and a promotion system with a strong political component had pushed to the top of the military hierarchy men who had learned to step lightly through the minefield of French civil–military relations. Consequently, they often had neither the authority nor the inclination to challenge the more strident ideas of some of their enthusiastic subordinates. 'The high command, grown old among obsolete ideas and distrustful among political agitators was sceptical and impotent', Joffre wrote. 'Against this background, young and dynamic officers went to dangerous lengths, confident that their new doctrine conformed with war traditions and transported by their own confidence and enthusiasm.'[19]

The weakness of army leadership meant that ambitious young aides-de-camp and ministry officers had relatively free rein and could foist their views on inert superiors; Messimy complained:

Too many general officers are sinking steadily into an ever deeper mental lethargy, letting their aides-de-camp think for them. Captains of industry and managing directors, whatever their age, however many their collaborators, make their own plans and themselves tell their subordinates roughly what to do. This is not the case in the army, where aides-de-camp are often all-powerful. Things run no less smoothly for it perhaps, but in the fateful hour when the leader must himself make the decisions upon which victory will depend, he will find that ability to think and plan for himself has atrophied through long idleness.[20]

This proved prophetically correct in 1914 when Messimy, Joffre, Weygand, General Trentinian and others noted the inability of many generals to make crucial decisions in the heat of battle. Ten years earlier General Zurlinden had complained that members of the *conseil supérieur de la guerre*, the designated army commanders, used their aides-de-camp and not their staffs to prepare for war. 'This arrangement could continue in wartime, and so undermine the general staffs', he said.[21] Jean de Pierrefeu, a reserve lieutenant assigned to Joffre's headquarters during the war, quickly learned that a seemingly straightforward hierarchy contained many subtle variations, one of which was that a lieutenant colonel, who served as the general's adjutant, or a young lieutenant aide-de-camp was 'a hundred times more powerful than his rank'.[22]

Without strong direction from above, many officers simply aped fashionable views. Once in power, Radical republicans dusted off the offensive, and it quickly captured the imagination and ambition of many French officers. 'People probably realised that the offensive was fashionable higher up, and so did their best to "carry out the offensive" – but in what conditions!' Joffre wrote.[23] One of his first tasks on his appointment as commander-in-chief in 1911 was to draw order and tactical doctrine out of confusion. He was not successful. His very appointment showed that Radicals like Messimy were prepared to hedge on their commitment to a powerfully led army. As a colonial outsider, devoted republican and possibly the army's most talented chief, Galliéni would have combined military efficiency with political acceptability, but because of age and ill-health, he withdrew from the running in favour of General Pau. Pau was doubly suspect as much because of his brilliant military reputation which earned him rare respect in high military circles as for his devout Catholicism. Pau's insistence that he be allowed to name his subordinate commanders extricated both him and Messimy from an embarrassing situation.

As third choice for generalissimo, Joffre was a Radical's dream commander: 'It is understood in the democratic style, that every fat man is a good man', wrote Jean de Pierrefeu with the generalissimo in mind.[24] Joffre was no soldierly prima donna, but an amiable, self-effacing man, the Eisenhower of the Western Front. He accepted opposition calmly, simply patting his head and muttering 'Pauvre Joffre!' His modest background, southwestern origins and masonic connections were also a source of comfort to Radical leaders, sound in the knowledge that they had named no Saint-Arnaud or Boulanger to lead their army.

Unfortunately, Joffre lacked the starch and the intellectual preparation for high command. A polytechnician who had joined the engineers, most of his career had been spent constructing fortifications in the colonies. In 1894, he briefly rubbed shoulders with fame and glory when he was conscripted to lead the column which secured Timbuctu after Colonel Bonnier's expedition was wiped out. Otherwise, he read little, exhibited no curiosity about questions of strategy or tactics, climbing the military ladder by virtue of colonial service and hard work, occupying technical posts in France which culminated in his nomination in 1910 as 'director of the rear'. When in the following year he became commander-in-chief, he was out of his depth, a poor choice to mould an army desperate for shape and direction. Joffre was not a weak leader – his sacking of many generals and senior officers in the heat of battle regardless of professional or personal considerations testified to his determination and strength of character. Far from lacking character, as some like Sarrail claimed, Joffre had a steady hand, which in the early weeks of the war helped the army recover from the mauling it had received in the Battle of the Frontiers. Joffre did not lack character, he lacked ideas; and here his leadership faltered, for he failed to command the prestige to impose some order on the intellectual and tactical anarchy which ruled the forces before 1914. Joffre's ignorance of tactical questions exaggerated some of the army's worst defects, one of which was the inordinate influence of young officers. 'Don't worry about his shortcomings', his staff officers regularly said, soothingly. 'We are in control, we know what to do. He will endorse our decisions and everything will be all right.'[25] In his eagerness to fill the gaps in his knowledge, Joffre approached the study of strategy and tactics as if they were so many technical formulae to be learned uncritically.[26] But generally, he left the initiative to his staff, quickly nicknamed the 'young Turks'. 'Out of fear of a generalissimo, we had many capitainissimos', wrote Frederic Engerand, deputy for the Calvados.[27] Jean de Pierrefeu complained that Joffre did not direct his staff, he merely chose from among the plans they presented.[28] Visitors to Joffre's headquarters during the war were surprised and not a little disturbed to find him sitting in a bare office, so that maps were hung and his desk littered with papers each time important visitors or photographers arrived, to be removed again as soon as the guests disappeared.[29]

Hostility to the 'young Turks' built up to such a fever pitch in both political and military circles that after several months of war many read the German press releases in preference to those coming from Joffre's headquarters. However, Pierrefeu, who was by no means sympathetic to the staff men, believed them much maligned. Their hard work and skill had proved invaluable during the siege of Verdun, as in the opening phases of the war when the staff had kept the French army in the frontier battles. They were constantly seeking new solutions, methods and weapons useful in the trench deadlock, and on more than one occasion intervened to stop some local offensive launched by a general out for publicity and promotion.[30] The main problem stemmed from the fact that they were not forcefully led: 'As the result of a long peace, the army, which had become the empire of old men, fell into the hands of the young generations', he wrote. 'Despite the grave dangers that their inexperience, pride and lack of culture initially inflicted on the country, they came to constitute the nucleus of vital forces and wills ready for any sacrifice, whose action weighed heavily in the balance.'[31]

The shortcomings of the general staff also sprang from the general decline in army prestige and the quality of the officer corps before 1914, which was soon reflected in the *Ecole de guerre*, to which the best officers applied in their fifth year of service, around the age of 25 or 26. Students were often considered too young to make the most of the college training. 'Because of their short service and young age, these candidates do not always show the professional knowledge and maturity they need to profit from the course', Messimy wrote in 1911, echoing General Pédoya.[32] Criticism was frequently levelled at college teaching which made much of memory and little of imagination. For instance, the 1906 entrance examination required officers to trace Napoleon's campaign of 1807 down to the battle of Friedland or to describe the operations of the German 3rd army on 19 August 1870, write a paper in German, draw a map either of the Pyrenees or the Alps, list the nationalities which made up the Austro-Hungarian Empire or describe how British colonies were so placed as to 'assure the free circulation of the English fleet'. They were asked to give the peacetime organization of the four combat arms and of an army corps, to write on the role of 'intermediary fortifications and forts' and to describe a tactical movement based on these forts, to draw another map and resolve a tactical problem. The *France militaire* complained that the questions in this examination, like so many others, either demanded an 'arid nomenclature', were so vague as to be virtually unanswerable, or, in the case of the tactical problem, far too complicated. 'It is above all necessary that the [tactical] problem does not become a sort of guessing game or a Chinese puzzle as has often been the case since the school's creation', it wrote on 17 January 1906. 'It is often easier to appreciate the tactical judgement of an officer with a very simple question about a small unit rather than with a problem which calls for a "mass manoeuvre".'

General Debeney, professor of infantry tactics at the *Ecole de guerre* in 1909, denied that the war college was responsible for the costly tactical offensive; 'One of the characteristics of the *Ecole de guerre*'s teaching was a great tolerance of opinions', he wrote. 'The four years which preceded the war was a period of great tolerance during which we concentrated on educating officers and not upon formulating a doctrine.' Colonel de Grandmaison, chief of the 3rd bureau, was responsible for drawing up the controversial 1913 infantry regulations, 'which flew in the face of the ideas on the preponderance of firepower taught at the *Ecole de guerre* by Colonel Pétain and so many others', like Colonels Maud'huy, Fayolle and Debeney.[33] 'In fact, the *Ecole de guerre* always refused to formulate a doctrine', Debeney continued, pointing out that many of the school's professors were very critical of Grandmaison's 1913 regulations.[34]

Nor did Debeney believe that the offensive was a product of the *Ecole de guerre*'s historical approach to military science and fascination with Napoleonic campaigns. Foch, Bonnal and Lanrezac were 'pseudo-historians', simply pulling from military history whatever illustrations suited their pre-conceptions: 'I believe that when one begins historical studies at 30 or 40 years of age without knowledge of historical methods, one can only ask one thing of the documents – to illustrate in one way or another an opinion formed elsewhere based on other considerations', he wrote.[35] Pierrefeu also believed that the historians of the general staff 'took from Napoleon whatever suited their ideas while neglecting the prudence and calculation of this great Captain'.[36]

The *Ecole de guerre* was not a laboratory where the army's elite boiled up a tactical doctrine, but a school where future staff men learned the nuts and bolts of military administration: 'The *Ecole supérieur de la guerre* today is not properly speaking a "school of war", but rather a special academic organization turning out good staff officers', the *Porte-Voix* noted on 10 April 1914. 'It is therefore a staff school – and if brevet officers will pardon the audacity – an administrative staff school... Military science must not be confused with the hotch-potch of abstraction and jargon which makes up today's deplorable *esg* curriculum... There is no real war school.'

General Pédoya complained that the *Ecole de guerre* did not build military leaders or tacticians; 'It is a training school uniquely concerned with preparing officers for top commands. It does not impart the qualities or the learning needed in these commands. The instructors... whether because of their relatively low rank or meagre war experience, do not have the authority to make a doctrine credible.'[37] On 28 August 1901, the *France militaire* also criticized the tendency to take promising young officers rather than experienced older men on the teaching staff.

The general staff should have been the army's brain. The *Ecole de guerre*'s top graduates were taken for immediate staff assignment while the remainder returned to their regiments as brevet staff officers, alternating every three years between a troop command and staff duty. This system centralized and systematized tactical thought and ensured staff officers the practical experience denied them in the old staff corps. This staff system, organized on the German model, inherited many of the vices of the old staff corps. Staff assignments were spent performing routine administrative tasks. The law of 24 July 1880, creating the *service d'état major* from the independent staff corps, charged it with 'the direction and running of the administrative and medical services'. 'From his entry into the staff service', Messimy wrote, '... he checks charts, arranges numbers, draws up new rosters, reads and files circulars; he is very busy... but his imagination and judgement are never taxed.'[38] The army's 1,800 staff officers were scornfully referred to as 'leather cushions... a real waste of government money and of the intellectual powers of many officers'.[39]

The spirit of the offensive

Staff time allotted to military theory was minimal. Messimy complained that morning mail duties bit into training time and that one staff ride, a compulsory training outing held annually, took place in a thick fog in Christmas week, having been delayed by the pressures of administrative work.[40] 'Find me in France a staff which sets aside a little time each week for a staff ride, any outside work, a historical study, a *Kriegspiel* [war game] with a map or a garrison manoeuvre', Charles Humbert challenged. 'I defy anybody to name even one.'[41] He held that the government's fear of an independent military leadership had stunted the growth of the general staff by encouraging a concern with minutiae.[42]

The bureaucratization of the general staff soon told in the high command, most of whose generals were products of the *Ecole de guerre* with long years in staff assignments. 1914 demonstrated that men who had been considered competent staff officers and even brilliant tacticians too often failed to act decisively under fire. Debeney argued that courage and character, vital for a successful general, were not revealed by the school examinations,[43] while Mayer blasted a system which promoted many staff men on the basis of their graduation mark at the war college rather than on their military qualities.[44] 'They made magnificent generals in peacetime, handsome soldiers who knew everything but war', Foch remembered.[45]

With all of these problems, tactics were in confusion. Staff training exercises revealed a mass of conflicting tactical theories. 'No-one, or almost no-one, can agree with his neighbour on tactical questions', General Lamiraux, ex-vice-president of the *conseil supérieur de la guerre*, told the *France militaire* on 29 November 1901. 'Some say: firepower is all important... Others tell you: Attack! Always attack!... How does one create a method from such dissimilar ideas? We cannot do it. We take a bit of one, add a pinch of the other and hope that any errors... will sort themselves out in combat.' In 1911, War Minister Messimy found the situation little changed: 'The high command has allowed a regrettable fluctuation in the thought of the general staffs and subordinate commanders on many points', he wrote. 'The examples are numerous: in the domain of tactics, the conduct of combat, the employment of advance guards, etc... divergent views have been heard throughout the winter of 1910 during general staff conferences. The role of the artillery in combat has raised controversies between the Permanent Inspector of the Artillery and the Director of Practical Firing Courses.' Virtually every vital decision on tactics, organization and *matériel* had been delayed because of the inability of the high command to come to a consensus.[46] General Chomer, inspecting staff *Kriegspiels* in the South in 1913, noted little – if any – tactical similarity in the solutions: 'This exercise [led by a staff colonel] was so unique and based on such questionable ideas that I had to change the plans in the middle of the session and express my dissatisfaction.'[47] 'The solutions adopted are masterpieces of ingenuity', Arès said of these exercises. 'They try for originality rather than the simple and clear ideas troops need, and the most convoluted solutions are held to be the best.'[48] In August 1911, Messimy ordered all divisional staff chiefs and their subordinates to Paris to discuss standardization of tactics and training.[49] But widespread staff prejudices demanded that the 'drudgery' of exercises be avoided whenever possible.[50]

The offensive had failed to percolate through to the mass of the forces, either officers or soldiers, in any coherent form. 'Only a small nucleus ... was affected by the new ideas', Joffre wrote. 'In 1911, the new doctrine had not yet penetrated very far in the mass of the army, but this had begun to move. Tossed about for years between the most extreme theories, led by officers opposed to all innovation, [the army] nevertheless conserved an apathy and indolence which was almost complete.'[51] 'The grand strategic and tactical principles, drawn up from studying the principal European wars of the last century, have not yet penetrated the mass of combat officers', the future General Mordacq wrote in 1913. 'This is why, even in manoeuvres, we see fundamental principles violated.'[52] 'From a tactical point of view, there was much work to be done', Joffre said of the 1912 manoeuvres, an observation which applied equally to those of 1913.[53] Those of 1914, according to Weygand, 'taught us what to avoid rather than giving us models to follow'.[54]

Officers had little chance to keep up with the latest tactical innovations, much less to apply them in training and manoeuvres. Many military leaders had no training beyond that received at Saint-Cyr or the *Ecole polytechnique*. 'We stuff our chickens and starve our horses', Messimy complained. 'With luck and savoir faire, a soldier can rise to the highest ranks at the age of 60 without having progressed intellectually since he haphazardly acquired more knowledge than he could possibly digest at the *Ecole polytechnique* or at Saint-Cyr when he was 20.'[55] Captain Jibé concurred: 'Many colonels and generals are well aware that without present organization, they go through their career on what they learned in the military schools ... and tactics have undergone profound changes since then.'[56]

The German army regularly returned staff officers to the *Kriegsakademie* for classes on the latest theory, but senior French officers had no way of keeping up to date.[57] Staff manoeuvres were infrequent, nor, as has been shown, were they based upon any centrally accepted principles. 'The staff officers are not trained because the numerous exercises which they attend during the year are established and directed without method and so do not prepare them for their role as the auxiliaries of the command', General Chomer complained in 1913.[58] A *Centre des hautes études militaires* was established in 1911 to train majors and lieutenant colonels for high staff positions, but refresher courses were suspended in 1912 after only one year because the army could not spare officers from troop commands.[59] The future General Weygand, one of the 27 officers who passed through the Centre in 1913, found that the instruction there bore little relation to the combat conditions he was to meet barely a year later: 'I never failed to be struck by how little attention was paid to manoeuvre', he remembered.

One posited a well-chosen initial situation upon which we worked. We wrote out orders for the different echelons of the command, which required a considerable amount of work. Because of the lack of time, this sometimes became a test of endurance. Afterwards, we presented our solutions for discussion. But the study was never pushed far enough to produce incidents or events which are always found in war, which upset programmes and plans and oblige a commander to manoeuvre.[60]

Very few officers had passed through the Centre by 1914, and Messimy said that it had given the high command no 'coherent doctrine'.[61]

The costly offensives of 1914 did not stem from a coherent tactical doctrine, but from the fact that the 'forward rush' had filled the yawning gap left by the lack of a doctrine, of leadership and training.[62] Before the war, Lyautey predicted that the army's lack of training would make it impossible to impose a tactical theory: 'We will have revised the regulations and pushed the offensive in all its forms in vain as long as field training rests in its present impoverished state', he wrote to Messimy in December 1911. 'The danger cannot be overstated. All the best wills will break, all the theories will dissolve into talk.'[63] This is precisely what happened in 1914: 'From all over the front I received reports of mistaken manoeuvre which resulted in heavy losses and sometimes nullified the offensive and defensive worth of the soldiers', Joffre wrote.

I was told that the advance guard, out of a misunderstanding of the offensive, almost always attacked without artillery support and fell under the shells of enemy artillery in rows. In other cases, large units advanced without covering their flanks and were quickly exposed to cruel adventures. The infantry almost always attacked at too great a distance from its objective ... Above all, there was hardly ever cooperation between artillery and infantry. As soon as these facts became known, I told the armies to be more prudent in their attacks and above all to pay more attention to inter-arm coordination. It was precisely this perfecting of the offensive doctrine that I had proposed in the training camps that was now imposed in the rude conditions of battle. Alas! One needs more than a written order instantly to transform the mentality of an army. One needs time to create a new spirit.[64]

The colonial experience contributed in no small measure to the development of the tactical offensive in France. The first Moroccan crisis announced that France faced a serious threat at home, forcing colonial men to reorientate their ambition and imagination toward Europe. Colonial troops would add muscle to French defence, but more, French soldiers could learn much from the colonial experience. On a superficial level, this meant pushing the daring attacks which often proved so successful against lightly armed and poorly disciplined natives. But the real contribution of colonial men was to the spirit rather than to the mechanics of the offensive. For soldiers abroad, France was a political and spiritual invalid, deprived of unity by self-inflicted divisions which made a concerted national policy impossible to realize. For several decades, colonial soldiers had dreamed of transporting the unity of purpose felt in the colonies back to the Fatherland, uniting Frenchmen in a common bond of fraternity and national purpose. Lyautey led a chorus of colonial soldiers who believed it their 'social duty to tear this country from decomposition and ruin. Not by changing the constitution, an empirical and transitory method, but by a violent reaction upon manners, inertias and worries . . . react upon metropolitan inertia, establish a continuing and regenerating current of life between France without and France within, which will be a revival for this country.'[65]

The Nationalist Revival offered colonial prophets their chance. But the offensive triumphed not because the army was gaining confidence after 1910, as historians have claimed, but because army confidence and morale had been laid so low. Grandmaison, whose attitudes had been formed by service in Tonkin, was responsible almost single-handedly for drawing up the controversial 1913 regulations which praised the offensive as the only possible battle tactic. Only an infusion of 'moral forces', he argued, could pull France from her 'decrepitude'.[66] This was especially true for the forces. The Dreyfus affair had not only divided Frenchmen, it had accentuated the worst features of the metropolitan army: a high command bullied by politicians and terrified of responsibility, a bureaucratized general staff buried in the minutiae of military life, an army organization in shambles leaving troop commanders leaderless in resolving important tactical questions topped an understaffed and undertrained army. These problems were virtually insurmountable in the short term. Only by importing the 'moral forces' unleashed in the colonies could Frenchmen hope to meet their stronger enemies on equal terms. Grandmaison's ideas caught fire among a generation of officers desperate for a doctrine: 'The *Ecole supérieure de guerre* therefore had nothing to do with the doctrine of which I speak', Debeney concluded. 'It was the *Instruction sur les grandes unités* [28 October 1913] which formulated the doctrine of the offensive *à outrance* . . . Unfortunately, the influence of such a gifted man [Grandmaison] was considerable and created an attractive school for the mediocre spirits keen on formulae: at last we had a doctrine!'[67] A number of military pundits deplored the avidity with which a famished officer corps devoured the offensive *à outrance*, without realizing that it was a feast of hope – no matter how illusory – placed before starving men: Mayer castigated the officers who treated the offensive as a 'revealed dogma'[68] while Foch called Grandmaison's 1913 regulations 'a donkey's guide'.[69] But it was the very failure of the military elite to develop a logical and coherent doctrine and of the high command to apply tactical common sense in the military schools, often through no fault of its own, which accounted for the popularity of Grandmaison's appeal for confidence.

The tactical offensive was also helped by techniques in modern warfare. It did not flourish, as historians would have it, in ignorance of those developments. General Fuller accused Foch of being a 'tactically demented Napoleon' and ignoring new developments in weaponry. 'Step by step,' he said, 'with few variations, he follows Napoleon in the face of magazine rifles and quick-firing artillery as if they were the muskets and cannon of Jena and Friedland.'[70] De la Gorce maintains the French 'ignored the firepower of modern armaments, especially of heavy artillery, and under-estimated the effectiveness of defensive tactics'.[71] Liddell Hart said that: 'The new French philosophy, by its preoccupation with the moral element, had become more and more separated from the inseparable material factors.'[72] But it was those very material factors that led to the logical evolution of the offensive. Armaments development required an almost constant reassessment of tactics. Colonel Langlois wrote:

The instability of the [tactical] regulations . . . results from the instability of our modern conditions. If tactics formerly changed every ten years, according to Napoleon, they change more frequently today, and the regulations must be constantly modified. This is a fact of life. However, the broader the terms in which the regulations are couched, the less the detail, the more durable they will be.[73]

The doctrine of the offensive, popularized by republicans and colonial soldiers, provided a durable tactical law. The only way to cope with the new technical developments despite poor French resources was to rely on the patriotic audacity of French soldiers.[74]

Increased firepower was the most critical technical development in late-nineteenth-century warfare. The modern rifle, machine gun and cannon compelled military pundits to re-think established tactical theory. Soldiers who once fought successfully in relatively close formation now had to spread out under fire or risk heavy casualties. With a greatly extended battlefield, officers and NCOs could no longer control or keep track of their men in combat. Simon feared that discipline would be the first casualty unless soldiers were fired by patriotic zeal:

When a company deploys in rank on a 290-metre front . . . many will not hear orders. The men will no longer see their leaders. They have no-one in front to lead them, no-one behind to push them . . . Nothing is left to keep them moving forward but the individual will to win . . . History testifies that the soldiers who fight best when dispersed are those with the strongest patriotism and will to conquer, and the strongest devotion to their leaders and comrades. Soldiers without these feelings can be led into the attack only in relatively close formation . . . . The more armaments are developed, the more dispersal becomes necessary and the more individual moral strength is needed.[75]

'Firepower does not weaken the offensive spirit', General Bazaine-Hayter, commander of the 13th corps, wrote in October 1906. 'Never forget that a defensive battle will seldom bring victory. However powerful weapons become, the victory will go to the offensive which stimulates moral force, disconcerts the enemy and deprives him of his freedom of action.'[76] 'The systematic study of history shows that, the more armaments are perfected, the more advantages are offered by the offensive', General Langlois concluded.[77]

The advantages of morale in the face of modern armaments were held to have been demonstrated in the Russo-Japanese War of 1904–5. The superior moral preparation of the Japanese soldiers had more than compensated for modern Russian armaments, discrediting those who maintained that the Boer War had put paid to the offensive. The devastating rifle fire of the Boer War was proof of exceptional Boer marksmanship, but more importantly revealed the sorry state of the British army – professional soldiers led by upper class officers.[78] 'Tactics . . . will depend more on the morale of the nation at the beginning of the war and on the individual energy of the soldier than on the power of armaments', one soldier concluded.[79] Joffre later wrote:

The Russo-Japanese War was a dazzling confirmation of General Langlois' view that the Boer War had not discredited the offensive. Under the direction of Foch, Lanrezac and Bourderiat, the young intellectual elite at the *Ecole de guerre* now threw out the divisive old doctrine [the primacy of the defensive based on the Franco-Prussian War experience]. But as always happens when

The spirit of the offensive

established ideas are challenged, the value of the offensive was exaggerated by this group. People have referred to the 'mystique of the offensive'. This is probably going too far. But it does demonstrate rather well the somewhat irrational character the cult of the offensive took after 1905.[80]

Moral training was placed high for a second practical reason – the ever increasing superiority of German military strength. The French birthrate had dropped after 1870 so that by the turn of the century Germany's population was larger by 15 million. France made prodigious efforts to overcome this deficiency in army terms, conscripting 5,620 men for each million inhabitants as compared to 4,120 per million in Germany. But in 1903 she was able to muster only 459,000 men and 25,000 officers to 621,000 men and 26,000 officers across the Vosges.[81] With the approach of war, the situation worsened. The 1913 military law voted by the Reichstag gave the German army an almost 2–1 edge over the French, creating places for 42,000 officers and 112,000 NCOs to 29,000 officers and 48,000 NCOs in France.[82] German numerical superiority was backed up by an advantage in weaponry. In August 1914, Germany counted 4,500 machine guns to 2,500 in France, 6,000 77-millimetre cannon to 3,800 French 75s, and an almost total monopoly in heavy artillery. The long-term projections were even more sobering: in 1932, Germany's military resources were estimated at 5,400,000 trained men, compared with a maximum of four million in France.[83]

Although French military expenditure accounted for 36 per cent of the national budget, against only 20 per cent in Germany, in real terms the French investment fell far short of the German figure.[84] Klotz, president of the parliamentary army committee, put the 1904 defence figures at 38,256,364 francs compared with the equivalent of 99,195,998 francs spent in Germany in the same year.[85] General Langlois calculated in 1908 that Germany spent the equivalent of 1,770 francs per soldier while France spent only 914. 'This shows the efforts our eastern neighbours have made to equip and train their army. ... Happily, we still have the moral emphasis which we must consider a head start', he said.[86]

France therefore had to look for superiority in other spheres. 'To fight dispersed, a soldier must compensate for the lack of material support by a more solid moral preparation', André wrote.[87] 'We want an army which compensates numerical weakness with military quality', Messimy stated in 1908.[88] 'Neither numbers nor miraculous machines will determine victory', he said in 1913. 'This will go to soldiers with valour and "quality" – and by this I mean superior physical and moral endurance, offensive strength.'[89] Patrice Mahon gauged that only drive could beat numbers: 'The truth', he said, 'is that the only possible way of overcoming Germany's more efficient mobilisation is to confront them with our offensive.'[90] With these substantial material handicaps, France had to oppose mind to Germany's main. '[The Russo-Japanese War] was an impressive demonstration of moral forces', General Négrier wrote. 'Now it is everywhere recognized that with modern armaments the individual worth of the combatant has never been more important. This must comfort our hearts. The character of our soldiers adapts itself marvellously to present requirements. Numbers no longer decide victory . . . A certain numerical inferiority does not trouble our soldiers.'[91] 'It is more important to develop a conquering state of mind than to cavil about tactics', Grandmaison concluded.[92]

Nor did the prospect of foreign military aid significantly ease the French soldiers' sense of insecurity. Attempts to squeeze a firm military commitment from Russia and Britain ultimately only served to point up French isolation. The Russian army, badly mauled in the Russo-Japanese War, was not expected to regain its fighting form before 1910. Its leaders who visited France were often more interested in getting to the tables at Deauville or Monte Carlo than in discussing joint strategy, while in Saint-Petersburg, French generals met a wall of secrecy and evasiveness. French strategists obviously hoped for Russian assistance, but they could not count on it. And even if it came, Russian mobilization was so slow that France would have to bear the full weight of the German army in the initial stages of a conflict. For these reasons, French soldiers had to rely on their own resources in drawing up their strategic plans and tactical theories.[93]

Relations between French soldiers and their British counterparts were excellent, mainly due to the efforts of Brigadier, later Field Marshal, Henry Wilson, Director of Military Operations from 1910, who drew up the detailed plans which permitted the British Expeditionary Force to intervene effectively in the war's opening weeks. But the eagerness of British soldiers to fight on the continent was matched only by the hesitations of their government to mortgage its policies to French action: 'English army: first quality; young, well-informed if small command', Millerand noted after a conversation with Foch in October 1912. 'In the event of war, the English soldiers ask only to fight. The machine is ready to go: will it be unleashed? Complete uncertainty. The cabinet is vulnerable in its domestic policies [Home Rule], very uncertain in foreign policy, not knowing what it wants to do. It will do what public opinion wants it to do, [but Englishmen] are only interested in earning money.'[94]

In the final analysis, while Britain was in no way responsible for the disastrous Plan XVII, the 'problematical' nature of British intervention had a harmful effect on French strategic planning. Because

British intervention could not be counted upon, French planners did not include the British army in their line of battle, continuing to rely on the 'spirit of the offensive' to make up deficiencies in arms and manpower. But because the likelihood of intervention hinged on German violation of Belgium neutrality, Joffre dropped plans for an offensive through the Belgian Ardennes in favour of strikes in Alsace and Lorraine. While a French offensive through the Ardennes would probably have met only limited success, it would have been preferable for two reasons: firstly, it would not have broken against prepared German defences and, therefore, might have been less murderous. Secondly, it would have put French troops in a better position to counter the wide sweep of the Schlieffen plan. 'If Joffre bears the final responsibility for succumbing to the madness of the offensive *à outrance*,' writes American historian Samuel Williamson, 'the elusive prospect of British help, or, more precisely, the ambiguous *entente*, shares the responsibility for creating the framework in which Plan XVII was elaborated.'[95] In the end, the small BEF was consigned to the left flank to counter German forces expected obligingly to remain on the right bank of the Meuse, so freeing more Frenchmen for the offensive against the German centre and left.

Nor did French intelligence provide information which could modify the army's commitment to the offensive. Before 1914, the French led the world in communications intelligence. By 1900, Major Etienne Bazerie, seconded to the Quai d'Orsay, had broken the diplomatic codes of most world powers. From 1904, his work was complemented by the codebreakers at the *Sûreté* – the French criminal investigation department – under Commissaire Haverna, who unravelled the codes used by the Japanese in the Russo–Japanese War. Prime Minister Clemenceau enlarged Haverna's operation in 1907, and in 1909 created a *Commission interministérielle de cryptographie* which included representatives of the ministries of war, the navy, colonies and post and telecommunications. He also set up a *section du chiffre* at the war ministry under Major, later General, Cartier, who worked closely with Haverna in the *Sûreté*. Tested for the first time in the spring manoeuvres of 1914, Cartier's work earned him a congratulatory telegram from the war minister. During the First World War, the *section du chiffre* under Captain Painvin deciphered over 28,000 enemy messages including the famous 'télégramme de la victoire' which announced that Germany's 1918 offensive was running out of steam. Some rated the French cryptographers more highly even than the redoubtable British team of 'Room 40' in the Admiralty which deciphered the Zimmermann telegram of 1917.

Before 1914, however, the potential advantages offered by France's relatively sophisticated intelligence machinery were largely squandered due to two failings commonly associated with the Third Republic: interministerial rivalry and the indiscretions of politicians. Co-operation between Bazerie at the Quai d'Orsay and Haverna at the *Sûreté* ceased in October 1905 after the *Sûreté*, under orders from Prime Minister Rouvier, turned over deciphered telegrams to the Russians. Foreign Minister Delcassé's resignation in June 1905 followed closely by the transfer of Octave Homberg, the chief of the Quai d'Orsay's 'cabinet noir', removed the two men who had been able to channel Bazerie's brilliant but erratic energies. Bazerie's best cryptanalysts joined Haverna at the *Sûreté*, leaving the deciphering section at the Foreign Office a mere phantom of its former self. The *Sûreté* continued to decipher diplomatic communications but kept the information to itself. The Quai d'Orsay, for its part, refused to join the interministerial intelligence commission.

The indiscretions of politicians also did much to lower the effectiveness of French intelligence. Between October 1906 and January 1912, French prime ministers also doubled as ministers of the interior and so commanded the *Sûreté*. The decoded messages provided by Haverna allowed them to keep an eye on the activities of their colleagues, while foreign ministers were provided with similar information by their own cryptanalysts. On at least two occasions, this interministerial eavesdropping touched off a public quarrel between politicians which alerted the Germans that their diplomatic codes had been compromised: during the Agadir crisis, when Foreign Office decrypts revealed to a very annoyed Foreign Minister Selves that Prime Minister Caillaux was holding secret talks with the Germans and in May 1913, when the Prime Minister discovered that President Poincaré and Foreign Minister Pichon were negotiating to re-open diplomatic relations with the Vatican. The first crisis resulted in the Germans changing their codes so that few German telegrams were deciphered in the three years before the war, while in 1913 the *Sûreté* was forbidden to decipher diplomatic traffic. Most other countries changed their codes on the eve of the war after Gaston Calmette, editor of the *Figaro*, was shot to death in March 1914 by Madame Caillaux because, it was rumoured, he had threatened to publish telegrams deciphered by the French which revealed her husband's perfidious contacts with the Germans at the time of Agadir. The 'cabinet noir', therefore, was blinded on the eve of war. In August 1914, the object of the codebreakers became military rather than diplomatic, but when most of them reported to the rue Saint-Dominique and to the GHQ, their efficiency was hampered initially by the code changes of the immediate pre-war period.[96]

In 1914, French intelligence did not suspect that the opening German offensive would sweep far to the west of the Meuse nor that the enemy would throw their reserves into the front lines. This is not to say that the indications were not there: in 1904, a German officer code-named 'le Vengeur' sold the French a copy of a German plan which resembled that drawn up by Schlieffen, while in 1927, French Colonel Loustaunau-Lacau claimed to have discovered a 1913 report by the chief of the 2nd bureau, the intelligence division of the French general staff, which indicated that the right flank of the German army would scrape the sea.[97] But if the signs pointing out true German intentions appeared clearly marked, French commanders were prisoners of their own preconceived ideas. They were also ill-equipped to evaluate information culled by methods which seemed to belong more properly to the realm of popular fiction than to those of military science. The Japanese attack on Pearl Harbour, Hitler's offensive against Stalinist Russia and the Normandy invasion of 1944 provide ample evidence that even with the greater experience and more sophisticated techniques of the Second World War, governments and generals frequently ignored intelligence warnings. Joffre and two of his predecessors, Generals Brugère and Hagron, realized that the German thrust would most likely come through Belgium, but concluded that this would weaken German defences in Lorraine and open them to a counter-attack there. The spirit of the offensive also tended to minimize the importance of intelligence to French planners: why should French soldiers allow their plans to be dictated by the intentions of the enemy?[98]

In the final analysis, the tactical offensive was not the product of a system, but of the lack of one. It was the very disorganization of the army which was responsible for its popularity. The high command, composed largely of timid old men, looked on helplessly as young, dynamic officers eager for a doctrine, any doctrine, took up the offensive. The *esg* refused to apply a corrective, taking refuge in their role as a school of military administration. Staff officers were too busy making war by shuffling papers to bother with relevant problems of tactics and firepower. In any case, a tactical doctrine was destined to be only half understood and poorly applied in an army which had no place to practice it. The ever-growing strength of the German army, rather than introduce a sobering note of reality, simply increased the atmosphere of fantasy in which war was studied. To admit that France was simply too weak to face war with Germany was, of course, impossible. The likelihood of war had been growing since 1905. Once French soldiers got over the shock of Tangier and began to reconcile themselves with the possibility, indeed the probability, of a war with Germany, it was unthinkable to back down. 'Moral force' became the substitute for the arms which French soldiers did not possess.

12

The heavy artillery

The French army's most glaring deficiency in 1914 was its almost total lack of heavy artillery. France's 4,000 odd 75s were excellent light artillery pieces, reckoned superior in range and rate of fire to Germany's 5,000 Krupp-produced 77s, but hardly a match for the Kaiser's 2,000 heavy artillery pieces and 1,500 light mortars. French attacks were shattered and supply lines were thrown into chaos under the hammer of German heavy guns firing from the safety of positions beyond the range of the light French weapons or nestled behind woods or hills, inaccessible to straight firing 75s.[1] Contemporaries and historians blamed the lack of heavy artillery on the army's obsession with mobility over firepower which was part and parcel of the offensive doctrine: 'The pivot of our tactic in 1914 was the almost general belief in the predominance of manoeuvre over firepower', wrote General Herr, commander of the 6th artillery division in 1914 and a strong advocate of heavy artillery. 'In the concrete domain of organization, this principle translated automatically into the preponderance of numbers over *matériel*.'[2] 'The general staff did not believe in heavy artillery', claimed Michon. 'In this as in other questions, the technicians refused to bow before the facts', writing off the heavy artillery as 'useless baggage'.[3] De la Gorce wrote that the French tactical offensive 'neglected the firepower of modern armaments, especially of heavy artillery'.[4]

While it was certainly possible before 1914 to find officers who thought heavy artillery so much useless ironmongery, the French army's deficiencies in heavy weaponry cannot be put down to their nefarious influence. The French army's lack of heavy artillery in 1914 testified, like so many other military shortcomings, to a general confusion on tactical questions. It also provided testimony to poor army organization, a severe shortage of manpower and to the government's reluctance to pour money into defence.

France's deficiencies in heavy artillery became critical around 1910 when steady German progress had nibbled away France's lead. Until 1905, France's 75s and 155s gave her an incontestable superiority in heavy weaponry. The Boer War and especially the Russo–Japanese War proved the worth of heavy artillery, reversing the late 19th century trend toward light guns.[5] 'In the present state of armaments, heavy artillery is necessary for campaigning armies', wrote General Lombard, head of the French military mission to the Japanese army in 1904–5. 'Heavy field artillery is necessary for its effect on [enemy] morale and for certain material destruction.'[6] But it was the Germans, not the French, who heeded these lessons. In 1905, they substantially improved the rate of fire of their Krupp-produced 77s while perfecting a brake which increased accuracy. Also in that year, a curved trajectory 155 was adopted. Armed with superior range, the German army began to practise counter battery tactics, almost unknown in France. In 1909, an 'excellent' 105 mm cannon was added to the Kaiser's arsenal and in the following year a delayed fuse was perfected to increase effectiveness against entrenched troops. In 1911, a shaken French government woke up to find its army severely disadvantaged by its lack of heavy and medium artillery, and opened the debate on French artillery reform.[7]

Opponents of heavy artillery argued that the adoption of more pieces would complicate the manufacture and supply of shells and reduce mobility. Furthermore, they argued, it was pointless firing a weapon further than one could see. Although the 75 had an effective range of 6,500 metres, it was seldom fired beyond 4,000 metres.[8] Lastly, the Boer War and the Russo–Japanese War had demonstrated that while artillery was extremely effective against troops in the open, it simply left entrenched soldiers covered with a thin layer of dust. The rifle, not the cannon, was the greatest killer.[9] The Great War showed many of these points to be valid. The German armies rolling through France in August–September 1914 often found their heavy artillery unable to keep pace – one of the principal factors in Joffre's victory on the Marne was the absence in any quantity of German heavy artillery, so that the French 75s for the first time could manoeuvre in relative freedom.[10] Once the war settled down into a trench deadlock, allied soldiers again came under German heavy guns, but if properly dug in, they remained relatively safe. Even as late as 1916, British troops attacking on the Somme discovered the shortcomings of shrapnel and direct impact shells on well-entrenched Germans.

While many technical problems existed to discourage the adoption of heavy artillery, they appeared to slip away as war approached, reducing to a handful the number of men who invoked them as arguments against the heavy artillery. 1870 had been a supply officer's nightmare, leading some officers to declare in favour of a single artillery calibre to avoid confusion behind the lines and empty cassons at the front. But by 1910, the French army possessed a supply network capable of coping with a diversity of weapons, including almost 700 120 and 155 mm cannon already in operation. Arguably, the modernization of the heavy artillery would rationalize rather than complicate artillery supply. In any case, supply problems did not prevent the adoption by Millerand in 1912 of the 65 mm cannon for the cavalry and mountain troops.

The lack of mobility also appears to be a specious argument. The charge resulted in part from unrealistically abbreviated manoeuvres during which a three-day battle would be reduced to a few hours 'so as not to tire the soldiers'. By the time the heavy artillery had received orders to move, the attacking troops had taken their objective and were headed home, leading some to conclude that the heavy artillery could not keep on the heels of advancing infantry.[11] But by 1912, the French had joined the German and Austrian armies in introducing tractors to pull heavy guns. With the introduction of tractors, if not before, the 155 mm cannon acquired, in the estimation of Artillery Director General Banquet, 'a very acceptable mobility'. The 105 was as light and mobile as the 75, combining the advantages of a curved trajectory with a bigger bang,[12] and, according to General Banquet, 'many staff officers and officers of all arms' called for their introduction into the line of battle.[13] Some officers argued that the extra range of heavy artillery made it even more manoeuvrable than the 75.[14] The heavy and certainly the medium pieces had the mobility to satisfy even the most fanatical advocate of the offensive *à outrance*. If the high command had been so concerned with mobility, then presumably it would have forced through mobile field kitchens, lighter knapsacks and other reforms designed to increase mobility. But these reforms were no more successful than the heavy artillery. The problems which slowed the adoption of the heavy artillery in France were more technical than tactical.

Probably the greatest stumbling block to the full development of heavy artillery, and recognizably a very temporary one, was the problem of observation. Increased firepower meant greatly extended battlefields. Artillerymen who once fought in or very near the front lines found themselves increasingly distant from the troops they were meant to support, complicating the problems of fire direction and control. The obvious solution was to place forward artillery observers in airplanes or with the infantry, linked by telephone to supporting batteries. 'The question of air observation dominates that of firing against a masked objective', the *conseil supérieur de la guerre* declared on 9 April 1914. 'The artillery which learns to organize it first will assure itself a crucial element of superiority over its adversary.'[15] Unfortunately for Joffre, the Germans were first. Although the French began to experiment with air observers in 1912, they never perfected a signalling system, while German heavy artillery was directed with devastating accuracy from the air.[16] Money for field telephones was voted only in July 1914, leaving French officers to rifle houses and public buildings in the opening weeks of war in search of telephones.

The last objections levelled against big guns concerned their lack of accuracy and destructive power, both faults due primarily to problems of shell technology. This more than any concern with mobility postponed the adoption of the 105 'short' or mortar and cast doubts on heavier pieces. Firing trials of the 105 were abandoned in 1905 because the shell was 'inaccurate' and because it failed to dent field fortifications.[17] Trials restarted in 1910, but, in the final firing exercises held in March 1913, the inaccuracy of the projectile was given as a major reason for favouring the 'Plaquette Malandrin', a device fitted on to a 75 shell to give it a curved trajectory.[18]

The Russo–Japanese War had revealed the limitations of heavy guns against entrenched troops: 'Short cannons [mortars], because of their lack of accuracy at the distances at which one is ordinarily obliged to fire, are almost without effect against shallow works, like field fortifications', reported Major Payeur in 1905. 'Long, high calibre cannons produce some destruction.'[19] Artillerymen sympathetic to the adoption of the 105 'long' fretted over its lack of punch during trials in 1914: 'The effects produced upon obstacles are always limited even with the largest calibres', Lieutenant colonel Lepelletier told them.[20] The destructive effects could be increased with the introduction of a delayed fuse[21] in service with the German army since 1910. But when Charles Humbert asked why this had not been developed in the French army, he was told by the army general staff that it was not suitable for the 75.[22] So the medium and heavy artillery pieces were found wanting in part because the artillery had yet to perfect the shells, but delayed fuses were not adopted because the army believed the 75 unsuitable.

While these technical problems had not been resolved by 1914, trials, manoeuvres and wars had proved that heavy artillery could combine acceptable mobility with required firepower and accuracy. Even convinced advocates of the offensive had to admit that heavy guns were necessary both for dominating enemy artillery and for breaking enemy strongpoints like Metz. The German heavy artillery had been organized offensively for these reasons, while French heavy artillery remained largely fortress-bound. Already, by 1911, heavy artillery was deemed vital by the army general staff: 'The army general staff believes that it is necessary to look for the means to form as soon as possible a serviceable mobile heavy artillery, even if it is provisional', General Dubail, chief of the army general staff, wrote to Messimy on 24 November 1911.[23] Opponents of heavy artillery received a further setback with the publication of General Herr's February 1913 report on the Balkan wars, which stressed the crucial role played by the heavy artillery. While Herr's report by no means converted the most ardent worshippers of the 75, Joffre remembered that it won over the undecided and tipped the balance in favour of partisans of heavy guns and resulted in the immediate order by the parliamentary budget committee of 220 105 'longs'.[24] In February 1913, Artillery General Lamothe told the war minister that improvements in mobility, observation and shell technology, as well as the experience of the Balkan wars, had removed all technical impediments to the adoption of the heavy artillery.[25] In January 1914, even Grandmaison's 3rd bureau recognized the need for heavy guns and especially for mortars,[26] thereby falling in behind the *conseil supérieur de la guerre* which had called officially for a new range of big guns since July 1911.[27]

The French army's lack of heavy artillery cannot be put down primarily to its obsession with the offensive. The attitude of officers to artillery reform bore testimony to the army's confusion in tactical questions. Heavy artillery pieces proved an embarrassment to manoeuvre commanders because they did not know what to do with them. 'We have heavy artillery. Do we have a doctrine for the employment of this heavy artillery? It does not appear so', wrote one general in 1913.

Ask one hundred officers picked at random of all ranks and arms: 'What is heavy artillery? What is it used for? How is it used? Whom does it support? Where is it positioned?' The odds are 100–1 that you will get no answer or that the same questions will be asked of you. It is this impression of general confusion which one sees in Kriegspiels, cadre manoeuvres and grand manoeuvres when there is a decision to take concerning the heavy artillery. Of course, the decision is eventually taken, but it is makeshift, taken when there is no way out.[28]

General Weygand remembered that the *Centre des hautes études militaires* was equally vague on the role of heavy artillery in offensive operations. 'As for the heavy artillery, several batteries were included for effect in the line of battle of the armies which we directed on paper, but we could never learn what we were to do with them', he wrote.[29] In his famous speech of 14 July 1914, when Charles Humbert laid bare for his fellow senators the hard facts of French military unpreparedness, the lack of heavy artillery was put down in large part to the inability of the high command and the army general staff to agree on rules for its use.[30] 'The committee for new weapons believes, on the contrary, that one must postpone any decision on the [105 long] until we are told what is the exact role which the command expects it to perform', General Lamothe, a strong partisan of artillery reform, wrote to the war minister on 1 February 1913.[31] General Banquet complained that after 1901 the artillery directors, men instrumental in the selection of weapons, were basically staff men whose notions of artillery tactics were as vague as their technical knowledge.[32]

The lack of heavy artillery was thus due more to the lack of a set of rules governing its use than to a dogmatic commitment to offensive mobility. Examination of the debates over heavy artillery leads toward the inescapable conclusion that the adoption of calibres above the 75 snagged on the smorgasbord of choice rather than on the question of whether or not to adopt heavy artillery. In the final analysis, it was the endless wrangling among staff men and technicians over the respective merits of 105s, the Plaquette Maladrin, 120s, 135s and 155s which time and again waylaid a solution, which split those who wanted 'immediate results'[33] even if this meant accepting a piece whose merits had not been proved beyond all doubt from men who wanted continued experiment and the perfect piece.[34] And here, the administrative anarchy of the ministry, the lack of power and authority of the high command, the indecision of the general staff proved decisive.

Messimy blamed Joffre for the lack of artillery reform: 'I am certain that if . . . Joffre . . . [had] done battle with the technical service and with the [war] minister, he would have surely won', he wrote. 'It is beyond question that Joffre and the general staff were wrong not to attack the problem.'[35] But the ability of the commander-in-chief and the *conseil supérieur de la guerre* to force their views on war ministers and service directors was limited by their constitutional situation, the realities of civil-military relations in Radical republic and long-standing practices which made service directors the petty barons of the rue Saint-Dominique and Joffre their King John.

Despite Ralston's claim that Joffre's 1911 appointment as generalissimo made him the most powerful French soldier since Bonaparte, the war minister remained the constitutional head of the forces and the acknowledged army chief. While Joffre enjoyed good relations with most of his bosses, he had little say in the running of the ministry. War ministers continued to deal directly with their departmental chiefs in assessing army needs, bypassing the general staff. But ministerial instability left the army leaderless in resolving many technical questions. 'They fell before they had time to become familiar with the complicated workings of their ministry', Joffre wrote of the war ministers. 'Too many departments depended directly on this ephemeral minister... The result was the omnipotence of the directors who submitted to no superior authority.'[36] General Réné Alexandre, too, complained that ministerial inexperience and instability increased the strength of the administrators who saw questions from a financial rather than a military viewpoint.[37]

Nor were senior soldiers able to fill the leadership gap left by ministerial instability. Radicals had deliberately devalued the post of the chief of the general staff after 1900 by naming rather junior major generals to fill it, while the vice-president of the *conseil supérieur de la guerre*, the generalissimo, was deprived of any effective power. Chiefs of the general staff and vice-presidents of the *csg* came and went almost as frequently as war ministers. 'The chief of the general staff changes far too often to produce the continuity of ideas necessary for a doctrine', General Langlois wrote in 1911. 'For this reason, [tactical doctrine] can only be the product of a tradition.'[38] Between 1874 and 1914, the German army had only four chiefs of the general staff. The French army counted 17 chiefs of the general staff between 1874 and 1914, and six vice-presidents of the *csg* between the creation of the post in 1889 and its abolition in 1911.

Ministerial instability and inexperience did much to undermine the continuity so necessary for a long-range armaments programme. If the technicians and staff men could not agree on what type of heavy piece to adopt, successive governments argued over sums to be put toward heavy weapons, which threw a shadow over the future of the heavy artillery and helped to deflate any sense of urgency to find a piece. A programme of expenditure laboriously negotiated between the ministers of war and finance disappeared with the fall of Caillaux in January 1912. The new ministers, Poincaré, Millerand and Klotz, slashed the programme to the bone, from 246 million to 50 million francs, eliminating money earmarked for mortars, heavy guns, metal platforms for siege guns and new powder.[39] In November 1912, as the lack of heavy artillery joined other military shortages as a political time bomb ticking away under the Poincaré ministry, a programme of expenditure was hastily established. But Millerand fell on 13 January 1913, and the cash disappeared with him. Finally, in March 1913, the Parliamentary finance commission authorized the expenditure of 720,400,000 francs for vital reforms including heavy artillery and the service directors were invited to state their requirements: 'One had never witnessed such enthusiasm nor such haste to satisfy national needs', Joffre wrote. 'Fear is the beginning of wisdom.'[40] In April 1913, War Minister Etienne asked for yet more money for heavy artillery, initiating another complicated set of negotiations with the finance minister and the parliamentary finance committee which eventually established a programme of expenditure of more than one billion francs: 'But at the beginning of December 1913 the ministry changed again, bringing a new postponement.' The new war minister, Noulens, negotiated yet another package worth more than one billion francs, but the vote was overtaken by the April 1914 parliamentary elections. Finally, the defence expenditures were voted in July 1914, literally days before the war, after an impassioned speech by Charles Humbert in the Senate laid bare the extent of French unpreparedness.[41]

Many of the ill effects of ministerial instability might have been off-set by the high command and the general staff, steady hands in a sea of shifting parliamentary fortunes. The high command should have drawn up a programme of general army needs based upon the army's strategic requirements and financial bills should have been voted on this basis. But in drawing up the budget the military chiefs were seldom consulted by a war minister who dealt directly with the service directors in the ministry. 'It is fair to say that one of the causes of this inability to push through reforms lay in the fact that the general staff had not until then exercised over the ministry 'directions' the power of stimulation and coordination proper to the command', Joffre wrote.[42] As a result, the general staff was considered 'as a direction equal to the others, and did not have the necessary pre-eminence to coordinate the various wheels of the ministry'. The vice-president of the *csg* 'lived completely removed from the administrative organs of the ministry which ignored the needs regarded as vital by the council'.[43]

The creation of a commander-in-chief with increased powers, in July 1911, was a step toward coordinating and centralizing military reform. But old habits died hard, and war ministers continued to bargain directly with their directors. Budgets were approved by the finance section, not on the basis of defence needs but according to the bargaining talents of the section chief. Millerand did not consult Joffre when he scrapped the 1911 programme, nor was he consulted when the finance committee voted more than 720 millions in extra funds for defence in April 1913.[44] Neither the *csg* nor the technical services were asked for their views on the programmes drawn up in 1912 and 1913.[45] All the generalissimo could and did do was to nudge the minister gently toward reforms he believed vital. And even when Joffre did come out strongly in favour of the 105 mortar in 1913, he was overruled and the Plaquette Malandrin adopted.[46]

The general staff and its commander had no control over the technical services which produced the cannon, nor the ministry directors who requested the funds. 'The finance section worked directly with the parliamentary committee reporters,' Joffre wrote, 'and played a role for which it was not made. It modified and changed the departmental requests, it coordinated them. It was [the finance section] which in reality prepared the budget. Its position was even stronger, for it remained when the minister had fallen.'[47] The general staff could ask the ministry directors to request funds for certain proposals, as on 12 December 1913 when Grandmaison's 3rd bureau sent a long shopping list to the finance director, which included heavy artillery and tractors to pull it, more shells, airplanes, field telephones and strengthened fortifications at Verdun.[48] But the general staff could not require the director of finance, the service directors or the war ministers to act on their requests. 'The army general staff is not privy to the transactions among the various ministerial departments to *obtain these funds*, and the results of negotiations are made known to it, sometimes very late and only if requested, only for information', read a general staff memorandum of July 1914.[49] The war minister, not the general staff and its chief, must unify and coordinate military policy: 'Only the war minister is able to regulate the various organs of the central administration', the general staff again wrote in an undated memorandum. 'The mission of the army general staff is to aid him in his task by providing the information he needs to make a decision and to see that it is carried out.'[50] If staff officers or service directors had sought to take the debate over the army's *matériel* deficiencies out of the ministry into the public arena, as Michon suggested they should have done to circumvent heavy-handed finance directors and ministers,[51] they certainly would have received little thanks from a republic which required its soldiers to behave like faceless civil servants.

Directors were virtually omnipotent within their ministry departments, and it fell largely to the director of the artillery to push through a programme of reform. The relative strength of the French artillery up to 1905 was due largely to three artillery directors – Berge, Mathieu and Deloye – who combined tactical and technical knowledge of artillery with the tenacity and strength of character to push their views. Deloye almost single-handedly forced the adoption of the 75 despite opposition from the artillery technical committee.[52] But Deloye was axed in 1901 because left-wing Radicals disapproved of his political views and independent spirit. His successors were mainly staff men with limited knowledge of the arm which they had been called upon to direct and little inclination to shake the inertia of Parliament or the technical committees: 'After 1901, when General Deloye was removed from the ministry, it seemed that an artilleryman who had followed technical questions for much of his career was ill-suited to direct the artillery', General Banquet reported.

Politics were not absent from the choice of directors. In any case, until 1912 the artillery directors were, above all, staff officers. They had hardly worked in the technical services and knew very little about the *matériel*. They had not held staff positions which allowed them to follow armaments questions. It is also very unlikely that any high-ranking staff officer would have voluntarily consented to lead a technical service where initiative had become difficult. Whatever the reason, General Deloye's successors had neither firm nor preconceived ideas . . . either on technical or tactical questions. They made no effort to acquire opinions nor to defend them with the faith which leads to decisions.[53]

The result, according to War Minister Noulens, was 'endless discussions' in the technical committees.[54] 'Count the number of artillerymen consulted on a technical matter, and you have that many different opinions on the same subject', wrote General Gascouin.[55]

[The general staff] knew very little about the artillery – as did also a part of the high command – before and at the beginning of the war . . . The many committees which sat in these years had some heated sessions which rarely enlightened, where agreement could not be reached and from which everyone emerged with ideas unchanged, having learned nothing because they listened to nothing.[56]

Because no-one could agree, more trials were ordered and a decision delayed still further. Caillaux complained that war ministers refused to intervene to force a decision because 'they admired the omnipotence of the committees from whose yoke they should have escaped'.[57] Nor was the decision hastened by the constant turnover of personnel on the technical committees or by the reorganization of the committees themselves. In 1910, War Minister Brun abolished the artillery technical committee claiming that its functions overlapped with those of the directory and that this had delayed decision on a piece.[58] In April 1912, Millerand named General Lamothe inspector of studies and technical trials for the artillery 'to bring more unity into the programmes and to speed up trials'.[59] The choice of Lamothe was not altogether a happy one: a strong personality and a cautious technician he refused to hasten the selection of artillery pieces despite constant prodding from Millerand: 'One does not construct matériel *in response to an embarrassing political situation*', he told Millerand. 'It is a long-term work which cannot be abbreviated without risking the worst uncertainties both from a financial and a military point of view.'[60]

Lamothe's appointment also served to point up the personal conflicts which sabotaged artillery reform. He quarrelled both with Millerand and with General Sylvestre, head of the fortress artillery, whose co-operation was vital in agreeing on heavy pieces.[61] Technical disputes often masked more personal conflicts among men and groups whose reputations and careers were at stake in committee meetings. Cliques and petty rivalry divided the artillery direction and technical committees, made up of ambitious polytechnicians and inventors, for whom the sobriquet 'petites chapelles' was frequently applied. 'The senior officers whose inventions and perfections had singled them out, were naturally called upon to sit on these committees', Caillaux wrote.

Each one of them looked for new technical progress and, following a natural human inclination, was inclined to refuse approval to anything which did not have his stamp or that of his friends. If the general staff or the minister proposed the adoption of a piece invented elsewhere, a coalition was rapidly formed among the disappointed, which included the majority of the committee. The ministerial suggestion was not rejected, of course. A preliminary investigation was ordered, a second if need be. Studies piled upon studies, reports upon reports. Time passed. Nothing happened.[62]

'In fact, the system of studies in the arsenals was only partially successful and encouraged more a spirit of anarchy than production', General Herr concluded in 1919.[63]

No-one appeared willing or able to impart the smack of firm direction into the artillery. Ministers were impressed and intimidated by the authority of the technicians[64] and seldom remained in power long enough to lay a successful siege even had they been so inclined. Artillery directors after Deloye lacked the authority and knowledge to push a programme through to completion. Even the president of the technical committee could not make the inventors and arsenals follow his wishes.[65] Consequently, the technical services continued to invent, debate, perfect and intrigue.[66]

The poor state of the technical services and the arsenals did little to hasten solutions. The arsenals had been run down after construction of the 75 at the turn of the century, so that many of the best technical officers left for more lucrative jobs in industry.[67] Polytechnicians were resigning from the artillery at an alarming rate: a 1908 report said that 50 per cent of the polytechnicians in the artillery had resigned because of poor career prospects,[68] while the *France militaire* calculated on 9 January 1914 that only 26 per cent of artillery officers were ex-polytechnicians. In May 1910, the general staff reported that the arsenals were so short of manpower that they could not cope with the projected expansion of the artillery without a substantial infusion of money to hire civilian workers,[69] and these presumably would not be skilled men.

The only obvious answer was to turn to private industry for heavy artillery and Messimy trumpeted his decision to do so in 1911 as a radical and revolutionary way to break the stranglehold of the army technicians and bureaucrats on reform and provide a rapid solution to the lack of heavy artillery.[70] In fact, private industry had for years been cooperating with government arsenals, usually producing parts to be assembled by the arsenals. By 1914, army orders alone to armaments firms totalled two million francs.[71] But the resort to private industry did not produce the immediate results hoped for by many of its partisans. In the first place, its pieces and parts were often dearer than those produced in the arsenals, which complicated the problem of finance still further.[72] Nor did private firms like Creusot have the productive capacity to fill army orders rapidly. Krupp, pushed by the Kaiser, had developed a large armaments division, but for French firms, arms remained a relatively minor sideline. Creusot thought it hardly worth the expansion required to produce the 120s and refused to expand its armaments division, so that orders of 105s took three years to fill.[73] What was needed was an intelligent and firm artillery director able to coordinate France's industrial capacity and talent, rather than pit private industry against army technicians and arsenals, which did little to speed up the selection of a piece.

The alacrity with which some politicians and soldiers called for the adoption of products of private industry naturally led to the whispered charge that money was changing hands. Humbert's jeremiads lost much of their effect because many suspected that they sprang more from personal interest than from a genuine concern for French defence.[74] In a September 1912 letter to Poincaré, Humbert in turn charged that some officers ordered certain weapons or parts to be produced privately because they stood to profit personally:

I can add here, in parenthesis, that certain almost irrefutable facts have recently been brought to my attention which lead me to ask very seriously if the purchase by different ministry services of some defective, obsolete or excessively onerous *matériel* has not been motivated by the abusive action of certain very influential officers in the ministry looking to increase the benefits of some firms in which they secretly have a preponderant interest.[75]

The whiff of scandal automatically hung over anyone who came out strongly in favour of a weapon produced by a private firm.

Georges Michon argued that the three-year service law of 1913 also delayed the heavy artillery, both because it devoured funds which should have gone toward big cannon and because it demonstrated the preference of the high command and the Nationalist Revival for bodies over hardware. 'The three-year law imposed large expenses on the finance direction (163 million in 1913) obliging it to put off any important programme of war *matériel* . . . The general staff, concerned with the three-year law, was only preoccupied with the question of numbers.'[76]

Michon ignores the fact that the Left, not the Right, traditionally opposed armaments expenditure. The finance ministry certainly complained that the three-year law imposed an extra financial burden, and opponents of expenditure no doubt used the extra year's service as an excuse to delay still further putting cash toward heavy artillery. But this 163 million represented only about one-tenth of the money which the army had requested for vital improvements in 1913 and about one-twelfth of the sum actually voted the following year.[77] Benazet, member of the parliamentary budget committee and reporter of the war budgets for 1913 and 1914, admitted that they had postponed requests for heavy artillery funds in 1913, not because the three-year law had absorbed all of the money but because to do so would have led to 'sterile discussions' and blown an already overloaded political circuit.[78] So funds for heavy artillery ultimately were waylaid for political, not financial, reasons, as in 1914 when the budget vote was delayed until after the April elections.[79]

Nor did Michon realize that the three-year law was vital if the French army hoped to expand its artillery. One of the greatest stumbling blocks to creation of new heavy batteries was the army's shortage of manpower. The resignation of officers and the shortfall of recruits not only meant that training suffered in existing batteries but also that the situation would become impossible if the artillery were expanded to include heavy batteries. 'One must recognize that the task of the command has become very difficult in action due to the failings of lower cadres whose training cannot be carried out in the present conditions', Galliéni noted in 1911.[80] When in January 1912 the artillery direction attempted to create ten 155 batteries, the general staff replied that they simply did not have the men to staff it: 'The army general staff agrees with the third direction to call for these pieces immediately, but due to the lack of trained artillerymen and above all of cadres, it seems absolutely impossible to constitute the new groups on the model of the present type of 155 groups.'[81]

General Herr may have proved that heavy artillery was an essential element in modern war, but where were the men to come from? 'It would be premature to decide upon ... the creation of a long-range army corps artillery which General Herr calls for, especially if one takes account of the fact that because of the crisis of manpower this creation will obviously be at the expense of the 75 batteries.'[82] Before the law's passage, the French army could muster only one mobile heavy artillery regiment,[83] and the army was debating a switch from four piece to six piece batteries, as in the German army, to conserve manpower.[84] But French artillerymen argued that four piece batteries offered more advantages under fire, that what was saved in captains with a six piece battery would be lost in lieutenants, and that in any case it would not economize enough men for more than a few mortar batteries.[85] With the three-year law, Joffre immediately organized 15 new heavy batteries and the following year five heavy artillery regiments were formed.[86] So the three-year law speeded up rather than retarded the constitution of the heavy artillery batteries by supplying the men to staff and train them.

However, the three-year law did not solve the problem of the shortage of officers. The expansion of the artillery, like that of the air corps, could only be at the expense of the already over-stretched infantry and cavalry. The infantry had already sent over 100 officers into the artillery and its officers might regard a further expansion of that arm with some trepidation, not to mention jealousy, at the promotion opportunities offered to their artillery colleagues.[87]

In the final analysis, the heavy artillery was not sabotaged by the tactical offensive or by a clique of right-wing officers and politicians more concerned with morale than *matériel*. For a decade after 1900, France and her army had dozed, somnambulant in the confidence that war with Germany was always avoidable. Deprived of any sense of urgency, technicians tinkered to no real end, with no real direction, in the knowledge that no politician was ever likely to commit the government to a substantial programme of armaments.[88] Joffre, Messimy and others put down the lack of heavy artillery basically to the fact that for the first decade of the 20th century, France had followed 'the chimera of idealism, the chimera of universal pacifism ... the country slowed down its effort'.[89] 'Before the war we went through a period of 12 years when the feeling that we must protect ourselves had significantly diminished', Benazet wrote in 1916.[90] When at last France woke up to the realities of her weakness in 1911, reformers attempted to make up over a decade of lost ground in a few months. Not surprisingly their programme stumbled over an army which was without confidence, without firm leadership to help it resolve vital tactical and technical questions, rich in bureaucrats, technical committees and confusion, poor in money and manpower. 'If the [artillery] directors who followed [Deloye] did not seem to possess all the necessary qualities, it is probably due to the belief which spread and thrived for too long in the nation that war could always be avoided', wrote Banquet. 'This is the primary reason for the delays in our armaments. The divergencies of opinion among the experts were only a pretext for those who did not know or did not want to take any decision whose utility they did not believe in, and also for those who preferred to put off the expenses which they believed inconvenient.'[91]

In the question of heavy artillery, like that of the offensive, the shortcomings of the nation-in-arms interpretation are only too apparent. By 1912 if not before, the question of mobility versus firepower had been resolved in favour of the heavier pieces. It had never been a problem for medium artillery or mortars. Soldiers were agreed on the need for big guns, but which piece to select? Here it was the old story of the lack of firm leadership, financial stringency, bureaucratic complacency, ministerial instability and institutional malfunctioning which intervened to sabotage vital reform.

13

Conclusion

The Great War is one of the most depressing episodes in modern history. Born in a muddle of diplomacy, its operations became a byword for military incompetence, lack of imagination and inhumanity which entombed the best of a generation in a furrowed, splintered landscape of mud and utter desolation. After 1918, historians seeking to explain the appalling military blunders of those four years and the enormous miscalculations which dogged the French war effort put them down to the failure of military system – the professional army. *L'Armée nouvelle*, written by Jean Jaurès in 1910, provided them with their bible.

The 'nation-in-arms' was born with the Revolution. The desire to place French defence in the hands of a militia, or at least of a large conscript army with length of service and the professional element reduced to a minimum, was motivated by domestic political considerations: the professional army was the hired assassin of republican mythology, a uniformed Sparafucile who had dispatched two republics and smothered several revolutions. Unfortunately for the Left, the Franco-Prussian War also proved that military expertise was necessary for national defence.

Civil–military relations, while an important element of government in every country, were a dominant political theme in the Third Republic. From its foundation in 1870, the republic sought a working relationship with its soldiers, debating how an authoritarian, hierarchical army could be slotted comfortably into the left-leaning, democratic republic. The Gambettists assumed correctly that as long as the patriotic sentiments and professional needs of its soldiers were satisfied, republicans could sleep safely in their beds. By the early 1890s, the anti-republicanism of the army was fast receding into a dim and distant past. The Dreyfus affair reopened the question of army loyalty to the regime. But while the general staff provided the pretext for the debate, its singular virulence was achieved in great part because Radicals exploited the miscarriage of justice to pry their way to power. Once successful, they attempted to redefine the relationship between the army and the government.

Conclusion

'Turning away from the splendours of the French military tradition, the Radicals, as the new political masters of France, now envisioned a reshaping of the spirit and ideals of the officer corps, to bring them into accord with current democratic concepts', wrote David Ralston.[1] This attempt at military reform failed, the theory goes, because an incorrigibly right-wing officer corps was rescued in the nick of time by the Nationalist Revival. But Radical politicians made no serious attempt to reshape the spirit and ideals of the officer corps. By posing as the champions of liberty and saviours of the republic, they successfully concealed the absence of ideals which came to characterize their passage in power. Examined closely, their slogans and claims assume the threadbare look of Third Republic electioneering, while their reforms sought to assure the loyalties of the soldiers by controlling their livelihoods. Although Radicals claimed to be seeking new officer attitudes and ideals, opening vents in the solid walls of reaction to let in the winds of change, in reality they sought control of promotion and thus of each man's career. Political loyalties were therefore assured by pressure rather than by persuasion. In the final analysis, it was the control of the military institution rather than of the ideals of its members which provided the Radical solution to the grossly inflated problem of civil-military relations.

The social role offered the only serious and, Girardet believes, one of the few successful attempts by Radicals to alter officer attitudes. But the impact of the 'social role' on the outlook of the forces must not be overstated. The indifference of officers to their men noted by Lyautey stemmed not from their anti-democratic prejudices – their modest social origins and the fact that many had been promoted through the ranks reduced aristocratic *hauteur* to a minimum – but from a neglect spawned by an excessive concern with administration, examinations and the minutiae of military life. The military system rather than social recruitment was to blame. The Radical period reinforced, rather than discouraged, the bureaucratic attitudes of the officer corps by creating more administrative demands while presiding over a decline in discipline which forced many into the safe refuge of paperwork. Many of those who pushed the 'social role' in the regiments did so with both eyes fixed on the promotion list, giving these undoubtedly beneficial reforms a bad name among officers who saw them exploited by opportunists or as substitutes for military training and efficiency.

Concern with the place of the army in domestic French politics underpins *L'Armée nouvelle*. Jaurès, too, recognized that French Radicals had sought no fundamental change in the nation's military institutions nor influence over the political sentiments of its officers, and it is his analysis of the shortcomings of the forces and the confusion of ideas resulting from Radical government which make up the most original part of the book. Jaurès sought to dispatch the problem of army–republican relations by virtually eliminating professional soldiers. The army was a relic of a bygone age, a dinosaur of discipline and patriotism lumbering toward the abbatoir of socialist internationalism. French defence, he argued, should rest with a militia system of the Swiss model. Professional soldiers would be reduced to a mere 4,000, recruited among sons of the working class and trained in universities rather than in elitist military colleges. Military service would be limited to six months followed by training periods in the reserve and the whole defence edifice would rest on a foundation of civic rather than military spirit. The barracks army would give way to the nation-in-arms, eliminating the compromises the republic was forever obliged to strike with its soldiers. It would also exorcise the force of oppression which blocked the legitimate aspirations of the working classes.

While this reform blueprint contained many interesting ideas, as a solution to France's defence problems it was neither particularly original nor convincing. Where it was revolutionary, however, was that it linked a form of military organization – the militia – with a strategic doctrine – the defensive. Some saw in this a military rationale: less well trained, militiamen were less apt at manoeuvre and therefore unprepared for offensive warfare which required well-drilled professional soldiers. However, many could and did argue the contrary: that the offensive was the only tactic suitable for men who compensated for lack of training with patriotic *élan* and 'moral force'. Neither historical precedents nor politicians were lacking to link the offensive to the Left and the untrained.[2] 'M. Jaurès' bill contains not only a plan of organization, it contains a plan of war and a plan of political organization', the staunch Dreyfusard deputy, Joseph Reinach, told his colleagues. 'It is inexact, historically inexact, inexact from all points of view that a defensive policy, a policy of peace and justice, requires a defensive strategy.'[3]

Historians of the 'nation-in-arms' school, by invoking arguments for the defensive based on the real or supposed fighting potential of the militia, overlook the fact that Jaurès' true motives for posing as the champion of the defensive were political ones – a strictly defensive army offered a compromise between pacifism and the requirements of national defence. Henri Paté, who examined Jaurès' proposal for Parliament, claimed that, in attempting to meet both the demands of his conscience and the country's defence needs, Jaurès had probably satisfied neither.[4]

The legacy of the *L'Armée nouvelle* to the post-war generation was the defensive orientation of the 'nation-in-arms'. Post-war reforms which reduced service time and the professional cadre to a minimum and committed France to a strictly defensive posture, bore the stamp of Jaurèsian pacifism, a reluctance to fight, as much if not more than they incorporated the supposed military lessons of the First World War. They also distorted the military debate of the inter-war years, for when de Gaulle called for the creation of a mobile tank force organized for offensive warfare, the tanks were to be driven by professional soldiers. In France, more than anywhere else in Europe after 1918, a recruitment policy imposed a strategic and tactical doctrine.

For many left-wing historians of the inter-war years with a political axe to grind, the temptation to read Jaurès' thesis back to the days before the war was great. Monteilhet, Michon and others could explain the blood and blunders as the logical and inevitable spin-off of the professional army with its in-built commitment to the offensive. The professional army was contrasted with 'nation-in-arms', the offensive with the defensive, the professionals with the humanists.

These conclusions were motivated by concerns more political than historical. An examination of the army before 1914 reveals that it was ruled more by confusion than by logic, afflicted by institutional malfunctioning rather than from the neat application of a coherent but wrong-headed system of thought inspired by professional principles and right-wing sentiments. Monteilhet and Michon charge that the Right voted for more men while ignoring *matériel*. If some soldiers constructed battle theories which played down the importance of *matériel*, it was largely because they had to make do with what they had, or did not have. Joffre gave this as his reason for drawing a dangerously optimistic picture of French defence in his January 1914 report to the *csg*: 'It was for reasons of morale, especially to avoid discouragement, that I couched this report in optimistic terms: our inferiority could escape no-one . . . As long as we lacked heavy guns, it was useless to insist on the advantages these pieces offered to the combatants.'[5] The Left, on the other hand, consistently opposed funds for new weapons. Nor, in the pre-1914 army, was there a correlation between a general's political view and his tactical theories. An outspokenly republican general like Sarrail announced to officers under his command in 1907 that '[The machine gun] will never have a place on the battlefield'. 'Despite his advanced political ideas, he was particularly reactionary in military matters', Mayer said of Sarrail.[6] Left-wing General Percin, an artilleryman and André's adjutant, also opposed the introduction of heavy artillery. Even André justified his budget cuts by claiming that forts were a waste of money because the army planned to take the offensive.[7] For those, like Caillaux, who praised André for his purchase of some heavy artillery, General Banquet noted that 'the great persuasive powers' of the inventor, rather than any general plan of army needs, was responsible for the purchase of the 155s in 1904.[8] Even General Michel, whom post-war historians canonized after he fell on his lone stand against the high command in support of his defensive strategic plan, also stood virtually alone against them in 1911 in his opposition to their call for more heavy artillery.[9] Good republican generals like Joffre and Galliéni stood shoulder to shoulder with the Catholic Castelnau and Pau in their advocacy of the offensive.[10] The offensive was common ground shared by Right and Left, civilian and soldier, atheist and believer.

Jaurès' defensive and the offensive both sprang from a recognition of French military weakness. Both were strategies based upon the inadequacies of French defence. So while the nation-in-arms historians have attempted to explain the military shortcomings revealed by the war in terms of the failure of the Left to impose their ideas in the army, this book has examined how Radical ideas and policies actually influenced military development before 1914, in order to strike a more balanced appreciation of the state of the forces, and thus the reasons behind the war's mistakes.

The war revealed an army short on training, leadership and armaments. While the Radicals can by no means take anything approaching total responsibility for these deficiencies, they had for over a decade presided over a steady decline in French military strength. Bad training was the result of the lack of training areas and personnel. But rather than hard cash, politicians held out near useless palliatives – the social role was substituted for marksmanship, civic spirit for manoeuvre, 'military preparation' for training camps.

Joffre's purge of the high command in the heat of battle in 1914 served to point up the poor quality of many senior French officers. Lower down, the decline in the quality of the officer corps was quantifiable. For at least a decade before 1900, good men had begun to look elsewhere for a career. This was only to be expected as the 1870 war slipped further into the past, taking the fire out of calls for revenge and recovery of the lost provinces. After 1900, both the numbers and quality of officer applicants plummeted, and the *Zeitgeist* was not entirely to blame. The army was in official disfavour. Radicals publicly discouraged the talented and the middle class from applying. The use of the army to break strikes and the doors of churches, the close watch kept on the political and religious convictions of officers and their wives, served to discourage many from embracing the career of arms, while parents of prospective Saint-Cyr cadets exerted every ounce of parental pressure to keep young men on civvy street. This decline in quality recruitment at Saint-Cyr soon told in the *Ecole de guerre*. Attempts

Conclusion

by Combes, André and Clemenceau deliberately to offend the pride and religious and political sentiments of many officers and, above all, the abolition of promotion committees, coaxed others into premature retirement, further eroding the quality of the officer corps. While by no means every officer who hung up his spurs in these years did so for political reasons, the official cloud, reflected in low pay and prestige, which drifted over the army after 1900 lowered military morale to the danger mark and convinced many talented men, especially polytechnicians, that a better future was to be had outside.

The high command soon began to reflect intellectual and moral anaemia as the rest of the army was bled. The generally poor quality of the army's top men cannot be put down exclusively to the preference given to left-wing officers on the promotion ladder. Men from traditional Catholic backgrounds could still climb to the top ranks. But with the abolition of the promotion committees, advancement certainly became more arbitrary and men with political connections stood a much better chance of drawing a winning number in the promotion lottery. Many officers now cultivated their political contacts rather than their brains, which resulted in a very uneven quality of senior officer. The promotion committees had had their faults, but they did guarantee solid standards among general officers. Now the door to the stars swung open and shut with every puff or political wind, or responded to the pull of invisible strings. Some good men were allowed to squeeze through, as were some bad ones. In general, the competence of service chiefs in 1914 had slipped several notches since 1900.

Politics on occasion operated directly as a rigid selection board for senior soldiers. But more important, it encouraged a caution and self-effacement which froze the energy of command posts. Before 1900 Lyautey noted that the army was slipping into bureaucratic habits, with initiative and imagination giving ground to administration and routine. Radical control confirmed and accentuated this trend, inculcating habits of caution, a fear of taking risks in men who found that, since Boulanger at least, republicans preferred desk-bound officers to the more flamboyant image traditionally cultivated in military circles. Men capable of showing the initiative and single-mindedness needed to push through reforms, to lift the dead weight of administrative intransigence, were fired, resigned or drifted to the colonies, leaving top jobs largely to affable administrators like Joffre: 'Democracies are uneasy', wrote General Zurlinden. 'They have a tendency to suspect men to whom talent and circumstances draw attention, not because they do not recognize their qualities and services but because they tremble for the republic.'[11]

The colonial army proved the exception to this rule. While, in

France, hierarchy and politics crushed initiative and imagination, in the colonies these attributes were encouraged, to the point that indiscipline was built into the system. It was this open attitude and energy, more than their actual war experience, which pushed many colonial men into the places vacated by their less able or more timid metropolitan colleagues. In the case of General Mangin, who ignored that separate sets of rules existed for home and colonies, that Rhenist separatists were not Touareg tribesmen to be tipped into revolt with the aid of secret government backsheesh, it pushed him into early retirement. For colonial men, French garrisons spawned textbook officer paper soldiers able to discuss and administer war, not to fight it: 'The functionaries' mentality . . . has no place in the colonies', wrote Lyautey.[12]

Short of energetic leaders, the army slipped deeper into administrative lethargy, clinging tightly to a system which favoured note-takers and where the study of war bore little resemblance to reality. Abel Ferry, Emile Mayer and others put the high command's inability to come to terms with the murderous reality of trench warfare down to the fact that artillerymen and engineers like Joffre, Nivelle and Foch had monopolized the army's senior commands. In 1915, GHQ was almost entirely in the hands of the 'armes savantes'.[13] Operational sanity arrived with Pétain, an infantryman well aware of the effect of bullets on human bodies and sensitive to the needs of his men. 'The system of our army condemns artillery officers, when they have a future, as one says, to go from one service to another without stopping in a fixed post and without specializing', Mayer wrote.

When barely arrived in a regiment, they already know they will soon leave for a new post. They spend their time preparing for the next job rather than concentrating their enthusiasm on present needs . . . They are the victims of a bad system which puts them in a bad position for getting experience. That is why so many officers from the 'knowledgable' arms ignore this important part of command which rests on the profound knowledge of the soldier.[14]

He reckoned that Foch had spent less than one-quarter of his career in troop commands.

Artillerymen suffered most from a system which placed great value on examination results and where administrative experience rather than troop command were rewarded. Senior commanders and staff men were bound to be remote from the hard realities of the fight, unable to feel the palpable resentment of front-line troops over inequalities and poor organization which eventually exploded in 1917. The general staff was composed of hardworking, patriotic men who spent much time and energy trying to make the offensive work, but who lacked the imagination and a touch of common sense to realize that the break-through was impossible. 'The mentality of [the staff officer] inclines him to remain a student all his life', wrote Jean de Pierrefeu.[15] The Great War was their sort of war, one to be administered and supplied rather than led.

Joffre's attempts to set things right by purging many generals thought incompetent ironically increased indecision in high places: 'Such was the terror of "limogeage" among most generals, that more than one sacrificed his subordinates to escape the punishment which hung over him', General Trentinian wrote. 'This took away their initiative and made palace mutes of many of them, henceforth incapable of giving a useful opinion, of daring to make an interesting proposal. Every attack was prepared only to satisfy the general staff still set on the offensive *à outrance*.'[16] Nor could the nerves of commanders have been steadied by War Minister Messimy's repeated demands in September 1914 that incompetent chiefs be summarily shot.

The decline of the high command hobbled military efficiency. The point allegedly at issue in the Dreyfus affair was who rules the army. Radicals confused rather than decided this debate. Governments and war ministers seldom intervened in any constructive way in important policy decisions. The concept of authority in the army was encouraged to wander in a bureaucratic maze, the myth of the hierarchy to vanish amid its twists and culs-de-sac. Nowhere was the absence of firm leadership more apparent than in the lack of armaments. No military Moses with imagination and force of personality existed to lead his Israelites through the morass of bureaucratic complacency, ministerial instability, institutional malfunctioning and financial stringency to the promised land of big guns. The shabby attempts by deputies to squirm out of their responsibilities for army deficiencies by claiming that they had voted every franc requested for defence were no more valid in 1914 than they were in 1940. Furthermore, they missed the point, for they did not tackle the basic question of authority in the forces. The Nationalist Revival, far from encouraging military decadence, voted men and money to put many of these problems right while half-heartedly attempting to boost the courage and confidence of the high command. But the politicians of the Nationalist Revival were far too republican to slice completely through government red tape and give the high command real power to coordinate an effective defence system. Some knots are Gordian and can only be cut.

In the final analysis, the Radical republic got the army it deserved – a characterless leadership bolstered by a bureaucratic and unimaginative general staff, largely out of touch with the men it controlled. Political indifference to military efficiency widened the gap between the French army and her Teutonic rival. Radical reformers who had set out to 'republicanize' the army in 1900 had succeeded beyond their wildest dreams, for they had put the finishing touches on the transformation of the forces to fit the image of other French government departments: 'The spirit of 1793 is down, bureaucracy is in the ascendant', Abel Ferry concluded in 1915. 'That is the trouble.' But the road to success had been bulldozed through a garden suburb of professional values and attitudes. The Dreyfus affair was not a hiccup in French civil-military relations from which the army quickly recovered, as historians have maintained. The accusations of moral cowardice and disloyal, perhaps treasonable, sentiments levelled at officers during the Dreyfus affair increased the soldiers' sense of isolation, throwing up a wall of distrust between the army and the republic which was breached only temporarily by the *union sacrée* of 1914. The inhabitants never forgave the republic this callous piece of redevelopment. When defeat seemed certain in 1940, a generation of soldiers who had suffered arrogant politicians since 1900 did not pass up the opportunity to pull the rug from under the feet of its tormentors.

APPENDIX 1

War Ministers, 1871–1914

	date of taking office
de Cissey	5 June, 1871
du Barail	29 May, 1873
de Cissey	22 May, 1874
Berthaut	15 August, 1876
de Rochebouët	23 November, 1877
Borel	13 December, 1877
Gresley	13 January, 1879
Farre	28 December, 1879
Campenon	14 November, 1881
Billot	30 January, 1882
Thibaudin	31 January, 1883
Campenon	9 October, 1883
Lewal	3 January, 1885
Campenon	6 April, 1885
Boulanger	7 January, 1886
Ferron	30 May, 1887
Logerot	12 December, 1887
de Freycinet	3 April, 1888
Loizillon	11 January, 1893
Mercier	3 December, 1893
Zurlinden	28 January, 1895
Cavaignac	1 November, 1895
Billot	29 April, 1896
Cavaignac	28 June, 1898
Zurlinden	5 September, 1898
Chanoine	17 September, 1898
de Freycinet	1 November, 1898
Krantz	6 May, 1899
de Galliffet	22 June, 1899
André	29 May, 1900
Berteaux	15 November, 1904
Etienne	12 November, 1905
Picquart	26 October, 1906
Brun	24 July, 1909
Berteaux	3 March, 1911
Goiran	28 May, 1911
Messimy	27 July, 1911
Millerand	15 January, 1912
Lebrun	13 January, 1913
Etienne	22 January, 1913
Noulens	9 December, 1913
Messimy	14 June, 1914

APPENDIX 2

Army corps areas, 1871–1914

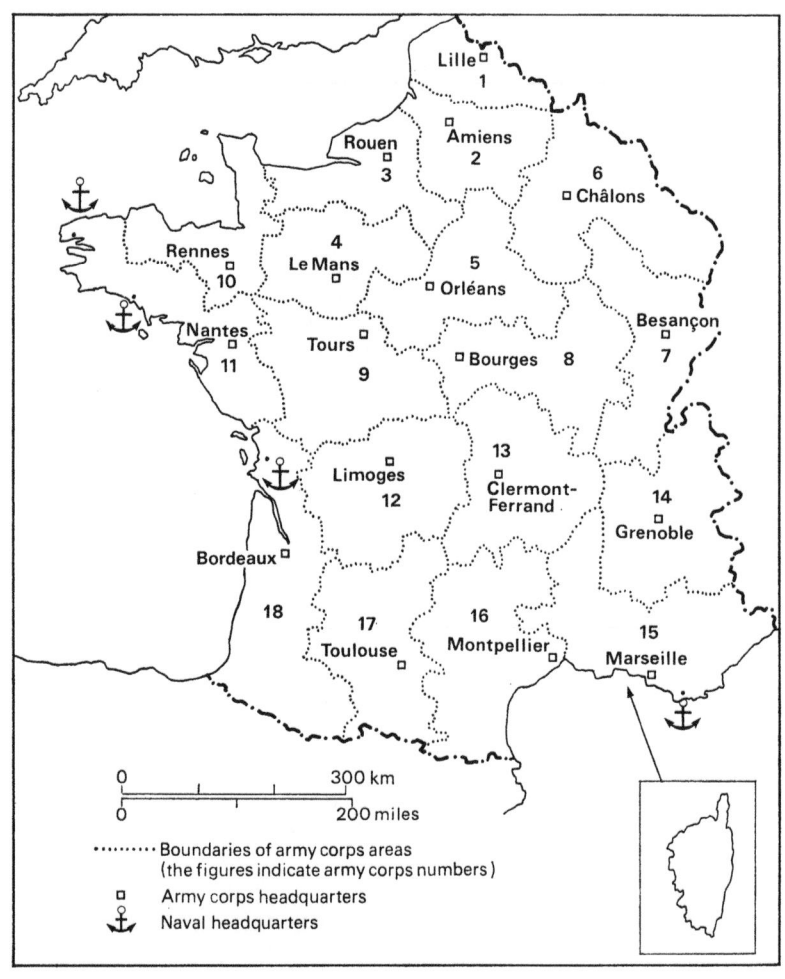

From Vidal-Lablache, *Atlas général*, Colin, 1895

Notes

The following abbreviations are used in the notes:

ACM   Archives de la Charante Maritime
AHG   Archives historique de guerre
AN   Archives nationales
BI   Bibliothèque de l'Institut
BN   Bibliothèque nationale
JO   *Journal officiel*
PRO   Public Records Office

I THE ARMY AND THE REPUBLIC

1. J. P. T. Bury, *Gambetta and the Making of the Third Republic*, London 1973, p. 21.
2. E. L. Katzenbach, *Freycinet and the Army of Metropolitan France*, unpub. Ph.D thesis, Princeton University 1952, pp. 202–3.
3. Bury, p. 369.
4. *Ibid.*, p. 372.
5. AN C 2816.
6. Emile Mayer, *Nos Chefs de 1914*, Paris 1930, p. 108.
7. du Barail, *Mes Souvenirs, 1820–1879*, col. 3, Paris 1896, p. 304.
8. Mayer, *Nos Chefs*, p. 96.
9. du Barail, p. 250.
10. David Ralston, *The Army of the Republic*, Cambridge, Mass. 1967.
11. R. Girardet, *La Société militaire dans la France contemporaine*, Paris 1953, p. 250.
12. See S. Scott, *The Response of the Line Army to the French Revolution*, OUP 1978.
13. Porch, *Army and Revolution*, London 1974, pp. 41–2.
14. Girardet, *La Société militaire*, p. 136.
15. F. Bédarida, 'L'Armée et la république: Les opinions politiques des officiers français et 1876–8', *Revue historique* 1964, p. 150.
16. Bury, p. 384.
17. *Ibid.*, p. 368.
18. *Ibid.*, p. 371.
19. du Barail, p. 421.
20. Charles de Rémusat, *Mémoires*, vol. v, Paris nd, p. 427.
21. *Avenir militaire*, 21 November 1873; Right: Generals Aumale, d'Aurelle de Paladines, de Chabaud-Latour, de Cissey, Ducrot, Robert, Martin de Pallières, Loysei and Lt.-col. Bastard. Left: Generals Chanzy, Letellier-Valazé, Chareton, Saussier, Billot, Frébault and Col. Denfert-Rochereau.
22. Quoted in Bury, fn. pp. 458–9.

23. L. Thomas, *Le Général de Galliffet*, Paris 1910, p. 93.
24. Katzenbach, p. 70.
25. *Ibid.*, p. 129.
26. Bédarida, fn. p. 139.
27. *Ibid.*, p. 154.
28. Bury, p. 369.
29. Weygand, *Mémoires*, vol. 1, *Idéal vécu*, Paris 1953, p. 30.
30. Bury, p. 21.
31. *Ibid.*, p. 162.
32. *Ibid.*, p. 21.
33. *Ibid.*, p. 98.
34. S. de Sacy, *Le maréchal MacMahon*, Paris 1960, p. 281.
35. Ralston, p. 79.
36. Bury, pp. 152–3.
37. *Ibid.*, p. 155.
38. *Ibid.*, p. 163.
39. S. de Sacy, p. 283.
40. Bury, p. 401.
41. A. Ranc, *Souvenirs*, Paris 1913, p. 281.
42. Bury, p. 459.
43. Ralston, p. 172.
44. R. Girardet, *La Société militaire*, pp. 198–9.
45. Katzenbach, pp. 202–3.
46. Bédarida, p. 157.
47. Weygand, *Histoire de l'armée française*, Paris 1938, pp. 174–5.
48. P. Chalmin, *L'Officier français de 1815 à 1870*, Paris 1957, p. 160.
49. *Ibid.*, p. 161.
50. Girardet, *La société militaire*, p. 186.
51. P. de la Gorce, *La République et son armée*, Paris 1963, p. 39.
52. *Ibid.*
53. Weygand, *Mémoires*, vol. 1, *Idéal vécu*, p. 21.
54. T. Zeldin, *France 1848–1945*, vol. 1, *Love, Ambition and Politics*, Oxford 1973, pp. 403–4.
55. Saint-Aulaire, *Confessions d'un vieux diplomate*, Paris 1953, p. 85.
56. Iung, *La République et l'armée*, Paris 1892, p. 204.
57. P. Delattre, *Les Etablissements des Jésuites en France 1540–1900*, Paris 1940–1957, vol. 3, p. 1372 and vol. 4, pp. 338, 1397.
58. *France militaire*, 6 October 1904.
59. John W. Bush, 'Education and Social Status. The Jesuit College in the Early Third Republic', *French Historical Studies*, vol. IX no. 1, Spring 1975, p. 136.
60. *France militaire*, 2 September 1905.
61. Girardet, *La Société militaire*, p. 276.
62. M. Larkin, *Church and State after the Dreyfus Affair, the Separation Issue in France*, London 1974, p. 84.
63. du Barail, p. 484.
64. Vallery-Radot, *Journal d'un volontaire d'un an*, Paris 1874, p. 27.
65. AN, C 3149.
66. Bush, p. 139.

Notes to pages 23–37

2 THE ARMY AND THE NATION

1. J. Monteilhet, *Les Institutions militaires de la France*, Paris 1932, p. 217.
2. *Ibid.*, p. 215.
3. *Ibid.*, pp. 214, 220.
4. Alan Mitchell, 'Thiers, MacMahon and the conseil supérieur de guerre', *French Historical Studies*, vol. 6, no. 2, 1969, pp. 232–52.
5. Freycinet, *Souvenirs*, vol. 1, Paris 1914, p. 291.
6. Monteilhet, p. 159.
7. Archives historiques de guerre (henceforth AHG), 7N 33 and X^s 184.
8. *Avenir militaire*, 9 October 1888.
9. AN, C 5436.
10. Freycinet, *Souvenirs*, vol. 2, p. 508.
11. *Avenir militaire*, 26 November 1884.
12. See *Ibid.*, 11 April 1884.
13. *Ibid.*, 6 July 1882.
14. Freycinet, *Souvenirs*, vol. 2, pp. 289–93.
15. AHG, 7N 33.
16. *Ibid.*, report of 21 May 1881.
17. Monteilhet, p. 177.
18. AHG, 7N 33.
19. *Ibid.*, dossier 15.
20. AHG, X^s 184 and *Le Petit Parisien*, 29 January 1880.
21. *Avenir militaire*, 23 August 1887.
22. AHG, 7N 33.
23. E. Mayer, *Nos chefs de 1914*, Paris 1930, p. 109.
24. AN, C 2807.
25. Lewal, *Lettre à l'armée*, Paris 1872, p. 240.
26. *Avenir militaire*, 6 March 1876.
27. AHG, X^s 184.
28. Quoted in E. L. Katzenbach, *Freycinet and the Army of Metropolitan France*, unpublished Ph.D thesis, Princeton, 1952, p. 231.
29. *Avenir militaire*, 26 March 1877 and 21 December 1881.
30. *Progrès militaire*, 21 April 1886 and 30 October 1889.
31. du Barail, *Mes souvenirs, 1820–1879*, vol. 3, Paris 1896, pp. 517–18.
32. *Avenir militaire*, 6 September 1882.
33. E. Weber, *Peasants into Frenchmen*, London 1977, p. 298.
34. Freycinet, *La Guerre en province*, Paris 1871, pp. 332–5.
35. *Ibid.*, pp. 356–7.
36. AHG, 7N 33.
37. Weber, *Peasants*, pp. 99–104.
38. *Ibid.*, pp. 105–8.
39. R. Girardet, *La Société militaire dans la France contemporaine*, Paris 1953, p. 168.
40. AHG, 7N 33.
41. Katzenbach, p. 171.
42. *Avenir militaire*, 2 June 1872.
43. Trochu, *Oeuvres posthumes*, Tours 1896, p. 211.
44. *Ibid.*, pp. 193–4, 213, 241–2.
45. *Avenir militaire*, 22 March 1872.
46. Lewal, *Etudes de guerre*, Paris 1873, pp. 61–2.
47. Berge, *Etudes sur la réorganisation des forces militaires de la France*, Tarbes 1871, p. 9.

48. Girardet, *La Société militaire*, p. 164.
49. *Débats parlementaires–Chambre*, 15 June 1881, p. 1,230.
50. Lewal, *Etudes de Guerre*, pp. 36–7.
51. *Ibid.*, p. 46.
52. *Ibid.*, pp. 10–11.
53. AN, C 2807.
54. Trochu, *Oeuvres posthumes*, pp. 222, 215. The six French schools were Saint-Cyr, the *Ecole polytechnique*, the cavalry school at Saumur, the artillery school at Metz, the staff college in Paris and the Prytanée, the military preparatory school.
55. Trochu, *Oeuvres posthumes*, p. 221.
56. AN, C 2807.
57. Trochu, *Oeuvres posthumes*, p. 242.
58. du Barail, p. 317.
59. L. Hanrion, *Saint-Cyr, Neuf années de commandement, 1871–80*, Paris 1888.
60. Emile Mayer, *Trois Maréchaux*, Paris 1928, p. 111.
61. *Avenir militaire*, 1 July 1882.
62. du Barail, p. 404.
63. *Avenir militaire*, 26 March 1885.
64. *Ibid.*, 13 January 1886.
65. *Progrès militaire*, 28 July and 23 October 1886.
66. Quoted in Katzenbach, p. 382.
67. Dilke, 'The French Armies', *The Fortnightly Review*, 1 November 1891, p. 622.
68. C. Bugnet, *En écoutant le Maréchal Foch*, Paris 1929, pp. 170–1.
69. P. Mason, *A Matter of Honour*, London 1974, p. 373.
70. AHG, 1N 13.

3 THE HIGH COMMAND

1. R. Holmes, *The Road to Sedan*, unpublished Ph.D thesis, Reading University 1975, pp. 314–15, 334–5.
2. F. A. Bazaine, *Episode de la guerre de 1870 et le blocus de Metz*, Madrid 1883, p. x.
3. Trochu, *Oeuvres posthumes*, Tours 1896, p. 126.
4. A. Soulier, *L'Instabilité ministérielle sous la Troisième République, 1871–1939*, Paris 1939, p. 483.
5. Ollé-Laprune, *La Stabilité des ministres sous la Troisième République 1879–1940*, Paris 1962, pp. 67, 41.
6. du Barail, *Mes Souvenirs, 1820–1879*, Paris 1896, vol. III, p. 384.
7. du Barail, p. 364.
8. *Ibid.*, pp. 387, 338, 364, 464–5.
9. Trochu, *Oeuvres posthumes*, p. 107.
10. *Progrès militaire*, 6 March and 3 April 1886.
11. du Barail, p. 364.
12. D. Ralston, *The Army of the Republic*, Cambridge, Mass. 1967, pp. 163–7.
13. Ralston, p. 173.
14. AHG, 7N 36.
15. du Barail, p. 303.
16. Ralston, pp. 189–91.

4 THE DREYFUS AFFAIR

1. E. Weber, *Peasants into Frenchmen*, London 1977, pp. 300–1.
2. *Ibid.*, pp. 301–2.

Notes to pages 55–70   261

3. R. Girardet, *La Société militaire dans la France contemporaine*, Paris 1953, p. 221.
4. *Ibid.*, p. 226.
5. A. Messimy, *Considérations générales sur l'organisation de l'armée*, Paris 1907, pp. 18–19.
6. André, *Cinq ans au ministère*, Paris 1907, p. 99.
7. W. Zaniewicki, 'L'Impact de 1870 sur la pensée militaire française', *Revue de défense Nationale*, August–September 1970, p. 1339.
8. Girardet, *La Société militaire*, p. 191.
9. Jean de Pierrefeu, *GQG, secteur 1*, Paris 1920, pp. 12–13.
10. Maurois, *Lyautey*, Paris 1931, pp. 85–6.
11. P. Heidsieck, *Le Rayonnement de Lyautey*, Paris 1947, pp. 186–7.
12. Emile Mayer, *Nos Chefs de 1914*, Paris 1930, p. 109.
13. A. Combarieu, *Sept ans à l'Elysée avec Emile Loubet, 1899–1906*, Paris 1932, p. 27.
14. P. Guedalla, *The Two Marshals, Bazaine and Pétain*, London 1943, p. 269.
15. P. Sorlin, *Waldeck-Rousseau*, Paris 1966, p. 409.
16. Louis Thomas, *Le Général de Galliffet*, Paris 1910, pp. 310–11.
17. Combarieu, p. 27.
18. Waldeck-Rousseau Papers, BI, Ms. 4567.
19. H. de Rolland, *Galliffet*, Paris 1945, p. 172.
20. Radziwill, *Lettres au Général Robilant*, vol. 2, Paris 1933, pp.341–2.
21. *L'Eclair*, 12 July 1909.
22. Rolland, p. 172.
23. T. Révillon, *Camille Pelletan, 1846–1915*, Paris 1930, p. 142.
24. Combarieu, p. 42.
25. Waldeck-Rousseau Papers, BI, Ms. 4579.
26. Radziwill, vol. 2, p. 341.
27. Waldeck-Rousseau Papers, BI, Ms. 4567.
28. Combarieu, p. 37.
29. Douglas Johnson, *France and the Dreyfus Affair*, London 1966, Chapter 11.
30. Waldeck-Rousseau Papers, BI, Ms. 4566, 13 September 1899.
31. Combarieu, p. 40.
32. Révillon, p. 144.
33. de Civrieux, *Du Rêve à la réalité, 1871–1908*, Paris 1909, pp. 88, 76–7.
34. Radziwill, p. 338.
35. Waldeck-Rousseau Papers, BI, Ms. 4567.
36. Waldeck-Rousseau Papers, BI, Ms. 4613.
37. *Ibid.*
38. André, *Cinq ans*, p. 144.
39. Zurlinden, 'Le Haut commandement des armées', *Revue des deux mondes*, 15 June 1903, p. 800.
40. Waldeck-Rousseau Papers, BI, Ms. 4207.
41. Rolland, p. 207.
42. Metzinger, *La Transformation de l'armée, 1897–1907*, Paris 1909, pp. 22–4.
43. Rolland, p. 190.
44. Metzinger, p. 25.
45. H. Langlois, *Questions de défense nationale*, Paris 1906, pp. 148–9.
46. Pierrefeu, *GQG*, p. 113.
47. Langlois, *Questions de défense nationale*, pp. 150–1.
48. *Avenir militaire*, 16 January 1894.
49. Sorlin, p. 409.
50. Langlois, *Questions de défense nationale*, pp. 150–1.

51. E. Mayer, *Nos Chefs de 1914*, Paris 1930, pp. 7–8.
52. Metzinger, p. 25.
53. Rolland, p. 190.
54. Radziwill, p. 344.
55. Sorlin, p. 415.
56. Waldeck-Rousseau Papers, BI, Ms. 4579.
57. André, *Cinq ans*, p. 11.
58. Radziwill, pp. 344–5.
59. D. Ralston, *The Army of the Republic*, Cambridge, Mass. 1967.

5 THE RADICAL SOLUTION

1. J. Caillaux, *Mes Mémoires*, vol. 1, Paris 1942, p. 215.
2. G. Clemenceau, *Le Cas Hartman*, Paris 1903, pp. 111–12.
3. T. Zeldin, *France 1848–1945*, vol. 1, *Love, Ambition and Politics*, Oxford 1973, pp. 715–16.
4. Waldeck-Rousseau Papers, BI, Ms. 4567.
5. Radziwill, *Lettres au Général Robilant*, vol. 2, Paris 1933, p. 345.
6. Legrand-Girard, *Un Quart de siècle au service de la France, 1894–1918*, Paris 1954, pp. 262, 264.
7. André, *Cinq ans au ministère*, Paris 1907, pp. 11–13. This conversation together with André's subsequent military reforms indicates that, far from being 'indifferent' to military matters as Pierre Sorlin suggests (Sorlin, *Waldeck-Rousseau*, p. 430), Waldeck-Rousseau saw army reform as an essential precondition to the republic's survival.
8. *Ibid.*, p. 24.
9. *Ibid.*, p. 42.
10. Legrand-Girard, p. 262.
11. A. Combarieu, *Sept ans à l'Elysée avec Emile Loubet, 1899–1906*, Paris 1932, p. 76.
12. D. Ralston, *The Army of the Republic*, Cambridge, Mass. 1967, pp. 291–2.
13. Louis Havet Letters, BN, naf 24506, 10 August 1900.
14. *France militaire*, 22 January 1902.
15. AHG, 5N 6, 31 March 1906.
16. d'Arbeaux, *L'Officier contemporain*, Paris 1911, p. 92.
17. Havet Letters, BN, naf 24506, 10 January 1901.
18. AHG, 5N 3, 30 July 1904.
19. d'Arbeaux, p. 113.
20. C. Arès, *La Décadence intellectuelle de l'armée*, Paris 1912, p. 6.
21. Legrand-Girard, pp. 482–3.
22. *Ibid.*, pp. 204, 434.
23. d'Arbeaux, pp. 69–70.
24. Legrand-Girard, p. 464.
25. E. Mayer, *Nos Chefs de 1914*, Paris 1930, pp. 128–30.
26. Combes Papers, Archives de la Charente Maritime, 13J 24.
27. *France militaire*, 27 January 1902.
28. Sarrail Papers, BN, naf 15007, ff 62–4.
29. Sarrail Papers, BN, naf 15007, ff 69.
30. A. Messimy, *Considérations générales sur l'organisation de l'armée*, Paris 1907, p. 126.
31. H. Langlois, *Quelques questions d'actualité*, Paris 1909, p. 74.
32. R. Girardet, *La Société militaire dans la France contemporaine*, Paris 1953, p. 276.

33. *Porte-Voix*, 21 May 1912. See also 11 January and 15 September 1913; 10 and 20 January 1914.
34. *France militaire*, 11 November 1913 and *Porte-Voix*, 1 September 1912.
35. Arès, pp. 17, 22–3.
36. Sarrail Papers, BN, naf 15007, ff 69.
37. *Ibid.*, pp. 32–4 and *France militaire*, 8 September 1912.
38. Sarrail Papers, BN, naf 15007, ff 69.
39. Messimy, *Considerations*, p. 126.
40. *Ibid.*
41. J. Jaurès, *L'Armée nouvelle*, Paris 1932, p. 236.
42. *Ibid.*, pp. 238, 240–1.
43. P. Mahon, 'La Loi des cadres d'infanterie', *Revue des deux mondes*, 1 June 1912, p. 655.
44. *Porte-Voix*, 1 September 1912.
45. See *Porte-Voix*, *Ibid.* and 10 and 20 January 1914. 186 candidates in 1900, 420 in 1905 and 500 in 1910.
46. *Porte-Voix*, 1 March 1913.
47. d'Arbeaux, p. 117.
48. Arès, pp. 73, 80.
49. AHG, 7N 33, War Minister to corps commanders 27 January 1914.
50. André, *Cinq ans*, p. 87.
51. *France militaire*, 6 January 1906.
52. A. Millerand, *Pour la défense nationale*, Paris 1913.
53. L. Thoyot, *Le Ministre contre l'armée*, Paris 1902.
54. Mayer, *Nos chefs*, pp. 204–5.
55. Roland Andréani, *Armée et nation en Languedoc méditerranéen, 1905–14*, Montpellier 1975, p. 135 and E. Etienne, *Son Oeuvre coloniale, Algerienne et politique 1881–1906*, vol. II, Paris 1907, p. 455.
56. Lyautey, *Vers le Maroc*, Paris 1937, p. 258.
57. Andréani, *Armée et nation*, p. 103.
58. d'Arbeaux, p. 58.
59. *Ibid.*, p. 81.
60. Vallery-Radot, *Journal d'un volontaire d'un an*, Paris 1874, pp. 226–7.
61. See *France militaire*, 14 June 1907 for a married captain's monthly budget.
62. Pédoya, *L'Armée évolue*, vol. III, Paris 1908, pp. 73, 75.
63. *France militaire*, 19 November 1908 for French pay scales and Pédoya, *ibid.*, p. 85 for German.
64. *Ibid.*, p. 77.
65. *France militaire*, 19 February 1913.
66. d'Arbeaux, p. 76.
67. *Ibid.*, p. 77.
68. Pédoya, *L'Armée évolue*, p. 88.
69. *Porte-Voix*, 1 June 1910.
70. *France militaire*, 3 October 1913.

6 THE 'AFFAIRE DES FICHES'

1. André, *Cinq ans au ministère*, Paris 1907, pp. 23–5.
2. Havet Letters, BN, naf 24506, 9 December 1901.
3. J. K. Tannenbaum, *General Maurice Sarrail, 1856–1929*, Chapel Hill 1974, p. 29.

4. Legrand-Girard, *Un Quart de siecle au service de la France, 1894–1918*, Paris 1954, p. 437.
5. *France militaire*, 5 November 1904.
6. E. Combes, *Mon Ministère, 1902–5*, Paris 1956, pp. 245–6.
7. AN, F⁷ 12476, 8 November 1904.
8. *Ibid.*, 4 November 1904.
9. *Ibid.*
10. Legrand-Girard, p. 435.
11. J. H. Mollin, *La Vérité sur l'affaire des fiches*, Paris 1905, p. 135.
12. Havet Letters, BN, naf 24506, ff 154, 23 August 1902.
13. Combes Papers, ACM 13J 24.
14. Waldeck-Rousseau Papers, BI, Ms. 4613, 24 October and *JO–Sénat*, 31 March 1905, p. 518.
15. E. Mayer, *Nos chefs, de 1914*, Paris, pp. 131–49 and Mollin, p. 167.
16. Combes Papers, AGM 13J 24.
17. A. Millerand, *Pour la défense nationale*, Paris 1913, p. 254.
18. *JO–Sénat*, 31 March 1905, pp. 519–20.
19. de Civrieux, *Du Rêve à la réalité, 1871–1908*, Paris 1909, p. 246.
20. d'Arbeaux, *L'Officier contemporain*, Paris 1911, pp. 22–3.
21. *Ibid.*, pp. 22–3.
22. André, *Cinq ans*, p. 25.
23. E. Etienne, *Son oeuvre coloniale, Algérienne et politique, 1881–1906*, vol. II, Paris 1907, pp. 448–9.
24. Saint-Aulaire, *Confessions d'un vieux diplomat*, Paris 1953, p. 168.
25. AHG, 5N 7.
26. Millerand, p. 296.
27. Tannenbaum, p. 29.
28. *Aurore*, 1 January 1906.
29. d'Arbeaux, p. 20.
30. de Civrieux, p. 123.
31. H. Langlois, 'Notre situation militaire', *Revue des deux mondes*, 15 October 1907, pp. 787–8.
32. See, for instance, Charles Bugnet, *En écoutant le Maréchal Foch*, Paris 1929, p. 180.
33. Based on figures taken from the *Annuaire*.
34. J. Veron, *Souvenirs de ma vie militaire, 1905–1940*, Rouen 1969, p. 16.
35. AN, F⁷ 12476.
36. d'Arbeaux, p. 62.
37. 'L'Officier de troupe', *Revue de Paris*, 1 August 1909, pp. 636–57.
38. Langlois, 'Questions de défense nationale', pp. 152–3.
39. de Civrieux, p. 349.
40. d'Arbeaux, p. 24.
41. Lyautey, *Vers le Maroc*, Paris 1937, p. 68.
42. *Ibid.*, pp. 312–13.

7 ANTI-MILITARISM AND INDISCIPLINE

1. R. Andréani, *Armée et nation en Languedoc méditerranéen, 1905–14*, Montpellier 1975, p. 137.
2. See Lyautey, *Vers le Maroc*, Paris 1937, p. 258.
3. Bapst, *Le Maréchal Canrobert*, vol. I, Paris 1898, pp. 141–2.

4. Quoted in Zeldin, *France 1848-1945*, vol. 1, *Love, Ambition and Politics*, Oxford 1973, p. 744.
5. *France militaire*, 11 February 1905.
6. See J. Juillard, *Clemenceau, briseur de grèves*, Paris 1965, pp. 23-4.
7. de Civrieux, *Du Rêve à la réalité, 1871-1908*, Paris 1909, pp. 196-7.
8. Lt. Z, *L'Armée aux grèves*, Paris 1904, pp. 95-6.
9. *Ibid.*, pp. 50-1.
10. *Ibid.*, p. 155.
11. de Civrieux, p. 201.
12. d'Arbeaux, *L'Officier contemporain*, Paris 1911, pp. 193-4.
13. de Civrieux, p. 212.
14. d'Arbeaux, p. 188.
15. *France militaire*, 26 May 1905.
16. J. Maitron, *Histoire du mouvement anarchiste en France, 1880-1914*, Paris 1915, pp. 283-4.
17. Millerand Papers, BN, Report of 31 January 1912, 'La Propagande révolutionnaire dans l'armée, le sou du soldat'.
18. AN, F7 13326.
19. *Ibid.*, F7 13323.
20. Maitron, p. 346.
21. J. J. Fiechter, *Le Socialisme français de l'affaire Dreyfuse à la Grande Guerre*, Genève 1965, p. 157.
22. AN, F7 13327.
23. *Ibid.*, F7 13326.
24. *Ibid.*
25. R. Andréani, 'Antimilitarisme en Languedoc avant 1914', *Revue d'histoire moderne et contemporaine*, vol. XX, Jan.-March 1973, p. 117.
26. AN, F7 13324.
27. *Ibid.*
28. C. Humbert, *Chinoiseries militaires*, Paris 1909, pp. 259-60.
29. C. Humbert, *Les Voeux de l'armée*, Paris 1908, p. 130.
30. G. Bonnefous, *Histoire politique de la troisième république*, vol. I, 1906-1914, Paris 1956, p. 29.
31. AN, F7 13323.
32. See E. Driant, *Vers un nouveau Sedan*, Paris 1906, p. 135.
33. M. Le Blond, *La Crise du Midi*, Paris 1907, p. 408.
34. AN, F7 12920.
35. *France militaire*, 14 September 1906.
36. AN, F7 12910.
37. *Ibid.*, F7 13323, 20 August and 5 September 1907; 10 and 16 August 1908.
38. *Ibid.*
39. J. Haroué, *La Détresse de l'armée*, Paris 1904, p. 173.
40. Le Blond, pp. 407-8.
41. J. Caillaux, *Mes Mémoires*, vol. I, Paris 1942, p. 263.
42. AN, F7 12920, report of 4 July 1907. See also Guy Bechtel, *1907, La Grande révolte du Midi*, Paris 1976, pp. 136-7.
43. AN, F7 13323.
44. *France militaire*, 26 June 1907.
45. Le Blond, p. 135.
46. Bechtel, pp. 257-8; Andréani, *Armée et nation*, p. 156.
47. Metzinger, *La Transformation de l'armée, 1897-1907*, Paris 1909, p. 53.

48. Pédoya, *L'Armée évolue*, Paris 1908, vol. II, pp. 191–4.
49. AHG, 6N 41.
50. Le Blond, p. 131; see also AN, F⁷ 12920 for Colonel Rabier's testimony.
51. Le Blond, p. 408.
52. AHG, 7N 109.
53. AHG, 6N 41.
54. *Ibid.*, 1N 13.
55. d'Arbeaux, p. 35.
56. AHG, 7N 35.
57. *Ibid.*, 6N 41.
58. *JO-Documents, Chambre*, 1907, no. 1233, p. 1425.
59. Le Blond, p. 489.
60. de Civrieux, pp. 118–19.
61. *Ibid.*, p. 119.
62. Le Blond, p. 394.
63. *France militaire*, 4 September 1906.
64. P. Simon, *L'Instruction des officiers, l'éducation des troupes et la puissance nationale*, Paris 1905, p. 431.
65. C. Ebener, *Le Role social de l'officier*, Paris 1901, p. 30.
66. AHG, 5N 6, 31 March 1906.
67. Sillion, *Vers l'armée démocratique*, Paris 1907, p. 38.
68. Marceau, *L'Officier, éducateur national*, Bordeaux 1905, pp. 61–2.
69. Sillion, p. 46.
70. Rata is a thick stew made either of beans or potatoes which was staple army fare. A favourite conscript song ran: 'C'est pas de la soupe, c'est la rata/ Ce n'est pas la merde, mais ça viendra.'
71. H. de Larzelles, *Lettres d'un réserviste*, Paris 1907.
72. André, *Cinq ans au ministère*, Paris 1907, p. 108.
73. d'Arbeaux, p. 156.
74. A. Messimy, *Considérations générales sur l'organisation de l'armée*, Paris 1907, p. 189.
75. AHG, 6N 43, Fonds Galliéni.
76. A. Millerand, *Pour la défense nationale*, Paris 1913, pp. 290–4.
77. *France militaire*, 13 June 1906.
78. Bonnefous, vol. I, p. 135.
79. Pédoya, *L'Armée évolue*, vol. I, Paris 1908, pp. 32–3.
80. de Civrieux, p. 385.
81. *France militaire*, 18 October 1911.
82. H. Langlois, 'Notre situation militaire', *Revue des deux mondes*, 15 October 1907, p. 790.
83. *Porte-Voix*, December 1907.
84. Le Blond, p. 421.
85. *France militaire*, 29 October 1909.
86. AHG, 5N 3, 1 October 1907.
87. *France militaire*, 6 November 1909.
88. *France militaire*, 19 April 1912.
89. Langlois, 'Notre situation', p. 790.
90. AHG, 7N 104.
91. Pédoya, vol. I, p. 80.
92. See, for instance, AN, F⁷ 12920.
93. *Ibid.*
94. *Ibid.*

95. Le Blond, p. 434.
96. *Ibid.*, p. 381.
97. AN, F⁷ 13323.
98. Freycinet, *Souvenirs*, Paris 1914, vol. I, pp. 253-5.
99. Humbert, *Chinoiseries*, p. 164.
100. d'Arbeaux, p. 53.
101. *Ibid.*, pp. 54-5.
102. Le Blond, p. 392.
103. *Ibid.*, p. 432.
104. *France militaire*, 16 June 1907.
105. AHG, 6N 41.
106. *Ibid.*
107. *France militaire*, 7 February 1905.

8 THE COLONIAL ARMY

1. Jules Harmand, *Domination et colonisation*, Paris 1910, p. 371, quoted in R. Girardet, *L'Idée coloniale en France*, Paris 1972, page 6, footnote.
2. H. d'Ideville, *Le Maréchal Bugeaud d'après sa correspondance intime*, Paris 1882, vol. III, p. 155, quoted in Kanya-Forstner, *The Conquest of the Western Sudan*, Cambridge 1969, pp. 8-9.
3. Girardet, *Idée coloniale*, p. 6.
4. Kanya-Forstner, *The Conquest of the Western Sudan*, pp. 53-4.
5. H. Brunschwig, *Mythes et réalités de l'impérialisme colonial français, 1871-1914*, Paris 1960, pp. 15-16.
6. Paul Cambon, *Correspondance*, vol. I, Paris 1940, p. 237.
7. Girardet, *Idée coloniale*, pp. 7, 17.
8. *Ibid.*, p. 9.
9. Brunschwig, pp. 73-81.
10. *Ibid.*, 139.
11. C. M. Andrew and A. S. Kanya-Forstner, 'France, Africa and the First World War', *Journal of African History*, XIX, no. 1, 1978, p. 17.
12. Lyautey, *Lettres du Tonkin et de Madagascar, 1894-1899*, Paris 1942, p. 59.
13. Kanya-Forstner, *The Conquest of the Western Sudan*, p. 207.
14. P. Varet, *Du Concours apporté à la France par ses colonies ... au cours de la guerre de 1914*, Paris 1927, p. 5. Quoted by Andrew and Kanya-Forstner, 'France, Africa and the First World War', p. 22.
15. Kanya-Forstner, *The Conquest of the Western Sudan*, p. 228.
16. *Ibid.*, p. 228.
17. *Ibid.*, p. 201.
18. Girardet, *Idée coloniale*, p. 44.
19. C. M. Andrew and A. S. Kanya-Forstner, 'The French "Colonial Party", Its Composition, Aims and Influence, 1885-1914', *Historical Journal*, vol. XIV, 1971, p. 100.
20. C. M. Andrew, 'The French Colonialist Movement during the Third Republic: The Unofficial Mind of Imperialism', *Transactions of the Royal Historical Society*, London 1976, pp. 150-3.
21. Girardet, *Idée coloniale*, p. 58.
22. BI, Terrier Ms. 5892, 30 June 1900, quoted in Andrew, 'The French Colonialist Movement', p. 149.
23. Kanya-Forstner, *The Conquest of the Western Sudan*, p. 266.

24. J. K. Munholland, *The Emergence of the Colonial Military in France*, 1880–1905, unpublished Ph.D thesis, Princeton University 1964.
25. Cambon, pp. 237, 201.
26. For campaigns in Western Sudan, see Kanya-Forstner, *The Conquest of the Western Sudan*.
27. Kanya-Forstner, 'Military Expansion in the Western Sudan – French and British Style' in Gifford and Louis, *France and Britain in Africa*, New Haven 1970, p. 422.
28. Cooke, *The New French Imperialism, 1880–1910*, Newton Abbot 1973, p. 58.
29. Kanya-Forstner, *The Conquest of the Western Sudan*, p. 13.
30. *Ibid.*, p. 237.
31. Munholland, p. 279; Cooke, pp. 127–9.
32. Kanya-Forstner, *The Conquest of the Western Sudan*, pp. 53–4.
33. Cooke, p. 23.
34. H. Lyautey, *Vers le Maroc*, Paris 1937, pp. 252, 307, 308.
35. Kanya-Forstner, *The Conquest of the Western Sudan*, pp. 17–20.
36. Andrew, 'The French Colonialist Movement', p. 155.
37. *Documents parlementaires-Chambre*, 1917, no. 3476, in Kanya-Forstner, 'France, Africa and the First World War', pp. 11–12.
38. Lyautey, *Vers le Maroc*, pp. 210, 301.
39. L. Grandmaison, *En Territoire militaire*, Paris 1898, pp. 181–3.
40. Ingold, *Sous l'ancre d'or, hommes et restes d'outre-mer*, Paris 1947, pp. 72–4.
41. Lt. col. K., 'L'Expédition de Madagascar', *Revue de Paris*, July–August 1895, p. 527 and Munholland, pp. 49–50.
42. William B. Cohen, 'The French Colonial Service in West Africa', in Gifford and Louis, p. 492.
43. Girardet, *Idée coloniale*, p. 77.
44. Lyautey, *Lettres du Tonkin*, p. 467.
45. Cohen, 'The French Colonial Service in West Africa', p. 492.
46. Lyautey, *Lettres du Tonkin*, pp. 46–7.
47. Brunschwig, Chapter 8.
48. C. M. Andrew, P. Grupp and A. S. Kanya-Forstner, 'Le Mouvement colonial français et ses principales personalités, 1890–1914', *Revue française d'histoire d'outre-mer*, LXII, no. 229, 4th quarter 1975, pp. 646–8.
49. R. E. Robinson and G. Gallagher, 'The Partition of Africa', *The New Cambridge Modern History*, vol. VI, pp. 610, 621.
50. Andrew and Kanya-Forstner, 'The French Colonial Party', pp. 126–7.
51. *Ibid.*, p. 127.
52. Andrew, Grupp and Kanya-Forstner, 'Le Mouvement colonial'.
53. Kanya-Forstner, *The Conquest of the Western Sudan*, p. 237.
54. Brunschwig, pp. 163–70.
55. *JO-Députés*, 8 December 1896. Quoted in Andrew, 'The French Colonialist Movement', pp. 153–4.
56. Cooke, pp. 122–3.
57. Lyautey, *Vers le Maroc*, p. 14.
58. *Ibid.*, p. 35.
59. *Ibid.*, pp. 114–15.
60. Cooke, p. 132.
61. P. Mason, *A Matter of Honour*, London 1974, pp. 400–1.
62. Munholland, p. 285.
63. Louis Baron, *Les Idées coloniales en France et le recrutement des officiers sortant de*

Notes to pages 151–164

Saint-Cyr dans l'infanterie de marine, 1872–1891, thesis, Paris Sorbonne 1969, p. 104. See also Chalmin, L'Officier français de 1815 à 1870, Paris 1957, p. 135.
64. A. Bournazel, L'Officier colonial, 1919–39, thesis, Paris 1967, p. 38.
65. Baron, p. 104.
66. Girardet, L'Idée coloniale, p. 186.
67. Baron, pp. 62–6; 392 of 571 students at Saint-Cyr received state grants.
68. Colonel Henri Charbonnel, De Madagascar à Verdun, Paris 1962, p. 24.
69. See Lyautey, Vers le Maroc, p. 211.
70. Baron, pp. 63–4.
71. Ibid., pp. 102–4.
72. Lyautey, Lettres du Tonkin, p. 232.
73. Lyautey, Vers le Maroc, p. 233.
74. Pellé Papers, BI, Ms. 4406, 23 November 1913.
75. C. Mangin, 'Lettres du Soudan', Revue des deux mondes, 15 September 1930, p. 347.
76. Marcel Blanchard (ed.), 'La correspondance de Félix Faure touchant les affaires coloniales, 1882–98', Revue d'historie des colonies françaises, vol. 42, no. 147, 1955, p. 159.
77. Munholland, p. 66.
78. Kanya-Forstner, The Conquest of the Western Sudan, p. 30.
79. Lyautey, Vers le Maroc, p. 213.
80. A. Maurois, Lyautey, Paris 1931, p. 108.
81. Munholland, p. 75.
82. H. Lyautey, 'Le Rôle colonial de l'armée', Revue des deux mondes, September 1900.
83. Lyautey, Vers le Maroc, p. 286.
84. Lyautey, 'Le Rôle colonial'.
85. H. Gouraud, Zinder-Tchad, Paris 1945, p. 232.
86. Lyautey, Vers le Maroc, p. 234.
87. Bulletin du Comité de l'Afrique française, Supplément 1900, p. 169.
88. Kanya-Forstner, The Conquest of the Western Sudan, p. 12.
89. Bulletin du Comité de l'Afrique française, p. 22.
90. Lyautey, Vers le Maroc, p. 285.
91. Cambon, pp. 190–1.
92. Emile Mayer, Nos Chefs de 1914, Paris 1930, p. 42.
93. P. Denis, L'Evolution des troupes Sahariennes, thesis, Rennes, pp. 204–5.
94. H. Lyautey, Lyautey l'Africain, vol. 2, Paris 1953, pp. 295–6.
95. Ibid., pp. 297–9.
96. Kanya-Forstner, 'Military Expansion in the Western Sudan', pp. 436–7.
97. Mason, p. 363.
98. Lyautey, Lettres du Tonkin, p. 321.
99. Lyautey, Vers le Maroc, p. 13.
100. H. Lyautey, Choix de lettres, Paris 1947, p. 147.
101. E. Peroz, Hors des chemins battus, Paris 1908, p. 6.
102. Grandmaison, En territoire militaire, p.p 34–5.
103. Lyautey, Lettres du Tonkin, p. 489.
104. H. Lyautey, Lettres du Sud de Madagascar, 1900–02, Paris 1935, pp. 91–2.
105. Lyautey, Lettres du Tonkin, p. 48.
106. Galliéni, 'Lettres de Madagascar', Revue des deux mondes, 15 April 1928, p. 312.
107. AHG, 5N 3, 1 October 1907.
108. See Ibid., 3 August 1901 for debate over control of colonial army.

109. H. Frey, *Campagne dans le Haut Sénégal et dans le Haut Niger, 1885-8*, Paris 1888, pp. 36-7.
110. Trentinian, *La Fusion des officiers de l'armée métropolitaine et l'armée coloniale*, Paris 1911, p. 10.
111. Lyautey, *Lettres du Tonkin*, p. 439.
112. Grandmaison, *En territoire*, pp. 265-6.
113. Deschanel, 'Programme d'action colonial', *Bulletin du Comité de l'Afrique Française*, supplément 1906, p. 240.
114. Munholland, 300-1.
115. André Dussauge, 'Le Recrutement des équipages de la flotte et de l'armée coloniale', *Questions diplomatiques et coloniales*, vol. 37, 1914, p. 65.
116. Debon, 'Le Rapport de M. Raiberti sur le budget des troupes coloniales', *Questions diplomatiques et coloniales*, vol. 34, 1912, pp. 294-5.
117. C. Mangin, *La Force noire*, Paris 1910, p. 324.
118. E. Peroz, *Armée coloniale, armée de métier, milices nationales*, Paris 1909, p. 12.
119. H. Gouraud, *Au Maroc 1911-14*, Paris 1949, p. 129.
120. Peroz, *Armée coloniale*, p. 13.
121. *Ibid.*, pp. 10-11.
122. M. Michel, 'Le Recrutement des tirailleurs en AOF pendant la guerre mondiale. Essai de bilan statistique', *Revue française d'histoire d'outre-mer*, LX 1973.
123. M. Michel, 'La Genèse du recrutement de 1918 en Afrique noire française', *Revue française d'histoire d'outre-mer*, vol. LVIII, 1971, pp. 437-8 and 'Un Mythe: La "Force Noire" avant 1914', *Relations Internationales*, vol. 1 (1974), pp. 83-90.
124. Andrew and Kanya-Forstner, 'France, Africa and the First World War', p. 16 and Michel, 'Un Mythe'.
125. Andrew and Kanya-Forstner, 'France, Africa and the First World War', p. 22.
126. Debeney, *La Guerre et les hommes*, Paris 1937, p. 129.

9 THE ARMY AND THE NATIONALIST REVIVAL

1. G. Michon, *La Préparation à la guerre. La Loi de trois ans, 1910-1914*, Paris 1935, p. 90.
2. J. Monteilhet, *Les Institutions militaires de la France*, Paris 1932, p. 220.
3. Michon, pp. 93-4.
4. H. Langlois, 'Le Haut commandement', *Revue des deux mondes*, 1 September 1911, p. 56.
5. AHG, 1N 1.
6. D. Ralston, *The Army of the Republic*, Cambridge, Mass. 1967, pp. 338-40.
7. A. Messimy, *Mes Souvenirs*, Paris 1935, p. 77.
8. J. Ollé-Laprune, *La Stabilité des ministres sous la Troisième République, 1879-1940*, Paris 1962, p. 47.
9. Messimy, *Mes Souvenirs*, p. 70.
10. E. Mayer, *Trois Maréchaux*, Paris 1928, p. 22.
11. Monteilhet, p. 281.
12. A. Maurois, *Lyautey*, Paris 1931, pp. 143-4.
13. C. Humbert, *Chinoiseries militaires*, Paris 1909, pp. 9-10.
14. Joffre, *Mémoires*, vol. I, Paris 1932, pp. 50-2.
15. S. R. Williamson, *The Politics of the Grand Strategy*, Cambridge, Mass. 1969, p. 209.
16. Millerand Papers (italics Millerand's), 'Note sur la préparation et la conduite de la guerre'.

Notes to pages 175–183

17. *Ibid.*, 8 March 1912.
18. Abel Ferry, *Les Carnets secrets*, Paris 1957.
19. A. Millerand, *Pour la défense nationale*, Paris 1913, p. 117.
20. AHG, 1N 1.
21. A. Messimy, *Considérations générales sur l'organisation de l'armée*, Paris 1907, p. 70.
22. André, *Cinq ans au ministère*, Paris 1907, p. 144.
23. Messimy, *Mes Souvenirs*, pp. 80–1.
24. R. Alexandre, *Avec Joffre d'Agadir à Verdun: Souvenirs, 1911–16*, Paris 1932, p. 13, quoted in Ralston, p. 335.
25. H. Lyautey, *Vers le Maroc*, Paris 1937, pp. 126, 133.
26. See also *Le Temps*, 4 October 1913.
27. AHG, 1N 13, 28 November 1913.
28. AN, C 7257, Messimy proposal, p. 90.
29. Mayer, *Trois Maréchaux*, pp. 29–30.
30. Pédoya, *L'Armée n'est pas commandée*, Paris 1905, p. 19.
31. *Porte-Voix*, 1 October 1913.
32. PRO, WO33.618 and *Le Temps*, 10 October 1912.
33. J. Jaurès, *L'Armée nouvelle*, Paris 1932, p. 402.
34. Messimy, *Mes Souvenirs*, p. 72.
35. *Ibid.*, pp. 74, 71.
36. AHG 7N 2.
37. *Ibid.*
38. Millerand Papers, note d'entretien, 27 January 1912.
39. Millerand, *Pour la défense nationale*, pp. 296–7.
40. *Ibid.*, pp. 317–18.
41. AHG, 5N 6.
42. *France militaire*, 8 January 1911.
43. Millerand, *Pour la défense nationale*, p. 311 and *France militaire*, 13 January 1912.
44. *Porte-Voix*, 1 March 1911, 1 March 1912 and 1 February 1913.
45. Messimy, *Considérations*, p. 61.
46. *Porte-Voix*, 1 March 1911 and 1 March 1912.
47. *Ibid.*, 1 February 1913.
48. Millerand Papers.
49. E. Weber, *The Nationalist Revival in France, 1905–1914*, Berkeley and Los Angeles 1959, p. 102.
50. Millerand Papers.
51. *Le Matin*, 11 February 1911.
52. *France militaire*, 8 May 1909.
53. d'Arbeaux, *L'Officier contemporain*, Paris 1911, p. 153.
54. AN F^7 13330.
55. *Ibid.*
56. *France militaire*, 13 April 1905.
57. *Le Journal*, 10 February 1911.
58. *Porte-Voix*, 21 February 1912.
59. *JO-Députés*, 15 March 1911, pp. 1178–9.
60. AN, F^7 13330.
61. C. Arès, *La Décadence intellectuelle de l'armée*, Paris 1912, p. 108.
62. d'Arbeaux, p. 174.
63. *Ibid.*, p. 179.
64. Jaurès, p. 247.
65. d'Arbeaux, p. 177.

66. *France militaire*, 11 July 1911.
67. *Ibid.*, 15 November 1910 and 24 October 1913.
68. Millerand Papers.
69. *Ibid.*
70. Michon, p. 90.
71. Millerand, *Pour la défense nationale*, pp. 271–2.
72. Messimy, *Mes Souvenirs*, pp. 118–19.
73. Millerand, *Pour la défense nationale*, pp. 180–6.
74. *Ibid.*, pp. 333–4.
75. *Ibid.*, pp. 342–3.
76. *Ibid.*, pp. 278–9.
77. C. Humbert, *Les Voeux de l'armée*, Paris 1908, p. 107.
78. *Ibid.*, p. 108.
79. Millerand, *Pour la défense nationale*, pp. 293–4.
80. *JO-Chambre*, 29 June 1912, pp. 1826–8.
81. Millerand, *Pour la défense nationale*, p. 384.
82. M. Paléologue, *Au Quai d'orsay à la veille de la tourmente, journal 1913–14*, Paris 1947, pp. 6–7.
83. Ralston, p. 340 and R. Girardet, *La Société militaire dans la France contemporaine*, Paris 1953, p. 277.
84. *Porte-Voix*, 11 March 1912.
85. Weber, *The Nationalist Revival in France*, p. 13.
86. *France militaire*, 24 and 29 October 1913.
87. *Porte-Voix*, 11 February 1912.
88. Mayer, *Trois maréchaux*, p. 29.
89. Joffre, *Mémoires*, pp. 302–3.
90. *Ibid.*, p. 52.
91. Girardet, *La Société militaire*, p. 277.
92. Weber, *The Nationalist Revival in France*, p. 101.
93. AN, F^7 13336.
94. *Ibid.*, F^7 13345.
95. *Ibid.*, F^7 13336.
96. *Petit Parisien*, 23 May 1913.
97. *Le Matin*, 23 May 1913.
98. Paléologue, p. 138.
99. AN, F^7 13336.
100. *Ibid.*, F^7 13326.
101. *Le Matin*, 19 June 1913.
102. AN, F^7 13345.
103. Paléologue, p. 139.
104. AN, F^7 13345.
105. Paléologue, p. 139.
106. *Ibid.*, p. 143.
107. *Ibid.*, pp. 139–40.
108. *Porte-Voix*, 20 June 1913.

10 THE THREE-YEAR LAW

1. J. Monteilhet, *Les Institutions militaires de la France*, Paris 1932, p. 263.
2. G. Michon, *La Préparation à la guerre. La Loi de trois ans*, Paris 1935, p. 93.
3. AHG, 7N 1737, Plan XVII.

4. Joffre, *Mémoires*, vol. I, Paris 1932, pp. 96, 167–8.
5. AHG, 7N 1737 and Joffre, *La Préparation à la guerre*, Paris 1920, pp. 10–11.
6. A. Millerand, *Pour La Défense nationale*, Paris 1913, pp. 13–18, 26.
7. *Porte-Voix*, 11 May 1913.
8. *France militaire*, 8 April 1913.
9. *JO-Documents*, 2096.
10. *JO-Sénat*, 20 June 1902, p. 847.
11. *JO-Chambre*, 2 June 1913, p. 1649.
12. C. Humbert, *Les Voeux de l'armée*, Paris 1908, p. 142.
13. *JO-Chambre*, 10 December 1912.
14. A. Messimy, *Le Problème militaire*, Paris, 1913, p. 26.
15. *Documents parlementaires-Chambre*, 1913, annexe no. 2716, pp. 332–3.
16. *JO-Chambre*, 2 June 1913, p. 1648 and AN, C 7257, Messimy report, p. 10.
17. Joffre, *Mémoires*, pp. 91–3.
18. *JO-Chambre*, 2 June 1913, p. 1648.
19. *JO-Chambre*, 2 June 1913, p. 1653.
20. J. Jaurès, *L'Armée nouvelle*, Paris 1932, p. 297.
21. A. Messimy, *Considérations générales sur l'organisation de l'armée*, Paris 1907, pp. 213–15.
22. AN C 7257, Messimy report 1903.
23. Messimy, *Le Problème militaire*, p. 10.
24. *JO-Chambre*, 2 June 1913, p. 1656.
25. *Documents parlementaires-Chambre*, 1904, vol. I, no. 1553, p. 151.
26. *Ibid.*, p. 155.
27. *Ibid.*, p. 157.
28. *Ibid.*, p. 159.
29. *Ibid.*, p. 156.
30. *JO-Sénat*, 20 June 1902, pp. 863–4.
31. Army Committee Report on Pay, 8 December 1913, *JO-Chambre*, annexe no. 3269, p. 123.
32. AHG, 7N 109.
33. R. Alexandre, *Avec Joffre d'Agadir à Verdun: Souvenirs 1911–16*, Paris 1932, p. 77.
34. Humbert, *Les Voeux de l'armée*, p. 139.
35. Joffre, *Mémoires*, p. 101.
36. *Echo de Paris*, 26 August 1911.
37. J. Veron, *Souvenirs de ma vie militaire 1905–1940*, Rouen 1969, p. 23.
38. AHG, 7N 109, 2 May 1912.
39. Messimy, *Considérations*, p. 205.
40. AN, F[7] 13330, Leroy Committee.
41. Army Committee Report on Pay, p. 122.
42. Pédoya, *L'Armée évolue*, vol. II, Paris 1908, p. 148.
43. AHG, 1N 13.
44. AHG, 1N 1, 4 March 1913.
45. AHG, 7N 2.
46. *France militaire*, 4 February 1911.
47. AN, F[7] 13330, 27 January 1913.
48. *Ibid.*
49. *Ibid.*
50. *Ibid.*
51. *Ibid.*

52. *Ibid.*
53. *Ibid.*
54. *Ibid.*
55. *Documents parlementaires-Chambre*, 1904, vol. II, no. 1553, p. 155.
56. *JO-Députés*, 31 May 1904, p. 1220.
57. de Civrieux, *Du Rêve à la réalité 1871–1908*, Paris 1909, pp. 319–20.
58. AHG, 6N 41.
59. See PRO, WO33.363, *Military Resources of France*, 1905, pp. 20, 75. Palat, 'Les Manoeuvres en Languedoc en 1913', *Revue des deux mondes*, 15 October 1913, pp. 814–15.
60. *France militaire*, 9 and 25 February 1912.
61. de Civrieux, p. 167.
62. Messimy, *Considérations*, p. 187.
63. Grandmaison, *Dressage de l'infanterie en vue l'offensive*, Paris 1906.
64. Humbert, *Les Voeux, de l'armée*, p. 212.
65. de Civrieux, pp. 338–9.
66. *Porte-Voix*, 11 February 1912.
67. d'Arbeaux, *L'Officier contemporain*, Paris 1911, p. 180.
68. Joffre, *Mémoires*, p. 33.
69. *Porte-Voix*, 11 February 1912.
70. PRO, WO33.618, p. 20.
71. *JO-Sénat*, 19 June 1902, p. 833.
72. Pédoya, *L'Armée évolue*, vol. II, p. 97.
73. Langlois, *Le Temps*, 25 February 1908.
74. C. Humbert, *Chinoiseries militaires*, Paris 1909, p. 251.
75. AHG, 5N 3, July 1906.
76. AHG, 7N 107, September 1910.
77. *France militaire*, 4 April 1912.
78. AHG, 7N 111, 23 April 1913.
79. Paté report, *Documents parlementaires-Chambre*, 1913, annexe no. 2716, pp. 332–3.
80. *Echo de Paris*, 13 November 1908.
81. Millerand, *Pour la défense nationale*, p. 366.
82. *Ibid.*, pp. 359–60.
83. AHG, 7N 107, 1 February 1910.
84. *Ibid.*, 11 February 1910.
85. H. Contamine, *La Revanche*, Paris 1957, p. 107 and D. Ralston, *The Army of the Republic*, Cambridge, Mass. 1967, p. 345.
86. *France militaire*, 9 and 12 February 1912.
87. AHG, 7N 107, 14 March 1910.
88. de Civrieux, pp. 280–1.
89. *Avenir militaire*, 27 March, 3 April and 1 May 1894; *France militaire*, 13 March 1901.
90. AHG, 7N 107, 18 March 1910.
91. *France militaire*, 26 and 27 January 1906.
92. de Civrieux, pp. 373–4.
93. J. Haroué, *La Détresse de l'armée*, Paris 1904, p. 17.
94. Legrand-Girard, *Un Quart de siècle au service de la France, 1894–1918*, Paris 1954, p. 495.
95. Messimy, *Considérations*, p. 193.
96. Legrand-Girard, p. 495.
97. Messimy, *Considérations*, p. 193.

98. Veron, pp. 30–1.
99. AN C 7342.
100. Messimy, *Considérations*, p. 288.
101. *Documents Parlementaires-Chambre*, 13 November 1908, p. 64.
102. *Ibid.*
103. *JO-Chambre*, annexe 2716, 14 March 1913, p. 325.
104. Millerand, *Pour la défense nationale*, pp. 12–20, 105.
105. *JO-Chambre*, 15 March 1911, p. 1194.
106. *Documents parlementaires-Chambre*, 13 November 1908, pp. 63–7.
107. Déroulède, *L'Education militaire*, Paris 1882, p. 3.
108. *Avenir militaire*, 16 August 1895.
109. Déroulède, pp. 4, 20.
110. *Ibid.*, p. 23.
111. A. Garçon, *L'Education militaire à l'école*, Paris 1886, p. 13.
112. *Avenir militaire*, 1 May 1885.
113. Barodet, Chambre des Députés, *Programmes et engagements électoraux*, vol. x, pp. 45–52.
114. *Echo de Paris*, 2 August 1911.
115. Messimy, *Considérations*, p. 286.
116. Messimy, *Considérations*, pp. 285–6.
117. *Ibid.*
118. *JO-Chambre*, 2 July 1913, p. 2369.
119. Millerand, *Pour la défense nationale*, pp. 103–5.
120. Michon, p. 164.
121. Jaurès, *L'Armée nouvelle*, and *JO-Chambre*, 10 December 1912.
122. *JO-Chambre*, 28 November 1912, p. 2850.
123. H. Contamine, 'Jaurès vu par les nationalistes français', *Actes du colloque Jaurès et la nation*, Toulouse 1964, p. 139.
124. *Les Armées françaises dans la grande guerre*, vol. I, Paris 1922, annexe 4, pp. 13–12.
125. *Ibid.*, annexe 942, pp. 768–9.
126. *Ibid.*, annexe 1193, p. 937.
127. E. Mayer, *Nos chefs de 1914*, Paris 1930, pp. 222–31.
128. Weygand, *Mémoires*, vol. I, Paris 1953, pp. 97–9.
129. Contamine, 'Jaurès vu par les nationalistes français', p. 141.
130. *Ibid.*
131. Contamine, *La Revanche*, p. 235.
132. Pellé Papers, BI, Ms. 4406.

11 THE SPIRIT OF THE OFFENSIVE

1. P. de la Gorce, *La République et son armée*, Paris 1963, p. 142.
2. Joffre, *Mémoires*, Paris 1932, vol. I, pp. 99–100.
3. Possony and Mantoux, 'Du Picq and Foch, the French School', in E. M. Earle (ed.), *The Makers of Modern Strategy*, Princeton 1944, pp. 222–3.
4. Fuller, *The Conduct of War*, London 1972, p. 128.
5. J. Monteilhet, *Les Institutions militaires de la France*, Paris 1932, pp. 271–2.
6. *Ibid.*, pp. 321, 330, 351.
7. D. Ralston, *The Army of the Republic*, Cambridge, Mass. 1967, p. 350.
8. Joffre, *Mémoires*, pp. 20–1.
9. E. Driant, *Vers un nouveau Sedan*, Paris 1906, p. 139.
10. PRO, WO 33.618, *Report on Foreign Manoeuvres in 1912*, pp. 15–16.

11. *Porte-Voix*, 1 March 1912.
12. André, *Cinq ans au ministère*, Paris 1907, p. 144.
13. *Ibid.*, p. 141.
14. P. Simon, *L'Instruction des officiers, l'éducation des troupes et la puissance nationale*, Paris 1905, p. 172.
15. Grandmaison, *Dressage de l'infantrie en vue de l'offensive*, Paris 1906, pp. 2–3.
16. *Ibid.*, p. ix.
17. A. Messimy, *Considérations générales sur l'organisation de l'armée*, Paris 1907, p. 175.
18. Joffre, *Mémoires*, p. 33.
19. *Ibid.*, p. 34.
20. Messimy, *Considérations*, p. 60.
21. Zurlinden, 'Les Hautes-études de la guerre et l'avancement dans l'armée', *Revue des deux mondes*, 15 December 1904, p. 777.
22. Jean de Pierrefeu, *GQG, secteur 1*, Paris 1920, p. 18.
23. Joffre, *Mémoires*, p. 33.
24. Pierrefeu, *GQG*, p. 244.
25. E. Mayer, *Trois maréchaux*, Paris 1928, p. 85.
26. *Ibid.*
27. F. Engerand, *Le Secret de la frontière*, Paris 1918, pp. 226–7.
28. Jean de Pierrefeu, *Plutarque à menti*, Paris 1923, p. 50.
29. Pierrefeu, *GQG*, p. 99.
30. *Ibid.*, pp. 163–4.
31. Pierrefeu, *Plutarque*, p. 53.
32. AHG, 7N 3 and Pédoya, *L'Armée n'est pas commandée*, Paris 1905, p. 14.
33. Debeney, *La Guerre et les hommes*, Paris 1937, p. 12.
34. *Ibid.*, pp. 277–8.
35. *Ibid.*, p. 265.
36. Pierrefeu, *GQG*, p. 228.
37. Pédoya, *L'Armée n'est pas commandée*, p. 14.
38. Messimy, *Considérations*, pp. 48–9.
39. *Ibid.*
40. *Ibid.*, p. 56.
41. C. Humbert, *Les Voeux de l'armée*, Paris 1908, pp. 162–3.
42. *Ibid.*, p. 164.
43. Debeney, pp. 242–3.
44. E. Mayer, *Nos chefs de 1914*, Paris 1930, p. 89.
45. C. Bugnet, *En écoutant le Maréchal Foch*, Paris 1929, p. 142.
46. AHG, 5N 4, 19 October 1911.
47. *Ibid.*, 1N 13.
48. C. Arès, *La Décadence intellectuelle de l'armée*, Paris 1912, p. 67.
49. *Echo de Paris*, 9 August 1911.
50. *France militaire*, 12 January 1910; see also AHG, 7N 2, September 1913.
51. Joffre, *Mémoires*, p. 33.
52. H-J-J. Mordacq, 'L'Officier au XX siécle', *La Vie militaire en France et à l'étranger, 1912–13*, Paris 1914, pp. 7–8.
53. Joffre, *Mémoires*, p. 38.
54. Weygand, *Mémoires*, vol. 1, *l'Idéal vécu*, Paris 1953, p. 62.
55. Messimy, *Considérations*, p. 137.
56. Jibé, *L'Officier dans l'armée nouvelle*, Paris 1906, p. 39.
57. Pédoya, *L'armée n'est pas commandée*, p. 14.
58. AHG, 14N 1.

59. *France militaire*, 9 February 1912.
60. Weygand, *Mémoires*, p. 45; Weygand claimed that he went to the Centre in 1912, but his name is on the list for 1913. See AHG 14N 1.
61. A. Messimy, *Mes Souvenirs*, Paris 1937, p. 81.
62. Pierrefeu, *Plutarque*, p. 49.
63. AHG, 6N 42.
64. Joffre, *Mémoires*, pp. 303–4.
65. H. Lyautey, *Lettres du Tonkin et de Madagascar, 1894–1899*, Paris 1942, p. 489.
66. Grandmaison, *En Territoire militaire*, Paris 1898, pp. 265–6.
67. Debeney, pp. 277, 281.
68. Mayer, *Trois maréchaux*, p. 153.
69. Bugnet, p. 60.
70. Fuller, p. 128.
71. de la Gorce, p. 140.
72. Liddell Hart, *A History of the First World War*, London 1972, p. 31.
73. *Avenir militaire*, 4 April 1893.
74. On this theme see John Bowditch, 'The Rationalization of Weakness', in E. M. Earle, *Modern France*, Princeton 1951, pp. 40–2.
75. Simon, *L'Instruction des officiers*, pp. 176, 184–5.
76. AHG, 6N 41, 19 October 1906.
77. H. Langlois, 'Le Haut commandment', *Revue des deux mondes*, 1 September 1911, p. 65.
78. Simon, *L'Instruction des officiers*, p. 218.
79. 'Quelques enseignements de la guerre Sud-Africaine', *Revue des deux mondes*, 15 June 1902, p. 723.
80. Joffre, *Mémoires*, pp. 32–3.
81. de la Gorce, pp. 82–3.
82. AN, C 7257, Messimy report p. 10.
83. Monteilhet, pp. 277–8.
84. AN, C 7257, Messimy report *op. cit.* Messimy includes hidden expenses.
85. L. Klotz, *l'Armée en 1906*, Paris 1906, p. 101.
86. *Le Temps*, 15 November 1908.
87. André, *Cinq ans*, p. 117.
88. AHG, 7N 35.
89. A. Messimy, *Le Problème militaire*, Paris 1913, p. 15.
90. P. Mahon, 'Le service de trois ans', *Revue des deux mondes*, 15 April 1913, p. 883.
91. Negrier, 'Quelque enseignements sur la guerre Russo-Japonaise', *Revue des deux mondes*, 15 January 1906, p. 333.
92. Grandmaison, *Deux conférences faites aux officiers de l'état-major de l'armée*, Paris 1911, p. 34.
93. See, for instance, AHG 7N 1538, report of Col. Janin of the 2e bureau, December 1911: 'Les Russes n'exerceront pas sur les Allemands une action quelconque avant le 30e jour, et cette action ne deviendra sérieuse que bien plus tard. Les défenses de toute nature, la distance permettent aux Allemands, s'ils veulent, de ne laisser de ce côté que des forces actives peu nombreuses ... jusqu'à ce qu'une décision fut intervenue du côté de l'Ouest.'
94. Millerand Papers, note 21 October 1912.
95. S. R. Williamson, *The Politics of the Grand Strategy*, Cambridge, Mass. 1969, p. 218.
96. C. M. Andrew, 'Déchiffrement et diplomatie: Le cabinet noir du Quai d'Orsay sous la Troisième République', *Relations internationales*, no. 5, 1976, pp. 37–64.

97. Contamine, *La Revanche*, p. 162.
98. Williamson, p. 122.

12 THE HEAVY ARTILLERY

1. Gascouin, *L'Evolution de l'artillerie pendant la guerre*, Paris 1920, p. 26; and F. Herr, *L'Artillerie*, Paris 1923, p. 26.
2. Herr, *Ibid.*, p. 1.
3. G. Michon, *La Préparation à la guerre*, Paris 1935, pp. 211–12.
4. de la Gorce, *La République et son armée*, Paris 1963, p. 140.
5. Péloux, 'Matériels de campagne et de siège à tir rapide', *Revue d'artillerie*, vol. 80, p. 6.
6. Pellé Papers, BI, Ms. 4405, file 3, p. 15.
7. Although 105s and 120s are medium pieces, most of the questions which affected their adoption were the same as for the 155s, so that they can be considered within the general debate on heavy artillery.
8. Herr, *L'Artillerie*, p. 4.
9. *Ibid.*, p. 14.
10. *Ibid.*, p. 28.
11. Banquet, *Souvenirs d'un directeur d'artillerie*, Paris 1923, pp. 31–2.
12. Herr, *L'Artillerie*, p. 29.
13. Banquet, p. 29.
14. General D, 'Une doctrine pour l'artillerie lourde', *Revue d'artillerie*, vol. 83, October 1913–March 1914, p. 431.
15. AHG, 9N 96, 'Note relative aux séances de tir', p. 29.
16. Herr, *L'Artillerie*, p. 11 and Gascouin, p. 71.
17. J. Challeat, *L'Artillerie de terre en France pendant un siècle*, vol. 2, 1880–1910, Paris 1935, pp. 480–1.
18. Herr, *L'Artillerie*, p. 19.
19. Pellé Papers, BI, Ms. 4405, file 3, p. 3.
20. AHG, 9N 96, 20 May 1914.
21. *Ibid.*
22. AHG, 7N 53.
23. AHG, 7N 50.
24. Joffre, *Mémoires*, Paris 1932, p. 68.
25. AHG, 7N 50, 1 February 1913.
26. *Ibid.*, 'Note sur l'emploi de l'artillerie lourde de campagne'.
27. Joffre, *Mémoires*, p. 63.
28. General D., p. 1.
29. Weygand, *Mémoires*, vol. 1, Paris 1953, p. 45.
30. *JO-Sénat*, 14 July 1914, p. 1206.
31. AHG, 7N 50.
32. Banquet, pp. 33–4.
33. Joffre, *Mémoires*, pp. 66–7.
34. Banquet, p. 32.
35. A. Messimy, 'Souvenirs de l'année 1911', *Revue de Paris*, 1 March 1937, pp. 31–2.
36. Joffre, *Mémoires*, p. 59.
37. Alexandre, *Avec Joffre: Souvenirs 1911–1916*, Paris 1932, p. 30.
38. Langlois, 'Le Haut commandement', *Revue des deux mondes*, 1 September 1911 p. 65.
39. Joffre, *Mémoires*, pp. 52–3.

40. *Ibid.*, p. 54.
41. *Ibid.*, pp. 54–8.
42. *Ibid.*, p. 50.
43. *Ibid.*
44. *Ibid.*, p. 55.
45. Humbert in Senate. *JO-Sénat*, 13–14 July 1914, p. 1200.
46. Joffre, *Mémoires*, p. 69.
47. *Ibid.*, p. 59.
48. AHG, 7N 53.
49. *Ibid.*, 2 July 1914 (Italics in the original).
50. AHG, 7N 53.
51. Michon, *La Préparation à la guerre*, p. 220.
52. P. Benazet, 'Le Parlement devant la Patrie,' *La Renaissance*, 15 April 1916, pp. 1–3.
53. Banquet, pp. 33–4.
54. J. Noulens, 'Le Gouvernement français à la veille de la guerre', *Revue des deux mondes*, 1 February 1931.
55. Gascouin, p. 12.
56. *Ibid.*, pp. 12–14.
57. J. Caillaux, *Mes Mémoires*, vol. I, Paris 1942, p. 246.
58. Challeat, *L'Artillerie de terre*, p. 389.
59. Millerand Papers, 1 April 1912 decree.
60. *Ibid.*, Lamothe letter, 18 December 1912 (Italics in the original).
61. See *Ibid.*
62. Caillaux, *Mes Mémoires*, vol. I, p. 246.
63. F. Herr, 'Rapport d'ensemble du Général Herr, président de la commission centrale d'artillerie, sur les enseignements à retirer de la guerre en matière d'artillerie', 1 October 1919, p. 119. Typed report in AHG.
64. Caillaux, *Mes Mémoires*, p. 247.
65. Challeat, *L'Artillerie de terre*, p. 445.
66. Humbert in Senate, *JO-Sénat*, 13–14 July 1914, p. 1202.
67. Banquet, p. 38 and Challeat, *L'Artillerie de terre*, p. 388.
68. AHG, 7N 49.
69. *Ibid.*, 7N 107.
70. Messimy, 'Souvenirs de l'année 1911', p. 29.
71. Banquet, p. 44.
72. Enjalbert, 'L'Organisation et le fonctionnement des établissements d'artillerie', *Revue d'artillerie*, vol. 83, October 1913–March 1914, p. 453.
73. Banquet, p. 39.
74. Noulens, p. 614.
75. Millerand Papers, 12 September 1912.
76. Michon, *La Préparation à la guerre*, p. 218.
77. Joffre, *Mémoires*, pp. 57–8.
78. Benazet, 'Le Parlement devant la Patrie'.
79. Noulens, p. 618.
80. AHG, 6N 42, 20 November 1911.
81. *Ibid.*, 7N 109.
82. *Ibid.*, 6N 43.
83. Joffre, *Mémoires*, p. 70.
84. Percin, 'La Question de l'obusier de campagne', *La Vie militaire en France et à l'étranger, 1911–12*, Paris 1913, p. 40 and *France militaire*, 22 February 1912.

85. See AHG, 9N 96 and Percin, *ibid*.
86. Joffre, *Mémoires*, pp. 70-1.
87. Gascouin, fn. pp. 25-6.
88. Challeat, *L'Artillerie de terre*, p. 202.
89. *JO-Sénat*, 14 July 1914, p. 1263; see also Joffre, *Mémoires*, p. 47.
90. Benazet, 'Le Parlement devant la Patrie'.
91. Banquet, p. 41.

13 CONCLUSION

1. D. Ralston, 'From Boulanger to Pétain: The Third Republic and the Republican Generals', in Brian Bond and Ian Roy (eds.), *War and Society*, London 1975, p. 184.
2. *Ibid.*, pp. 187-8.
3. *JO-Chambre*, 29 November 1912, p. 2866.
4. *Documents parlementaires-Chambre*, 1912, annexe 1683, p. 133.
5. Joffre, *Mémoires*, vol. 1, Paris 1932, pp. 72-3.
6. E. Mayer, *Nos Chefs de 1914*, Paris 1930, pp. 252-3.
7. *France militaire*, 1 February 1906.
8. Banquet, *Souvenirs d'un directeur d'artillerie*, Paris 1923, p. 34.
9. H. Contamine, *La Revanche*, Paris 1957, p. 129.
10. Ralston, 'From Boulanger to Pétain', p. 186.
11. Zurlinden, 'Le Haut commandement des armées', *Revue des deux mondes*, 15 June 1903, p. 711.
12. P. Heidsieck, *Le Rayonnement de Lyautey*, Paris 1947, p. 197.
13. A. Ferry, *La Guerre vue d'en haut et d'en bas*, Paris 1920, p. 38.
14. Mayer, *Nos Chefs*, p. 69.
15. Jean de Pierrefeu, *GQG, secteur 1*, vol. 2, Paris 1920, p. 13.
16. Trentinian, *L'Etat-major en 1914*, Paris 1927, pp. 84-5.

Select bibliography

PRIVATE PAPERS

Combes Papers, Archives de la Charente Maritime
Etienne Papers, Bibliothèque nationale
Fonds Galliéni, Archives historiques de guerre, Château de Vincennes
Louis Havet Letters, Bibliothèque nationale
Millerand Papers, Bibliothèque nationale
Pellé Papers, Bibliothèque de l'Institut
Sarrail Papers, Bibliothèque nationale
Thiers Papers, Bibliothèque nationale, naf 20624 'Organisation et administration de l'armée, 1871–77'
Waldeck-Rousseau Papers, Bibliothèque de l'Institut

OFFICIAL PUBLICATIONS

Journal officiel
Ministère des affairs étrangères, *Documents diplomatiques français, 1911–1914*, 3rd series, Paris 1929
Ministère de la guerre, *Les Armées françaises dans la grande guerre*, Paris 1922

NEWSPAPERS AND JOURNALS

Armée et democratie
Avenir militaire
Echo de Paris
France militaire
Journal des sciences militaires
La Lanterne
Progrès militaire
Revue des deux mondes
Spectateur militaire
Le Temps
La Vie militaire en France et à l'étranger

GENERAL WORKS

All following works published in Paris unless otherwise stated
Anon. *Les Appellations des officiers dans l'armée*, 1910
    L'Armée française en 1884 et le Général Galliffet, Antwerp 1884

L'Armée et la démocratie, 1885
L'Armée et l'ordre publique, 1891
L'Armée française en 1887, 1887
L'Armée jugée par les nationalistes, Saint-Denis nd
L'Armée sans chef, 1891
L'Armée selon la nation, 1908
La Crise de l'offensive, 1912
L'Echo de la vieille armée, 1910
Encore un mot sur le rôle social de l'officier, 1895
L'Etat Major de l'armée et le haut commandement, 1902
Etude sur le recrutement des officiers. Les officiers d'artillerie, 1907
Les Généraux de l'armée française, 1904
'L'Officier de troupe', Revue de Paris, 1 August 1909
Les Officiers et la crise d'avancement, 1910

Agathon, Les Jeunes gens d'aujourd'hui, 1913
Alexandre, Gen. R., Avec Joffre d'Agadir à Verdun; Souvenirs 1911–16, 1932
André, Lt. col, Les Forces morales. Deux conférences faites à l'école d'instruction des officiers de reserve, 1914
André, Gen., Cinq ans au ministère, 1907
Andréani, R., 'Antimilitarisme en Languedoc avant 1914', Revue d'histoire moderne et contemporaine, vol. xx, Jan.–March 1973
　Armée et nation en Languedoc méditerranéen, 1905–14, Thèse d'état, Montpellier 1975
Andrew, C. M., 'Dechiffrement et diplomatie: Le cabinet noir du Quai d'Orsay sous la Troisième République', Relations internationales, no. 5, 1976
d'Arbeaux, Cpt., L'Officier contemporain, 1911
Arès, C., La Décadence intellectuelle de l'armée, 1912
Astier et Gouzy (deputies), Le Service de deux ans, Troyes 1900
Barail, Gen. du, Mes Souvenirs, 1820–1879, 3 vols. 1894–6
Baratier, M. A., L'Intendance militaire pendant la guerre de 1870–71, 1871
Baudin, P., La Préparation au service militaire, 1907
　L'Armée moderne et les état majors, 1905
　Notre armée à l'oeuvre aux grandes manoeuvres de 1908, 1909
Bechtel, Guy, 1907. La Grande révolte du Midi, 1976
Becker, J. J., Le Carnet B, 1973
　1914, Comment les Français sont entrée en guerre, 1977
Bédarida, F., 'L'Armée et la république: Les opinions politiques des officiers français en 1876–8', Revue Historique, 1964
Belhomme, Gen., Histoire de l'infanterie en France, vol. v, 1907
Berge, Gen. H., Etudes sur la réorganisation des forces militaires de la France, Tarbes 1871
Bert, P., L'Instruction civique, 1882
　L'Education civique, 1883
Bethouart, Lt. H., Le Réglement de manoeuvre d'infanterie en France et en Allemagne, 1913
Blanqui, L-A., Armée esclave et opprimée, 1880
Bocquillon, E., La Crise du patriotisme à l'école, 1905
Bonnald, Gen. H., Infanterie, méthodes de commandement, d'éducation et d'instruction, 1900
Bonnamour, G., Enquête sur l'antimilitarisme, 1911
Bonnefous, G., Histoire politique de la troisième république, vol. 1, 1906–14, 1956
Boucher, A., La France victorieuse dans la guerre de demain, 1911
　L'Offensive contre l'Allemagne, 1911
　Les Doctrines dans la préparation à la grande guerre, 1925

Select bibliography 283

Boudenot (deputy), 'L'Armée en 1903', *Revue politique et parlementaire*, January 1903
Bouniols, G., 'Justice militaire', *Revue de Paris*, 1 May 1907
Boyer, A., *Le Tour de France d'un compagnon de devoir*, 1957
Brincourt, Gen., *Lettres, 1823–1909*, 1923
Brisson, *La Congrégation, aperçu historique*, 1902
Brun, L., 'L'Ecole supérieure de la Guerre', *Spectateur militaire*, no. 27, 1885
Bruntière, F., 'Après le procès', *Revue des deux mondes*, 15 March 1898
Bugnet, Charles, *En écoutant le Maréchal Foch*, 1929
Bury, J. P. T., *Gambetta and the Making of the Third Republic*, London 1973
Bush, John W., 'Education and Social Status. The Jesuit College in the Early Third Republic', *French Historical Studies*, vol. IX, no. 1, Spring 1975
Caillaux, J., *Agadir, ma politique extérieure*, 1919
  Mes Mémoires, 3 vols., 1942–7
Cambon, Paul, *Correspondance*, 3 vols., 1940–6
Carrias, E., *La Pensée militaire française*, 1960
Cartier, V., *Un Méconnu, Le Général Trochu*, 1914
Challener, R. D., *The French Theory of the Nation in Arms*, New York 1955
Chappin, *Souvenirs d'un capitaine de cavalerie*, 1909
Charnay, J-P., *Société militaire et suffrage politique en France depuis 1789*, 1964
Christophe, R., *Vie tragique du Maréchal Bazaine*, 1948
Chuquet, A., *Le Général Chanzy*, 1884
Civrieux, Commandant de, *Du Rêve à la réalité, 1871–1908*, 1909
Claretie, J., *Souvenirs du dîner Bixio*, 1923
Cognet, G., *Le Problème des réserves*, 1914
Colin, Gen. J., *Les Transformations de la guerre*, 1911
Combarieu, A., *Sept ans à l'Elysée avec Emile Loubet, 1899–1906*, 1932
Combes, E., *Mon Ministère, 1902–5*, 1956
Contamine, H., *La Revanche*, 1957
  'Jaurès vu par les nationalistes français', *Actes du colloque Jaurès et la nation*, Toulouse 1964
Cosseron de Villenoisy, Gen., *La Désorganisation de l'armée française*, 1886
Dansette, A., *Le Boulangisme*, 1946
Daudet, L., *La Vie orgueilleuse de Clémenceau*, 1938
Debeney, Gen., *La Guerre et les hommes*, 1937
Delattre, Pierre, *Les Etablissements des Jésuites en France 1540–1900*, 5 vols., 1940–57
Déroulède, P., *L'Education militaire*, 1882
Descaves, L., *Les Sous-offs*, 1891
Desmazes, Gen., *Saint-Cyr*, 1948
  Joffre, 1955
Digeon, C., *La Crise allemande de la pensée française, 1870–1914*, 1959
Drachkovitch, M., *Les Socialismes français et allemands et le problème de la guerre, 1870–1914*, Geneva 1953
Driant, Lt. col. E., *Vers un nouveau Sedan*, 1906
Dunop, Gen., *Le Rôle social de l'officier*, 1908
Duruy, V., *Le Sous-officier dans l'armée moderne*, 1906
  L'Instruction du sous-officier de l'infanterie, 1909
Earle, E. M. (ed.), *The Makers of Modern Strategy*, Princeton 1944
Ebener, C., *Le Rôle social de l'officier*, 1901
Engerand, F., *Le Secret de la frontière*, 1918
Erlanger, P., *Clémenceau*, 1969
Etienne, E., *Son Oeuvre coloniale, Algérienne et politique, 1881–1906*, 2 vols., 1907

Farrère, C., *Histoire de la marine française*, 1956
Ferry, Abel, *Les Carnets secrets d'Abel Ferry*, nd
   La Guerre vue d'en haut et d'en bas, 1920
Fesch, P., *La Franc-maçonnerie contre l'armée*, 1905
Fiechter, J-J, *Le Socialisme français de l'affaire Dreyfus à la Grande Guerre*, Geneva 1965
Fix, Col., *Le Service des état-majors*, 1891
   Souvenirs, 1898
Foch, F., *Des Principes de la guerre*, 1911
   Mémoires, 1943–4
Freycinet, *La Guerre en province*, 1871
   Souvenirs, 2 vols., 1914
Garçon, A., *L'Education militaire à l'école*, 1886
Garnier-Thenon, M., 'Jaurès et l'armée nouvelle', *Revue socialiste*, December 1961
Garros, L., *L'Armée de grand-papa, de Galliffet à Gamelin, 1871–1939*, 1955
Gilbert, Capt. G., *Loi et institutions militaires, six études organiques*, 1895
   La Guerre Sud-africaine, 1902
Girardet, R., *La Société militaire dans la France contemporaine*, 1953
Goguel, F., *La Politique des partis sous la troisième république*, 1946
Gohier, U., *L'Armée nouvelle*, 1897
   L'Armée contre la nation, 1898
   La Congrégation et les prétoriens, 1899
   L'Antimilitarisme et la paix, 1905
Golaz, A., 'L'Organisation du haut commandement de 1870 à 1914', *Note du service historique de l'armée*, March 1955
Goldberg, H., *The Life of Jean Jaurès*, Madison 1962
Goltz, Colmar von der, *La Nation armée*, 1884
Gorce, P. de la, *La République et son armée*, 1963
Grandin, Gen. C-V, *Dix-huit ans au généralat, 1878–96*, Besançon 1901
Grandmaison, Col., *Dressage de l'infanterie en vue de l'offensive*, 1906
   Deux conférences faites aux officiers de l'état-major de l'armée, 1911
Grouard, Lt. col. A., *France et Allemagne, la guerre éventuelle*, 1913
Guedalla, P., *The Two Marshals, Bazaine and Pétain*, London 1943
Hanrion, Gen. L., *Saint-Cyr, Neuf années de commandement, 1871–80*, 1888
Haroué, J., *La Détresse de l'armée*, 1904
Hauriou, A., 'Jaurès et le problème de l'armée', *Cahiers internationaux*, July–August 1959
Hermant, A., *Le Cavalier Miserey*, 1887
Holmes, R., *The Road to Sedan*, unpublished Ph.D thesis, Reading University 1975
Humbert, C., *Sommes nous défendus?*, 1907
   Les Voeux de l'armée, 1908
   Chinoiseries militaires, 1909
Iung, Gen., *Des Principes de l'organisation de l'armée*, 1874
   La République et l'armée, 1892
Jackson, J. H., *Clemenceau and the Third Republic*, London 1946
Jamais, E., *L'Armée et l'école*, 1883
Jaurès, J., *L'Armée nouvelle*, 1932
Jibé, *L'Officier dans l'armée nouvelle*, 1906
Joffre, *La Préparation à la guerre*, 1920
   Mémoires, 2 vols., 1932
Juin, Maréchal, *Je suis soldat*, 1960

Select bibliography

Julliard, J., 'Le CGT devant le problème de la guerre 1900–10', *Mouvement social*, no. 49, October–December 1964
Clémenceau, briseur de grèves, 1965
Katzenbach, E. L., *Freycinet and the Army of Metropolitan France*, unpublished Ph.D thesis, Princeton 1952
King, J. C., *Generals and Politicians, Conflict between France's High Command, Parliament and Government, 1914–18*, Berkley 1951
Klotz, L., *L'Armée en 1906*, 1906
Korganon, G., *La Question des réserves dans la réorganisation de l'armée de 1872 à 1898*, DES Paris 1954
Kovacs, A., 'French Military Legislation in the Third Republic, 1871–1940', *Military Affairs*, vol. XIII, Spring 1949
Kuntz, F., *L'Officier français dans la nation*, 1960
Lamarque, L., *Un An de caserne*, 1901
Langlois, Gen. H., *Conséquences tactiques des progrès de l'armament*, 1903
Questions de défense nationale, 1906
'Notre situation militaire', *Revue des deux mondes*, 15 October 1907
Quelques questions d'actualité, 1909
'Le Haut commandement', *Revue des deux mondes*, 1 September 1911
'Les Sociétés de préparation militaire et la politique', *Le Temps*, 7 August 1911
Larzelles, H. de, *Lettres d'un réserviste*, 1907
Laure, Lt. E., *L'Offensive française*, 1912
Le Problème de la bataille dans le domaine tactique, 1914
Lavisse, Col., *Devoirs d'officiers*, 1910
Vers la fusion, 1908
Le Blond, M., *La Crise du Midi*, 1907
Legrand-Girard, Gen., *Un Quart de siècle au service de la France, 1894–1918*, 1954
Lewal, Gen., *La Réforme de l'armée*, 1871
Lettres à l'armée, 1872
Etudes de guerre, 1873
Liddell Hart, Cpt. H. B., *Foch, The Man of Orleans*, Boston 1932
Lyautey, H., 'Role social de l'officier', *Revue des deux mondes*, 15 March 1891
Madre, J., *La Fondation des cercles militaires*, 1876
Mahon, P., 'La Loi des cadres d'infanterie', *Revue des deux mondes*, 1 June 1912
Maitron, J., *Histoire du mouvement anarchiste en France, 1880–1914*, 1951
Maitrot, Gen. C. A., *Nos Frontières de l'est et du nord: le service de deux ans et sa repercussion sur la défense*, 1912
Malcor, A., *L'Armée homogène ou l'unification du corps d'officiers*, 1872
Marceau, Lt., *L'Officier éducateur national*, Bordeaux 1905
Marchand, A., *Plans de concentration de 1871 à 1914*, 1926
Masse, J., 'L'Antimilitarisme dans le Var avant 1914', *Cahiers d'histoire*, vol. XIII, 1968
Mayer, Emile, *Trois Maréchaux*, 1928
Nos Chefs de 1914, 1930
Merlier, G., 'L'Esprit de l'offensive dans l'armée française en 1914 à la lecture de Grandmaison', *Bulletin de la société d'histoire moderne*, no. 8, 1966
Messimy, A., *Considérations générales sur l'organisation de l'armée*, 1907
L'Armée et ses cadres, 1909
Le Problème militaire, 1913
Mes Souvenirs, 1937
Metzinger, Gen., *La Transformation de l'armée, 1897–1907*, 1909

Michon, G., *La Préparation à la guerre. La Loi de trois ans*, 1935
Millerand, A., *Pour la défense nationale*, 1913
Mitchell, Alan, 'Thiers, MacMahon and the conseil supérieur de guerre', *French Historical Studies*, vol. 6, no. 2, 1969
Mollin, J. H., *La Vérité sur l'affaire des fiches*, 1905
Monteil, V., *Les Officiers*, 1955
Monteilhet, J., *Les Institutions militaires de la France*, 1932
Mordacq, Gen. H-J-J., *Politique et stratégie dans une démocratie*, 1912
    'L'Officier au XX siècle', *La Vie militaire en France et à l'étranger, 1912–13*, 1914
    Clémenceau, 1939
Motte Rouge, Gen de la, *Souvenirs et campagnes*, vol. III, 1856–1883, Nantes 1889
Nanteuil, R., *Le Dossier de M. Guyot de Villeneuve, l'armée cléricale*, 1907
Négrier, Gen., 'Quelques enseignements sur la Guerre Russo-Japonaise', *Revue des deux mondes*, 15 January 1906
Nickerson, H., *The Armed Horde, 1793–1939*, New York 1940
Ollé-Laprune, J., *La Stabilité des ministres sous la Troisième Républlque, 1879–1940*, 1962
Orano, R., *Gouvernement et haut commandement en régime parlementaire français, 1814–1914*, Thesis, Aix-en-Provence 1958
Palat, Gen., 'Les Manoeuvres en Languedoc en 1913', *Revue des deux mondes*, 15 October 1913
Paléologue, M., 'Comment le service de trois ans fut rétabli en 1913', *Revue des deux mondes*, 1 May 1935
    Au Quai d'Orsay à la veille de la tourmente, journal 1913–1914, 1947
Pédoya, Gen., *L'Armée n'est pas commandée*, 1905
    L'Armée évolue, 4 vols., 1908
    Désirs et plaintes des officiers, 1909
Pedroncini, G., *Les Mutineries de 1917*, 1967
Percin, Gen., *1914, Les erreurs du haut commandement*, nd
    La Guerre et la nation armée, 1919
    Lille, 1919
    Deux hommes de guerre, Sarrail et Galliéni, 1919
    L'Armée de demain, 1920
Pessard, H., *Mes petits papiers*, 1887–8
Philebert, Gen., *Des Cadres des armées de réserve et territoriale*, 1895
Picquart, G., 'La Discipline et la répression dans l'armée', *Grand Revue*, 1 February 1903
    'L'Affaire', *Gazette de Lauzanne*, 2 May 1903
    'Conseils de Guerre', *Gazette de Lauzanne*, 1 February 1904
Pierrefeu, Jean de, *GQG, secteur 1*, 2 vols., 1920
    Plutarque a menti, 1923
Poincaré, R., *Au Service de la France*, 1926–33
Pont, Cpt. C., *Les Indisciplinés dans l'armée*, 1912
Prudhomme, S., 'Patrie, armée, discipline', *Revue des deux mondes*, 15 June 1898
Radziwill, Princess, *Lettres au Général Robilant*, 4 vols., 1933
Raiberti, 'La Crise de notre organisation militaire', *Revue de Paris*, 1 March 1913
    'Une Nouvelle organisation de l'armée', *Revue de Paris*, 15 March 1913
Ralston, David, *The Army of the Republic*, Cambridge, Mass. 1967
Reinach, J., *Mes Comptes rendus*, 1911–18
Renault, Cpt. E., *Du Mariage militaire*, 1995
Révillon, T., *Camille Pelletan, 1846–1915*, 1930

Revol, Col. J., *Histoire de l'armée française*, 1929
Riet, C., *L'Armée moralisatrice*, 1896
Robuchon, J., *Les Grandes heures de Georges Clémenceau*, Fontenay-le-Comte 1967
Rolland, H. de, *Galliffet*, 1945
Rousselet, L., *Nos Grandes écoles, militaires et civiles*, 1888
Rousset, Lt. col., 'La Bonne a tout faire', *La Liberté*, 17 October 1911
Schlumberger, G., *Mes Souvenirs, 1844–1928*, 1929
Serman, W., 'Les Généraux français de 1870', *Revue de défense nationale*, September 1970
Sillion, *Vers l'armée démocratique*, 1907
Simon, P., *L'Instruction des officiers, l'éducation des troupes et la puissance nationale*, 1905
Le Formalisme, 1913
Simon, T., *L'Antimilitarisme vu à travers le Petit Marseillais, 1900–1913*, Maitrise, Aix-en-Provence nd
Sorlin, P., *Waldeck-Rousseau*, 1966
Soulier, A., *L'Instabilité ministerielle sous la Troisième République, 1871–1939*, 1939
Swart, K. W., *The Sense of Decadence in Nineteenth Century France*, The Hague 1964
Tannenbaum, J. K., *General Maurice Sarrail, 1856–1929*, Chapel Hill 1974
Tardieu, A., *Avec Foch*, 1939
Terquern, E., *Comment on fait une armée réactionnaire*, 1906
Thomas, Louis, *Le Général de Galliffet*, 1910
Thoumas, C., *Les Transformations de l'armée française*, 1887
Thoyot, L., *Le Ministre contre l'armée*, 1902
Tison, H., *La Loi de trois ans et l'opinion publique française*, DES Paris 1966
Titeux, Lt. col., *Saint-Cyr et l'Ecole spéciale militaire en France*, 1898
Trentinian, Gen. de, *L'Etat-major en 1914*, 1927
Trochu, Gen., *L'Armée française en 1867*, 1879
Oeuvres posthumes, Tours 1896
Vallery-Radot, *Journal d'un volontaire d'un an*, 1874
Veritas, *La Verité sur le ministère Thibaudin*, 1883
La Verité sur l'affaire Boulanger, 1888
Veron, Gen. J., *Souvenirs de ma vie militaire, 1905–1940*, Rouen 1969
Watson, D., *Georges Clemenceau*, London 1974
Weber, E., *Action Française*, Stanford 1963
The Nationalist Revival in France, Berkeley and Los Angeles 1959
Peasants into Frenchmen, London 1977
Weygand, Gen., *Histoire de l'armée française*, 1938
Mémoires, 3 vols., 1953–57
Williams, W., *The Tiger of France*, New York 1949
Williamson, S. R., *The Politics of the Grand Strategy*, Cambridge, Mass. 1969
Winock, M., 'Socialisme et patriotisme en France 1891–94', *Revue d'histoire moderne et contemporaine*, vol. xx, July–September 1973
Wright, G., *Raymond Poincaré and the French Presidency*, Stanford 1942
Lt. Z., *L'Armée au grèves*, 1904
Zaniewicki, Maj. W., 'L'Impact de 1870 sur la pensée militaire française', *Revue de défense nationale*, August–September 1970
Zurlinden, Gen., 'Le Haut commandement des armées', *Revue des deux mondes*, 15 June 1903
'Les Hautes études de la guerre et l'avancement dans l'armée', *Revue des deux mondes*, 15 December 1904

ARTILLERY

Alvin, Capt., *L'Artillerie de campagne dans les Balkans*, 1914
Banquet, Gen., *Souvenirs d'un directeur d'artillerie*, 1923
Benazet, P., 'Le Parlement devant la Patrie', *La Renaissance*, 15 April 1916
  Benazet report, *Documents parlementaires - Chambre*, no. 3491, p. 635, 9 February 1914
Bornecque, Commdt., *L'Artillerie de campagne, état actuel de la question*, 1908
Bourget, P., *Echo de Paris*, 1 November 1914
Buat, Commdt. E., *L'Artillerie de campagne . . . son état actuel*, 1911
Caillaux, J., *Agadir, ma politique exterieure*, 1919, pp. 241-2
Challéat, J., *La Question de l'obusier léger*, 1913
  L'Artillerie de terre en France pendant un siècle, vol. 2, 1880-1910, 2 vols., 1935
Général D., 'Une Doctrine pour l'artillerie lourde', *Revue d'artillerie*, vol. 83, October 1913-March 1914, p. 431.
Engerand, F., *Le Secret de la frontière*, 1918, pp. 153-4
Enjalbert, 'L'Organisation et le fonctionnement des établissements d'artillerie', *Revue d'artillerie*, vol. 83, October 1913-March 1914
Gascouin, Gen., *L'Evolution de l'artillerie pendant la guerre*, 1920
Herr, Gen. F., *L'Artillerie*, 1923
  'Rapport d'ensemble du General Herr, président de la commission centrale d'artillerie, sur les enseignements à retirer de la guerre en matière d'artillerie', 1 October 1919. Typed report in Archives historiques de guerre, Vincennes
Humbert, C., *Journal officiel-Sénat*, 13-14 July 1914
Klotz, *Journal officiel - Chambre*, 18 July 1916
Langlois, Gen. H., *Lessons from Two Recent Wars*, London 1909
  Revue bleu, 19 July 1913
Le Bon, G., *Les Premières conséquences de la guerre*, 1917
Messimy, A., 'Souvenirs de l'année 1911', *Revue de Paris*, 1 March 1937
Michon, G., *La Préparation à la guerre*, Appendix 'l'Etat-major et l'artillerie lourde', 1935
Millerand, A., *Pour la défense nationale*, 1913
Noulens, J., 'Le Gouvernement français à la veille de la guerre', *Revue des deux mondes*, 1 February 1931
Percin, Gen., *Artilleurs et fantassins, fâcheuses polémiques*, Angoulême 1912
  'La Question de l'obusier de campagne', *La Vie militaire en France et à l'étranger*, *1911-12*, 1913
Sautereau du Part, Lt. col. E., *Etablissement d'un matériel d'artillerie de campagne*, 1913
Schneider, *La Question de canons de gros calibres*, nd

COLONIAL ARMY

Abrams, L. and Muller, D. J., 'Who were the French Colonialists? A Reassessment of the "Parti colonial", 1890-1914', *Historical Journal*, vol. XIX, no. 3, 1976, pp. 687-725
Andrew, C. M., 'The French Colonialist Movement during the Third Republic: The Unofficial Mind of Imperialism', *Transactions of the Royal Historical Society*, series 5, vol. 26, London 1976, pp. 143-66
Andrew, C. M. and Kanya-Forstner, A. S., 'The French "Colonial Party": Its Composition, Aims and Influence, 1885-1914', *Historical Journal*, vol. XIV. no. 1, 1971

'The *Groupe Colonial* in the French Chamber of Deputies, 1892–1932', *Historical Journal*, vol. XVII, no. 4, 1974
'Gabriel Hanotaux, the Colonial Party and the Fashoda Strategy', *Journal of Imperial and Commonwealth History*, vol. III, no. 1, October 1974
'France, Africa and the First World War', *Journal of African History*, vol. XIX, no. 1, 1978
Andrew, C. M., Grupp, P., and Kanya-Forstner, A. S., 'Le Mouvement colonial français et ses principales personnalités, 1890–1914', *Revue française d'histoire d'outre-mer*, vol. LXII, 1975
Archinard, Gen. L., *L'Autre France*, 1914
  Le Soudan français, 1888–89, 1889
'Le Soldat colonial', *Bulletin du Comité de l'Afrique française*, 1910, pp. 290–2
Azan, Gen. P., *Franchet d'Esperey*, 1949
Baron, Louis, *Les Idées coloniales en France et le recrutement des officiers sortant de Saint-Cyr dans l'infanterie de la marine, 1872–1891*, thesis, Paris Sorbonne 1969
Bernard, Gen., 'Les Forces morales pour la guerre', *Revue général militaire*, January–April 1908
Betts, R. F., *Assimilation and Association in French Colonial Theory, 1890–1914*, New York 1961
Blanchard, Marcel, (ed.), 'Correspondance de Felix Faure touchant les affaires coloniales, 1882–98', *Revue d'historie des colonies françaises*, vol. 42, no. 147, 1955, pp. 133–85
Borgnis-Desbordes, Gen., 'Au Vieux Soudan, lettres inédites', *Bulletin du Comité de l'Afrique française*, 1910
Boucabeille, Gen., *Sur l'organisation des troupes coloniales*, 1926
Bournazel, A., *L'Officier colonial, 1919–39*, thesis, Paris 1967
Brunschwig, H., *Mythes et réalités de l'imperialisme colonial français, 1871–1914*, 1960
Charbonnel, Col. Henri, *De Madagascar à Verdun*, 1962
Corbin, Col. C., 'L'Armée coloniale', *Revue des deux mondes*, April 1898
Cornet, Capt., 'Etude sur les troupes noires', *Revue des troupes coloniales*, vol. 1, 1911
Davis, S. C., *The French War Machine*, London 1937
Denis, Pierre, *L'Evolution des troupes Sahariennes*, thesis, Rennes 1963
Deschamps, H. (ed.), *Galliéni pacificateur*, 1949
Ditte, Lt. col. A., *Observations sur la guerre dans les colonies*, 1905
Duchemin, Gen., La Défense des colonies', *Journal des sciences militaires*, series 10, no. 22, 1904
Durosoy, Gen. M., *Avec Lyautey*, 1976
Dussauge, André, 'Les Troupes indigènes', *Questions diplomatiques et coloniales*, vol. 34, 1912
Froelicher, J., *Trois colonisateurs: Bugeaud, Faidherbe, Galliéni*, nd
Galliéni, Gen. J. S., *Galliéni au Tonkin*, 1899
  Lettres de Madagascar, 1928
  Neuf ans à Madagascar, 1908
Girardet, R., *L'Idée coloniale en France*, 1972
Gouraud, Gen. H., *Au Maroc, 1911–14*, 1949
  Zinder-Tchad, 1945
Grandmaison, Col. L., *En Territoire militaire*, 1898
Hanotaux, G., *Le Général Mangin*, 1925
Heidsieck, P., *Le Rayonnement de Lyautey*, 1947
Huré, Gen. A., *La Pacification du Maroc*, 1952
Ibos, P. (pseud. Pierre Khorat), *Scènes de la pacification Marocaine*, 1914

'En Colonne au Maroc', *Revue des deux mondes*, 1 August, 15 September, 1 November 1911
Joffre, Gen. J., *My March to Timbuctoo*, New York 1915
Julien, C. A., *Histoire de l'Algérie contemporaine*, 1964
Kanya-Forstner, A. S., *The Conquest of the Western Sudan*, Cambridge 1969
Kaplin, M., *The Radicals and the Army in France, 1899–1905*, unpublished Ph.D thesis, City University of New York 1976
Kuntz, Lt., *Souvenirs de campagne au Maroc*, 1913
Lanessan, Jean de, *La Colonisation en Indo-Chine*, 1895
Lewal, Gen., *Les Troupes coloniales*, 1894
Lyautey, Gen. H., 'Le Rôle colonial de l'armée', *Revue des deux mondes*, September 1900
  Choix de lettres, 1947
  Lettres du sud de Madagascar, 1900–02, 1935
  Lettres du Tonkin et de Madagascar, 1894–1899, 1942
  Lyautey l'Africain, 4 vols., 1952–7
  Vers le Maroc, 1937
Mangin, Col. C., *La Force noire*, 1910
Mason, P., *A Matter of Honour*, London 1974
Michel, Marc, *La Mission Marchand*, 1972
  'La Genèse du recrutement de 1918 en Afrique noire française', *Revue française d'histoire d'outre-mer*, vol. LVIII, 1971
  'Un Mythe: La "Force Noire" avant 1914', *Relations Internationales*, vol. I, 1974
Ministère de la guerre, *Les Armées françaises d'outre-mer, les grands soldats coloniaux*, 1931
  Biographie des coloniaux illustres, 1935
Mordacq, Gen. H., *Pacification du Haut Tonkin*, 1901
Munholland, J., *The Emergence of the Colonial Military in France, 1880–1905*, unpublished Ph.D thesis, Princeton 1964
Peroz, Lt. col. E., *Armée coloniale, armée de métier, milices nationales*, 1909
  Hors des chemins battus, 1908
Sainte-Aulaire, Comte de, *Confessions d'un vieux diplomate*, 1953
Scham, A., *Lyautey in Morocco: Protectorate Politics, 1912–1925*, Berkeley 1970
Taillandier, G. Saint-René, *Les Origines du Maroc français, récit d'une mission, 1901–6*, 1930
Trentinian, Gen. de, *La Fusion des officiers de l'armée métropolitaine et de l'armée coloniale*, 1911

Index

Administration; colonial, 140–3, 144, 147, 157, 160; military, 40, 41, 42, 43, 46, 84, 121, 127, 131, 132, 180–1, 184, 195, 196, 220
Aenoult affair, 187
affaire des fiches, 20, chapter 6
aide-de-camp, 216
Algeria, 6, 16, 23, 35, 38, 66, 103, 134, 135, 136, 140, 148, 151, 154, 166, 167, 168, 189
Almereyda, Miquel, 110
André, General, 63, 68, 69, 71, 72, 75–80, 85, 86, 87, 90–9, 101, 104, 115, 116, 124, 127, 129, 149, 169, 171, 173, 176, 177, 181, 185, 215, 227, 249, 251
anti-militarism, 54, 55, 56, 57, 59, chapter 7, 157, 167, 187, 188, 189, 203–4
anti-semitism, 59, 60
Archinard, General, 140, 141, 146, 147, 150, 151, 154, 160, 181
aristocrats (in the army), 1, 17, 18, 19, 151–2, 247
armaments (*see also* artillery), 33, 43, 52, 90, 173, 175, 225, 226, 231, chapter 12, 249
artillery, 6, 9, 27, 28, 37, 41, 42, 43, 59, 70, 77, 78, 84, 93, 126, 170, 195, 200, 206, 211, 223, 225, 226, chapter 12, 249–50, 252
Association Internationale Antimilitariste, 110
Aumale, Duc d', 6, 14

Banquet, General, 234, 237, 240, 245, 249
du Barail, General, 3, 4, 8, 15, 21, 31, 40, 42, 47, 48, 49, 51, 52
bataillon d'Afrique, 129, 130, 156, 185
batillons scolaires, 207–9
Berge, General, 11, 37, 38, 240
Berteaux, Maurice, 78, 98, 126, 128, 173, 174, 195, 200
Billot, General, 2, 3, 39, 44, 49, 59, 61, 69
Boisdeffre, General, 21, 53, 60, 61, 70, 212
Bonaparte, Louis-Napoleon, 6, 7, 12, 14, 15, 23, 25

Borel, General, 2
Boulanger, General, 1, 8, 16, 26, 29, 31, 37, 42, 48–51, 61, 63, 67, 74, 217, 251
Bourbaki, General, 2, 3, 15
bourse du travail, 109, 110, 111, 113, 118, 119, 188
British Expeditionary Force, 228–9
Brugère, General, 63, 69, 77, 80, 231
Brun, General, 173, 177, 241
Bugeaud, General, 135, 136, 156
Bureau Arabe, 135, 156

Caillaux, Joseph, 73, 95, 117, 166, 230, 238, 241–2, 249
Cambon, Paul, 136, 140, 159
camouflage uniform, 184–5
carnet B, 109
Carrey de Bellemare, General, 4, 8, 13, 19
Castellane, General de, 135
Castelnau, General, 70, 77, 80, 120, 171, 176, 250
cavalry, 28, 40, 41, 42, 62, 70, 103, 107, 124, 132, 193, 195, 197, 198, 200, 201, 202, 245
Centre des hautes études militaires, 223, 236
Chambord, Comte de, 7, 13, 14, 15
Changarnier, General, 8
Chanzy, General, 2, 3, 10, 16, 208
chaplins, 21
Charenton, General, 27
Church, 69–70, 73, 74, 76, 77, 78, 86, 87, 92, 98, 102, 105, 106, 124, 146, 169, 209, 217, 250, 251
Clémenceau, George, 18, 59, 61, 65, 74, 75, 87, 105, 106, 107, 117, 118, 119, 128, 132, 138, 167, 168, 169, 174, 176, 180, 189, 251
Clinchant, General, 1, 3, 8, 14
colonial army, 41, 116, 127, chapter 8, 172, 181, 224, 251–2
colonial party, 144–6, 149, 150
Combes, Emile, 20, 74, 80, 87, 93, 94, 96, 97, 100, 146, 149, 251

Comité de l'Afrique française, 137, 139, 145, 147, 158, 167
Comité du Maroc, 145, 147
Comité supérieur de la défense nationale, 175
Commune, 1, 2, 11, 62-3, 74, 75, 106
complementary cadres, 192
Confédération générale du travail, 105, 107, 110, 111, 113, 188, 189, 203
conscription, 23-32, 34, 35, 55, 106; three-year service law of 1889, 25-6, 55, 195, 200, 203, 205; two-year service law of 1905, 75, 81, 87, 113, 192-6, 200, 202, 203, 205, 211; three-year service law of 1913, 114, 170, chapter 10, 243, 244
conseil supérieur de guerre, 22, 24, 47, 52-3, 67-8, 119, 170, 171, 176, 178, 192, 211, 216, 221, 234, 236, 238, 239, 249
court martials, 128, 129, 130, 185

Debeney, General, 219-20, 221, 225
Delanne, General, 77
Delcassé, Théophile, 140, 141, 146, 148, 149, 150
Deloye, General, 240-1, 242, 245
demi-soldes, 5
Déroulède, Paul, 64, 138, 208
desertion, 111, 112, 113, 130, 188
dowry, 79, 85, 88
Dreyfus affair, 2, 11, 18, 21, 22, 27, 32, 44, 53, chapter 4, 73, 74, 75, 76, 83, 87, 101, 112, 123, 162, 166, 170, 173, 184, 187, 206, 224, 246, 253, 254
Driant, Major, 182, 183, 214
Drumont, Edouard, 59
Dubail, General, 171, 177, 235
Ducrot, General, 2, 8, 9, 13, 14, 15, 21, 52

Ecole polytechnique, 20, 27, 40, 48, 75, 78, 81, 82, 83, 84, 116, 124, 144, 151, 172, 217, 222, 241, 242
Ecole supérieure de guerre (war college), 36, 40, 41, 57, 85, 88, 154, 156, 169, 213-14, 218, 219-20, 221, 225, 226, 231, 250
education (of officers – secondary), 19-20, 21, 22, 38, 39, 40, 58, 78, 81
engineers, 6, 9, 28, 41, 42, 48, 70, 78, 84, 126, 195
Espivent, General, 8
Etienne, Eugène, 86, 87, 99, 104, 116, 124, 128, 140, 144, 145, 146, 148, 149, 150, 173, 185, 189, 192, 238

Faidherbe, General, 135, 141, 147, 151, 154, 155, 156
Fashoda, 139, 146, 147-8, 158, 162, 165
Ferry, Jules, 50, 136, 139, 146, 208

Foch, Marshal, 43, 120, 169, 211, 213, 214, 219, 221, 225, 226, 252
Foreign Legion, 144, 156, 161
Freycinet, C. L. de S. de, 3, 10, 12, 18, 19, 24, 26, 32, 35, 36, 37, 42, 49, 50, 51, 52, 53, 58, 67, 69, 72, 74, 77, 131, 145, 146, 173

Galliéni, General, 70, 118, 119, 121, 122, 127, 132, 138, 139, 146, 147, 148, 149, 151, 152, 155, 156, 157, 159, 160, 161, 162, 164, 172, 178, 217, 244, 250
Galliffet, General de, 8, 9, 11, 14, 19, 50, 58, 62-71, 74, 75, 79, 80, 85, 92, 96, 97, 158
Gambetta, L., 1, 2, 4, 7-8, 9-15, 20, 28, 30, 31, 32, 34, 35, 36, 51, 54, 61, 63, 97, 99, 138, 145, 246
'Gambettist generals', 2-4, 50
general staff (*see also* high command), 33, 41, 42, 49, 51, 52, 57, 59, 60, 61, 70, 71, 76, 77, 83, 85, 163-4, 171, 176, 184, 213, 218, 220-1, 222-3, 231, 234, 239-40, 241, 243, 244, 246, 252-3
German (Prussian) Army, 17, 24, 27, 32, 36, 38, 39, 42-3, 45, 46, 49, 55, 89, 90, 124, 171, 172, 174, 175, 177, 192, 194-8, 201, 203, 210, 212, 220, 222, 227, 230-1, 232, 233, 234-5, 238, 244
Gohier, Urbain, 111
Goiran, General, 171, 173
Gouraud, General Henri, 157, 164, 166
Grandmaison, General de, 143, 163, 164, 165, 201, 213, 215, 219, 224, 225, 236, 240
Gresley, General, 15
Guerre sociale, 111, 112, 133
Guesde, Jules, 105, 109, 112, 183
Guyot de Villeneuve, 93, 97

Hagron, General, 80, 119, 169, 231
Herr, General, 232, 236, 242, 244
Hervé, Gustave, 109-12, 115, 131, 157
high command, 44, chapter 3, 54, 58-9, 61, 67-8, 70, 71, 76, 90, 101, 102, 103, 170-8, 196, 213, 216-18, 220, 224, 230, 231, 237-9, 246, 250-2
Humbert, Charles, 77, 83, 92, 95, 96, 131, 179, 185, 197, 202, 221, 235, 236, 239, 243
hygiene, 55

indiscipline, 33, 35, 36, 101, chapter 7, 159, 185, 205; 17th infantry regiment 1907, 114-21, 123, 128-32, 189; anti-three-year service law riots 1913, 114, 187-9
infantry, 28, 30, 40, 41, 42, 43, 63, 193, 194, 197, 200, 202, 206, 210, 214, 215, 223, 245
intelligence, French, 229-31

Index

Jamont, General, 69, 77
Jaurès, Jean, 61, 65, 73, 81, 83, 87, 98, 109, 111, 113, 119, 146, 148, 149, 150, 166, 178, 183, 193, 200, 210, 246, 247-9, 250
Jesuits (influence in officer corps), 1, 9, 19-20, 21, 22, 40, 69, 70, 92, 99
Joffre, General, 70, 120, 153, 159, 164, 166, 171-8, 187, 191, 194, 197, 202, 204, 212-14, 216-18, 222, 223, 226, 229, 231, 233, 236-9, 244, 245, 249-53
Jonnart, Charles, 147, 149, 167, 174
July Monarchy, army in the, 5, 6, 7, 16, 23, 134, 135

Khenifra, 159-60
Klotz, L. L., 131, 205, 227, 238

Lamoricière, General, 136, 156
Lamothe, General, 236, 241
Langlois, General, 68, 69, 80, 82, 101, 102, 119, 129, 213, 225, 226, 227, 238
Lewal, General, 11, 30, 36-8, 41, 42, 48
Ligue antimilitariste, 110
Lyautey, Marshal H., 19, 58, 70, 72, 85, 87, 95, 100, 104, 124, 137, 138, 141, 144, 146-53, 155-62, 164-5, 174, 223-4, 247, 251-2

MacMahon, Marshal, 2, 3, 12-15, 24, 30, 41, 49, 52
Mangin, General Charles, 138, 154, 164, 166-8, 252
manoeuvres (*see also* training), 177, 178, 194, 200, 202, 204, 234, 236
Marchand, General, 115, 147
masons, 68, 76, 86, chapter 6
Mercier, General, 49, 59, 60, 61, 64, 65, 75
mess, officers', 42-3, 79, 85, 88, 103, 185
Messimy, Adolphe, 50, 80, 82-3, 100, 122, 127, 129, 167, 169, 171-3, 176, 178, 182, 184, 186-7, 190, 195, 202, 206, 209, 215, 217, 219, 220-1, 222, 223, 237, 242, 245, 253
Michel, General, 119, 178, 211, 250
military preparation societies, 194, 195, 206-10, 211, 250
military unions, 180-4, 198-200
Millerand, Alexandre, 64, 66, 72, 85, 98, 119, 128, 169, 170, 171, 173-6, 178-80, 184-7, 190, 192, 202-3, 207, 209-10, 238-9, 241
Miribel, General de, 19, 52, 53, 212
Mollin, Captain, 94-7
Montaudon, General, 8, 15
'moral order', 12-15, 21
Morocco, 139, 141, 146, 148-9, 151, 155, 159-60, 165-7, 169, 171, 230-1

Mun, Captain Albert de, 125

National Assembly, 1, 7, 12, 13, 23, 28
Nationalist Revival, chapter 9, 213, 224, 247, 253
Négrier, General, 67, 69, 80, 154, 155, 228
non-commissioned officers (NCOs), 3, 6, 10, 15, 17, 26, 28, 30-1, 34, 38-41, 54, 75, 78-9, 81-3, 107, 112, 114, 117-18, 120-4, 127, 129, 131-2, 153, 166, 170, 182, 184-5, 187, 189, 192-201, 205-6, 210-12, 226-7, 244
Noulens, J., 173, 238, 241

offensive (*see also* tactics), 24, 170, chapter 11, 253
'one-year volunteers', 25-6, 55, 88, 205
Orleans, Duc d', 12-13

Paty de Clam, Major du, 60, 186
Pau, General, 172-3, 179, 188, 217, 250
pay, 17, 42, 88-90
Pédoya, General, 88-90, 128, 130, 199, 219-20
Peigné, General, 94
Pelletan, Camille, 63, 65, 87, 128, 146
Pelloutier, Ferdinand, 109
Pendezec, General, 77, 80, 149, 166
pensions, 90
Percin, General, 77, 92, 95-7, 249
Petain, Marshal, 219, 252
Picquart, General, 60-1, 77, 80, 87, 100-1, 118-19, 128, 173, 181, 201, 204
Plan XVII, 191, 212, 228-9
Poincaré, Raymond, 105, 169, 186, 188-9, 230, 238, 243
promotion, 2-5, 17, 38, 42, 69-70, 76-8, 88, 91, chapter 6, 158, 179-81, 192, 196, 251

Rank Revision Committee, 2-4, 50
regional recruitment, 29-32, 119-24
replacement, 24-5
reserves, 25-8, 30, 34, 42, 112-15, 118, 126-7, 170, 186, chapter 10
Restoration, army in the, 4-7, 21, 23, 29, 66, 69, 119
Rochebouet, General, 14
Roget, General, 64
Rousset affair, 112
Russian army, 194, 228

Saint-Arnaud, General, 6, 15-16, 74, 217
Saint-Aulaire, Comte de, 99
Saint-Cyr, 17-20, 38-40, 57, 77-9, 81-4, 96, 101, 124, 135, 144, 151-3, 156, 182-3, 215, 222, 250

Saint-Maixent, 77-8, 81-4, 92, 126
Sarrail, General, 77-8, 81, 86, 92, 100, 126, 217, 249
Saumur, école de, 81-2
Saussier, General, 2-3, 8, 16, 50, 53, 62, 69
Second Empire, army in the, 1-2, 6-7, 16-18, 25, 30, 32, 35, 37-8, 41, 45-6, 57, 135
Second Republic, 6
'Seize mai' crisis, 14-15, 74
social role, 125-8, 185-6, 201-2, 215, 247
sou du soldat, 110
strikes, use of army in, 89, 102, 106-9, 111-12, 117, 250
Sylvestre, General, 241
Syveton, G., 93

tactics, 24, 170, 200, 202, chapter 11, 233-4
tache d'huile, 156
Thibaudin, General, 8, 37, 48-51
Thiers, Adolphe, 11, 13, 24, 27-8, 33, 35, 52, 106-7
training, 33, 90, 193-6, 200-2, 204-5, 211-15, 221-4, 234

Trentinian, General, 164, 216, 253
Trochu, General, 2, 7, 9, 24, 27, 32, 36-9, 46, 48
Tunisia, 140, 154, 159
vote for officers, 108
Waldeck-Rousseau, Réné, 61-8, 71, 74-6, 80, 96-7
war ministry (*see also* high command and general staff), 41, 45-51, 53, 58, 92, 94-101, 123, 158, 163, 173-6, 178, 190, 230, 237-42, 253
   Galliffet in, 62-72
   André in, 76-80
Western Sudan, 137-8, 140-1, 145, 147-9, 151, 156, 160
Weygand, General, 11, 200, 211, 216, 222-3, 236
Wimpffen, General, 8, 19

Yvetot, Georges, 109-10

Zurlinden, General, 53, 62, 64, 68-9, 216, 251

For EU product safety concerns, contact us at Calle de José Abascal, 56–1°,
28003 Madrid, Spain or eugpsr@cambridge.org.

www.ingramcontent.com/pod-product-compliance
Ingram Content Group UK Ltd.
Pitfield, Milton Keynes, MK11 3LW, UK
UKHW041431180426
11947UKWH00007B/391